How Children Develop Social Understanding

Understanding Children's Worlds

Series Editor: Judy Dunn

The study of children's development can have a profound influence on how children are brought up, cared for and educated. Many psychologists argue that, even if our knowledge is incomplete, we have a responsibility to attempt to help those concerned with the care, education and study of children by making what we know available to them. The central aim of this series is to encourage developmental psychologists to set out the findings and the implications of their research for others – teachers, doctors, social workers, students and fellow researchers – whose work involves the care, education and study of young children and their families. The information and the ideas that have grown from recent research form an important resource which should be available to them. This series provides an opportunity for psychologists to present their work in a way that is interesting, intelligible and substantial, and to discuss what its consequences may be for those who care for, and teach children: not to offer simple prescriptive advice to other professionals, but to make important and innovative research accessible to them.

How Children Develop Social Understanding

Jeremy Carpendale and Charlie Lewis

Blackwell Publishing

BLACKWELL PUBLISHING

350 Main Street, Malden, MA 02148-5020, USA
9600 Garsington Road, Oxford OX4 2DQ, UK
550 Swanston Street, Carlton, Victoria 3053, Australia

First published 2006 by Blackwell Publishing Ltd

1 2006

Library of Congress Cataloging-in-Publication Data

Carpendale, Jeremy I. M., 1957–
How children develop social understanding / Jeremy Carpendale
and Charlie Lewis.
p. cm. — (Understanding children's worlds)
Includes bibliographical references (p.) and index.
ISBN-13: 978-1-4051-0549-1 (hardcover : alk. paper)
ISBN-10: 1-4051-0549-6 (hardcover : alk. paper)
ISBN-13: 978-1-4051-0550-7 (pbk. : alk. paper)
ISBN-10: 1-4051-0550-X (pbk. : alk. paper) 1. Social perception in
children. I. Lewis, Charlie. II. Title. III. Series.
BF723.S6C37 2006
155.4′18—dc22
2005034215

A catalogue record for this title is available from the British Library.

Set in 10/12.5pt Sabon
by Graphicraft Limited, Hong Kong
Printed and bound in Great Britain
by TJ International, Padstow, Cornwall

The publisher's policy is to use permanent paper from mills that operate
a sustainable forestry policy, and which has been manufactured from
pulp processed using acid-free and elementary chlorine-free practices.
Furthermore, the publisher ensures that the text paper and cover board
used have met acceptable environmental accreditation standards.

For further information on
Blackwell Publishing, visit our website:
www.blackwellpublishing.com

To Caroline, Hannah, Max, Rosemary,
Tom, and Camilla

Contents

Series Editor's Preface

How do children come to understand the complexities of human social behaviour – why people behave the way they do, the connections between people's feelings and beliefs and their actions, and the motivation underlying particular actions? Where does the acquisition of language fit into the developmental story? What are the messages from the most recent psychophysiological and brain research and how do these influence accounts of children's developing social understanding? These questions have a long history in psychology, but they have become in the past 25 years unquestionably the hottest topic for developmental psychologists. Jeremy Carpendale and Charlie Lewis have written a book which tackles the complexities of the different theoretical arguments, and marshals the extraordinary wealth of experimental and observational research from the past 25 years into a clear and coherent argument about the key psychological processes underlying children's developing understanding of the mind. It is a timely and extremely welcome contribution, with its core theme a social constructivist account in which children's social relationships are seen as central in explanations of how social understanding develops.

They begin with the key different theoretical positions concerning understanding of mind that are set out in an initial chapter, and then drawn upon throughout the book. The approach is extremely scholarly, and critical – the limitations in each approach are set out, and the diversity of perspectives acknowledged. But the core theme provides a map to this complex territory, as the book takes us from the details of infant development, with the evidence for the capacity to engage in shared attention as basic to later social understanding, through the preschool years and beyond; each of the current ideas on what are the core issues is examined – for instance in considering autism they take the *cognitive* account and contrast it with views of autism as a disruption in the ability to engage in *emotional* interaction. The key topics of how social relationships are linked to developments in social understanding and vice versa, and how language and communicative abilities are implicated are considered at length. There is an impressive breadth of approach to children's social understanding – the authors take us way beyond the evidence from the "false belief test" (a research literature examined with perspicacity) to consider the far wider implications of the astonishing developments in children's grasp of how inner states are linked to the way people behave. Relations between social understanding and understanding of complex emotions, aggression and bullying, and moral issues are considered, always with a sharp eye for problems in drawing causal inferences, and a sensitivity to the complexity of children's social lives. The book covers a massive literature with clarity. In the final chapter the authors draw together the threads of their argument and summarize their own account of the centrality of social relationships in the developmental story, addressing the various criticisms raised concerning this account in a coherent and accessible way. It is a powerful argument clearly and plausibly presented, concerning issues that are crucial in children's development and their social lives.

Preface

People may be the most complex aspect of our everyday world, and we spend considerable time thinking about and talking about the actions and talk of others and ourselves. It is hard to emphasize strongly enough just how embedded our lives are within complex webs of social interaction. It is this complexity that children must gradually come to understand as they begin to engage in more and more complex forms of social interaction.

The development of children's understanding of their social worlds is the topic of this book. We acknowledge that the topic described by our title is too vast for one book to be able even remotely to cover adequately. We also acknowledge that most of the material we review is more narrowly located in an area of the research literature on social cognitive development usually referred to as "children's theories of mind." This research is primarily concerned with how children come to understand themselves and others in terms of beliefs, desires, and intentions. Since this is the primary area that has dominated much of the research on social cognitive development in the past 25 years, it is the material that we were obliged to address in some detail. One reader of a draft of this book helpfully suggested that an alternative title such as "How children understand the mind" would more accurately describe the content of the book. Although there is some truth to this, we have resisted changing the title for two interrelated reasons. First, although we focus on issues like children's understanding of beliefs, we also mean to encourage a broader inquiry into social development from infancy through childhood and beyond. We attempt to broaden the discussion of what social understanding consists of in some of the chapters in this book. Secondly, the phrase "understanding the mind" may contain a hint of an assumed theoretical position in that it could give the impression that the mind is a biological given and that children gradually come to understand it. However, we wish to bring more attention to a less recognized view that minds develop within the social process of interaction. The broader term "social understanding" allows for the possibility that such social competence may be rooted in children's social interaction.

This issue is related to the terminology we use. The general area of research on social cognitive development has been described in many different ways, including: "children's theory of mind"; "mindreading"; "mentalizing"; "belief–desire reasoning"; and "folk psychology." In the field these terms are often used somewhat interchangeably when researchers are simply referring to children's ability to think about their social world. But at other times these terms come attached to theoretical assumptions regarding the nature and development of children's social knowledge – assumptions that we believe need to be examined. We occasionally use some of these terms but in general we prefer to stick with the broader term social understanding.

The social process is evident in the cover photograph of Hannah and Max apparently deeply engaged in discussion. But is this really possible for children of this age? Hannah at about 3 years was certainly talking a lot, but Max, under a year old, would not generally be considered a good conversational partner. However, Hannah seems happy to engage with him and provide anything that he cannot contribute to the interaction. This hints at the role of social engagement in development and it also highlights the dramatic changes in children's social competence occurring during these ages.

As we have mentioned above, people are embedded in complex social webs. And this holds for us as authors as well. Naturally, many people have contributed to this book in different ways. We first mention our families, Rosie, Camilla, and Tom, and Caroline, Hannah, and Max. Examples from our children that we use in this book raise the issues we discuss. They also put up with the two of us working together on this book and other related projects during various visits in Lancaster and Vancouver. We have worked on this book in several different countries, at conferences, on walks, in airports, on trains, and over e-mail.

We have benefited from discussions with many of our colleagues and many people have read and commented on chapters in the book, including: Tim Racine, Ulrich Müller, Michael Chandler, Norman Freeman, Bryan Sokol, Bill Turnbull, Grace Iarocci, Jo Lunn, Karen Shimmon, Kathy Leadbitter, Maki Yasui, Tracey Anbinder, Chris Moore, Stefan Vogt, and Seungmi Oh. Thanks are also due to Judy Dunn who read the whole book and has consistently given us support, as her own writings have given us inspiration.

We also wish to thank many more of our colleagues but the list is too extensive to complete in detail. Our debt to them is evident in our engagement with their ideas through this book. This book is partially based on an extension of our target article published in the journal *Behavioral and Brain Sciences* in 2004. We also thank the 38 commentators on our article for raising important questions that encouraged us to further develop our ideas.

We acknowledge support from grants from the Social Sciences and Humanities Research Council of Canada. We thank Sarah Bird, formerly with Blackwell and now exploring other adventures, for making the suggestion that first started us thinking about this book. Sarah's consistent support and encouragement as well as advice have now been taken over by Will Maddox.

Jeremy Carpendale
Charlie Lewis
Vancouver and Lancaster, April 2005

Chapter 1

Social Understanding and Social Interaction: An Introduction to the Issues

"How do you go from a bunch of cells to something that can think?"

This question was posed by a 9-year-old boy[1] who said that all his other questions came down to this one and it was even more important than other problems like, "Does the universe go on forever?" Although we cannot claim to address all the implications of this far-reaching problem, it is the question above, or rather some much narrower aspects of it, that motivates this book. The evolutionary (phylogenetic) aspect of this question is intertwined with the developmental (ontogenetic) aspect. Not only do we ask "How did organisms that can think evolve?", but also "How do such organisms develop thinking in the process of development?" We will keep both in mind but the book will focus mainly upon the second, developmental, dimension. In doing so we need to reflect on how our social relationships structure our unfolding ability to think about the social world. Thus, our question could be more narrowly formulated as how do children come to understand and think about themselves and other people? Throughout the book it will become clear that we think that social interaction plays an essential role in this development. That children, like developmental psychologists, grapple with such questions reveals a reflective form of thinking that is only possible because of the forms of social interaction that humans become able to engage in. In this book we explore how children develop this fundamental skill.

What Is Social Understanding?

One way to begin describing social understanding is to consider a range of examples of children struggling to understand the social world. Even very young children are already surprisingly competent in engaging in social interaction. Consider the following examples.

Even years before social competence is evident in young children's talk, more basic forms of social understanding are beginning to reveal themselves. At around their first birthday infants are already beginning to follow other people's attention by following gaze direction and pointing gestures and also directing other people's attention with pointing gestures. For example, one day, just before Max's first birthday, he had just woken up and he was a bit grumpy. I (JC) said, "Would you like to read a book?" He smiled and laughed, and pointed to some of his books that were on the shelf. To carry out such a "simple" task, Max had to understand the word "book," as revealed by his smiling, and to show that he knew what was being discussed by pointing, as well as showing agreement with the suggestion. The smile and laugh also show that early social understanding is immersed in the thrill of emotional interaction between children and others. Skills like pointing are essential in directing others' attention, particularly before children can do this simply by speaking. In this anecdote it is not clear if Max glanced at me before or while he gestured. This is significant because explicitly checking on the other's attention is taken by some theorists as essential in revealing an infant's level of social understanding. However, it is just one of the debatable points in this extremely important, yet highly controversial, area of children's social development.

More complex forms of understanding begin to emerge with the development of language. "I'll hold his hand so that he won't be scared when we go over a bump," said Hannah (2 years, 9 months) as she was sitting in the car beside her little brother, Max (3 months) (both in their car seats). This comment reveals at least a rudimentary understanding that others have emotions, what causes such emotions, and what can be done to regulate emotions. An elementary form of such understanding seems to emerge early. In another example, one day when Max was 2 years and 4 months he saw Hannah's friend and her friend's mother drive away in their car. Max said, "Anne went away from her house. Hannah really sad." Again, this comment reveals an early understanding of what will make someone sad. It could be the case that statements like that simply reflect the child echoing "emotion talk" that they do not fully understand. However, there are examples in children's everyday talk in which they generate novel statements that they cannot possibly have heard and which reflect their understanding. For example, on walking up a steep hill with Tom (age 6), carrying Camilla (2 years, 7 months) in a baby-carrier on my back, I (CL) lay face down on a rock panting. When Tom asked why I was tired I said "You try carrying two stones up that hill" (i.e., 28 lbs or 12.7 kg). An indignant voice came from behind me: "It's not two stones, it's a little girl." Even though she may not have understood my reference (the word "little" might have been an indication that she thought she wasn't heavy), Camilla was demonstrating an ability to reflect upon herself from a third person perspective. Before age 3 children are grappling with issues about their place in social interactions.

At a slightly older age children begin to understand something about beliefs. For example, one day I (JC) knew that Max (age 4) wanted to get a cookie, and then he asked me to leave the kitchen. This shows that he understood that if I wasn't there and didn't see him take a cookie I wouldn't know about it. That is, he understood that I would have a false or mistaken belief. And he knew how to engineer the situation by having me leave the kitchen so that I ended up having a false belief. This is quite a sophisticated level of social understanding, but for adults it is clear that there are still important things Max had to learn about people. That is, Max didn't realize that I would be suspicious. He didn't consider what I might think about his reason for asking me to leave the kitchen. Such skills involve thinking about the other people's thinking. This topic will be discussed through the book, as it is assumed in much recent developmental psychology that this is a fundamental achievement in the development of social understanding.

These anecdotes are meant to begin this introduction to the topic of social understanding by providing examples of some of the areas of development that we will be exploring in more depth throughout this book. Many of these examples involve children's understanding of beliefs, emotions, and intentions. These everyday examples also show how these are all interrelated aspects of children's understanding of their social world.

Asking the Questions that Structure the Book

The problem of how children develop an understanding of their social world might appear to be a nicely contained topic area and it should be straightforward to review research on what is known regarding this important area of children's development. However, as we begin to examine this question in more detail we hope to make it clear that many complex issues are raised. One of the first obstacles we must deal with stems, ironically, from the fact that we, as adults, are so good at understanding and interacting with other people. That is, our common-sense psychology is so natural and taken for granted in our everyday social interactions that we have to make it problematic to even notice it and justify studying it. Thus, one of our first goals in this chapter is to cause problems – to make readers aware of what is taken for granted in order to set up the issues that we will deal with in the rest of the book. Just as the last thing to discover water would be fish, our understanding of the everyday features of our social interaction is so taken for granted that it is rarely noticed.

To rephrase this, part of the problem is that social interaction is just not problematic for most people, it is a natural way of thinking about others and thus tends to be invisible. One way in which this issue becomes visible is when we encounter other people who lack such natural social competence. Although we all know that there are great individual differences in competence in social interaction, it is only when we interact with (or attempt to interact with) people who are at the extreme end of the continuum of social understanding that we realize that not all people are able to engage in everyday forms of interaction. Here we are referring in particular to the unfortunate disorder known as autism. Children and adults with autism have great difficulty with the usual forms of social interaction that most people take completely for granted.

Autism, Apes and Evolution: How Much Is Social Understanding Biologically Determined?

This book is about how children come to develop sufficient social understanding to function as skilled members of their cultures. In this section we address three key questions which have dominated general debates on this subject and undoubtedly will continue to do so. The first concerns the place of social understanding within our evolutionary history. How do our nearest biological relatives compare with us in terms of their ability to engage in and understand social relationships? This question was the driving force behind an article which many people argue launched the main debates that set the scene for the rest of the book (see chapter 2). The second question concerns the issue of what happens when individuals find social interactions and relationships hard to achieve and maintain. The film *Rain Man* depicted the problems faced by someone with the syndrome of autism; a disorder in which social interaction is hard or even impossible to achieve. We explore here how autism has been defined in the recent literature on social understanding. The theoretical reflections on autism and primates that we describe reflect a fundamental principle in developmental psychology, that we must be mindful of the evolutionary place of our skills and activities.

Yet, we discuss these topics here for another reason. This is that there has been a general shift in recent years toward the "nature" side of the nature–nurture continuum. We consider this trend here because one of the fundamental aims of the book is to show that developmental processes, or how children construct social understanding within relationships, are a vital part of the story that is in danger of being swamped by "exciting," "new" biological determinist models. This is an issue we pick up on in the final part of this section. There have been advances in recent work in which the neurophysiological correlates of social understanding are demonstrated in experiments using expensive new pieces of apparatus involving positron electron tomography (PET) or magnetic resonance imagery (fMRI). While the move to such work is interesting, and on a few topics highly revealing, we argue that it can only throw light (or rather magnetic sensitivity or deep x-rays) upon physiological processes which underpin the psychological issues that concern us. It cannot explain social understanding.

What are the main achievements in the development of social understanding? In traditional accounts a number of issues have received attention. For example, a great deal of attention was focused on the development of children's ability to take others' perspectives – an approach that was inspired by Piaget and Inhelder's (1948/1967) research on visual perspective taking. For Kohlberg (e.g., 1976), major achievements include the development of moral reasoning, which becomes increasingly sophisticated over the teenage years. Over the past 20 years one issue has come to dominate the field of social cognition and this concerns how children come to understand themselves and others as psychological beings. The chapters of this book attempt to evaluate the contribution and chart recent developments in this tradition. Two landmarks have been discussed in particular and these concern very early achievements: preschoolers' understanding that people act on their beliefs even when these are wrong and the ability demonstrated by infants (i.e., those under age 2) to engage in shared attention. For most researchers who are in the former tradition (see chapter 3), work on joint attention in infancy has been framed in terms of "precursors" to the important later achievement of understanding the mind. However, Tomasello (1995a) has argued the opposite: that preschoolers' understanding of mental states might be better thought of as a "post-cursor" to children's ability to engage in joint attention. This is because the basic level of social understanding consisting of the capacity to engage in joint attention or triadic interaction is a fundamental human ability which allows infants to experience interaction and acquire language in which they will later develop more sophisticated understandings of the social world. The rest of social understanding is "icing on the cake" compared to the importance of joint attention in human cognition (Tomasello, 1999a). It is for this reason that we start this book with an analysis of basic attentional skills. Chapter 4 evaluates the nature of this ability. Here we consider whether we should adopt a paradigm that downplays traditional developmental psychology in favor of a biological approach to development.

How different are we from chimpanzees?

To address the issue of how children develop social understanding requires us to ask many sets of questions that usually are asked by different disciplines, including developmental psychology, philosophy, cognitive science, primatology, and developmental psychopathology. To start with we need to ask what biological adaptations made human social cognition possible. What have we evolved: a discrete ability to understand social relationships and/or to read intentions into others' actions, or a more general ability to develop such an understanding? To begin to address such a question research with nonhuman primates is relevant because it gives a broad indication of those aspects of human social cognition that are shared with species close to humans in evolutionary terms. We get more deeply into the two sides of the dilemma in the next section. Research on nonhuman primates is also interesting because it reveals the sophistication that researchers have to employ to be able to ask such questions. We cannot ask a chimpanzee, or a baby, about their social understanding and it is all too easy to anthropomorphize – to read into simple acts all sorts of skills that may not be there. Thus researchers have had to come up with ingenious ways of testing social understanding in our nearest relatives.

Consider the following anecdote about the behavior of two chimps:

> Brandy . . . sees a banana protruding from a pile of nearby hay and starts to make her way toward it. But at just that moment, she spies the dominant male, Apollo, lumbering toward her. Brandy stops in her tracks and turns her back to the banana, leading Apollo to turn and just miss seeing it. Soon, Apollo is disappointed with Brandy's reactions to his overtures,

and heads away in search of other females. Brandy follows for a short distance, but once she is sure of his direction, she doubles back to the pile of hay, and stealthily retrieves her prize. (Povinelli & Giambrone, 2001, p. 691)

Such observations have raised heated debates in the literature on primates. Some authorities use them to attribute high-level social-cognitive skills underlying such actions – that chimps can "read" each other's minds by anticipating what they might or might not see. There is evidence that higher order primates have access to such information. For example, chimpanzees can also follow others' gaze direction just like children (Povinelli, 1999; see also Köhler, 1925). So, they can collect the right sort of data to infer "Apollo cannot see the Banana" (without of course using language). But the question is what does this behavior mean about the extent of chimpanzees' social understanding? A rich interpretation that gaze following in chimps necessarily indicates sophisticated social understanding appears to be blocked by recent research. Careful experimentation has led Povinelli (1999) to conclude that although chimpanzees are skilled at learning about and predicting the behavior of conspecifics (i.e., members of their own species), they do not understand others' psychological states (Povinelli & Giambrone, 2001; Tomasello & Call, 1997).

Initial optimism about chimpanzees' social cognitive abilities turned to pessimism after further research had been published (Heyes, 1998). In a series of experiments Povinelli (1999; Povinelli & Eddy, 1996) found that chimpanzees do not seem to understand the psychological significance of seeing. For example, after being trained to beg for food from experimenters by extending their reaching arm, the chimpanzees were presented with two experimenters, only one of whom could be asked for food with a gesture. They were just as likely to beg from the one who had a bucket over her head (see Figure 1.1) or her eyes covered with a blindfold as from an experimenter with her eyes open. The chimpanzees could eventually learn to beg from the right person, but it took many trials. Young children, however, would demonstrate an understanding right away. This suggests that although chimpanzees may have learned to follow head turns they do not seem to understand the psychological significance of seeing. Povinelli and his colleagues suggest that this sort of experimentation shows that chimpanzees' ability to follow gaze direction is due to a complex understanding of others' behavior rather than an understanding of psychological states. Under a more formal training regime to get the animal to predict another's

Figure 1.1 One trial presented to the chimpanzees in the study by Povinelli and Eddy (1996). Reprinted with permission from the Society for Research in Child Development. Photo courtesy of Cognitive Evolution Group, University of Louisiana at Lafayette

actions (placing an object to mark where a reward is), mature chimpanzees fail where 4-year-old humans have no problem (Call & Tomasello, 1999). Povinelli et al. (2003) have also advanced similar arguments that even though chimpanzees can learn to extend an index finger in order to obtain food it is simply a socially shaped way to get something and they do not understand the pointing gesture in the way human children do.

However, recent research is leading to a reconsideration of chimpanzees' understanding of what others know and intend. David Leavens and his colleagues challenge this pessimistic view of chimpanzee social cognition with evidence of referential communication in a series of experiments with large numbers of non-language-trained chimpanzees. These chimpanzees had no explicit training and only the first trial was analyzed to ensure that the chimpanzee's response was not simply due to training. Of the 101 chimpanzees in one experiment, half of them gestured toward a banana beyond their reach but only when the experimenter was present. Leavens, Hopkins, and Thomas (2004, p. 55) "favor an operational perspective on intentional communication; namely, these animals are communicating intentionally because they require an audience to exhibit the behavior and they exhibit a coordinated pattern of gestural and visual orienting behavior that is determined by the locations of both an observer and food."

Further recent research is also leading to a reconsideration of chimpanzees' understanding of what others know and intend. Tomasello, Call, and Hare (2003) now question the pessimistic view of chimpanzees' social cognition. They studied competitive situations in which a dominant and a subordinate chimpanzee were both watching from separate rooms as pieces of food were being placed in a central room. When the doors were opened the subordinate chimpanzee generally went toward the piece of food that the dominant chimpanzee was not able to see. This shows that the subordinate took in to account what the dominant had seen when choosing which piece of food to attempt to retrieve. That is, the chimpanzee's behavior was based on what the other conspecific knew.

In another line of research Tomasello and his colleagues found that chimpanzees also seem to know something about others' intentional action. Across a series of conditions chimpanzees behaved quite differently when an experimenter was unable, due to clumsiness or inability, to give them food, or was instead simply unwilling (i.e., teasing). The chimpanzees were more impatient and more likely to leave the area if the experimenter was *unwilling* to give them food than when the experimenter was simply *unable* to give them the food, suggesting that they understood something about the experimenter's intentions. This research has led Tomasello and his colleagues to revisit their earlier view of chimpanzee social cognition and to suggest instead that "chimpanzees can understand some psychological states in others – the question is only which ones and to what extent" (Tomasello, Call, & Hare, 2003, p. 156).

These experiments are exemplary in terms of the ingenuity of their design. To test chimps' understanding observation is not enough. It is useful because it provides crucial evidence about possibilities, but experimental manipulations are required to test the sophistication of observed skills. The same principles hold for children and the research we focus on in this book relies upon a rich blend of studies using observations, recordings of what children say, and experimental manipulations. Experiments are by no means fool proof – the results still have to be interpreted. Eddy (2004) points out that the behavior of chimps in the Povinelli and Eddy (1996) experiments we have presented here may not be representative of their interactions with conspecifics – how they interact with humans may not fully inform us about their capabilities with other chimpanzees. Thus, the paradigm developed by Tomasello and his colleagues may be more appropriate. A second conclusion can be drawn from this literature on chimpanzees. If we compare the abilities witnessed here strategically to select food that a dominant chimpanzee cannot see with the statements made by the children in the first section of this chapter, we see that human capabilities are far more sophisticated, notably in how we use language to construct elaborate ways of depicting the mind. A last lesson that we draw from research with chimpanzees is to note that the different ways in which chimpanzees are reared has a large effect on their communicative abilities (Leavens, 2002). The most well-known example of this is Sue Savage-Rumbaugh's research with the bonobo named "Kanzi." Savage-Rumbaugh and her colleagues (Savage-Rumbaugh, Murphy, Sevcik, Brakke, Williams, & Rumbaugh, 1993) found that Kanzi and other bonobos and chimpanzees raised in a human linguistic environment developed greatly increased understanding of language, although clearly they did not become human. Their linguistic skills were somewhat similar to a 2-year-old child.

Whatever the biological adaptations that distinguish us from the great apes, these have made the complexities of human social life possible, including language, culture, and history. Not only have humans evolved the ability to engage in complex social interaction and relationships but such developments form a platform for our cultural traditions and histories which influence the nature of individuals' social developments. This book explores how human children come to understand the complexities of the social world. We turn now to explore whether the very differences between humans and chimps necessarily lead to the conclusion that human skills can be defined in terms of a specialist genetic adaptation. This issue has been examined with reference to a small part of the population who have profound problems in social understanding.

Autism: joint attention and "mindreading" skills

Norbert Elias (1978, p. 107) asks "Which biological characteristics of man make history possible?" Or what adaptations made human culture possible? Many would argue that the ability to share a topic of interest is central. In addition to its place in human evolution we must consider the issue of how infants develop the capacity for joint attention. How much does its development depend either on infants' interaction with their social and physical environments, or on some sort of pre-prepared mechanism, module, or form of thinking set to unfold with maturity? Over the past 20 years this latter nativist position has become increasingly popular, and much of the evidence on the subject comes from individuals with autism and other genetic disorders. We need here to reflect upon the nature of autism and to consider how a biological model disorder generalizes to the study of social development in typically developing children. First we describe the key symptoms of the disorder.

Autism has come to be identified by three defining characteristics: impairment of "social interaction" and "communication" and engagement in repetitive or stereotypical behaviors (DSM-IV, APA, 1994). Individuals with this disorder show severe problems in social interaction and understanding. Discussing autism serves to emphasize what life would be like without the forms of social understanding that we take for granted. Perhaps the best way to provide a brief picture of it is to follow Simon Baron-Cohen's (1995, p. 61) lead and quote Kanner's (1943) original descriptions of the children he worked with in first identifying this syndrome:

"He seems to draw into his shell and live within himself. . . ."

"When taken into a room, he completely disregarded the people and instantly went for objects. . . ."

"When a hand was held out to him so that he could not possibly ignore it, he played with it briefly as if it were a detached object. . . ."

All these examples point to the key features of autism, which "include lack of normal eye contact, lack of normal social awareness or appropriate social behavior, "aloneness," one-sidedness in interaction, and inability to join a social group" (Baron-Cohen, 1995, pp. 62–63). In other words, these children have great difficulty in simply engaging in everyday forms of social interaction. All of the children in these examples were boys and, in fact, autism is much more common in boys than girls. The genetic component to autism is shown in the risk of autism being substantially higher in a family with a child with autism (Rutter, 2000). It is a severe, although rare, childhood condition affecting about 4 to 15 children in 10,000, and it is often associated with other problems such as mental disability, although not always (for a detailed introduction to these points see Frith, 2003).

How do we account for autism in this small minority of children? Some authors have suggested that the disorder reveals the importance of the biological determinants of social understanding in typically developing children. Baron-Cohen (1995, p. 12) writes about a fundamental human ability which he calls "mindreading" – the ability to grasp others' goals, beliefs, and intentions: "mindreading has an innate, biological, modular basis." He proposes that social understanding is supported by a series of four evolved mechanisms or modules. His approach is based on Tooby and Cosmides's (1992) claim that the mind consists of a series of modules that have evolved to solve particular problems in the ancestral environment. These are "cognitive mechanisms selected over evolutionary time" (Baron-Cohen, 1995, p. 107).

Figure 1.2 describes Baron-Cohen's (1995) four modules or mechanisms that are involved in social understanding, or "mindreading." A biological model cannot simply state that there is a gene for a particular skill – such a "model" would be useless as it would be circular: we have a skill because we have a skill. Here we will consider the first three modules to illustrate the basis of Baron-Cohen's model and some of the assumptions he adopted. As Figure 1.2 shows, he described the eye direction detector (EDD), the intentionality detector (ID), and the shared-attention mechanism (SAM). Each is self-contained but within this framework is related to others in terms of receiving input and sending output. SAM "builds" what are termed triadic representations (i.e., representations of three-way relations between self, other, and object) based on input (dyadic representations) from the earlier emerging EDD and ID. The EDD detects eyes and whether they are looking at the self or something else. ID reads any apparently self-caused motion in terms of an agent's goals and desires. The fourth mechanism is the theory of mind module (ToMM); the ability to "mindread" is triggered by input from SAM from about 18 to 48 months.

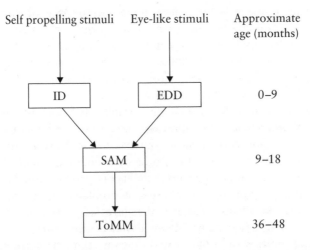

Figure 1.2 A simplified version of Baron-Cohen and Ring's (1994) model of the four components of the "Mindreading" system. Reprinted by permission of Lawrence Erlbaum Associates Ltd. and by permission of the authors Simon Baron-Cohen and Howard Ring

Just how right is Baron-Cohen's model here and what purpose does it serve? Although it identifies a number of different skills that might be central to an understanding of interactions and people, it is not clear how it can be tested. Some authors have pointed out potential problems. For example, Chris Moore (1996, p. 25) suggested that an empirical difficulty with the proposed eye direction detector (EDD) is that it might not capture just how babies start to orient themselves to others' signals because "initially infants are unaffected by changes in eye direction and only follow gaze indicated by changes in head direction." We return to the details of infant development in chapter 4.

Certainly Baron-Cohen (1995) has helped to show that joint attention skills are an important part of human infants' typical pattern of development; we do not notice when it is present but if it is missing psychopathology may be indicated. This has had clear effects on the clinical practice of health professionals screening for early disorders. Lack of joint attention behaviors at 18 months of age, especially pointing to direct the adult's attention, may be an indicator in the early diagnosis of autism. This was found in a study using the Checklist for Autism in Toddlers (CHAT) (Baron-Cohen, Allen, & Gillberg, 1992). This is a simple checklist for family physicians or home visitors consisting of two parts: 9 questions for parents and 5 questions for the physician or home (health) visitor. Items include lack of pretend play and forms of joint attention such as following, or making, pointing gestures. Children who fail 5 key items have a higher risk of later being diagnosed with autism or related disorders (Baron-Cohen, Allen, & Gillberg, 1992; Baron-Cohen, Cox, Baird, Swettenham, Nightingale, Morgan, Drew, & Charman, 1996).

Although it is now fairly well agreed upon that impairments in joint attention in infancy are diagnostic of autism, there is lack of agreement regarding why children with autism have such problems. In summarizing the literature, Sue Leekam (2005) offers two main accounts. According to the cognitive account (she calls it the metarepresentational hypothesis – see chapter 2), autism is the result of problems in the mindreading mechanisms, like those described in Figure 1.2, that evolved to solve particular social reasoning problems (Baron-Cohen, 1995). On the other hand, the problems of children with autism might be more accurately defined in another way. Leekam describes the "interpersonal-affective hypothesis." This refers to the ability to engage in social and emotional exchange, not to the business of processing such interactions. According to this perspective, autism is the result of "a disruption in the system of child-in-relation-to-other" (Hobson, 2002, p. 183). That is, impairment in joint attention in autism is rooted in problems in engaging emotionally with other people. From this perspective there may be different paths to autism through factors such as congenital blindness or severe social deprivation that may disrupt parent–infant engagement and lead to the development of autism-like symptoms (Hobson, 1993, 2002) (we explore the issue of social relationships and social understanding in chapter 6).

The evidence provides some support for the interpersonal-affective hypothesis. That children with autism have problems engaging in dyadic face-to-face interaction, as well as triadic interaction (i.e., self, another person, and an object), may well indicate that they have a basic impairment in orienting to other people. This would lead to difficulties in participating in the kinds of interpersonal emotional engagement within which typical children develop joint attention. Of course, there may be different explanations for problems in interpersonal dyadic interaction. Difficulties in orienting to others could be due to emotional and motivational factors. Alternatively, they could be traced to basic problems in interpreting sensory input (Frith, 2003; Iarocci, 2002; Plaisted, 2000). Thus there are several contenders for an explanation of autism that involves the ability to process information in interaction.

If there is debate about the cause of autism, does Baron-Cohen's theory explain typical development? There are three issues to address which we apply to the theory and which also allow us to reflect more generally upon the use of models that heavily load the biological bases in explaining social development. The first boils down to the question of how much social interactional skills can be captured within the "modules" that he proposes. Baron-Cohen (1995) drew on Cosmides and Tooby's (1992) evolutionary psychology in proposing a series of modules or mental mechanisms evolved to solve particular problems in our ancestral environment. We do not question the importance of basing psychological theories on evolutionary theory. However, Tooby and Cosmides' approach is just one application of evolutionary theory and taking evolution seriously does not necessarily mean endorsing their approach (Donald, 2004; Moore, 1996; Oyama, 1999). They combine evolutionary theory and a "computational view of the mind." Accordingly, evolution has provided us with sets of discrete abilities: "[w]e inhabit mental worlds populated by the computational outputs of battalions of evolved, specialized neural automata" (Tooby & Cosmides, 1995, p. xii). This explains the evolution of retinal cone cells and visual cortex for color vision. However, Tooby and Cosmides are quick to extend this model to "everything in our experienced worlds: the warmth of a smile, the meaning of a glance, the heft of a book, the force of a glare" (p. xi). Such explanations for social understanding break down in their attempt to deal with meaning. Human natural language is very different from formal languages (such as computer languages). Communication such as a glance, a pause, gestures, words, or utterances do not have evolved, fixed meanings that can be decoded in a mechanistic way using the "computations" that Tooby and Cosmides propose (Turnbull, 2003). A problem for a computational view of the mind is that it is difficult to deal with meaning and understanding: "Computers don't understand anything, nor do they care" (Hobson, 2002, p. xiv). Rather, meaning depends on the location in an ongoing sequence of interaction (Budwig, Wertsch, & Uzgiris, 2000; Goldberg, 1991). So, we need an alternative to the modular approach which captures such complexity in human interaction and language.

The second concern over Baron-Cohen's theory involves the lack of clarity concerning the responsibility attributed to learning in social understanding. He acknowledges that "the extent to which each of the four mindreading mechanisms is innate or develops as a function of some learning seems to be still open to investigation" (Baron-Cohen, 1995, p. 57). However, he goes on to claim that "clearly, a lot must be prespecified, as I have hinted, though there may be a role for learning in some of these – especially ToMM." Elsewhere (Baron-Cohen & Swettenham, 1996, p. 161) he argues that because joint attention is universal and independent of culture this "implies that its development is partly, if not completely, driven by individual, biological factors within the child." Even if we can assume from these differences in emphasis on innate knowledge and learning that there is some contribution from each, we must be careful about the assumption that human capacities for joint attention must be prespecified. In refuting this sort of argument Bates (1984) reminds us to be careful of such reasoning: just because eating with our hands is universal we do not therefore conclude that it must be innate. Furthermore, the fact that only humans cook their food does not mean that we should expect to find a gene for cooking (Tomasello, 1995b, 137–138). Such issues further question the validity of the modular approach to children's social understanding.

Clearly humans have evolved the capacity to *develop* joint attention. The third issue in Baron-Cohen's theory concerns the validity of the assumption that humans have evolved a skill as complex as "mindreading." Michael Tomasello (1999a) has strongly argued that there has not been enough time for all these modules to have evolved. Humans shared a common ancestor with chimpanzees about 5 to 6 million years ago and there is suggestive archeological evidence from about 40,000 years ago of some level of social understanding. It is more likely that human social cognition evolved in something like 250,000 years or less. This is a moment in evolutionary history and Tomasello argues that it is too short for the elaborate network of modules depicted in Figure 1.2 to have evolved. Instead Tomasello suggests that we should be looking for "a small difference that made a big difference – some adaptation, or small set of adaptations, that changed the process of primate cognitive evolution in fundamental ways" (Tomasello, 1999c, p. 510). According to Tomasello (1999a, p. 204), the problem with modularity approaches is that "they attempt to skip from the first page of the story, genetics, to the last page of the story, current human cognition, without going through any of the intervening pages. These theorists are thus in many cases leaving out of account formative elements in both historical and ontogenetic time that intervene between the human genotype and phenotype." This provides us with further justification to explore whether developmental psychology can provide a better alternative.

Mental state understanding and the brain

In addition to the study of primates and children with autism there is a third area of research which has attracted increasing attention over the

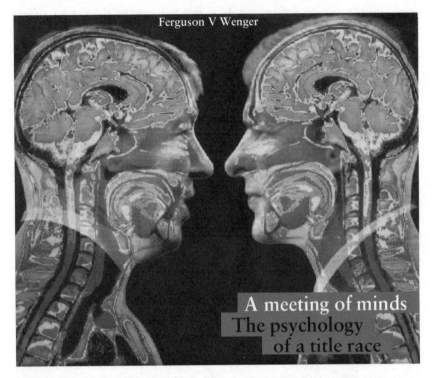

Figure 1.3   A popular analysis of the relevance of brain functions to psychology. *Source: The Guardian*, 26 April 2003. Reprinted by permission of Gavin Rodgers/Pixel

past decade in its attempts to explore the biological foundations of human social understanding. We discuss it here for two reasons. First, and in keeping with the issues described above, it reflects a move in psychology and indeed in industrial cultures as a whole toward a model of human action and understanding that is reducible to the study of brain functioning. Figure 1.3 displays an example taken from a sports page of the *Guardian* newspaper in April 2003, just as the UK soccer championships were nearing the climax of a dramatic two-horse race. It shows the two competing managers, Arsene Wenger and Sir Alex Ferguson, "psyching" one another out in this battle. The caption "A meeting of minds" is depicted by a mock-up of a brain scan – each firing on overdrive. Such an association between the mind and brain physiology has become all the rage: it captures the state of the art in terms of current popular conceptions of psychology. As we discuss now and at various times throughout this book, this move is a mixed blessing. It produces interesting data, but may not be the key to understanding how children or adults function in the social world.

The second reason for mentioning the brain here is that we wish to flag important work in two areas of neuropsychology. The first concerns research using positron electron tomography (PET) and functional magnetic resonance imaging (fMRI) techniques to examine metabolism within brain areas while participants perform a range of tasks involving, for example, considering the psychological state of a protagonist in a cartoon, or assessing someone's knowledge of events or their emotional reaction to them. Sometimes the participants reflect upon their own thoughts or feelings in a particular setting. While performing these activities brain images are taken to discern changes in activity, particularly activations over and above typical baseline levels. This work is carried out with adults firstly because PET scans are not safe for children (they involve radioactive substances) and secondly because the participant has to remain still over many minutes so that the particular brain area can be constantly measured without movement-induced artifacts. In typical fMRI studies recording times last 20–40 minutes and the data are excluded if participants move their heads more than 5 mm during the period (personal communication by my colleague Stefan Vögt).

This research suggests that two areas of the brain seem to be particularly associated with activities in which participants think about protagonists', or their own, mental states (see Abu-Akel, 2003, for a detailed review). Most commonly, the anterior cingulate cortex (ACC), a curved structure in the middle part of the front of the brain, shows greater activity when volunteers reflect upon issues like emotions aroused by photographs, or monitor their actions. In a review of these studies Frith and Frith (2000) summarize evidence which shows that there are slightly different areas of the ACC associated with tasks in which respondents monitor their own mental states, consider another person's thoughts or wishes, as opposed to just reflecting upon the movement of people. For example, Gallagher, Jack, Roepstorff, and Frith (2002) carried out a PET study in which they asked participants to play a computerized version of the game "stone, paper, scissors." There were two groups. One was told they were competing against the experimenter, implying that they were trying to outwit one another, while the other group was told they were playing a computer programmed to employ a strategy. In fact, for both groups the computer randomly generated one of the three symbols. They found greater activity in the anterior paracingulate cortex, adjacent to the ACC, in the group who thought they were

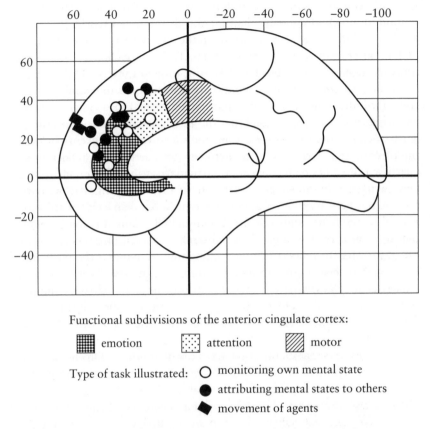

Functional subdivisions of the anterior cingulate cortex:

▦ emotion   ⬚ attention   ▨ motor

Type of task illustrated: ○ monitoring own mental state
                             ● attributing mental states to others
                             ◤ movement of agents

Figure 1.4 The areas of activation when monitoring one's own or another's mental states in relation to the three areas of the anterior cingulated cortex. *Source*: Frith & Frith, 2001, p. 153. Reprinted by permission of Blackwell Publishing

competing with a person. Gallagher et al. interpret this evidence as suggesting that this part of the brain is used when we are thinking about others' intentions. Figure 1.4 shows the summary presented by Frith and Frith (2001, p. 152) on the ACC. Given that patients with lesions in the ACC also show problems in inferring mental states without impairments in comparable cognitive tasks, these data seem to show the importance of the medial frontal region in tasks involving social understanding.

The other brain area discussed by Frith and Frith is the temporo-parietal junction (TPJ), just above the ear. This area lies midway between the ventral stream, which is associated with identifying "what" is in the environment, and the dorsal stream, which identifies "how" the environment is currently configured, as it is involved in the visual guidance of one's own actions and in the visual processing of the actions of others. Thus Frith and Frith (2001, p. 155) "speculate that this is the ideal location to act as interface" allowing mental states to be inferred: "the main requirement for a mentalizing system is the ability to represent the relationship between agents and their actions."

In addition to these studies which show that these neural activities are associated with participants' performance of tasks involving social understanding, there is a further reason why we raise the neuropsychological studies here. This concerns some fascinating data and debate concerning a particular type of cell associated initially with the premotor cortex, but now with other adjacent areas. Much of this stems from the careful analyses of single cell functioning in the comparable area of the macaque monkey's brain.[2] This research has identified neurons that are differentially associated with individual activities, like "holding," "tearing," or specific movements of the hand or mouth. In this work Gallese et al. (1996) found that some cells became active when the monkey performed an action *and* when it watched someone else performing it. These are therefore termed "mirror neurons." The implication is that in some cells the same neural substrate underlies the generation of one's own actions and the attention to the actions of others. On this level an "action" is represented independently of its agent. Such cells appear to fire under a variety of conditions. Kohler, Keysers, Umiltà, Fogassi, Gallese, and Rizzolatti (2002) found that a number of actions stimulated these neurons: when the monkey executed a noisy action like breaking open a peanut but also when they saw or just heard the noise of this happening. Likewise, Umiltà, Kohler, Gallese, Fogassi, Fadiga, Keysers, and Rizzolatti (2001) showed that only part of an action is sufficient to trigger these neurons – for example observing someone reaching toward an object that is obscured from vision.

Data like these have led to a frenzy of theoretical debate about the nature of our understanding of others and ourselves. If the same neurons fire when we are doing something or just watching an action, this suggests that our "mind-brain systems" work in a particular way – we understand others by "simulating" their actions. This is not a conscious activity, it is just the way the nervous system works: "The simulation process I am discussing is . . . *automatic, unconscious* and *pre-reflexive*" (Gallese, 2003, p. 521, italics original). Thus, the parts of the brain associated with social understanding make no distinction between self and other – in this respect Gallese argues that the neural activity underpinning social understanding occurs in "shared intersubjective space." We take this point up again when considering the nature of mental simulation in chapter 2.

Current research on the neurophysiological and neuropsychological correlates of social understanding is producing some very interesting results. At the moment the interchange with psychology is speculative. Some work is attempting to draw parallels between the work on brain areas and the particular theories that we will discuss in the next chapter. For example, Gallagher and Frith (2003, p. 78) suggest that the location of neural activity in "a highly circumscribed region of the brain, the anterior paracingulate cortex" lends support to a modular account of mindreading like those discussed in the section on autism above. While interesting, it is hard to see how such theoretical connections between the activation of neural pathways and how we understand the social world can ever be tested empirically. Likewise, the work of Gallese and his colleagues is fascinating, but even more speculative. On one level they appear to show how an understanding of the neural activity engaged in when we attempt to understand our own and others' actions is so intertwined as to require us to take what goes on between people as the lowest common denominator for social understanding, not individuals' inner thoughts about themselves and others. We take up similar issues in the rest of this book – the fundamental one is what is the basis of social understanding.

Yet Gallese takes this idea further to argue that neurons actually *represent* actions: "Our claim is that the mirror system makes a centrally relevant microfunctional contribution . . . it helps to code the representational content in question" (Metzinger & Gallese, 2003a, p. 557). In this ambitious attempt to blend the study of nerve cell activity and a theory of human understanding, Gallese seems even more ready to switch between different levels of theoretical analysis that simply bear no relation to one another. This position is highly speculative. Wolfgang Prinz's (2003, p. 572) response is that he finds "it difficult to understand and, in fact, impossible to believe that such complex things like conscious models of intentional relations can be coded by single neurons or even assemblies of those neurons." The issue here concerns just what psychologists should take the word "representation" to mean. The problem is to "explain the transition from causal processes in the brain to conscious, meaningful experience" (Müller, Sokol, & Overton, 1998b, pp. 229–230; see also Hacker, 1991). It is important to spell this point out, as it sets out a foundation for many of the perspectives explored in this book.

Attempts to equate the study of the mind with the study of the brain are described by their critics as "reductionist." Such approaches lead to the claim that the only thing we can be sure about is that representations or one's knowledge of the world is stored in the particular pattern of synaptic connections in one's brain (Churchland, 1995, p. 5; Craig & Barrett, 2004, p. 103). As Russell (1992, p. 500) points out, the problem is that "representation" is a Humpty-Dumpty word. Just as Humpty-Dumpty in *Alice in Wonderland* said he could use words to mean anything he wanted, psychologists mean very different things by the term "representation." How do Metzinger and Gallese use the word? Perhaps it could be said that in some sense neurons can "represent" because they contain information in the same way that exposing the film in a camera "represents" a particular scene or the way that a key that fits a lock contains information about that lock. However, neither the camera nor the key *knows* anything (Müller, Sokol, & Overton, 1998a, 1999b; Prinz, 2003). This reductionist view collapses the important distinction between information and knowledge. For example, a train schedule contains information but it has no *knowledge* of departure times (Kenny, 1991, pp. 158–159, emphasis in original), just as "the illiterate slave on whose shaven scalp the tyrant has tattooed his state secrets does not *know* the information which his head contains." It may be in this sense that Metzinger and Gallese (2003b) responded to Prinz's (2003) statement that "neurons don't represent" by claiming that "of course they do." Of course neurons respond to stimulation but they don't know anything, just as a computer responds to our key strokes but computers don't know anything. Clearly, investigation at the neurological level is important and such processes are obviously required for psychological processes. But if we are concerned with meaningful human conduct, as psychology must be, then psychology cannot be reduced to neurology. We should heed Terrance Brown's (2003, p. 16) warning that "in the interest of being scientific, psychology has opted out of being psychology." The tradition of research that we describe in this book has at its starting point the view that we must explain the origins of such "conscious, meaningful experience".

What Is This Book About?

This book explores how developmental psychology has attempted to grapple with the issue of how children come to understand the social world. Clearly biological issues are important, but we place at the center the question of how forms of social interaction influence social development. What kind of a book is this? How would you write an introduction to this topic? One possibility we considered was a straightforward textbook. That is, an attempt even-handedly to review the literature on social cognitive development. Although not usually acknowledged, no textbook can actually do this. A review is by necessity selective in some way. Choices must be made about what topics and pieces of research to cover in depth. And, of course, the structure of the presentation will also betray some bias. In fact, it is part of the nature of knowledge that it is interpretive. And one aspect of this book is to trace the gradual emergence of children's realization of the interpretive nature of the process of knowledge acquisition. Such bias tends to be overlooked in standard texts because they usually take the currently dominant position. But this is not always the case; in fact, some textbooks play an influential role in defining and structuring a field. But what kind of a textbook would it be? We argue in chapter 2 that in this field it is not clear that there is a dominant view anymore. In any case, a diversity of perspectives is emerging in response to a range of new empirical evidence. Thus the current state of the field is so theoretically diverse that the reader would be left with no clear conclusion.

Alternatively, we could have written a polemical account – that is, putting forward a particular position, in fact, our own position – we did this in Carpendale and Lewis (2004a, 2004b). Rather than reproduce these articles we offer a way to integrate the research in this book. The chapters are structured around particular topic areas. We attempt even-handedly to review research and theory, and outline how this work has been critically evaluated in the field. Yet, of course, this process is necessarily a way of making sense of the field from a particular perspective – our perspective. We (naturally) tend to structure the chapters so that by the conclusion we end by hinting (perhaps strongly) toward the position that just happens to be ours. We present our position more explicitly in chapter 10. Although it is not possible to be completely exhaustive in a field of this size, we hope to have presented enough of the research and theory and in a fair enough way for the reader to decide for her or himself whether to agree or disagree with us. We take it that the mark of a good reader is to question critically the material being presented. The chapters are structured in this way. However, the reader may need to continue such a critical evaluation when it comes to our own position, which we may not be critical enough of (although for critical reviews see the 38 peer commentaries on Carpendale & Lewis, 2004a).

The historical context of this book

The literature we review in this book is primarily from the past 25 years. This body of research is generally referred to as "children's theories of mind" because it has been argued that children's knowledge of the mind is in some ways like a theory. Furthermore, the empirical paradigm that this research has drawn on is the point at about 4–5 years of age when children begin to realize that beliefs can be mistaken or false. Of course, this general area of how children come to understand their social world is intuitively seen to be of such importance for children's lives that it has been a topic of perennial interest to developmental psychologists. Thus there have been a number of previous research literatures devoted to studying children's social cognitive development. The research tradition that preceded the current work was known as perspective taking or role taking. The perspective-taking literature was inspired by Piaget and Inhelder's (1948/1967) research on visual perspective taking. The general idea of visual perspective taking was then applied to social understanding in order to study when children become able to take other people's perspectives, or put themselves in other people's shoes. We briefly discuss this research in chapters 3 and 8. Other approaches have been referred to as person perception and metacognition – or what children know about thinking. In this book we cannot discuss the details of this research and we refer readers to reviews of this literature (Chandler, 1978; Chandler & Boyes, 1982; Shatz, 1975, 1983).

Thus older developmentalists sometimes see the "new" area of "theory of mind" as just old wine in new bottles. And they point out that researchers have studied these issues for many years under the different names of metacognition, person perception and role or perspective taking. How should we respond to such criticism? First, it is clear that a new area of research has not been created. All of these areas of research are concerned with the same topic of how children come to understand their social worlds. John Flavell (1992) is one of the few developmentalists who has done research in the areas of metacognition, role taking, and now "theories of mind," and he has argued for a continuity among these areas. Thus it is not the topic area that differs but rather the theoretical explanations meant to account for how it is that children come to understand their social worlds or take the perspectives of others. Each area of research tends to draw on different theoretical approaches. The goal of this book is to evaluate critically the research and theory during the past 25 years on the topic of children's social cognitive development.

The structure of the book

The organization of the topics covered in the chapters to some extent follows the recent history of this field. We begin in chapter 2 with a review of the current theories that are meant to explain the development of children's understanding of the mind. We discuss critiques of the theories and debates among them as well as emerging alternative positions. We then go on in chapter 3 to review the extensive body of research, including many variations of what has become the main procedure for assessing this understanding, the false belief task.

In chapter 4 we discuss the recently renewed interest in what aspects of social understanding are already developing in infancy and form the foundation on which later psychological understanding is built. As we stated above, the focus in infancy is on the development of infants' ability to coordinate their attention with others – what is referred to as joint attention. This is important in language development and in further social development. We focus on the contrast in accounts of early development between proponents of one view that babies develop such skills early versus those who argue that they emerge slowly over the first two years.

A further question that arises is whether general abilities such as memory and attention are related to social understanding. There is accumulating evidence that this is the case, which means we need to understand the relations between social understanding and domain general abilities, and how these general abilities help in the area of thinking about social matters. Chapter 5 is devoted to this topic and considers the central issue of whether these general skills underpin social understanding, have little or no relation to it or whether social interactions and understanding actually drive cognitive achievements in working memory, inhibitory control, and the ability to change from one rule to another.

Chapter 6 covers research related to the notion that aspects of social interaction may facilitate the development of social understanding. If the child's social experience plays a role in social development, and there is now considerable evidence reviewed in chapter 6 that it does, then what aspects of social interaction are especially important in facilitating social development? Much of this work began with Judy Dunn's pioneering longitudinal studies on the role of family interaction in social development. The relations between language and social understanding, as well as an examination of conceptions of language, are covered in chapter 7. In organizing this book we have attempted to group topics by chapter. However, the issues are not so obliging in neatly dividing themselves into separable areas. Some topics, in particular language, cannot be neatly packaged into one chapter. Although we do devote a chapter to the topic, reviewing research and theory explicitly on language, we find that it cannot be pinned down so easily and it makes itself felt in several other chapters in this book. The same can be said for emotion. Emotion cannot be simply separated from cognition, thus it comes up in most of the chapters in various ways. The division between chapter 6 on the influence of social interaction on social development and chapter 7 on the relations between language and social understanding is somewhat artificial. In our defense, one practical reason for dividing these chapters is that there is simply too much important research and theory on these topics to deal with in one chapter.

As well as studying children younger than 4 years of age, the field has now turned its attention to what it is that children older than 4 years still have to learn about the mind and emotions. This topic is discussed in chapter 8, where we consider the achievements of children in the school years, and in which we explore evidence suggesting that there is still much to learn about the social world once the preliminaries of social understanding are achieved.

Furthermore, we can ask what a child's understanding of belief and how beliefs are acquired influences her or his development. What difference does it make in the child's life? How do children become competent at engaging in social interaction? Are there further developments in understanding the mind and emotions? Is such understanding connected to the rest of the child's social life, and if so how? For example, how is social cognition related to getting along with one's mates? Does this help in understanding aggression, bullying, and morality? Understanding other people is also related to understanding the self and to insight regarding one's own emotional reactions. Such self-awareness is important in the development of children's social and emotional maturity and their ability to deal with complex social situations. As we will discuss in chapter 9, children's social understanding is related to many other aspects of their social development such as their competence in social interaction and also to moral development. Social competence is required in most domains of people's lives, from dealing with peers, teachers, and bullies in school to managing people within any form of occupation. Indeed such competence is essential for achieving one's potential in other areas of life, from realizing one's intellectual goals to achieving stable relationships and to becoming productive citizens engaged in maintaining and improving their society. Chapter 9 deals with the "so what" question, that is, what difference does an understanding of mind and emotions have in actual application to practical aspects of children's social lives?

In chapter 10 we summarize and attempt to integrate the theory and research discussed throughout the book. We should also warn the reader that this is where our own perspective will become most evident. While it makes explicit our own perspective, we realize that chapter 10 makes explicit many of the points that we allude to in previous chapters. Our main aim is to discuss the role of social and cognitive processes in the child's social understanding. We review key issues that theories of social development should address and we present our position on these issues. We summarize our relational view of infant social development, according to which infants gradually differentiate self, other, and the world from their activity. This leads to the capacity to engage in triadic interaction with others and the world, a form of interaction that provides the foundation on which language is built. Language then allows the child to learn how to talk about the psychological world, and in turn to think about this dimension of human activity. This development is embedded in social relations with others. Particular types of relationships, especially cooperative relationships, facilitate the child's understanding of people's activity, and thus facilitate the development of social understanding.

Although we are critical of many theoretical positions that we turn to next, the main aim of the book is to show how a range of factors are needed together to explain how children come to develop such skills. The aim is to show how analysis of the data and theory in the "theory of mind" tradition allows us to synthesize an account of social understanding that draws from each of the perspectives to be summarized in the rest of the book. It is this tradition, with all its complexities and differences of opinion, that we summarize in chapter 2.

Notes

1. The son of JC.
2. These studies are invasive and as vegetarians we do not applaud the use of surgery on animals in order to conduct research. However, the findings of these studies are significant enough for us to feel we should talk about them here.

Chapter 2

Contemporary Theories of Social Understanding

For the past 20 years a large proportion of research on the development of children's social understanding has focused upon the topic with the somewhat grand title of "theory of mind." This term is used in many different ways. For some researchers it signals an endorsement of the claim that children's understanding of the psychological world is theory-like in nature. More generally it has come to be used simply to indicate a broad area of research on how children come to understand the mind, without an assumption about which theoretical account best explains such a skill. For others, including us, the theoretical connotations of the phrase are too strong and they either avoid the term or distance themselves by using it within quotation marks. Objections to such references to children's social knowledge as a "theory" will be discussed in this chapter and throughout this book. We choose the more general and encompassing term, social understanding. In this chapter we aim to achieve two goals. First, we want to show that the phrase children's "theory of mind" refers to a highly visible and influential debate within developmental psychology. Secondly, by charting a brief history of this area we hope to provide an introduction to the very different theoretical positions within this debate.

The "theory" metaphor was the first in this movement and it has had most influence, so we turn to it first. A brief section on the origins of the movement is followed by a longer one in which we show that the dominant "theory" is really two perspectives rolled into one, without much analysis of the problems of having such a marriage of convenience. The third section deals with two "official opposition" accounts of mental state understanding that reject the claim that children's understanding is theory-like in its nature and development. The fourth briefly summarizes the state of play between these positions, arguing that they share more common ground than it might appear. The fifth and final section is the starting point for the rest of this book. It briefly describes a wide range of perspectives on the child's understanding which reject the theory of mind metaphor and those of the official opposition. These were labeled the accounts of the "great unwashed" by Michael Chandler because until very recently they have not been considered to be worthy of discussion within the theory of mind debate. The main aim will be to show why these accounts make an important contribution to a theory of children's developing social understanding. A secondary objective is to provide the starting point for each of the subsequent chapters, because general debates between "theory of mind" theorists and their critics raise a diversity of topics that we discuss throughout the book.

The "Theory of Mind": Origins of the Debate

Anyone reading the current literature in the "theory of mind" tradition could easily get the impression that the field began in either 1978 or 1983. All fields have their creation myths and this area is no exception.[1] The year of 1978 stands out because this is when Premack and Woodruff's target article was published in *Behavioral and Brain Sciences*, a journal that presents a series of commentaries after each paper. In their article Premack and Woodruff asked the question: "Do chimpanzees have a theory of mind?", concluding that the evidence on deception is sufficient to show that they do. The paper stimulated the primate research that we reviewed in chapter 1. In the commentaries on this article several philosophers argued that a convincing answer to this question would require that chimpanzees, other animals, or young children demonstrate an understanding that beliefs can be false. And they went on to discuss the minimum complexity of any tasks meant to assess such an insight. Dennett (1978) described Punch and Judy puppet shows where, for example, Punch is laboring under the misconception that Judy is in the box he is gleefully pushing off the stage. The smiles and laughter from the young audience show their understanding that Punch's belief about Judy being in the box is false. They, unlike Punch, had seen Judy slip out of the box while Punch's back was turned. This sort of event reveals young children's understanding of an essential aspect of social understanding; that is, beliefs can be mistaken or false, yet people's action is still based on the way they believe the world to be. It is only when a protagonist's beliefs do not square with the world that we can distinguish what children know about the world from what they know about the protagonist's understanding. As a result, Dennett's minimum criterion for a test of a "theory of mind" was one in which the child's understanding of a state of affairs is at odds with a protagonist's mistaken belief.

Then, in 1983, Heinz Wimmer and Josef Perner published an article reporting a series of studies based on this criterion. These "false belief tasks" were designed to reveal whether children understand that it is possible to hold beliefs that are different from reality – that is, beliefs that are false. The now well-known story line that such tasks turn on involves the mistaken belief of a puppet, Maxi, which is due to him being out of the room when his mother moves his chocolate. The mischievous character Maxi is drawn from German folk tales about the misdeeds of Max and Moritz and their manipulation of Widow Tibbit's beliefs about the identity of the culprit of various misdemeanors (Perner, 1991). In this task a simple series of events leads Maxi to "think" his chocolate is in the green cupboard, because he was out of the room and so doesn't know that his mother has moved it to the blue cupboard. It is a surprise to parents and researchers alike that 3-year-olds generally fail to realize that Maxi would have a false belief. Instead, preschoolers tend to state that Maxi would know about the chocolate's new location. It is not until the age of 4 or 5 that most children say that the Maxi puppet would have an outdated and now false belief about where his chocolate is, and thus would look for it in its original location. We describe variations on this task in detail in chapter 3.

Over the past 20 years there has been a proliferation of explanations of the development of mental state understanding as revealed in children's performance on false belief tasks. Why did this happen? All the right conditions have been in place: [1] Discussion between people from a variety of disciplinary backgrounds – philosophers interested in the problem of other minds, cognitive scientists from a variety of disciplines trying to model the workings of the "mind–brain" system, evolutionary biologists and primatologists exploring the differences between humans and closely related species, and developmental psychologists examining how children come to understand the social world; [2] An explosion of research, mainly on typically developing preschool children, but also compared with nonhuman primates and individuals with specific problems like autism and Williams' syndrome; [3] Theories in a range of disciplines have been drawn on to explain how children develop social understanding. So, how can we analyze the main theories that have been discussed since the 1980s? In the following sections we present a description of each of the leading perspectives in terms of:

1 its underlying assumptions and origins;
2 what it was trying to achieve;
3 the processes it attempts to describe;
4 its explanation for how these skills develop.

The Dominant Perspective:
The Child's "Theory of Mind"

The past 20 years of theorization on children's understanding of the mind has been dominated by the perspective that introduced this catchy title. It argues that the child constructs an understanding of mind that is theory-like. It is important here to spell out just what is meant by the term theory, as used in science, and how it might apply to young children's early understanding of the social world.

Theory theory

The dominant account was termed "theory theory" by the philosopher Adam Morton (1980), as it proposes a theory that the child's understanding of mind is theory-like in nature. In this section we describe it so that you can decide whether it is the most appropriate account or whether it falls foul of the very problems that it attempts to overcome. This has been the dominant position, but is really a cluster of theories, which can be divided into two groups, spearheaded by two theoreticians who have made major contributions to the field since the onset of the debate in the early 1980s: Henry Wellman and Josef Perner.

The term "theory" filtered into developmental psychology because of two concerns that were raised about Piaget's theory. First, it was claimed that Piaget's theory of development failed to take into account the role of social factors in social cognitive development – a claim that we revisit in chapter 10. Secondly, it was argued that Piaget's account of development was too overarching and all-inclusive. This idea that the cognitive system is a whole – change one part and everything changes – has been very commonly but we believe mistakenly attributed to Piaget (see Chapman, 1988, for the argument that, in fact, Piaget never did propose such a view of stages). As part of a reaction to that holism, a series of papers attempted to examine the idea that the child's knowledge base may in fact be divided into different and relatively unrelated parts, known as "domains." Gradually the metaphor of the child-as-scientist emerged alongside this view and research came to focus upon how children come to develop naïve theories within particular domains. A landmark paper by two of Piaget's colleagues was entitled "If you want to get ahead, get a theory" (Karmiloff-Smith & Inhelder, 1974), and gradually the idea of the child as scientist or theoretician filtered into textbooks on child development (e.g., Ross, 1980).

This movement gained momentum, hand in hand with the critique of Piaget's theory (Carey, 1985a), when researchers like Susan Carey (1985b) attempted to show that children's understanding of domains like biology or physics develops as a result of small-scale changes that cannot be couched in terms of general developmental shifts. Carey showed that the child's understanding of concepts like "living" vs. "dead" or "inanimate" changes by simpler concepts either becoming differentiated or joining together (coalescing). She describes very clearly how her daughter's understanding of death slowly changed as a result of her own deep thoughts and through mother–daughter conversation (Carey, 1988). For example, when the child asks such questions as "When you are dead, how do you go to the bathroom?" this shows both that she is thinking about concepts like death and is at first mistaken in believing that bodily functions [and possibly even consciousness] continue after we die. Carey's work opened the way for researchers to ask questions about the child's understanding of psychology.

The theory theory approach has other origins. The main impetus from philosophy came from the dramatic decline in two major doctrines about the mind. First, Descartes' (1637) view that understanding of others' minds can be achieved by introspection of one's own mental states and generalizing to others' mental states. Through the twentieth century a number of problems were raised about this view, as it presupposes firstly that "mind" and "body" are in some ways separate [known as "dualism"] and the fact that if "you" have to look into your mind in the first place then "you" must be a person within a person who is doing the reading [the "homunculus" problem]. The alternative presented by psychology was behaviorism, a theory that suggests that the problem of understanding the mind is impossible to solve as minds are inaccessible to us. Its solution was to suggest that psychologists should theorize only about overt behavior. The fault line in this theory is that it left out all the interesting bits that define us as human – our beliefs, values, and feelings. As an alternative the philosopher David Lewis (no relation) (1966, 1972) suggested that we formulate theory-like understandings of the mind that we test in our everyday social interactions. This idea seemed to fit in with an older tradition within social psychology in which the ability to infer others' intentions from their actions was considered to be a vital ingredient to social understanding. This view was developed into one about "naïve psychology," the view that we need to take seriously the individual's understanding of the mental world (Heider, 1958). A converging line of thought from philosophy concerned the debate over the reality of folk psychology – our everyday way of talking about psychological matters. One side took the extreme "eliminativist materialist" position that folk psychology would eventually become outdated when neuroscience has sufficiently developed a language for explaining human behavior (e.g., Churchland, 1984; Greenwood, 1991). (For more on the theoretical roots of theory theory see Leudar & Costall, 2004.)

Following both the general philosophical shift toward understanding adults' theories about the mind and the work on domain-specific understanding in developmental psychology, a frenzy of research in the 1980s explored the idea that young children's understanding of the mind develops in a theory-like way. Several conferences culminating in a series of books (Astington, Harris, & Olson, 1988; Butterworth, Harris, Leslie, & Wellman, 1991; Frye & Moore, 1991; Perner, 1991; Wellman, 1990) put the topic squarely on the map. In these volumes a leading group of theoreticians argued that children understand the mind by a process of theoretical reflection. It is important to understand how the term "theory" is used because this is a complex metaphor that is not used in a uniform way. In Wellman's original account the term has three definitional criteria: a theory [1] has *coherence* (i.e., it is not just a group of isolated facts); [2] *makes "ontological" distinctions and commitments* – in the case of the "theory of mind" this concerns the distinction between objects in the physical world and "mental entities" that are the contents of minds but have no physical substance; and [3] *it provides a causal-explanatory framework*, which integrates different elements of the child's understanding of the domain of mental states. It is the very opacity or "hiddenness" of mental states that requires the construction of a theory:

> If no neutral observational or experiential data dictate the inferences of mental states, what does? Observation and experience play their parts but, in addition, some intervening conceptual filter seems to stand between observation or experience and knowledge of mind, a theoretical lens that organizes the latter out of the former. (Wellman, 1990, p. 95)

Although we as adults quite easily distinguish events from mental states, this theoretical position holds that children have slowly to acquire such knowledge. Wellman holds that the two crucial constructs in the understanding of mind are desires and beliefs. Drawing upon the philosophical analysis of John Searle (1983), Wellman argues that the former emerge from within (e.g., your stomach wrenches and you start wanting chocolate chip cookies) and are satisfied when the world fits such desires (you open the cookie tin and find one in there). Beliefs are both different and more complex. Information originates in the world and hits our senses so that we have to process it in order to understand events. When the acorn falls onto Chicken Little's head she immediately thinks that the sky has fallen on her. So for beliefs the direction of fit is opposite to that of desires. An understanding of this causal network develops gradually in the preschool years:

> Beliefs "are a special sort of hybrid construct, spanning mind and world in a particular fashion. . . . [B]eliefs are thoughts about (potentially) actual states of affairs. . . . [I]n our everyday psychology, beliefs constitute mental causes for actual behaviors. . . . When we say that someone "believes" something rather than "knows" something we are acknowledging this potential lack of correspondence. . . . I wish to claim that by age three, children's naïve psychology is commensurate with adults' in several fashions: (1) in including a conception of belief and (2) in contrasting beliefs with desires while (3) at the time joining them in a causal reasoning scheme. (Wellman, 1990, pp. 61–63)

For theory theorists mental states like beliefs and desires fit into a causal network. Not only do we act on our beliefs, desires, and intentions, but these influence one another at many levels. So, to believe that a horse is a mammal is to believe many other things about horses – e.g., that they respire and reproduce in particular ways, that they are more like some types of animals than others, etc. In other words, each individual piece of knowledge fits into a conceptual framework within a domain. For Wellman the child passes through two phases. At age 2 s/he is a "desire psychologist," understanding that people act upon desires and that mental states do not have observable or tangible qualities – e.g., they cannot be touched. Then at around age 4 children come to differentiate beliefs from desires and their understanding of psychology becomes more complex. For Wellman and his followers the child's theory becomes enriched as his or her knowledge of the domain develops.

How much like a scientific paradigm is such a naïve theory? Wellman contrasts the conceptual framework approach with the use of the term theory within science:

Within science empirical data make contact with specific theories, which are revised accordingly; framework scientific theories are much less subject to empirical test. Within everyday cognition, observations and new data cause one to formulate, refute, and revise specific explanations; but commonsense framework theories, the global ontologies and causal presumptions that guide and constrain the formulation of specific explanations, are not up for empirical revision in the same way. (Wellman, 1990, p. 132)

There are a number of key questions that Wellman's theory attempts to address. It aimed to examine the domain of mental state understanding and to present a developmental account of an understanding of the domain. Yet the comparison which he makes here reveals both a strength and a weakness in his application of the term framework theory to children. It provides a useful metaphor for how children's knowledge fits into a general belief system, yet it makes the notion of theory hard to test.

The representational theory of mind

A closely related account of the child's understanding of mind also draws upon the metaphor of the child as a theoretician. This is the perspective of Josef Perner (1988, 1991). His interest lies in how the child comes to make representations of the world. It draws upon two nineteenth-century thinkers, Gottlob Frege, a mathematician and logician, and Franz von Brentano, a philosopher, who were interested in the relationship between thought as a representational system and the world. For Frege, in particular, thought is reducible to a system of logical relations – an idea that influenced Piaget's life work (Smith, 1999). Perner drew upon Frege's distinction between "representing" and "representing as." As Frege pointed out, there is an ambiguity in the notion of representation, which refers to both the processes of constructing a mental image of an event in the world ("representing") and the idea that the mind is a medium for representing objects ("representing as").

Drawing upon these philosophical analyses, Perner argues that in order to understand mental representations as representations, we need to be able to compare what is represented with how the mind represents it. Often the mind is actually misinformed in its mappings onto the world. I may be "sure" that I saw my keys on the cupboard but then did not find them when I went to look there. Such mistakes alert us to the problems in human cognition, and we need an account of mental understanding that can allow for them. To do this Perner uses the term "metarepresentation" that we mentioned in chapter 1. This is the ability to understand mental representations as representations – we must hold in mind and compare what we remembered or "saw" with what we see now, and we must also tacitly understand the nature [i.e., frailty] of mental representations. For Perner, a landmark in development is the acquisition at around age 4 of the ability to grasp that mental representations have such a loose relation to the world – our minds are not simply a copy of reality:

> by conceptualizing the mind as a system of representations, the child switches from a *mentalistic theory of behavior*, in which mental states serve as concepts for explaining action, to a *representational theory of mind*, in which mental states are understood as serving a representational function. One can think of the concept of "representation" as playing a catalytic role in children's reconceptualization of what the mind is, similar to the catalytic role that important scientific concepts play in the development of new scientific theories. (Perner, 1991, p. 11, emphasis original)

This quotation pinpoints both the similarities and differences between Wellman's and Perner's positions. They both use the metaphor of the child as a scientist, constructing more complex accounts of the relation between the mind and the world. However, for Perner, the notion of "representation" is vital for understanding how this process occurs. Wellman describes a more gradual process by which concepts of belief are contrasted with existing theoretical understanding based upon desires and within a general theoretical framework. For Perner, development occurs in a more dramatic realization that the mind is independent of the world.

Wimmer and Perner's (1983) false belief task became a key demonstration of the emergence of the ability to understand that representations serve a particular function in the development of an understanding of mind. For Perner, it marks the third of three stages of development in the preschool years (see Perner, 1988, 1991): (1) *Presentation* (0 to about 18 months): concerns having a mental model of the world but no knowledge that this model is constructed by the representational system; (2) *Representation* (about 18–48 months): involves being able to create new models of the world by rearranging perceptual information – for example, the child has an elementary ability to engage in symbolic play, treating an object in a way that it was not typically used (at this stage a child has a mentalistic theory of behavior); (3) *Metarepresentation* (from about 4 years): is the ability to construct a model of the relationship between a representation and what it models – this involves the ability to compare two representations of the world. Such a skill allows the child to understand both misrepresentation (that we can be wrong in our beliefs) and the hypothetical – we can plan a set of strategies for understanding the world and work out the best strategy. All that is needed is the ability to relate such mental states to one another, using progressively more complex procedures of mental recursion. Thus at about age 6, children can grasp second order false beliefs – the ability to understand that one person's representations of another's mental representations can be wrong. We return to the issue of second order belief understanding in chapter 8.

The Official Oppositions: Innate and Simulation Accounts

Although the term "theory of mind" has received a lot of attention in developmental psychology over the past 20 years, not all theoreticians have been happy with the image of the child as a scientist. In this section we describe two perspectives that have continued to be contrasted with the theory view, the innate module and the simulation accounts. They share a focus on early development, but from radically different theoretical vantage points.

The innate module account

One of the key motivators behind the notion of an innate module stems from a perceived problem in Piaget's theory that it does not attribute the infant with innate knowledge. Yet some research has been interpreted as evidence that babies are born with a range of skills that are "hard wired" into their psychological make-up, as discrete abilities. Spelke (1994) and other theoreticians within the same tradition suggested that our ability to attend to particular domains of knowledge must be innately constrained. This approach also drew on a tradition that includes Fodor's (1983, 1992) views about the modular nature of the mind. This is the idea that aspects of cognition are self-contained or encapsulated and thus restricted to particular domains. This general idea was taken up by Alan Leslie (1987) in an analysis of pretence (see chapter 3). Like Josef Perner, Leslie emphasizes the role of metarepresentation in cognition. Unlike Perner, Leslie (1988, 1994; Scholl & Leslie, 1999) does not suggest that each child elaborately constructs an understanding of this capacity at around age 4. Rather he argues that the child is born with a special brain mechanism that allows her or him to grasp "metarepresentation." Rather than developing a theory of belief or pretence, a brain mechanism, known as the "Theory of Mind Mechanism" or "ToMM," allows the child to represent mental states, so that in the false belief task the child can grasp that the protagonist or "agent" has a mental attitude toward the real world that is at odds with the real world.

Leslie's account emerged in part in order to explain why children demonstrate the ability to perform symbolic play actions in the second year of life. Like false beliefs, such actions involve holding two mental representations in mind simultaneously. So when a child holds a banana to her ear and says "hello," she has to hold in mind the representations "This is a banana" and "This is a telephone." To do this the child needs a metarepresentational capacity which quarantines off the reality-based representation in favor of the symbolic one. Otherwise the child would be surprised if she didn't get a dialing tone when she put the banana to her ear. The reason that 3-year-olds might fail the false belief task is that the default answer in most everyday circumstances is that people's beliefs correspond to what is actually true (Leslie, 1991). Thus in the false belief task the child has to learn not simply to apply this "default" answer to the test question. Alongside the ToMM is another cognitive mechanism called the selection processor or "SP," which inhibits the default response and allows for possible alternatives to be considered. This gradually improves over the preschool period. The existence of such general capacities will be a central focus of chapter 5. Here it is important to distinguish Perner and Wellman's ideas about the construction of a theory and Leslie's suggestion that the cognitive system is in place but needs to be accessed with improvements in a more general processing capacity.

In addition to the theoretical accounts of symbolic play, another strand of research evidence which has contributed to the idea that we have an innate module dedicated to understanding mental states concerns research on special populations, particularly children with autism. In an early false belief experiment, Baron-Cohen, Leslie, and Frith (1985) demonstrated that children with autism of around 11 years of age tended to fail the false belief test whereas a matched group of children with learning disabilities (children with Down syndrome also aged 11) and a preschool sample of 4-year-olds mostly sailed though the test. Data such as these gave rise to a debate about whether the nature of autism can be attributed to the problem with such a specific ability and whether children with autism present us with evidence that the innate module account is the best one to explain how typically developing children come to understand the mind (Baron-Cohen, 1995). In chapter 3 we return to the evidence for the association between autism and false belief.

The simulation perspective

The second opposition account also developed alongside the theory theory view, long before the use of the term in the research on mirror neurons that we described in chapter 1. It criticizes the claim that a child constructs a theory as being too elaborate. Rather, children possess the ability to imagine themselves taking a position that is different from their own. This position has several origins. Within philosophy, Jane Heal (1986) in the UK and Robert Gordon (1986) and Alvin Goldman (1989) in the USA put forward the idea that human competence in explaining and predicting the behavior of others involves what has come to be termed "mental simulation." Within developmental psychology, Carl Johnson (1988) and Paul Harris (1989) put forward accounts of the development of children's understanding of the mind based upon this fundamental ability.

Simulation theory is based upon the idea that it is simply too mentally taxing to refer constantly to a set of hypotheses about the mind, particularly when we apply such an ability to young children. The example that is often used is of two people walking up a hill in the Rocky Mountains and one suddenly turns and flees as if her very life depends upon it. Does the puzzled companion try to work out a theory for his companion's behavior? The answer given by simulation theorists is "No!" The puzzle is solved by imagining why someone would act like that, probably with the image of a huge grizzly bear coming to mind, and by the person turning tail themselves. According to Johnson, the child draws upon a set of organized experiences rather than hypothetical constructs like "beliefs." Mental state understanding is thus "intuitive," particularly in the preschool child.

Harris (1991, 1992) takes up this idea and proposes a four-stage developmental sequence in which the child comes to learn how and when to use mental simulation, or what he terms imagination. In the first of two steps to take place in the first year of life, the infant demonstrates an inbuilt ability to synchronize their interactions with others, but only in a rudimentary way. At the end of the first year the second step is when the child begins to "act on, rather than merely reproduce, another's current attitude" (Harris, 1992, p. 126). However, it is not until around 3 that children begin to "anticipate or enact the reaction of people or toy characters whose current mental stance differs from their own" (p. 126). Step 4 involves the ability to imagine hypothetical circumstances and those in which a person's perspective is so blatantly at odds with reality – as in false belief. So, in sum:

> The important step taken between 3 and 5 years according to ST [Simulation Theory] is not the discovery that the mind is a representational device, but rather the appreciation that mental states (notably seeing and believing) can be directed at situations which the child rules out as part of reality as it stands. This discovery is part of a more wide-ranging ability to think about and describe counterfactual substitutes for current reality. (Harris, 1992, p. 131)

Current Debates over the Dominant Theories

Most of the theoretical debates within the "theory of mind" movement over the past 15 years have been between the dominant perspectives – the two versions of theory theory, the innate module approach, and simulation theory. Discussion developed at such a pace that Carruthers and Smith (1996, p. 2) described it as a "small industry." What has the industry produced? Any answer to this question must account for the complexity of the data on the topic: the subject of the following eight chapters in this book. Here we consider the theoretical debates that have developed over the past decade.

Developments of the theory, simulation, and innate model perspectives

Given the early development of theory theory and the prominence of Wellman and Perner's work, their ideas are still taken as the gold standard of the new approach to the child's understanding of the social world. Few theorists have attempted to separate out their contributions even though Perner's interest is in the development of a metarepresentational "insight" at around age 4 whereas Wellman's account fits together different types of mental state understanding and their relation to action. Many issues raised over 10 years ago have been left unaddressed. For example, in their books on the subject each raised problems with the other's accounts. Wellman (1990) criticized Perner on two counts: on his idea that the young child initially has a "nonrepresentational" understanding of belief and his and others' lack of clarity about just what a representation is. Perner (1991), likewise, felt that Wellman's distinctions between belief and desire reasoning do not sufficiently grasp the crucial issue in development – the understanding of the mind as a representational device – a point acknowledged by Wellman. However, their shared view is that the child constructs successive accounts of how the mind works that are theory-like and this process forms the basis of the development of social understanding. The main debates have occurred at a number of different levels, but mainly compare this hybrid version of Perner and Wellman's accounts with those of others.

One common development of the theory perspective has been to extend the "child-as-scientist" metaphor in order to draw closer parallels between children's development and the ways in which theories change within science. Although Wellman's earlier work (e.g., 1990) rejects the association in favor of the notion of a theory as a framework of connected ideas, his more recent writing with Alison Gopnik (Gopnik, 1993, 1996; Gopnik & Wellman, 1992, 1994) has pushed the idea that the connections with the history and philosophy of science can be used to understand children's development. Like others within this tradition, Gopnik and Wellman (1994) acknowledge that children may have innately given "starting state" theories, thus conceding some ground to the "innate module" account described above. Nevertheless, for them, the important feature of development is that these are revised by the child as soon as he or she gains sufficient experience. Thus it is fair to suggest that over the past decade the theory theory position has come to stress the narrower definition of the term theory over the framework account in Wellman's earlier work that was described above.

However, this narrower definition of the term has made the theory theory view more open to criticism (e.g., Mitchell & Riggs, 2000). German and Leslie (2000) are typical in their claim that the analogy between children and scientists is difficult from the outset because there is little agreement about the mechanisms of change within science. If it is the case that philosophers and sociologists of science do not agree on how theory change takes place within science, and indeed there is great diversity in this area of debate (Kuhn, 1962; Feyerabend, 1975; Lakatos, 1970), then it does seem slightly problematic to apply the idea of the child-as-scientist to the child's development. We have to ask "Which view of science?" before we can begin to find parallels in children's development. Thus there has been a reluctance on the part of many theoreticians in this area to take this metaphor too literally – a point we explore in the next major section.

The main focus of attention concerning the theory theory has been between this position and related ones, particularly the official oppositions described above. Over the past 10 years there has been an impasse between the innate module perspective and the other two, while there has been something of a fusion between theory theory and simulation theory. In response to Harris's earlier work, Wellman (1990, p. 199) suggests that it is misleading to assume (as Harris does) that theorization and simulation are necessarily separate skills. He points out that simulation theory does not explain the knowledge base upon which we draw in order to imagine a particular point of view; this requires the sort of framework theory that Wellman proposes – we must organize the knowledge upon which we imagine a particular state of affairs. In work that has followed it has been hard to keep the simulation and theory perspectives apart – each side admits that the two abilities are not incompatible. Theory theorists, like Peter Carruthers (1996, p. 23), acknowledge that "the picture of two- and three-year-old children as little scientists constructing their theories through a process of data collection, hypothesis formation, and testing, is otherwise apt to seem extravagant." Stone and Davies (1996, p. 133) summarize the state of play in a review of simulation theory by quoting Perner's (1996, p. 103) chapter in the same volume:

> since any theory use involves an element of simulation and since simulation on its own cannot account for the data, the future must lie in a mixture of simulation and theory use. However, what this mixture is and how it operates must first be specified in some detail before any testable predictions can be derived.

Russell's critical analysis

Although within the theory of mind tradition moves toward a consensus between the three dominant perspectives have been made, criticism of the enterprise has continued. James Russell (1992, 1996) has been particularly incisive in his criticisms of these major positions, taking each in turn and raising major objections to its theoretical foundations. He attacks the innate module approach on philosophical grounds as it relies on a doctrine of thinking proposed by Fodor (1981), known as the Language of Thought (LoT) doctrine. This suggests that knowledge is innately constrained. Each "atomic" component skill must initially be separate – otherwise the child would be born with a complete knowledge-base and development would be irrelevant. The task for the child is to "parse" or separate out mental state propositions to the effect that "A subject has a mental attitude towards a content." Yet, Russell holds, a grasp of belief fits into a network of understandings – to think about apples is to imply an ability to think about concepts of fruit, what is edible, etc. Russell (1996, p. 11) claims that if our beliefs fit into a semantic network, this undermines the LoT doctrine: "if the merest strain of holism is allowed to seep into the definition of an LoT symbol then its truly symbolic nature will evaporate."

Russell (1996) raises objections to simulation theory. To think of the mind in the way proposed by Harris and Johnson, the individual has to imagine how he or she would perceive a problem and generalize their perspective to others – this is the classic "problem of inferring other minds" in philosophy that derives from Descartes and as far back as the solipsists. Such an ability presupposes that young children have an awareness of "inner feelings" from which they generalize to others. However, there are serious grounds for assuming that such generalizations from the self are unlikely to account for an understanding of mind. First, Russell points out that the simulation perspective is based on the assumption that the meanings of mental state terms are grounded in private experience. But the philosopher Ludwig Wittgenstein's "private language argument" "seems to establish that the meanings of linguistic expressions cannot be fixed by reference to the 'private' experience of the speakers of a language" (Russell, 1996, p. 186). Wittgenstein's conclusion is that the meanings of mental state terms are determined by the shared use of such words by members of a culture: not by introspection. We further discuss the relevance of the private language argument for social development in chapters 7 and 10. Secondly, Russell draws on an analysis from P. F. Strawson, known as the "generality constraint," according to which "there are no possible grounds on which 'pre-analogy' children can think 'I am thinking' if introspection is all they have to go on; for they are not in a position to classify that experience as their own if there can be no thoughts about other experiences" (p. 187). Russell's analysis, if correct, makes the simulation account highly problematic.

Russell (1996) identifies similar problems with the theory theory accounts. He takes the position typified by Gopnik that all children construct a series of theories of mind which result in the mature theory. He asks why it is that every child may follow such a journey *de novo*. His question raises a serious concern for the perspective, as it underlines the possibility that there might be other reasons why 3-year-olds fail false belief. They might, he argues, be overwhelmed by the demands of mentally processing the information required to solve false belief tasks and therefore plump for an answer that simply states where the object is now. We take up Russell's alternative in chapter 5 when we look at the relationship between "theory of mind" and more domain general skills.

The "Great Unwashed": Social Alternatives to the Official Theories

Not only have there been internal debates and divisions between the theory, simulation, and innate module accounts of how the child comes to develop a "theory of mind," the tradition as a whole also has consistently been criticized from a broader perspective. These criticisms largely reflect an unease about cognitive science, the study of systems of the mind, for its neglect of traditional theories of social understanding. In particular, they question those accounts that neglect the child's social relationships. In this section we describe this alternative perspective and how it fits in with both traditional social cognitive theories described in chapter 1 and the official accounts of theory of mind described in this chapter.

Early social reflections on the "theory of mind"

As soon as theory theory accounts were put forward feelings of disquiet were voiced by researchers with the longer view in mind. Jerome Bruner, an architect of the cognitive science movement in the 1950s, was noticeable for his critique of the insularity of the "theory of mind." In two books Bruner (1986, 1990) criticized the computational metaphor in contemporary accounts of cognitive development, raising fundamental problems with the idea that the route into understanding social cognition is through examining the child's theoretical reflections alone. Rather, he suggested that we should consider the nature of folk psychology itself – the complexity of belief systems, narratives, and metaphors that are organized in everyday practices and talk. From this perspective, everyday concepts of mind are based upon such practices and ways of talking, and understanding minds does not require a scientist's abstract reflections. For Bruner the child has to be introduced into a "culture of meaning," learning the ways in which his or her culture frames the notion of mental states and relationships. He has been accused of proposing a system in which we abandon studying the process of development in favor of looking at the conventions to which cultures introduce us – the enculturation perspective (e.g., Astington & Gopnik, 1991). However, Bruner (1990, chapter 3) is clear that he is proposing a model in which there is a subtle blend between genetic predispositions (he even talks about "innate representations"), the development of individuals (ontogeny), and the culture's communication system. Our innate representations are "triggered by the acts and expressions of others and by certain basic contexts in which human beings interact" (Bruner, 1990, p. 73). Such is the stuff of social life and interaction.

Bruner's ideas have not had a clearly direct influence upon the work that has been established within, or in opposition to, the "theory of mind" movement. However, the idea that we should look at the social relational issues has been championed by others with a similar perspective. Notably, the work of Judy Dunn stands in contrast to the three dominant perspectives on mental state understanding. She has pioneered the claim that social development has to be understood within the study of social interaction. Her longitudinal studies of the development of sibling relationships within the context of mother–child interaction served as a landmark in the study of family relationships because they showed the importance of family relationships for the child's later functioning (Dunn & Kendrick, 1982), including symbolic play (Dunn & Dale, 1984) and the influence of factors like sibling quarrels upon social cognitive skills (Dunn & Munn, 1985). In chapter 6 we will return to Dunn's work because more recently she has examined such family influences on social cognitive development. For this analysis, Dunn's (e.g., 1996) reflections on the role of relationships in "theory of mind" development serves as a timely reminder that the major accounts lack a crucial social dimension.

At the same time Michael Chandler (e.g., 1988) criticized the emerging "theory of mind" tradition for neglecting the longer view of development. He took part in the debate between followers of Piaget and the critics of the notion of egocentrism which were discussed in chapter 1. In the 1970s he continued to question the claim that children's success on simple perspective-taking tasks shows that they are not egocentric. Rather, he pointed out that simplifying tasks may result in assessing earlier competences rather than those required for taking perspectives in more complex situations (see, e.g., Chandler & Greenspan, 1972). Chandler made similar comments about the new tradition. For example, in an earlier analysis he argued that "theory of mind" researchers have focused too narrowly upon the preschool period and particularly on the shift that appears to develop around the child's fourth birthday (Chandler, 1988). In that and subsequent articles he has suggested that we should be looking for both earlier skill acquisition and indeed for later achievements in social cognition during childhood and well into the teenage years. We will explore some of the data that Chandler has collected to demonstrate his claims regarding children's early understanding of false beliefs in chapter 3, and his theory and research on adolescent epistemic development in chapter 8.

Somewhat outside the mêlée of debate over theory, the general approach has always been questioned for its focus on individual minds (Jopling, 1993). Some take a radically social perspective and claim that the issue of mental state understanding must be understood as a social enterprise in which people collectively construct the mind. For these theoreticians, the lowest common denominator is the dyad (i.e., the interaction between two people: Feldman, 1992; Forrester, 1992; Raver & Leadbeater, 1993):

> Theory-of-mind research focuses upon the single mind of the individual child as a rational empiricist, processing incoming perceptual data and reporting on the results of those observations. In contrast, social developmentalists focus on the interaction of at least dyads and the development of social minds of children actively communicating in a peopled world. (Raver & Leadbeater, 1993, p. 355)

From this perspective cynicism has been largely directed at the idea that a child could possibly develop a theory, when such an achievement is the culmination of a lengthy training rather than part of the early process of knowledge acquisition (Gellatly, 1997). Similarly, Campbell and Bickhard (1993) suggest that if the term "theory" is used loosely in the sense that knowledge is interconnected in a framework then it is general enough to include any form of human knowledge. However, it is hard to discern how much these and other critiques (e.g., Leudar & Costall, 2004; Sharrock & Coulter, 2004) have influenced the development of the major positions and their criticisms.

Development of social perspectives:
the role of language and communication

A small group of researchers, like Dunn, have worked within the "theory of mind" tradition to attempt to reopen some basic questions about how children's understanding of mind develops. There are four issues that have emerged over the past decade, which we will raise in brief here but each will be explored in subsequent chapters. Each stems from the idea that "theory of mind" research needs to take into account social interaction as an essential ingredient in social cognitive development.

The first issue concerns an overemphasis in the field on false belief understanding with a resulting neglect of earlier social cognitive development in infancy and the process of development. Two researchers in particular attacked the "theory of mind" tradition for focusing on skills that were at too high a level of competence. Vasudevi Reddy (1991) examined social interactions in infancy (i.e., the first 18–24 months of life). Reddy rejected the individualistic perspective of theory theory and argued instead that development occurs within the context of rich sequences of social interaction experienced by even young infants. She studied the early examples of what she termed "teasing and mucking about" that characterize adult–infant interaction from the second half of the child's first year. In her own daughter she reported a game that emerged at nine months in which Shamini

> offers object to F saying "ta" and waving her fingers with it as an additional call, looking at F's face intently; F stretches hand out to take it, as F's hand comes closer, Shamini with eyes intently on F's face begins to smile, then withdraws object with smile broadening and turns away, then looks back, F laughs, and says in a voice acknowledging being teased "You, gimme, gimme, gimme." (Reddy, 1991, p. 146)

Not only do such episodes become a familiar routine in infants' daily lives, they also need explaining. Reddy suggested that it is in such encounters that the child derives an understanding of the social world, consistent with Raver and Leadbeater's (1993) claim that the social mind is a dyadic one. She has maintained and developed this position (Reddy, 2003; Reddy & Morris, 2004) and we shall return to her perspective on infancy and of the nature of social understanding when we consider the theory and evidence on infants' social understanding in chapter 4.

While Reddy was reflecting on how babies might come to develop a social understanding within interaction, Peter Hobson (1991) was developing a strand of research and theory that attempted to question the application of the abstract notion of a theory of mind to the problems of autism. Such are the problems of autism – impoverishments in language and social interactions – that Hobson argues that deficiencies in much more basic skills are far more likely to be at the heart of these than more abstract "theoretical" abilities. At the very heart of autism is a difficulty in engaging in shared interaction. Typically developing children learn very quickly to engage in social exchanges. Individuals with autism find such interactional skill hard and even intellectually very able individuals report that shared affect is particularly difficult.

Hobson's (1993, 2002) view of autism is very much in keeping with that of two major autism scholars, Marian Sigman and Peter Mundy (e.g., Mundy & Sigman, 1989; Mundy, Sigman, & Kasari, 1994). For them, a major problem which children with autism face is shared affective engagement with others, particularly that involving shared attention to objects. Hobson takes this idea further to propose a model for the study of early developments in infancy. He has long claimed that it is the ability to read others' behavior that is central to the nature of autism and is therefore so central in the young child's understanding of the mind:

> intersubjective engagement and mental coordination between infant and caretaker entail that the infant's attitudes are altered and shaped by the infant's perception of those aspects of the caretaker's behavior that we as adults conceptualise as manifestations of attitudes, especially emotional attitudes. (Hobson, 1994, p. 74)

For Hobson, conceptual knowledge emerges slowly out of such interactions. The mechanism for development is what he terms the "relatedness triangle," between the child, the other, and objects of shared attention. Such a structure pays attention to the claim that learning about the world and other people is mediated through social interaction with others. Hobson's approach also leads to a particular view of language:

> Out of the infant's experience of *inter*personal co-referential attitudes the young child distils out an understanding of the nature of co-reference itself (p. 83). . . . We psychologists think of "symbolic thought" as a highly abstracted process, but the source of such thinking is the infant's

psychological engagement with the world . . . it is people, not symbols or "representations," that represent things and situations. (p. 84)

Hobson's account of infant interaction is in keeping with the work of Vygotsky and more recently Michael Cole (1992), but as we shall see in chapter 10 is also consistent with the views of Piaget and followers (Chapman, 1991).

The second area of research concerns the role of social interaction as children acquire mental state understanding. Janet Astington, a fully paid-up member of the "theory of mind" tradition (Astington et al., 1988), has consistently attempted to analyze the boundaries of the theory metaphor. Her earlier work explored the relationships between mental state understanding and broader concepts, like plans, actions, or intentions (Astington, 1990a). She stood out in her attempts to compare research within the tradition with the ideas of critics like Bruner (Astington, 1990b). More recently Astington has emphasized the role of communication (Astington & Olson, 1995) and broader social interactions (Astington, 1996) in the child's formulation of a theory. This work has taken on an explicit reference to the work of the Vygotsky, who argued that all human skills develop first in social interaction and then become "internalized," allowing the child to perform them without help from a more skilful interactant. Thus, Astington explicitly includes such a social dimension to her theory.

A third group of approaches places language at the center of the process by which the child comes to grasp mental states (Astington & Baird, 2005). There are a number of theorists who have attempted to account for the evidence that language is closely linked with children's social cognitive development. Paul Harris (1996) suggested that conversation may be a crucial factor in exposing the child to what the mind is about because it presents the child with other people's differing perspectives. From a "theory" perspective, Astington (2001) has recently stressed the importance of language as a means by which the child gains access to mental state terms. A third view is put forward by Katherine Nelson (1996, 2005). She attempts to integrate a perspective on the role of cultural factors, language, and "theory of mind." Like Astington, she grapples with the means by which children come to grasp terms like "think."

The fourth perspective takes a more radical approach to language (Carpendale & Lewis, 2004a; Montgomery, 1997, 2002, 2004; Sharrock & Coulter, 2004). It starts with the view that language is an activity, not just a means of labeling objects (Turnbull, 2003; Turnbull &

Carpendale, 1999a). It draws from Wittgenstein's Private Language argument, mentioned above with reference to Russell's critique of simulation, but extends it to all mental state understanding: children cannot learn the meaning of mental state terms by introspecting upon their own experiences, rather they do so by learning the varied uses of such words. From this perspective language mediates children's knowledge of reality. Children learn what Wittgenstein called the "criteria" for words to talk about human activity. By this he meant the publicly agreed ways of talking about such activity. Language, or communicative interaction, is the means through which children learn about other people's experience and so develop a more complete set of criteria. We discuss these and other theorists (e.g., Fernyhough, 1996; Symons, 2004) in chapter 7 where we examine the data linking language development with social development and evaluate the theoretical perspectives grappling with this evidence.

Summary and Conclusions

As we have outlined in this chapter, researchers working on young children's understanding of the psychological world have been fascinated by children's development of an understanding that false beliefs are possible. This insight is thought to be an essential aspect of young children's social understanding, also referred to as "commonsense psychology," "folk psychology," or "belief–desire reasoning." The significance attributed to false belief understanding is that children now understand that the mind works by representing the world, and that misrepresentation is possible but people still act in terms of their beliefs. Initially, three main theories were proposed to explain this development: theory theory, simulation theory, and the innate module approach. According to the theory theory, young children formulate a theory to explain the talk and action of people. The simulation theory, in contrast, assumes that rather than a theory, children's understanding of the mind is based on simulation. The innate module account, on the other hand, argues that children's way of understanding mental life is based on an innate module – an evolved mechanism for computing mental states. We also reviewed the current state of debates between these theories. More recently, a number of alternative theories have been advanced that focus more centrally on various aspects of the social dimension to social development. Some of these theories have emphasized the evidence of early social understanding in infancy and the role of interpersonal engagement in social development. A second approach has centered on the influence of social interaction on development, drawing on Vygotskian theory. The role of language in social cognitive development has been focused on in various ways by a third group of theorists. We will discuss the continuing debates among these approaches throughout the book. In the next chapter we turn to a review of the extensive research on the development of children's false belief understanding.

Note

1. We have borrowed this metaphor from Bryan Sokol.

Chapter 3

Understanding False Beliefs

In everyday life, beliefs rather than reality determine what people do. Hence the acid test of mentalizing is understanding a false belief. False beliefs play an important role in social communication, especially in the detection and use of deception, persuasion and trading.

(Frith & Frith, 2001, p. 151)

there is a danger in letting a single task become a marker for a complex development.

(Astington, 2001, p. 687)

In 1983 Heinz Wimmer and Josef Perner published the landmark "Maxi" study that we briefly described in chapter 2. In their original procedure, children had to assess how the belief of a protagonist contrasts with what they knew to be true. As Frith and Frith state, the "false belief" task has become the "acid test" of an understanding of mental states. One of the main aims of this chapter is to show why one procedure, or really a set of procedures, has been so central and so influential upon developmental psychology as well as the "theory of mind" tradition. Yet the task has always been subject to fierce critical scrutiny from both within and outside the "theory of mind" movement. So, it is important here to chart a history of both the connections between false belief and related skills and the variations of the procedure that have been established to test the central claim of "theory of mind" accounts that 3-year-olds have little insight into others' minds. This is the focus of the first section of the chapter. The second part presents a brief analysis of the debate about what the false belief task tells us about development. It analyzes the contribution of just one paper – a key meta-analysis of the many false belief experiments that have been conducted. The third section describes some recent developments in methodology that will serve as a bridge to the next six chapters.

Methodological Debates in the
Theory of Mind Movement

The false belief task

There are two main versions of the false belief test. The original task involving a character called "Maxi" is often referred to as the *unexpected transfer test*, because the character leaves an object (e.g., a chocolate bar) in one location and while he is "outside" it is moved to a new location. As Maxi did not see his chocolate moved, the child should expect him to act upon his, now outdated, belief and look in the old location for his chocolate. The reason why such a simple procedure has been so closely inspected is that 70 percent of young 3-year-olds failed this task, claiming that Maxi would say that his chocolate is in the new location, as if everyone's understanding of events must reflect current reality – children at this age appear to assume that Maxi could not be mistaken in his belief. In contrast, Wimmer and Perner (1983, experiment 1) found that almost 100 percent of 6-year-olds attributed Maxi with a false belief, when asked "Where will Maxi say the chocolate is?"

This age-shift in performance has been the source of much discussion, hinged mainly on the theoretical issues that we described in chapter 2. The focus of this section is mainly methodological and examines whether this represents a genuine shift in development across this age-span, or simply a failure of younger children's basic skills over and above their ability to understand mental states. Wimmer and Perner (1983) conducted a series of experiments which have checked for these extraneous influences. They hypothesized that the age gap might be caused by the younger children being less involved in the task. In the first experiment a reason was given for Maxi placing the chocolate in a cupboard – either to hide his chocolate from his brother or as part of a cooperative task in which Maxi's commitment to looking in that cupboard is enhanced by him needing his grandfather to help him place the chocolate there. They conducted two further tasks. In the first, the children were told to "stop and think" before the test question was asked in order to stop the child from impulsively stating where the chocolate actually is. In the second, they dispensed with the chocolate [Maxi's mother used it in her cooking]. Despite these manipulations of the task, the 5–6-year-olds were perfect in both conditions and the 4–5-year-olds were 68 percent correct, while only 15 percent of the 3–4-year-olds were successful (experiment 2). These data appeared to suggest that "a novel skill seems to emerge within the period 4–6 years" (Wimmer & Perner, 1983, p. 126) and this is not explained by the child's attention to the task.

In the 1980s and early 1990s a concerted effort was made to test these findings to destruction. Early work standardized the unexpected transfer test to assuage possible criticisms. Following Perner, Leekam, and Wimmer (1987), two control questions were added to the procedure of the unexpected transfer test to check the child's memory of events ("Where did Maxi put his chocolate in the beginning?") and awareness of the object's current location ("Where is the chocolate now?"). In most published papers since, only those children who pass these questions are included in the statistical analysis, as such knowledge is essential for an understanding of the contrast between reality and the protagonist's actions or thoughts. In addition to these memory and reality control questions, two phrasings of test question have become most used – either "Where will Maxi look for his chocolate?" or "Where does Maxi think his chocolate is?"

Perhaps young children fail the unexpected transfer test because they are poor at attending to tasks with dolls or which do not directly involve them as thinkers/actors? To address this question Wimmer and Perner devised the *deceptive container* [or deceptive box] test. In this the child becomes the protagonist. She is shown a familiar-looking (e.g., confectionery) box, like a Smarties tube (now replaced by a box – life is not as exciting as it used to be), and asked what is inside. Having guessed that appropriate items would be inside (e.g., chocolates) and been shown than something else was present (e.g., pencils), the child is asked to recall what she had said/thought was inside and/or what some-one else would think was in there. Early research using this technique (Hogrefe, Wimmer, & Perner, 1986; Perner, Leekam, & Wimmer, 1987) suggested the same split between 3-year-olds and older children. When asked, "What did you think was in the box?", younger children now state that they thought all along that the box contained pencils. Hogrefe et al. also produced an interesting dissociation. In a series of experiments they found consistently that 3-year-olds failed false belief questions in a variety of formats (e.g., "What will [Name of another person] say is in this box?" or the forced choice "Does s/he think there are pencils in the box or chocolates?"). However, they were significantly better at answering questions about the protagonist's ignorance (e.g., "Does [Name of another person] *know* what is really in the box or does she not know that?"). This suggests that 3–4-year-olds may be aware that another person's understanding may be different from their own or from reality but, paradoxically, may be unable to use this knowledge to infer what they think or how they might act. This dissociation provided crucial evidence for Perner's claim that at about 4 years of age children experience a dramatic insight that the mind serves as a "representational device" – that you can use your knowledge of another's mental state to predict their actions, statements, and even their commitment to a point of view. We return to Hogrefe et al.'s finding in the final section.

Does the false belief test underestimate children's competence?

Wimmer and Perner (1983) devised the false belief test in part to test the claim attributed to Piaget that before the age of 7 children are profoundly egocentric and unable to see the world from another person's perspective. In many ways they attempted to show that children as young as 4 were able to demonstrate social perspective taking (understanding that someone may represent the world from a different vantage point) as John Flavell and his colleagues (1974) had shown for visual perspective taking (being able to comment upon or even reproduce the view of a scene from another's position). It may therefore appear to be surprising that the main early criticism of "theory of mind" research was that it did not credit preschoolers with enough social skills. There were two main areas of debate about the false belief test. The first, that younger children fail because the task demands place too great a burden upon them, will be the focus of this section. The second concerns the three-way links between the task, what it purports to measure (i.e., the theoretical inferences we can draw from it), and related skills, notably pretense, deception, and other mental states, like desires and intentions. Such links will be the focus of the third section.

There are many researchers who question the validity of the test. For a start, it is a "one-off" procedure, in that once you have conducted it, you cannot reproduce the same procedure again. If you do, children's answers may be contaminated by previous answers to the test question. One of us (CL) once took a BBC film crew into the university playgroup at Lancaster to demonstrate children's performance on false belief. Some eight months before, my PhD student had tested children there. The first child whose parents had given permission for them to be filmed was brought into the playroom and Charlie held up a Smartie container and asked, "What is in this box?" The 4-year-old cast his eyes up to the heavens and responded dejectedly, "Pencils." Some attempts have been made to get round this problem by altering the materials used and/or the instructions given to the child. This way, test–retest reliability can be explored if children are tested within a relatively short time period. The evidence is mixed. One team reported very low reliability, which questions whether the task really does tap stable cognitive skills (Mayes et al., 1996). However, a more recent replication of this study found sufficiently consistent performance in children at two time periods (Hughes, Adlam, Happé, Jackson, Taylor, & Caspi, 2000). Thus, it is possible to present the false belief task in a way that appears to show construct validity – i.e., that the hypothesized underlying skill is present.

An alternative way to test the validity of the false belief task is to manipulate the procedure so that it becomes more meaningful to younger children. They might, for example, fail the test because it is somewhat abstract to them: a point made by Michael Chandler (1988) at the first major conference dedicated to exploring "theory of mind." There followed a spate of studies which attempted to explore the limits of competence in children below 4. One of my (CL's) early preoccupations concerned the child's understanding of both the experimenter's intent and the wording of the test question: e.g., "Where will Maxi say the chocolate is?" I supposed that the correct answer to that question should be "Dunno" as it is not possible to predict what people will say, particularly when they are 5-cm-high dolls. Alternatively, the question does not refer to any particular place in time, so the respondent is perfectly within her or his rights to assume that Maxi would search high and low for the object before both identifying it and stating where it actually is – the "incorrect" response. Members of the "theory of mind" movement thought of this and made the test question very specific. For example, Astington and Gopnik (1988, p. 195) phrased the question in the deceptive container experiment, "Now . . . when you first saw the box, before we opened it, what did you think was inside it?" Still 3-year-old children failed at the task.

Amanda Osborne and I worried about the phrasing of that "helpful" test question, as it included an embedded clause "when you first saw the box." The literature on early language development suggests that preschoolers struggle with such clauses. We therefore designed a deceptive container task in which we both presented a simplified test question which included clear temporal reference ("What did you think was in the box before I took the top off?") and we asked such questions about the next child (whose thoughts we also asked about) within the context of a whispering game – the experimenter and child had moved to one side while CL fetched the next participant. Under these testing conditions children's performance was greatly improved, but not in the standard task with the question "What did you think was in the box?", or in another condition with a more complex second clause, "What did you think was in the box when the top was still on it?" This was particularly the case in children above the age of 3½, 75 percent of whom answered the first test question correctly. We were not trying to say that preschoolers have a skill that is masked by the standard task. Rather we concluded that:

> a clearer understanding of preschoolers' theories of mind should make children's interactions the central focus of study, particularly their interpretations of the discourses in which experimenters attempt to assess their knowledge and skill. (Lewis & Osborne, 1990, p. 1519)

The early 1990s witnessed a debate about the significance of findings like these (see, for example, Lewis & Mitchell, 1994). During this period two camps appeared to be squaring up to one another. Some authors claimed that these were minor influences when compared with the findings from a rapidly growing number of papers that reported the "standard" test. The issues hinged around personal involvement and relevance to the child. One possibility was that the young child errs because he or she is embarrassed about guessing the contents of the box wrongly, so tries to get the true contents of the box right in the test question. Wimmer and Hartl (1991: experiment 3) tested this by involving an Austrian puppet, Kasperl, who is shown the box and asked what is inside while the child watches. The child is then asked the test question about Kasperl's false belief. Three-year-olds still were less than 50 percent correct. In the deceptive container test it could be argued that the child has a 50 percent chance by guessing either the usual contents or the novel ones, as only these two choices have been connected with the box. A similar attempt to get the child to understand the task was conducted by Moses and Flavell (1990). They were concerned that the task lacked ecological validity as it did not provide cues about the fact that the protagonist's expectations were breached. Thus they set up new versions where the child saw a video clip in which a false belief was shown to cause surprise in the actor. For example, Mary is desperately looking for Bandaids ("Ouch my finger hurts . . . I'm looking for a Bandaid") and finds a Bandaid box on the kitchen table ("Ah here are some Bandaids"), only to find that the box contains a toy car and no plasters. The film freezes with the car poking out of the Bandaid box and Mary looking surprised. All the way through the experimenter gives cues like "She's looking for Bandaids" and when she is thwarted prompts "Look how surprised Mary is," before asking the child what Mary thought was in the box before she opened it. Moses and Flavell found that 53 percent of preschoolers said that Mary expected to find the car in the box, despite the narrative from Mary, which reinforced the experimenter's commentary. They concluded: "young children's difficulties are extremely robust and if they do possess an understanding of false beliefs as some have argued, it must be either extraordinarily difficult to access or remarkably easy to shake" (p. 942).

Such results are intriguing and certainly show that the preschooler is easily misled by the false belief test. However, other data suggested that the picture is more complicated. The issue of personal involvement was central to many such studies. Freeman, Lewis, and Doherty (1991) turned the unexpected transfer task into a "hide-and-seek" game, with a Daddy who cheats and sees Sarah go into one of two adjoining sheds. While Daddy turns back to count, she then goes into the other shed. Children answered the verbal question "Where will Daddy look for Sarah?" by pointing to where Sarah is now. However, when asked to "Take daddy to find Sarah," the 3-year-olds took him to the first shed and often said "Sarah? Oh you're not here. Let's try the red shed . . . There you are." They were not successful in a control condition in which Daddy and Sarah were out for a walk and Daddy casually notices her going into the first shed. So, the study appeared to demonstrate competence but only under very specific circumstances. Thus understanding may be "scaffolded" through interactions, but is not easily available to the 3-year-old. Other teams claimed that such understanding can be found in false belief tests that are set up so that the child can trick another experimenter (Sullivan & Winner, 1993).

The issue of tricking someone was also taken up by Chandler, Fritz, and Hala (1989). They set up a task to test competence in children around their third birthdays. The aim was to see if a child could help a doll, "Toni," to lay false trails or erase footprints to where a reward is hidden. Toni was a doll mounted on a stick with feet attached to a wheel, so that the child can push her along a whiteboard. Her feet were immersed in an ink bed so that when she "walks" to one of four bins, she leaves a trail of footprints. Children had to take Toni to hide a reward from a second experimenter and then, with encouragement, use a sponge to erase her inky trails or lay false tracks. In one study (Hala, Chandler, & Fritz, 1991: experiment 2), 19 out of 20 three-year-olds *both* erased Tony's tracks to the correct location in a deception condition and spontaneously laid tracks to the correct bin when asked to do something to make it easy for the second experimenter to find the treasure. However, other studies using deception did not find consistent results (e.g., Russell, Mauthner, Sharpe, & Tidswell, 1991; Sodian, Taylor, Harris, & Perner, 1991). We will describe Russell et al.'s methodology in chapter 5. Sodian et al. carried out a similar task in which the child had to either help one doll (a king) or deceive another (a robber). Although almost all the children laid false trails, only 21 percent of 3-year-olds who laid such trails did so for the robber only while 42 percent of them got completely muddled and did so for the king whom they were supposed to be helping. The same patterns did not hold for the 4-year-olds: 62 percent laid trails for the robber while only 6 percent did so for the king. Sodian et al. concluded that 3-year-olds may know about deceptive strategies like laying false trails but children do not fully understand the reasons behind such actions until they have a more mature "theory of mind" (for further discussion see the chapters by Sodian and Chandler & Hala in Lewis & Mitchell, 1994). The contrast between these results is puzzling. Slight differences in methodology influence 3-year-olds' performance dramatically: an issue to which we return later.

The False Belief Re-observed: Recent Re-analyses of the Task

The meta-analysis of Wellman, Cross, and Watson (2001)

The heated debate over the importance of the many modifications performed on the false belief task continued through the1990s. So many had been published that Henry Wellman and his colleagues (Wellman et al., 2001) conducted what is known as a meta-analysis. This is a method for pooling data from a range of studies and performing statistical tests on manipulations that are shared across groups of studies. As so many variations on the task had been conducted in the period 1983–98, Wellman and his colleagues were able to do a careful, conservative analysis. For example, they decided to take only studies in which the vast majority of children passed the control trials that tested their knowledge of the movement of the objects in the unexpected trials or the true content of the container in the deceptive box task. Such a starting point guarded them from obtaining non-significant results simply because they included some poorly conducted investigations. They identified 77

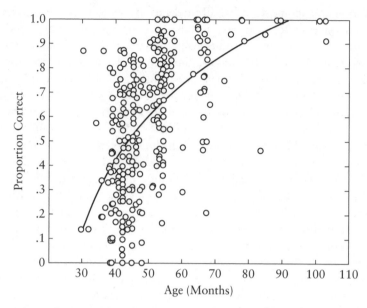

Figure 3.1 The patterns of data found in the meta-analysis of Wellman, Cross, and Watson (2001). Reprinted with permission from the Society for Research in Child Development

reports and studies that met these criteria and took pains to include some unpublished papers to ensure that any significant findings obtained were not the product of a simple bias in the acceptance of papers for publication. Within these papers, they examined 178 experiments with 591 conditions and the studies were conducted across a number of countries, mainly in the industrial world (48 percent were from the UK and the USA), but with a few from the developing world (e.g., Africa and South America).

Wellman et al.'s first task was to explore the general pattern of findings across these many studies. In Figure 3.1 each condition is represented by a small circle. It shows performance of children between 30 and 100 months, but concentrated mainly over the fourth year of life. Wellman et al. plotted the curve to display the line at which it is 50 percent likely that the child will succeed in the task. As would be expected, there is a rapid increase in the child's likelihood of success over her or his fourth year. Just after their third birthdays children have less than 40 percent chance of passing. A year later children are almost three times as likely to pass the test. However, Figure 3.1 also shows that there is great variability in test performance across trials.

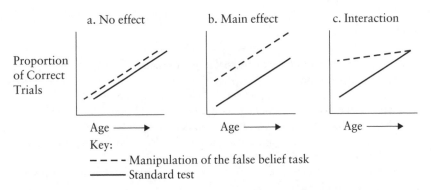

Figure 3.2 is shown with three graphs labeled "a. No effect", "b. Main effect", and "c. Interaction". The y-axis is labeled "Proportion of Correct Trials" and each x-axis is labeled "Age →".

Key:
– – – – Manipulation of the false belief task
——— Standard test

Figure 3.2 The three patterns of results hypothesized by Wellman, Cross, and Watson (2001). Reprinted with permission from the Society for Research in Child Development

To address this variability, Wellman et al. explored the possibility that particular task manipulations might boost the performance of 3-year-olds. They put forward three competing hypotheses that are presented in Figure 3.2, in which the two types of condition are shown in two different types of line – dashed and continuous. In the left-hand graph (Figure 3.2, section a) there is a slight difference between the two conditions, but as this difference is not statistically different it is labeled as "no effect." The graph in the center of Figure 3.2 (section b) presents a "main effect" in that it shows that in a manipulation of the test (the top line on the graph), children consistently score more highly at all ages tested. It is the right-hand graph of the figure that Wellman et al. claim would show an influence of a task manipulation upon children's performance, in that it would bring 3-year-olds' below chance performance "up" to the "above chance" levels of 4-year-olds.

Wellman et al. examined 11 such manipulations to test the three hypothetical patterns of data displayed in Figure 3.2. These derive from the debates that were initiated as a result of the studies explored in the previous section. Table 3.1 lists the issues examined in their analyses. It shows that six factors, like the type of task performed, or whether the target question focused on the protagonist's thoughts or her actions, did not vary systematically across studies. Five factors did show significantly improved performance in preschoolers across studies: a motive for the protagonist is made explicit; the child actively participates in the procedure; the object is either not shown to the child or is destroyed [i.e., eaten] before the test question is asked; the protagonist's mental state is made salient – for example, by the child being told that Maxi is

Table 3.1 The factors examined in Wellman et al.'s meta-analysis of false belief

---

Factors not found to influence false belief performance
- Year of publication
- Type of task (e.g., unexpected transfer vs. deceptive box)
- Type of question (e.g., whether the protagonist will think, know, or say what the object is, or where s/he will look)
- Nature of protagonist (e.g., a real person, a videotaped person, a doll, a puppet, or a storybook character)
- Nature of target object (e.g., a real item like a piece of chocolate, a toy, a picture of an object)
- Whether the holder of the false belief was the child or someone else

Factors found to relate to performance
- When the protagonist has a motive for transforming the object (e.g., to deceive someone)
- The child actively participates in the task (e.g., makes the essential transformation)
- The object ceases to exist (e.g., the chocolate is eaten or put into a cake mix)
- The salience of the protagonist's belief is increased (e.g., it is clearly stated or a picture is made of it)
- Country of origin (children in Australia and Canada perform best; those in Korea, the USA, and the UK show similar levels of competence, which are better than those from Austria and Japan)

---

gone and cannot see the object being moved; the child is shown a picture which represents the protagonist's belief or is reminded of it. None of these factors interacted with age. This suggests that none has a magic effect of revealing false belief understanding which is hidden in standard procedures. Indeed Wellman et al. found consistent improvement across the fifth year of life, suggesting that the task does assess a skill which is mastered at about this time. Only one factor, temporal marking (following Lewis & Osborne, see above), interacted with age, but this seemed to show greater effects in older, not younger, preschoolers.

Game, set, and match to Wellman et al.?

Figure 3.1 shows a consistent increase in performance with age and Wellman et al.'s meta-analysis shows that age is the most statistically significant predictor of success in the false belief task. Their close inspection of the hundreds of studies seems to provide strong support for the claim that mental state understanding undergoes dramatic change at around the age of 4. However, the analysis did not appear to end the disputes over whether the false belief test is an acid test of the developing "theory of mind." The article was followed by four brief commentaries that are well worth close examination. Two of these suggest that the patterns of data do not necessarily restrict us to a narrow focus on the achievement of mental state understanding. Moses (2001) points out that the data presented by Wellman et al. can be explained by more general cognitive skills than a simple "theory of mind." Astington (2001) [whose quotation starts this chapter] calls for both a wider range of assessments of children's understanding of mind and puts her money on the role of language in the acquisition of such skills. We return to these issues, respectively, in chapters 5 and 7.

Perhaps the severest criticism of Wellman et al.'s claim that the age shift is indicative of a theory shift came from Scholl and Leslie (2001, p. 700): "In other words, this view makes the single daring prediction that children should get better as they get older!" To the idea that this indicates a conceptual change, they state emphatically "We disagree." In the place of a theory theory explanation (described in chapter 2), Scholl and Leslie argue that change is equally well described by an innate account in which general cognitive skills act as a constraint on the development of the ability to "read minds." Their response reminds us that a key issue is to describe the process of change as clearly as possible. Using one test alone is unlikely to do this. Indeed the paper has led some recent accounts away from the need to concentrate upon the complexities of change: "the meta-analysis of Wellman et al. (2001) demonstrated that the age effect in false belief is substantial, unmoderated by other factors, and universal. Hence biological maturation goes a long way to achieve it" (Jenkins & Oatley, 2004, p. 112). We have cautioned against analyses that resort to notions of "biological maturation" in chapter 1.

A meta-analysis has many uses. It can test specific hypotheses, particularly those that might require a large sample or where the data in a field remain controversial. However, it does not seem as if the air has been cleared by this particular analysis. In the section before this we charted what appear to be subtle variations in young children's performance and the apparently large effects of small manipulations of the task. While Wellman et al.'s paper has served to focus our attention on a very interesting change over the fourth year of life and across a diversity of cultures, it may have obscured some key features of that change. Moses (2001, p. 688) points out that among the types of studies not included are studies involving explanations of false beliefs, deceptive behavior [like the studies of Chandler and his colleagues cited above], and other simplifications of the task. In one such manipulation, Wellman et al. found that children's performance improves if the protagonist's motive is made explicit or if the child actively participates in the procedure. Such patterns are worthy of further investigation.

For example, Suzanne Hala and Michael Chandler (Chandler & Hala, 1994; Hala & Chandler, 1996) followed up their earlier work with systematic assessments of when and how deception might work. They found that a number of factors have to be combined before the child can be seen to understand an act of deception. It is not sufficient to be a witness to one experimenter deceiving another or to plan a move in the unexpected transfer test without a deceptive intent. The child only understands deception if it is an act which is strategically planned with the aim of that deception clearly marked. If this is the case (and Hala and Chandler's data are persuasive) then the lumping together of all conditions in which some trickery has occurred would not bring out such subtleties. The point also applies to other manipulations such as temporal marking (i.e., structuring the test question to remind the child that the question refers to where Maxi would look first). So, collapsing many variations may wash out important differences. In order to understand the development of false belief understanding it is these differences that should be examined to discover why some manipulations of the social context of the false belief task improve performance whereas others do not.

The debate about methods has theoretical implications. Wellman et al. criticize what they call the "early competence model," attributed to Chandler and others discussed above. What Wellman et al. mean by this is the idea that 3-year-olds already understand false beliefs but something about the test procedure masks this competence. As the quotation from Lewis and Osborne (1990) in the previous section suggests, the aim of those who analyze false belief performance in 3-year-olds has always been more than the search for early competence (see Chandler & Hala, 1994, for further discussion). Indeed Chandler has long been concerned with the assumption that all the developmental achievements have been made once the child can pass false belief (see chapter 8). Wellman et al. also claim that support for such a model would come only from the statistical interaction depicted in section c of Figure 3.2. However, the main effect (section b) may be agued to provide equal support as it raises 3-year-olds' performance to the level of 4-year-olds in the standard condition. So perhaps Wellman et al. are overly conservative in their analysis?

Thus false belief continues to receive critical scrutiny in the literature. Bloom and German (2000) published a recent article entitled "Two reasons to abandon the false belief task as a test of theory of mind." "Reason 1" was that there is more to passing false belief tests than "theory of mind." Following a claim made by the philosopher Jerry Fodor (1992) that younger children may simply use the wrong heuristic "people will act in accord with their desires," they cite evidence that suggests that children fail related tasks which are not restricted to a grasp of false beliefs. "Reason 2" is that there is more to "theory of mind" than false belief. Bloom and German pinpoint evidence which shows that younger children do not have a blanket ignorance of alternative perspectives on the world that failure on false belief may suggest. We turn to such evidence in the next section. Bloom and German's (2000, p. 30) argument serves as a conclusion for this section: "the false belief task should be considered in its proper context. It is an ingenious, but very difficult task that taps one aspect of people's understanding of the minds of others. Nothing more, nothing less."

False Belief: The "Acid Test" or One Skill Amongst Many?

The false belief task has been depicted as "a single task" that has "become a marker for a complex development," but Astington (2001), who was quoted at the start of this chapter, is fully aware that there have always been attempts to explore other aspects of mental state understanding. The aim of this section is to sketch in the variations on the task that have been employed to test the validity of the theoretical positions that we present in chapter 2. We explore four issues that were generated in the debates between the three rival mainstream theoretical camps. We start with the very early acquisition of skills in pretend play – some two years before an understanding of false belief. Such an age gap might appear to support the innate module view but in fact the debate has been heated on this topic. Each theoretical perspective presented in chapter 2 accounts for some but not all of the data. The rest of the section explores issues that are central to debates over the validity of theory theory. The second part examines a key feature of this position, that an understanding of false belief develops from an initial framework theory involving beliefs and desires (Wellman, 1990). We present some evidence that questions this assumption. The third section examines a contention of theory theory that false belief should fit into a network of theoretical propositions concerning how beliefs originate. The fourth and final part considers the long-term perspective, to consider the skills that might foster early false belief understanding.

Pretend play: support for an innate module perspective?

The most popular area of research on this topic concerns the nature of pretense and how it relates to an understanding of mind. Very soon after Wimmer and Perner's paper was published, Alan Leslie (1987) drew attention to a possible link. In a seminal article he analyzed the skill of using one object to represent another. Children of 18–24 months usually engage in this activity. For years I have shown a clip to my students of a 12-month-old who pretends to drink tea from a toy tea cup. Two points are of interest here. First is the claim that pretense and false belief are similar in terms of requiring two perspectives on the same event to be taken into account. Let's return to an example we considered in chapter 2. When holding a banana to one's ear one has to suspend the usual "representation," "this is a banana," for another, "this is a telephone." So, Leslie argued, the child has to have a metarepresentational capacity which allows both perspectives to be held in mind. Pretense "is an early symptom of the human mind's ability to characterize and manipulate its own attitudes towards information" (Leslie, 1987, p. 416). The second is that it led Leslie to the belief that pretense emerges so early and so readily in development that it must be innately constrained and develops in the child with minimal environmental input. He continues to maintain the view that the domain of mental state understanding can best be understood in these terms with general cognitive skills which develop slowly, explaining the lag between the onset of pretense at 18 months and false belief at 48 months.

The origins and nature of pretense have intrigued scholars for centuries. The early emergence of this skill is certainly an issue within the "theory of mind" debate, but thus far has not resolved the divisions between the three theoretical camps described in chapter 2. Leslie (e.g., Scholl & Leslie, 2001) continues to maintain that pretense provides crucial evidence for the child's access to mentalizing skills. In contrast, Paul Harris (e.g., 1991, 2000) has written extensively about the role of pretense in the child's developing imaginative or simulation skills. As we suggest in chapter 2, for Harris the ability to simulate is a developmental achievement, not simply the switching on of a mental module. His empirical work suggests that children acquire these skills very early in development. Harris and Kavanaugh (1993) provide strong support for this position in a series of experiments which show that 2-year-olds easily distinguish real from pretend actions and their consequences. So, if one naughty toy animal spills pretend tea on another animal the child might help to clean up the mess, but will also acknowledge that the animal is not really wet.

At the same time pretense has been explored from a theory theory perspective. According to a framework approach, children may learn to "pretend" in the second year of life, but this will initially lead to realizations about desire and only subsequently beliefs once the child develops belief–desire reasoning. Such a view was explored by Lillard and Flavell (1992) within a unified research design. They told preschoolers short stories, like (with the test and control questions in brackets): "This is Julie. She's running to get a snack. She wants there to be juice on the table. (What does she want?) Let's look. Oh it's really milk, but she wants it to be juice. (What is really on the table, milk or juice? And what did Julie want to be on the table, juice or milk?)" They found that children actually were above 70 percent correct on "want" stories, were slightly less clear about a protagonist who "pretends" there's juice there, and were worse about what Julie "thinks" is on the table. The order of difficulty stimulated further research. Lillard (1993a, 1993b, 1998) has presented children with a range of tasks to explore whether they understand the intentionality underlying pretense. For example, if a story character jumps up and down like a kangaroo, but has never seen or heard of kangaroos before, he or she cannot be *pretending* to be a kangaroo. But equipped with such information 3-year-olds still claim that the story character is doing just this. It seems that children's "theory" of pretense is actually slower to emerge than their theory of belief.

In the 1990s some attempts were made to reconcile the innate module, theory, and simulation perspectives on pretense (see chapters 10–13 in Lewis & Mitchell, 1994). Perner, Baker, and Hutton (1994), for example, coined the term "prelief" to refer to a form of pretense representation that retains Leslie's claim that pretense actions are demonstrations of mental relations (pretending that a banana is a telephone receiver), but does not have the same status as belief because pretenses cannot be true or false (any pretend action is acceptable, so I am allowed to pretend that I am riding a bicycle even though I am not), while beliefs necessarily have a relation to reality. Lillard's work seems to be consistent with such a view as it shows that children can pretend without having a clear understanding of the relationship between a person's actions and their intentions. However, this view was criticized from the innate module perspective. German and Leslie (2001) hypothesized that 4–6-year-olds might fail tasks like Lillard's because of the performance demands rather than an ability to understand pretense. They found that children make the same errors when the inference to be made is about a false belief that does not involve pretense, even though the children were above the age at which they should, in theory, have mastered false belief. They also found that general demands like the salience of the character's ignorance had a significant effect on children's ability to infer whether the actor was pretending or had a false belief. Thus they showed that Lillard's finding that children are slow to make inferences about pretense may well be in large part a reflection of the task demands.

The research on early pretense is fascinating, but simply reveals its complexities as a concept and in its development. We need to explain its early onset and how it relates to the child's early understanding of the mind. This is important because some forms of pretense have long been shown to be linked to false belief understanding (e.g., Astington & Jenkins, 1999; Youngblade & Dunn, 1995). Lillard's research shows that children's grasp of its complexities is relatively slow to unfold, although research is still divided over whether complex pretense is a form of counterfactual reasoning that is equivalent to false belief (Amsel & Smalley, 2000; Robinson & Beck, 2000). We pick up the point about slow development in chapter 4 in which we explore how mental state understanding gradually unfolds in infancy as the child develops related skills, chapter 6 where we focus upon children's social interactions, and chapter 5 where we explore the issue of counterfactual reasoning. Pretense is, after all, often a social skill in which participants negotiate shared meanings. We need more close observations of how this remarkable skill emerges. For example, Walker-Andrews and Kahana-Kalman (1999) describe a sequence in which adults may scaffold pretense behaviour, with 15–18-month-olds imitating pretend gestures. This gradually leads to the child grasping such pretend stipulations of the adult before, around the child's second birthday, being able to employ such understanding to enter into collaborative pretend play. Only later in development is the ability to tailor one's pretend actions in that interaction in evidence. Thus perhaps all the three perspectives we have described, the innate module, simulation, and theory theories, are each partly correct on the issue.

Belief–desire reasoning: a precursor of false belief understanding?

Throughout the debate stimulated by the publication of the first false belief experiments (Wimmer & Perner, 1983), there has been a continuing analysis of another key mental state skill, belief–desire reasoning. This topic has been associated with one particular version of theory theory, that of Henry Wellman (1990). We summarized this position in chapter 2. It rests on the assumption that the child constructs a framework "theory" into which a developing understanding of constructs like desires, beliefs, and intentions fit. Wellman's collaborations with David Estes, Jacqueline Woolley, and Karen Bartsch in the 1980s produced data which were consistent with his perspective on theory theory. His initial research with the first two co-authors was to establish that young children are aware that states of mind have a different ontological status to states of the world. So, within an interview 3-year-old children can tell that real objects can be seen, touched, and manipulated by self and others, whereas mental states like thoughts, dreams, memories, and acts of pretense cannot be (e.g., Wellman & Estes, 1986). For example, when asked to explain a dream, one child said: "It's in his head, it's only pretend" (Wellman, 1988, p. 77), demonstrating not only that mental states are different from reality, but also a connection between dreams and pretenses within a causal-explanatory framework.

Wellman also explored children's grasp of the precursors of false beliefs. He tested his hypothesis that beliefs and desires are initially separate, indeed that children understand desires before beliefs and initially desire overrides belief. He had a good philosophical foundation for such a claim since, as we described in chapter 2, desires emanate from different origins – you feel a churning in your stomach (an internal sensation) and that prompts you to *desire* pizza; you smell a familiar scent (an external stimulus) and thus *believe* that your daughter is cooking pizza. Wellman and Bartsch (1988) asked 3-year-olds simple stories about the distinction between thoughts and desires and whether they are fulfilled. For example: "Sam wants to find his puppy. His puppy might be hiding in the garage or under the porch. Sam thinks his puppy is under the porch. Where will Sam look for his puppy, in the garage or under the porch?" They manipulated the story so that they could test a number of different possibilities. For example, the child might be asked where she thinks the puppy is. She is told that in fact Sam thinks it is in the other location and then asked where Sam will look. This establishes a contrast between two "representations" of the same reality. Wellman and Bartsch found that 3-year-olds were significantly above chance on tasks like this: they appeared to go against their own guess that it was in one location to choose the other as Sam's looking place. Similarly, if Jane saw magic marker pens at location "A" but the child is told that there are some also at location "B" they will still predict that Jane will look at "A" even though a strategy based upon reality would predict that she could look in either "A" or "B." In contrast, they failed the false belief test even when told that the protagonist's beliefs are in error. This suggests that before the age of 4 the child has a good knowledge of beliefs, but not false beliefs.

Wellman initially claimed that such data supported the position that children's understanding of belief is built onto their understanding of desire. They develop belief–desire reasoning. Belief is a difficult construct because beliefs can be wrong. Desires firstly fit more into the child's everyday language experience and secondly they are inherently more straightforward. Some data clearly supported this view. For example, Wellman and Woolley (1990) set up an experiment in which the child's desires were in conflict with those of a protagonist, in the same way as the conflicting belief tasks were set up above. Even 2-year-olds were able to predict that the protagonist would go where she, and not the child, would prefer to go. Wellman and Liu (2004) have followed up such research recently. In a meta-analysis they examined studies comparing children's reasoning about a variety of different types of social understanding. They found that in 46 experimental manipulations across 16 published papers children appeared to understand desires before beliefs, then knowledge and ignorance, before, finally, false beliefs. In a study with relatively comparable task formats, Wellman and Lui confirmed the following sequence of acquisition: understanding that two people can have different desires about the same objects, that they may have different beliefs about those objects, that a person has to have perceptual access to information in order to formulate a belief, false belief, and finally that a person may express one emotion while feeling a very different one.

However, other research has explored whether children really understand desire first or whether tests of understanding desire are simply not as complex as the false belief task. When appropriate controls are in place the picture changes. Chris Moore and his colleagues (1995) suggested that preschoolers find the false belief task difficult not because they are unable to represent beliefs as mental states, but because it imposes significant cognitive, or executive, demands (see chapter 5). In a first experiment, they set up a task where the child's desires were established at the start of the procedure; the child was asked to choose one of two stickers to take home with them. This was followed by a narrative in which a protagonist is frightened by the same type of animal on the sticker that the child had chosen. Next, the story character is offered a choice of one of two stickers, one of which is a picture of that animal that frightened him or her. Only 5-year-olds infer that the child will not want a sticker of that animal. Three- and 4-year-olds were unable to make the inference even though they remembered what had frightened the protagonist. In a second experiment 3-year-olds were given a false belief task as well as a conflicting desire task, in which in a competitive game to build a jigsaw puzzle, the child and an opponent, Fat Cat, pick up cards indicating the puzzle pieces they could receive. The order of the cards was fixed so that the child and Fat Cat ended up needing different cards. The children were then asked, "Which color card does Fat Cat want now?" (other's desire) and "Which color card did you want last time?" (own outdated desire) (Moore et al., 1995, p. 476). These 3-year-olds were as bad at this task as they were on false belief. This finding has important implications for interpreting performance on the standard false belief task, particularly as in the second experiment 3-year-olds performed similarly on the two tasks.

Indeed, desires are far more complex than simple "wants." Leslie and Polizzi (1998) pointed out that they are not necessarily positive. They used the examples of desiring not to burn one's fingers or of avoiding putting a piece of fish into a box where one's sick kitten is recuperating. In the latter setting Renee has a piece of fish to place in the box not including the kitten. They set up a false belief task as the kitten moves from one box to another while she is collecting the fish. This task is difficult even for 4-year-olds: 62 percent failed while 94 percent pass standard tests. Leslie and Polizzi explain false belief and false desire problems in terms of how they influence shifting attention to an alternative target location. They suggest there is a "default attributional response" in many intellectual tasks. For example, we usually assume that a container holds the contents that it usually contains – pictures of Smarties on the box reinforce such an attribution. In such tasks the route to success is to inhibit this default response, not the sudden acquisition of a theory of mind (see Leslie et al., in press, for a development of this argument). We return to the tension between "theory of mind" and such "domain general" accounts in chapter 5.

In Wellman and Bartsch's experiments, described above, 3-year-olds' false belief understanding appeared to develop from prior belief–desire reasoning. In these tasks the protagonist acts upon his or her false belief and the child is asked why she or he did this. So, in an experimental condition the child sees the experimenter move sticking plasters (i.e., Bandaids) from a commercially identifiable container to a plain box and then witnesses a puppet searching for plasters and looking in the labeled box. In a control condition where the puppet did not act, 69 percent of 3-year-olds said that he would look for the plasters in the plain box. In the experimental condition 66 percent attributed the puppet with a false belief when explaining why he looked in the commercial box. Originally Bartsch and Wellman (1989) considered the suggestion that the traditional test underestimates their skills and that 3-year-olds are capable of false belief reasoning. However, Wellman (1990, p. 262) rejected such a claim as it cannot explain why 3-year-olds still fail the Smarties experiment, described at the start of the chapter. Here the "canonical" response to "What will your friend say is in here?" should be "Smarties" as the child is staring at a box with the sweets pictured on the outside. Wellman also speculated that there would likely be tasks in which 3-year-olds may well fail to explain a protagonist's actions.

Wellman's suspicions have been confirmed in subsequent research (Moses & Flavell, 1990; Wimmer & Hartl, 1991). For example, Wimmer and Hartl showed a "Milka" chocolate box to children and set up the deceptive box test by showing mock surprise that there was a pencil inside. When asked "Why did you think that there were chocolates in here?" only 30 percent were able to justify their response. When they answered the prediction question correctly the children could say "Because it is a Milka box" (Wimmer & Gschaider, 2000, p. 257). Wimmer and Gschaider describe a further task in which no young 3-year-olds explained why a protagonist acted upon a false belief, there was a 50 percent success rate at 3.5–4 years and 100 percent success at age 5. Taken together, these studies suggest that Wellman's claims about an understanding of false belief emerging from belief–desire reasoning are not fully supported in the data.

Concurrent links with false belief: a key conceptual advance or a restricted test?

From the late 1980s two issues were hotly debated about the validity of the false belief test. The first issue emerged from within the theory theory and the representational theory of mind perspective traditions (see chapter 2). For them a major quest was to explore the building blocks of the intellectual skills required for understanding mental states as mental states. A number of interesting pieces of data seemed to show that false belief is just one problem faced by preschoolers. For example, Gopnik and Graf (1988) tested whether preschoolers could identify the origins of their beliefs. They allowed them to look into a box, gave them a clue, or told them what was inside. While 3-year-olds could recall the contents they could not reliably remember how they had come across such information. Four-year-olds were significantly better, suggesting that the shift toward false belief understanding is accompanied by a range of other skills like a grasp of the sources of their knowledge.

Such data appear to provide strong support for "theory"-based accounts as they conform to Wellman's (1990) assumption of the "theory of mind" that it is consistent and coherent: perception leads to knowing, while no perception leads to ignorance. Although in chapter 8 we will review studies that show that these problems continue well beyond the fourth year, the picture with reference to preschoolers is more complex. For a start, asking children simpler questions about the origins of their knowledge leads to improvements in their ability to identify the source (Pratt & Bryant, 1990). In addition, a simple rule-based account, that "seeing leads to knowing" and "not seeing leads to not knowing," makes predictions that are not borne out. For example, Friedman, Griffin, Brownell, and Winner (2003) gave simple tasks in which the application of the above rules would be straightforward. In one condition a puppet "sees" a toy being placed into one of two differently colored boxes and then leaves. Four-year-olds could say which one the puppet "thinks" it is in, but then tended to answer "no" when asked a "true belief" question, "Does [puppet] know where it is?" Similarly, the ability to infer whether another person knows something is slow to develop. Sodian and Wimmer (1987) found that even 5-year-olds had difficulties in inferring what was in a box when informed that that person had been told that one of the two contents had been removed. This phenomenon is known as inference neglect. Clearly there is more to an understanding of beliefs that involves the application of two simple rules.

A second issue concerns just why children fail false belief. A debate in the 1990s centered around an intriguing finding of Wimmer and Hartl (1991) in which another variant on false belief was introduced. In this, children are shown a familiar container and asked to say what is inside. Their guess is confirmed and the contents are then exchanged for something new – for example, dominoes in a domino box exchanged for pencils. Wimmer and Hartl hypothesized that 3-year-olds in this task would pass on the grounds that having little insight into the mind would interpret the question "What did you think was in the box?" as

"What was in the box?" Their hypothesis was confirmed in that most children who failed the standard task passed this "state change" test. However, at the same time, Peter Mitchell drew together research which seemed to point to another conclusion, that children get hooked on current reality. According to this view, children say Maxi will look where the chocolate is or state "pencils" in the deceptive box task, as they are hooked on reality. It is further supported in studies that show improvements in tasks where the "lure" of reality is reduced. For example, the child may simply be told that the object was first in one location in the unexpected transfer test and then moved (Zaitchik, 1991) or she "posts" (i.e., puts in a mail box) a picture of the expected objects (Smarties) in the Smarties box before looking inside and finding pencils (Mitchell & Lacohée, 1991). In Zaitchik's procedure, the child is less committed to the lure of current reality, while in Mitchell and Lacohée's case posting the picture works either because it serves to locate the child's original belief in reality or because the picture itself is a representation that helps the child to retain their usually fragile grasp of their prior belief (Freeman & Lacohée, 1995).

How does Mitchell explain the poor performance on the state change task, where children appeared to override current reality to answer correctly? Saltmarsh, Mitchell, and Robinson (1995) devised four experiments to compare their reality masking hypothesis with the theory account advanced by Wimmer and Hartl. In these tasks they used a hand puppet, Daffy the Duck, so that they could test the child's current and past belief against another's. If Wimmer and Hartl were correct they should answer "What does Daffy think is in the box now?" as if it meant "What is in the box now?" In various conditions they replaced one set of contents with another. They replicated the Wimmer and Hartl procedure, but also added a condition in which the Smarties tube was found initially to contain a key. This was replaced with a new object – a spoon. Saltmarsh et al. did not find that children stated the first contents of the Smarties tube in the question about the past or the present contents in response to the protagonist's current view. They conclude that the data support the view that under most conditions reality is a lure to the child. Unfortunately, Perner (2000) reaches a different conclusion, that Mitchell's data do not support any theoretical viewpoint. He suggests that all the switches of the contents of the boxes lead to a variety of responses in 3-year-olds rather than a clear pattern. The lesson here is that false belief has given rise to complex series of experiments that do not in themselves support one of the leading theoretical positions more than any other.

False belief: the longer-term view in typical development and autism

The claim made by Janet Astington at the start of this chapter is that there has been a tendency for researchers to rely upon false belief, as if it is the only test of mental state understanding and as if it is used only as an acid test and not as a means of assessing a wider range of skills. As a means of concluding this section we review the current state of play and chart some exceptions to these rules. There have been interesting alternative tests, additions to the main procedure and means of linking this one skill with other related skills within the context of the issues which the child faces over their fourth and fifth years.

One reason why false belief has dominated the "theory of mind" debate is that research in the 1980s suggested that the core problem faced by children with autism concerns their ability to "read" minds. We have described this literature in brief in chapters 1 and 2. We report here the current state of play concerning the state of the use of the test to explore the key diagnostic features of the disorder. This literature matches that on typically developing children that we have described above. Children with autism tend to fail the false belief test and measures of understanding and engaging in pretense (Baron-Cohen, 1987), the relationship between seeing and knowing (Leslie & Frith, 1988), and a range of related skills. Baron-Cohen (2000, p. 4) lists 20 such skills that are associated with "theory of mind" in such children. However, these data have to be understood within the continuing debate over the nature of the disorder (see chapter 1).

The "theory of mind" hypothesis cannot explain why children with autism appear to show different performance profiles in other areas of social, linguistic, and cognitive functions. For example, they also have difficulties with general cognitive tests involving the control of one's actions which do not necessarily involve social understanding (Russell, 1997 – we focus on these tests in chapter 5), they have specific skills which cannot be explained by the theory of mind hypothesis like the ability to construct a pattern using differently colored blocks (see Frith, 2003, for a review), and they seem to find it difficult to relate parts of the perceptual field to the whole field (e.g., Plaisted, 2000). Another reason why the relevance of the theory of mind hypothesis to autism has not been agreed upon is that "many studies have confirmed the finding that children with autism have difficulty with a wide variety of theory-of-mind tasks (Baron-Cohen, 2000). Nevertheless, there has been relatively little research that has explicitly examined the relationship between theory of mind deficits and the core symptoms or severity of impairments in autism" (Tager-Flusberg, 2003, p. 197). Tager-Flusberg's current research project examines the links. Her preliminary finding is that mental state understanding is one of a number of skills that are associated with the defining features of autism, notably the problem of social interaction, which is independent of other problems like their language development. However, the literature suggests that the skills focused upon in tests like false belief cannot identify all the problems in autism and much of the debate that we touched upon in chapter 2 concerns the precursors to mental state understanding both in children with autism and their typically developing counterparts. We focus exclusively on these precursor skills in chapter 4.

We have already touched upon such skills. In a previous part we described research within theory theory that has attempted to link children's belief reasoning to earlier skills like belief–desire reasoning. Such work has continued, so that now there is much evidence to suggest preschoolers develop coherent accounts of what happens "in the head" (Watson, Gelman, & Wellman, 1998). How do such skills relate to other abilities and how do they emerge? Alison Gopnik and her colleagues (see Gopnik, Capps, & Meltzoff, 2000) have attempted to show how such knowledge is built upon a range of previous skills. For example, they summarized evidence in the perspective-taking literature which suggests that there are shifts in the ability to see the world from another angle that coincide with the acquisition of false belief. In addition, these skills may derive from earlier interactions in which attitudes toward objects are negotiated. Repacholi and Gopnik (1997) conducted an interesting experiment in which they explored whether 18-month-olds would show a sensitivity to someone else's stated desires during interaction. The experimenter presented two bowls of food to the child, one containing raw broccoli and the other goldfish crackers. The child was offered "one" to eat and most of them preferred the goldfish crackers. In the condition in which the experimenter's desires differ from the child's the experimenter pantomimes disgust at eating the crackers and delight at eating the broccoli. When the experimenter asked the child "Can you give me some more?" [not specifying which food], the children used the recent behavioral cues to select the food that had been preferred. That is, most of these 18-month-olds gave broccoli to the experimenter. However, we await confirmation of this finding because replications of this study have not yet been published. Other researchers have not replicated this finding with 18-month-olds (Müller, Zelazo, Frye, & Lieberman, 2002).

Nevertheless, Gopnik's work opens the door to the exploration of a range of skills that might feed into the developments in children's social understanding in the fifth year. A similar strand of research has attempted to explore the precursors to full false belief understanding. An interesting study by Clements and Perner (1994) used the unexpected transfer test to assess younger children who would be expected to fail false belief. As the experimenter told the false belief story she said "I wonder where he's [the protagonist] going to look" and the children's eye movements were examined. Clements and Perner found that many children over the age of 2 years, 11 months looked toward the correct location (i.e., where the protagonist should falsely believe it to be) but these young children tended to fail the typical false belief question by verbally reporting that the protagonist would look in the location where the object now was. They concluded that before children acquire a fully fledged understanding of the mind, they have "implicit" understanding, akin to an awareness of ignorance, which they cannot articulate because they do not have a full understanding of representations. More recent work using this procedure has suggested that this implicit looking effect is related to the children's confidence in their judgments. They appear to be fully confident about their wrong judgment, having looked at the correct location, and then as they go through the transition to a successful verbal judgment they appear initially to be less confident (Ruffman, Garnham, Import, & Connolly, 2001). Thus, learning a particular skill like false belief may be a process in which the child gradually acquires new skills (Ruffman, 2004).

The research on implicit understanding draws our attention to a key issue in false belief understanding, concerning how this skill emerges. Much of the research which we have described in this section of the chapter explores possible precursor skills. However, it does not realize earlier optimism concerning the way in which the theory account pieces together the various skills into a framework (see Astington & Gopnik, 1991, for an excellent progress report). As a result, the period before the development of false belief understanding has been referred to the "dark ages" of the "theory of mind" field (Meltzoff, Gopnik, & Repacholi, 1999). My own work with Joanna Lunn (Lunn & Lewis, 2003) has been attempting to explore how false belief emerges by simplifying the task into its component skills. Two versions of the task appear to be passed reliably a year before standard false belief – before children are 3;6 years and in some as early as 2;6 years. In the first the task is presented in a nonverbal format (Call & Tomasello, 1999). Over a succession of trials the child has to identify which of two identical boxes (in our studies) Freddie the glove puppet will mark when he has a false belief about the presence of a reward. To succeed the child has to impute Freddie with a false belief. In the second task the standard false belief task is administered in a book format and the only other difference is that the child is allowed two "runs" through the story before turning to the last page when the protagonist is returning to the scene (following Lewis, Freeman, Hagestadt, & Douglas, 1994). These tasks share a high degree of redundancy and provide support for the child in every way except in their extrapolation of the crucial false belief information. Thus this work, like that on implicit understanding, suggests that research should focus more upon the precursor skills to mental state understanding as represented by success at false belief.

Conclusion

False belief is a particular skill – the ability to suspend one's own knowledge of reality and to contrast it with another's mistaken view of reality. Fundamental to the debate which has continued for 20 years has been the relationship between false belief as a particular skill and social understanding more generally. In many respects the task has been so successful that it has distracted us from the development of other means of studying social development and other periods than the late preschool years. Many of the chapters that follow attempt to identify such areas of study. As Bloom and German (2000) suggest, there is a danger of equating success at false belief with social understanding. Yet, at the same time, there are good grounds for concluding that the task deserves its center-stage position. Wellman et al.'s meta-analysis shows how robust the task is. Given the proliferation of studies involving false belief, it is also important to use it as a yardstick against which to compare other measures. Finally, we must also be aware that we still know relatively little about which skills feed into false belief and which later skills it feeds into. Most of the remaining chapters in this book attempt to address these issues. Our conclusion is that existing research with false belief tasks do not allow us to deliberate between the theoretical positions presented in chapter 2. German and Leslie (2004, p. 107) put this case well, by identifying the links that need to be made with the task:

> it is only by developing models of successful performance on various component "theory of mind" skills, such as recognition of agency in

infancy (e.g., Johnson, 2003), pretend play (Leslie, 1987, 1994), belief–desire reasoning (Leslie & Polizzi, 1998), and recall of the contents of one's own past mental states (Barreau & Morton, 1999), and by studying their specific neuro-cognitive basis (Frith & Frith, 1999; Gallagher & Frith, 2003) that we can hope to understand how the brain has been organized to acquire this important knowledge base.

However, German and Leslie present a theoretical conclusion which falls foul of some of the problems that we identified with biological determinism in chapter 1. The Wellman et al. meta-analysis and the commentaries on it suggest that the debates between the main theories reviewed in chapter 2 will not easily be resolved. However, in chapters 7 and 10 we suggest that all these theories share the same problematic view of the nature of language and the mind. We explore alternative positions throughout this book.

Chapter 4

The Development of Social Understanding in Infancy

Even before infants start using their first words they are already beginning to engage in complex forms of social interaction. For example, one day shortly after his first birthday Max was being picked up by his father from his babysitter. Max pointed out of the door, next to his red boots which were up on a shelf, then to the two bags for his clothes and finally to his coat which was hanging on a doorknob. He made a sound (like "uh") each time he pointed. He gestured toward all the things that were to be taken home with him, having perhaps first pointed in the direction of "home." With these simple acts Max was actively engaging in social interaction. They are typical examples of how infants' pointing gestures seem to reveal their understanding of others' attention. Even before this age infants begin to follow a person's direction of gaze, suggesting that they understand that the other person has seen something worth looking at. All this seems to indicate an important level of social understanding which emerges in the first two years in humans but which, we suggested in chapter 1, is apparent in simpler forms and in some contexts in mature chimpanzees. The emerging ability to coordinate attention with others is known as *joint attention* (Moore & Dunham, 1995). Such "triadic" interaction involving the self, other, and objects develops from earlier forms of "dyadic" interaction with either a parent or an object (Bakeman & Adamson, 1984; Trevarthen & Hubley, 1978). The miraculous development of such joint or triadic interaction makes language and new forms of interaction possible, yet it almost goes unnoticed by parents because it is such a natural and taken for granted part of human interaction. We notice if such interaction is missing but not when it is present.

Over the past 15 years interest in the development of children's social understanding has extended down the age span from the three- to four-year shift into infancy. This is partly because aspects of babies' interaction have been taken to be precursors of later achievements and a "theory of mind" (Moore & Dunham, 1995). Although theoreticians in the area have "discovered" these achievements in infancy, a rich tradition explored social development in early development during the 1970s. A few highlights include: [1] Daniel Stern's (e.g., 1977) close examination of the way in which short bursts of adult–child proto-conversations [babbling, gurgling, and eventually smiling] gradually increase in the numbers of turns taken over the first three months and how the adult's initial work to maintain the child's involvement in the interaction gradually reduces; [2] Colwyn Trevarthen's (e.g., 1979) analysis of babies' contribution to communication in the early months of life in which they demonstrate "pre-speech," a movement of the mouth in synchrony with the adult, and "primary intersubjectivity," the ability to share attention within this "dyadic interaction"; [3] Jerome Bruner's (Bruner & Sherwood, 1976) focus upon games with contingency, like peek-a-boo, in which the child learns both about turn taking and timing in interaction. So rich was this tradition that it is not surprising that Bretherton, McNew, and Beeghly-Smith (1981) suggested that infants soon develop an "implicit" "theory of mind" – an understanding of the person with whom they interact. This literature demonstrates that there are several forms of interaction that infants begin to engage in during their first year that seem to show some understanding of other people: mutual face-to-face interaction and games with great excitement and timing, culminating in the gradual emergence of the ability to engage in interactions which involve objects, not simply face-to-face gestures ("triadic" interaction, as described above).

In this chapter we focus on joint attention because it has been singled out by recent theories as a foundation for later social understanding, notably "theory of mind." In a broad sense it is tied up with our participation in culture (Bruner, 1995). After providing some examples of forms of interaction involving joint attention such as pointing gestures, gaze following, and social referencing, we turn to the task of defining this important skill. Understanding it in terms of mutual awareness immediately raises the problem of knowing what infants comprehend about other people's attention. How much does the infant understand of what he or she is doing when pointing to direct another's attention or following their gaze? There is a tendency to interpret these forms of interaction richly and to assume an adult level of social under-standing, which involves a grasp of the other person's attention. Other researchers are more conservative in how much they assume about what the infant knows regarding others' attention. This issue is tied up with the question of how this essentially human form of interaction develops during infancy. Many approaches are individualistic in their assumptions and often rely on what is called the analogical argument – the generalization from self to other. We present this position as well as critiques and then offer an alternative, relational approach to infant development. The middle two sections of the chapter examine the development of pointing gestures, in particular, and theories of social development in infancy, in general. Finally, we discuss joint attention as a foundational skill for language development.

Rich and Lean Interpretations of Infant Skills: The Example of Joint Attention

Joint attention skills include pointing to make requests or to direct others' attention, following another's direction of gaze or pointing gestures, and "social referencing," i.e., looking toward a parent in an ambiguous situation, apparently for the parent's reaction. A clear definition of this skill, however, is not easy to formulate, because different interpretations have been proposed about what joint attention is and what it signifies. Although definitions vary, there is general recognition of the importance of infants' emerging ability to coordinate attention with others. This ability seems to underpin language and more general social cognitive development. Longitudinal research shows that infant joint attention skills are correlated with later development in social understanding (Charman, Baron-Cohen, Swettenham, Baird, Cox, & Drew, 2000) and language development (Carpenter et al., 1998). It is thus not surprising that this capacity to coordinate attention with others is considered of "cosmic importance" (Bates, 1979) because it seems to form the foundation for the development of human culture and is perhaps the essential difference between humans and nonhuman primates (Tomasello, 1999a). Also, difficulties with joint attention, especially a lack of pointing at 18 months of age to direct others' attention, may be an early indicator of psychopathology and, in particular, autism (Baron-Cohen, Allen, & Gillberg, 1992; Baron-Cohen, Cox, Baird, Swettenham, Nightingale, Morgan, Drew, & Charman, 1996).

What is joint attention?

Here we briefly describe several forms of interaction involving joint attention. One clear example is when infants begin to point to objects

and may glance at another person, apparently to confirm joint awareness (Figure 4.1). Two main functions of pointing have been distinguished (Bates, 1976; Bates et al., 1975). Infants' use of pointing
in order to make requests has been termed a *"proto-imperative."* This
involves the use of the gesture to make a request or to get another
person to do something and it is essentially understood as "get that for
me." For example, in Bates, Camaioni, and Volterra's (1976) longitudinal case study the infant, Carlotta, at 13 months, "pointed toward the
sink. Mother gives her a glass of water, and Carlotta drinks it eagerly"
(p. 55). In contrast to attempts at obtaining things, a second function
of infants' pointing is to direct adults' attention. The use of pointing
in order to share attention with an adult has been referred to as a
"proto-declarative." Carlotta began using pointing to serve this function at about 12 months (Bates et al., 1976). Adults may also use
pointing gestures to inform others about locations. It has been found
that infants at 12 and 18 months of age use pointing gestures in order
to inform an adult experimenter about the location of an object that the
experimenter was looking for (Liszkowski, Carpenter, Striano, &

Figure 4.1   (a) Most infants learn how to point shortly after their first
birthdays. (Photo: Gerhard Vosloo)

Figure 4.1 (cont'd) (b) Raphael, *Madonna and Child with the Infant St John* (*the Esterhazy Madonna*), 1508. Museum of Fine Arts, Budapest/ Bridgeman Art Library, London

Tomasello, in press). Other uses of pointing, like asking questions, have been described anecdotally by parents.

A second form of joint attention includes *following other people's attention*, either by looking at where they are pointing or following their direction of gaze. In one of the early classic studies on gaze following that we shall describe in detail below, Scaife and Bruner (1975) reported that even at 6 months infants' gaze following could be discerned in a laboratory. However, more complex forms of this behavior continue to develop after this age and later we turn to how this skill develops.

The third early form of social interaction that develops at about 9 months is *social referencing*. This is infants' tendency to look toward their parents when faced with ambiguous events (Walden & Ogan, 1988). The usual reading of this phenomenon is that when faced with an uncertain situation such as a visual cliff (i.e., a transparent surface that looks like a vertical drop) or a toy spider, infants look at their parent's face to gauge their emotional reaction before proceeding accordingly. When their mothers smile infants are more likely to cross the visual cliff or play with ambiguous toys than when their mothers frown or appear to be uninterested.

Having described examples of joint attention we turn to the contrasting ways of defining this skill. A first definition to consider is "looking where someone else is looking" (Butterworth, 1998, p. 171). However, this could be more simply described as "simultaneous looking" (Tomasello, 1995a, p. 105) or "onlooking" (Bakeman & Adamson, 1984). There is more to joint attention than is captured by this simple definition (Bruner, 1995; Butterworth, 2001). Tomasello (1995a, p. 105) argues that "joint attention is not just a geometric phenomenon concerning two lines of visual attention." It requires that "two individuals know that they are attending to something in common" (Tomasello, 1995a, p. 106). Both must be *aware* that they are paying attention to the same thing. If two people happen to look out of different apartment windows on the same street scene their attention is on the same thing at the same time, but, by most definitions, this would not be considered joint attention because the people involved do not even realize that their attention is directed toward the same thing (Tomasello, 1995a).

If we revisit the example of Max's pointing described at the start of this chapter, we face an immediate difficulty in assessing his joint attention skills, since we do not know what he understood about his pointing gestures. This issue has profound theoretical implications, particularly for the developmental psychologist. The definitional problems we have described thus lead to the question of what forms of joint attention, like pointing gestures and gaze following, reveal about infants' level of social understanding. Do manifestations of particular behaviors indicate a basic level of social understanding that the infant has acquired, or are there simpler explanations when these gestures first appear – i.e., might infants display some behaviors such as gaze following without being aware of sharing attention with someone else?

Rich interpretations of infants' social understanding and criticism

It is tempting to interpret the forms of joint attention we discussed above (pointing, following others' attention, and social referencing) as evidence that one-year-old infants already have an "implicit" "theory of mind" (Bretherton, 1991; Bretherton et al., 1981). This has become known as a "*rich interpretation*," because it suggests that when infants use these skills they demonstrate an understanding that other people have goals, intentions, and attention that can be directed to various aspects of the world (Carpenter, Nagell, & Tomasello, 1998; Tomasello, 1995a, 1999a, 1999b). There are various forms of rich interpretations. Colwyn Trevarthen has argued for the past 30 years for his theory of "innate intersubjectivity – that the infant is born with awareness specifically receptive to subjective states in other persons" (Trevarthen & Aitken, 2001, p. 4). In taking a developmental rather than an innate perspective, Michael Tomasello claims that joint attention behaviors should be correlated in development because "what underlies infants' early skills of joint attention is their emerging understanding of other persons as intentional agents" (Tomasello, 1995a, p. 103):

> The central theoretical point is that all of the different joint attentional behaviors in which infants follow, direct, or share adult attention and behavior are not separate activities or cognitive domains; they are simply different behavioral manifestations of this same underlying understanding of other persons as intentional agents. (Tomasello, 1999b, p. 64)

Theories that interpret joint attention richly are generally based on individualistic assumptions, according to which the starting point for social development is individual self-knowledge of some form. From this perspective, the infant learns about her or his own inner experience and then reasons by analogy to understand others. For example, Meltzoff, Gopnik, and Repacholi (1999, p. 35) assume that an innate ability for imitation provides the basis for the infant to see other people as "just like me" (see also Meltzoff, 2002). Meltzoff et al. then outline the analogical argument as: "(a) When I perform that bodily act I have such and such a phenomenal experience, (b) I recognize that others perform the same type of bodily acts as me, (c) the other is sharing my behavioral state; ergo, perhaps the other is having the same phenomenal experience" (p. 35, see also Meltzoff & Brooks, 2001). Tomasello (1999b, p. 68) agreed that infants view other persons as "like me" (Tomasello, 1999b, p. 68), and "because infants view other persons as 'like me' from a very early age, any new understanding of their own functioning leads immediately to a new understanding of the functioning of others." From this it follows that when infants "understand themselves as intentional, they understand others as intentional" (p. 69). Furthermore, "infants begin to engage in joint attentional interactions when they begin to understand other persons as intentional agents like the self" (Tomasello, 1999a, p. 68).

Meltzoff and his colleagues (e.g., Meltzoff, 2002; Meltzoff & Brooks, 2001; Meltzoff, Gopnik, & Repacholi, 1999) claim that there is evidence that newborn babies can imitate. In a series of experiments, when shown particular facial gestures like tongue protrusion, or a surprised expression with a wide open mouth, very young babies "copy" these expressions (Meltzoff & Moore, 1977). Interpreting such results as an innate ability to imitate, Meltzoff has argued that this imitation forms the foundation for recognizing similarity between self and other. However, this position rests on claims that newborn infants can imitate a *range* of facial expressions and this evidence has been challenged (Moore & Corkum, 1994). In contrast to Meltzoff's claims, critical reviews argue that it is only tongue protrusion that is reliably reproduced by very young infants in response to an adult model (Anisfeld, 1991, 1996; Anisfeld, Turkewitz, & Rose, 2001; see also Müller & Runions, 2003, p. 31). If this is so, then explanations other than a *general* innate ability are more likely. A puzzle for Meltzoff's interpretation is why very young infants can imitate but they lose this ability around 2 to 3 months of age and then start imitating again at the end of the first year. Jones (1996) questions whether infants' matching of tongue protrusion is really imitation. In a series of experiments with 4-week-old infants Jones found that "infants who looked longer at a nonsocial light display also produced tongue protrusions at higher rates than infants showing less interest" and "infants showed more interest in (looked longer) at a tongue-protruding adult face than a mouth-opening face" (p. 1952). Furthermore, infants produced more tongue protrusions than mouth openings when they were presented with interesting objects dangled in front of them. Thus, Jones (1996, p. 1952) suggests that, rather than imitation, "infants' tongue protrusions in response to a tongue-protruding adult reflect very early attempts at oral explorations of interesting objects."

Recently Tomasello and his colleagues have reconsidered their position that identification with others is based on neonatal imitation (Tomasello, Carpenter, Call, Behne, & Moll, in press). Instead, they speculate that identification with others "depends crucially on the skills and motivations for interpersonal and emotional dyadic sharing characteristic of human infants and their caregivers (Hobson, 2002)" (Tomasello et al., in press, p. 25). However, they retain their position that "infants begin to understand particular kinds of intentional and mental states in others only after they have experienced them first in their own activity and then used their own experience to simulate that of others" (Tomasello et al., in press, p. 25).

There are a number of fundamental theoretical problems with the idea that this analogical argument explains the development of conceptions of self and other (e.g., Merleau-Ponty, 1960/1964; Müller & Carpendale, 2004; Müller & Runions, 2003; Scheler, 1913/1954; Soffer, 1999). The main one is that the argument attempts to explain how the infant comes to distinguish self from other, but it already presupposes such a capability (Müller & Runions, 2003). Not only is this tautological, it also skates over some potential problems. For example, a baby does not see herself smiling, so her *experience* of her own smile is very different from the experience of seeing someone else smile. No account of how such issues are overcome is offered. Once children have a distinction between self and other, they may be able to reason by analogy in some cases, but they cannot *form* this distinction through analogy. Furthermore, Tomasello's position requires the assumption that intentions exist as inner mental entities that can be introspected upon. This is the view that Wittgenstein (1968) has argued against (Carpendale & Racine, in press) and we return to it later. Difficulties such as these have led others to consider an alternative approach to social development based on what is termed a relational framework.

Lean Interpretations of a Self–Other Distinction

As well as the conceptual problems with the analogical argument discussed above, there are also other reasons to be cautious about overly rich interpretations of infants' behavior. We have to be careful about the "psychologist's fallacy" (Piaget, 1971). That is, just because forms of activity look similar on the surface we should not assume that they are always based on the same underlying causes. Moore and Corkum (1994) refer to the rich interpretation of joint attention as the "commonsense view." For example, it assumes that infants understand an adult's head turn as the adult "looking" at something. Moore suggests caution in simply accepting the commonsense view when infants' early cases of joint attention are open to simpler interpretations.

Moore and Corkum's (1994; Corkum & Moore, 1995, 1998; Moore, 1998, 1999) leaner view holds that infants engage in joint visual attention with an adult, without having yet developed an *understanding* of attention, through processes such as conditioning. Conditioning occurs when a pleasurable response (a reward) follows a behavior. So, if babies get a reward (a pleasurable stimulus to look at) every time they follow someone's head turn, they may simply do this without having to *understand* the other's attention. Rather than joint attention necessarily revealing infants' understanding of other people's attention, Moore and Corkum (1994) suggest that understanding others is constructed within their interactions. Regarding social referencing (checking the parent's expression in reaction to a potential "threat"), a leaner interpretation of this behavior is that infants may engage in it at first because it is an evolved attachment response to potential danger. That is, in situations of uncertainty and possible danger infants may look toward their parent for reassurance rather than information. Of course, further social understanding may develop within such interaction (Baldwin & Moses, 1996). We should be clear that lean approaches do not mean to explain away these phenomena, but rather to outline a developmental theory that provides an explanation for the development of these capacities.

Which theories have developed a relational framework?

Because of the problems with individualistic approaches, discussed above, some theorists have considered an alternative framework – the relational framework (Carpendale & Lewis, 2004a; Fogel, 1993; Hobson, 2002; Jopling, 1993: Müller & Carpendale, 2004). This is also the starting point for arguably the major theorists in twentieth-century developmental psychology (e.g., Piaget, 1954, 1970/1972; Baldwin, 1906; Vygotsky, 1998; Merleau-Ponty, 1964), that initially there is a lack of differentiation between the infant and the world of objects and other people. Such distinctions gradually develop through the infant's daily interactions and experiences. Perhaps it is unfortunate that this position has been defined in different and slightly floral terms by these authors: as "adualism" (Baldwin, 1906), the "great-we" (Vygotsky, 1998, p. 233), "radical egocentrism," as if the infant "were the centre of the universe – but a centre that is unaware of itself" (Piaget, 1970/1972, p. 21), a "primordial sharing situation" (Werner & Kaplan, 1963), a "primordial soup" (Hobson, 1993), or "we-centric space" (Gallese, 2003). The new reader should not be put off by the diversity or relative inaccessibility of these terms. They simply refer to the assumption that newborn infants do not yet have a clear understanding of the distinctions between self, other, and the world. That is, although they are engaged in activity with others and the world they do not at first understand how their action is separate from others and objects.

Before considering this approach it is important to address a common criticism that would appear to undermine relational approaches. It is sometimes assumed that they are based on the assumption "that infants at first are unable to differentiate between stimuli belonging to the self versus the environment" (Gergely, 2002, p. 27). However, there is evidence that infants can differentiate stimuli from the self and from the environment (see Gergely, 2002; Rochat, 2001). For example, Rochat and Hespos (1997) reported that newborn and 4-week-old infants respond differentially to their own hand touching their cheek in comparison to an experimenter's finger touching it. In addition, by 4 months of age infants appear to respond differently to video images of themselves in contrast to an experimenter mimicking them (Rochat & Striano, 2002). In response to such a criticism, we point out that infants' ability to respond differentially in different conditions reveals little about their understanding of self and other. Rochat and Striano (2002, p. 44) acknowledge that their results do not mean that infants at this age "actually recognize themselves or express conceptual self-awareness." Secondly, and contrary to Gergely's interpretation of Piaget, an ability to distinguish self from other stimulation would be required in order to experience the self as an agent (Russell, 1996), an ability that seems necessary for cognitive and social cognitive development from a Piagetian perspective and is not inconsistent with relational approaches. What is claimed by relational approaches is that infants may initially distinguish at a behavioral level but will not understand the contrast between their own perspective and others' perspectives (Carpendale, Lewis, Müller, & Racine, 2005).

How does a relational approach explain development?

The infant may interact with others and with objects but, according to this view, at first has not developed these distinctions (Piaget, 1977/1995; Vygotsky, 1998). A separation of inner and outer, subject and object, and self and other is gradually constructed by the infant through activity. The infant starts from intersubjectivity, and developing awareness involves a differentiation of self and other. That is, "the infant must discover her own mind in interaction with others" (Müller & Runions, 2003, p. 47). From this perspective, "psychogenesis begins in a state where the child is unaware of himself and the other as different beings" (Merleau-Ponty, 1964, p. 119). Thus social understanding is grounded in what is often termed "interpersonal relatedness." Through such interaction infants develop expectations consistent with an understanding of others as having attention and intention, and then later children construct a more sophisticated understanding of the mind.

Peter Hobson (2002, p. 258) describes this as a "differentiating out" approach, which contrasts with "joining together" approaches that assume that "the baby perceives bodies and then infers the existence of minds":

> The joining-together account says that children begin with their own thoughts, and learn how to communicate these thoughts to others. The differentiating-out approach says that children begin with an ability to communicate with others, and through communication they distil out thoughts-for-themselves. It is this developmental grounding that dissolves the mystery of why it is possible to convey thoughts from one person to another. Symbols *begin* life between people, and only as a secondary development do they become vehicles for an individual's thoughts. (Hobson, 2002, pp. 258–259, emphasis in original)

How does this increasing differentiation between self and other occur? Infants can respond to others' attitudes without yet having a conception of what these attitudes are (Carpendale & Lewis, 2004a; Hobson, 1994). The infant's early experience in face-to-face interaction with others is important in this process. Vasudevi Reddy (2001, 2003) argues for the importance of infants' experience of being the object of attention of others. She points out that even two-month-olds sometimes respond to adults' attention to the self in various ways such as with shy or coy smiles. If mothers stop normal interaction by looking away or by presenting a "still-face," infants show signs of distress (for a review of this research see Adamson & Frick, 2003, and for discussion see Tronick, 2003; Muir & Lee, 2003; Cohn, 2003). Furthermore, Reddy argues that beginning at about 8 months infants try to attract attention to themselves by "showing off," "clowning," and "teasing." This sort of research suggests some early competence in responding to adults' attention. The earlier research by Bruner (Bruner & Sherwood, 1976) on infants' interaction in the game of "peek-a-boo" and Watson's (1972) research on what he called "the game" is also relevant, because it shows how the infant is immersed in social interactions that facilitate the gradual dawning of social awareness. Newson and Newson (1975; see also Shotter & Gregory, 1976) pointed out that the fact that adults are impelled to treat the baby as a psychological being provides the best medium for such learning. That is, in the development of an understanding of others, the experience of others' attention directed to the self during the first months in face-to-face dyadic interaction may be very important. The question, however, is what to make of this account. That is, how richly should these forms of infant interaction be interpreted? We suggest a lean interpretation according to which the infant does not yet have a clear understanding of others' attention but instead has acquired expectations about interactions with others. In other words, this is an "understanding in action" or a sensorimotor "understanding" of attention.

Gradual Development of Joint Attention: The Research Evidence

In this section we review evidence on the emergence of two joint attention skills, gaze following and pointing gestures, to see if the evidence supports the claim that there is a gradual development of such skills. One of the lessons we attempted to draw out in chapters 1 and 2 in the context of experimental debates was that in taking a developmental approach we should look for various forms of understanding. And we should resist the (current) tendency to think that the earliest appearance of some form of a particular understanding or ability is equivalent to more mature forms (Chandler, 2001). In the spirit of this developmental approach we will describe various forms of gaze following and pointing gestures. We should not necessarily expect to see a particular form of knowledge or ability or understanding appear overnight. Instead we should expect to observe forms of knowledge gradually developing.

Forms of gaze following and pointing gestures

Gaze following is an important social cognitive skill that has been found in many nonhuman primates (Tomasello, Call, & Hare, 1998), and there is also some evidence for gaze following in domestic goats (Kaminski, Riedel, Call, & Tomasello, 2005). Furthermore, it appears that dogs (Call, 2004; Hare, Brown, Williamson, & Tomasello, 2002) and dolphins (Tschudin, Call, Dunbar, Harris, & van der Elst, 2001) can make use of some communicative cues from humans including gaze direction. The evidence suggests that in human infants gaze following is an early form of joint attention that develops through a series of increasingly more sophisticated forms that we describe here. Infants' abilities are generally assessed with variations of a procedure used by Scaife and Bruner (1975) in which an adult experimenter establishes eye contact with an infant and then turns her head 90 degrees to fixate on a target to one side. After reestablishing eye contact, this procedure is repeated with a head turn to the other side. Scaife and Bruner found that 30 percent of 2- to 4-month-old infants in this early study made at least one head turn in the correct direction on two trials. The percentages increased up to 100 percent in an 11- to 14-month-old group.

In research conducted since this early study the reported age for the development of gaze following varies from 3 months to 18 or more depending on the nature of the task and the strictness of the criteria for passing. Using liberal criteria, such as those of Scaife and Bruner (1975), infants were considered to have followed an adult's gaze if they looked toward the area around the target. Whether infants had looked first toward the target is not considered. In contrast, more conservative criteria consist of just scoring the direction of infants' first looks and requiring looking exactly at the target. Procedural differences such as the location of the target objects, whether objects are actually present or not, and the way in which the adult's directedness is indicated all contribute to the relative difficulty of following gaze in particular situations. We will explore some of these procedural variations here.

There is evidence that infants as young as 3 months show some ability at gaze following under certain conditions. At this age infants turn to the correct side in response to an adult's head turn significantly more than to the incorrect side when the targets are close by and in the infants' visual field – i.e., 80 cm away and 15 degrees to the infant's left or right (D'Entremont, 2000). However, at 3 months infants cannot reliably follow gaze to moving targets or objects that are 25 or 40 degrees to the side. This may be related to difficulty in disengaging from the adult's face. In a series of experiments with infants and their mothers Butterworth and Jarrett (1991) explored the increasing robustness of infants' gaze-following ability from 6 to 18 months. At 6 months of age infants generally turned in the right direction but they tended to stop at the first object they encountered in their scan path even if it was not the object their mother was looking at. As this ability depends on the structure of the environment, Butterworth (2001) refers to it as involving an "ecological" mechanism. At the age of 12 months infants could correctly find their mothers' target of focus even if it was the second object in their scan path. This, according to Butterworth (2001, p. 220), involves a "geometric" mechanism because it "appears to require extrapolation of a vector between the mother's head orientation and the referent of her gaze." Finally, by 18 months, infants rely on what Butterworth terms a "representational" mechanism and are able to follow an adult's gaze to objects located behind themselves (Butterworth & Jarrett, 1991).

It should be noted that the experiments described above were conducted in controlled laboratory situations with no distracting objects. Furthermore, there are still more complicated forms of gaze following in situations with obstacles in the line of sight. In this "barriers paradigm" the experimenter's line of sight to the target is blocked by a barrier in some conditions. Butler, Caron, and Brooks (2000) found that 18-month-olds but not 14-month-olds demonstrated some understanding that an experimenter's sight of a target would be blocked by a barrier but not if there was a window in the barrier. This conclusion was refined by Caron, Kiel, Dayton, and Butler's (2002) research showing that 15-month-old infants but not 12-month-olds seemed to understand that an experimenter could see a target through a window. In any case, Moll and Tomasello (2004) argued that this paradigm gives infants conflicting cues and is quite unusual. A more natural event is when an adult sees something but the infant's line of sight is blocked. Using this type of situation Moll and Tomasello found that both 12- and 18-month-old infants will actually walk or crawl around a barrier in order to able to see what the adult is looking at. By 18 months infants were better at this task than the 12-month-olds and this gaze-following situation was somewhat more difficult than the control condition used in which there was no obstacle in the infant's line of sight to the target.

We now turn to the development of infants' pointing gestures. Infants begin pointing sometime between 8 and 13 months of age, on average at about 11 months (e.g., Butterworth, 2003; Camaioni,

Perucchini, Bellagamba, & Colonnesi, 2004). As with gaze following, the evidence suggests that increasingly sophisticated forms of pointing gestures emerge over the second year of life. Furthermore, it is not just the form of the pointing gesture that changes with development, but also the context of the infant's other actions that allows increasing attribution of sophistication of social understanding.

Infants even as young as 9 to 15 weeks have been observed to extend their index finger in a hand configuration resembling a pointing gesture during the flow of hand activity (Fogel & Hannan, 1985). However, this is most likely not a communicative gesture. In considering the development of pointing we should be skeptical about just what infants understand when they begin pointing. One key marker is whether or not the pointing gesture is associated with a look toward the adult. This is "visual checking" of the other person, apparently to see if the gesture has been understood. At 12 months infants often point without such checking (Murphy & Messer, 1977), suggesting that the gesture emerges in a less sophisticated form before being used to try to direct others' attention. If the infant just points without looking at the other person this may be a less communicative form, or an earlier form of pointing. If the infant wants to direct someone's attention then he or she should see if it is working, i.e., he or she would have to look at the other person. However, from a skeptical perspective visual "checking" may not be so sophisticated. For example, if an infant is playing with a toy and is startled by an adult's voice and looks at the adult, this could be just shifting attention, not monitoring another's attention. Checking might just be looking at the parent for other reasons, such as the infant expecting some response from the adult (Moore, 1998, pp. 169–170; Moore & Corkum, 1994).

Bates et al. (1975) followed three infants of different ages longitudinally, and suggested that one of them appeared so confident of communication that she only checked if it failed. Thus Bates et al. (1979) suggest that checking may actually decrease with age. Although Bates' caution serves as a reminder to ensure that our inferences about infants' actions are correct, recent research suggests that typical developmental patterns involve a shift from initial pointing to pointing with a visual check. Desrochers, Morissette, and Ricard (1995) found that at 12 months of age over 50 percent of the 49 infants in their longitudinal studies were using pointing gestures, but it was not until 15 months of age that over 50 percent of these same infants were producing pointing gestures accompanied by a look toward their mother. Franco and Butterworth (1996) reported that at 12 months of age 47 percent of pointing gestures were associated with visual checking and this increased to 65 percent of pointing gestures at 18 months. But what also changed across these months was the timing of the visual checking. They found that at 12 months infants usually looked toward their mother after pointing, at 14 months checking tended to be during the pointing, and at 16 months checking was most often just before the pointing gesture. This seems to indicate a series of different forms of pointing and different levels of understanding.

The differences in pointing gestures between 1 and 2 years of age suggest that infants change in their understanding of others' attention. Moore and D'Entremont (2001) presented children with an interesting sight while their parent was either looking toward that side of the room or not. The pointing gestures of 1-year-olds did not depend on whether or not their parent had already looked at the interesting sight. Instead they pointed more when their parent was looking at them. Moore and D'Entremont (2001) argue that this suggests that infants at this age are using pointing to enhance interaction. In contrast, 2-year-olds seem to understand that what others see may differ from what they see. They used pointing to direct attention more when the parent had not seen the interesting sight or was not looking at the sight. However, Liszkowski, Carpenter, Henning, Striano, and Tomasello (2004) argue that at 12 months infants point in order to direct others' attention because their gestures depend on the adult's response. In their study, when an experimenter responded to the infants' point by ignoring it or only looking either at the event or at the child's face, the infants repeated the gesture more than when the experimenter shared attention by looking at the infant and the event. The fact that infants persisted suggests that they were not satisfied with the experimenter's partial responses. Furthermore, across a series of 10 trials infants in the condition in which the experimenter shared attention by looking at both the infant and the event and commenting pointed more than infants in the other conditions, suggesting that these infants felt successful in their communicative attempts. Liszkowski et al. argue that this shows that already at 12 months infants point with a declarative motive in order to direct others' attention and share interest.

Which comes first, the child's ability to point or her/his ability to follow another's gesture? That is, does the production of pointing precede comprehension or vice versa? As in other areas of theorization, there is some controversy about the relationship between infants' production and comprehension skills. Bruner's (1983, p. 75) longitudinal study of two infants suggested that the child's "ability to comprehend an adult point precedes his own production by a month or two in our records." Carpenter et al. (1998) found that comprehension of pointing precedes the production of imperative and declarative pointing. Thus, Butterworth (2003, p. 23) concluded that "many studies agree that the comprehension of pointing, at about 10 months, slightly precedes its production" (see also Camaioni et al., 2004). However, the picture is not this clear. Murphy and Messer (1977), in a cross-sectional study of 24 infants at either 9 or 14 months of age, reported that production seemed to precede comprehension by a few months. Desrochers et al. (1995) produced support for this latter position in a longitudinal study of 25 infants. They found that over half of the infants in their sample were using pointing gestures at 12 months but it was not until 15 months that this number could follow their mothers' pointing gestures. They also found no correlation between the infants' comprehension of their mothers' pointing gestures and their own production of pointing gestures (either non-communicative pointing – not looking at their mothers when pointing – or communicative pointing – looking at their mothers in relation to the gesture). Thus, there seems to be no obvious single or causal relation between comprehension and production of pointing. To us this complexity suggests that, as we have described above, there are various forms of these joint attentional interactions. If we put all the evidence that we have described in this section together, the age at which children demonstrate comprehension of pointing seems to depend on the nature of the situation; that is, following pointing gestures to close objects develops somewhat earlier than the ability to follow points to more distant objects (Butterworth, 2003). Also, the production of imperative pointing seems to develop before declarative pointing (Camaioni et al., 2004). The case for a gradual and complex developmental pathway seems clear.

Theories of the origins of pointing

Having outlined the various forms of progressively more sophisticated pointing gestures, we now turn to theories of their development. Can we can devise an adequate account of the way in which these skills unfold? There are many explanations for their emergence, one being that gestures like this are strongly determined by genetic factors. Even Bruner (1983, p. 75), who is not noted for an adherence to nativist perspectives, argued that it "seems more likely that pointing is part of a primitive marking system for singling out the noteworthy." Butterworth

(1998, p. 180) agreed and took this argument further: "it seems likely that pointing will prove to be a specialised human adaptation. . . . Manual pointing seems to be based on a species-specific modular coordinative structure which operates in the interpersonal context" (Butterworth, 1991, p. 231). He went on to argue that "[t]he specialized function of the index finger in relation to shared attention may be innate. The developmental changes are to be explained by successive acquisition of arm control, fine manipulative skills and cognitive integration of the communicative roles of infant and adult" (Butterworth, 1991, pp. 229–230). However, it is important to think about just what is meant by the claim that pointing may be innate. It does not seem plausible to assume that pointing could be innate in the sense of a fixed action pattern, because the very same gesture can be used to serve at least two, if not more, functions, i.e., imperative and declarative. This means that the "cognitive integration of the communicative roles of infant and adult" most likely has a large part to play in this development.

In concluding a chapter on "some observations on the origins of the pointing gesture" Lock, Young, Service, and Chandler (1990) state that "Its origins are not straightforward" (p. 55). In the rest of this subsection we explore the issues that make gestures, like pointing and referential looking, complex in theoretical terms. One of the best known of the many theories is Vygotsky's (1978, p. 56) idea that pointing develops from reaching: "Initially, this gesture is nothing more than an unsuccessful attempt to grasp something. . . . When the mother comes to the child's aid and realizes this movement indicates something, the situation changes fundamentally. Pointing becomes a gesture for others." This claim follows from Vygotsky's general developmental position that forms of thought are originally social and only later individual.

Bretherton, McNew, and Beeghly-Smith (1981) present the Vygotskian position that:

> Functional reaching and grasping behavior gradually becomes abbreviated and ritualized as it turns into a communicative gesture. Similarly, the arms-up gesture emerges out of cooperation with the mother: As the mother extends her arms toward the baby in order to pick him or her up, the baby responds by lifting its arms. Later, the baby may start to raise the arms as soon as mother enters the room in the morning in the *expectation* of being picked up. Eventually, an infant comes to use the arms-up gesture communicatively, that is, the child spontaneously approaches his or her mother in order to *request* a pick-up. (p. 338, emphasis in original)

Bretherton et al. (1981) found that all the infants in their sample used this "arms-up" gesture by the age of $10^1/_2$ months. The development of gestures in this way is what Tomasello (1999a, pp. 31–33; Tomasello & Camaioni, 1997) termed "ontogenetic ritualization": "Ritualizations are gestures in which the infant simply employs an effective procedure for getting something done" (Tomasello, 2003, p. 32). Tomasello argues that such repeated actions seem to be the way in which chimpanzees acquire most if not all their gestures.

The Vygotskian hypothesis that pointing develops from reaching only accounts for imperatives or requests. It does not explain the development of protodeclaratives because it does not seem likely that the process of directing someone's attention would develop from failed grasping. It is still necessary to provide an account of how infants begin to use this gesture to serve a declarative function merely to direct others' attention. Werner and Kaplan (1963, p. 78) argued that pointing does not develop from grasping, but they do suggest that there is "some element of reference to the bodily acts of *reaching*." They describe two forms of reaching, only one of which is "quasi-referential": "reaching-for-touching is genetically related to reference; reaching-for-grabbing is not." (Here "genetically related" means developmentally related.) The implication here that pointing may originate in attempts at finger-tip exploration fits with observations from Shinn (1900/1975, p. 220) in her longitudinal observation of one infant: "First the baby began to use her forefinger tip for specially close investigations; at the same time she had a habit of stretching out her hand towards any object that interested her – by association, no doubt, with touching and seizing movements." This hypothesis is consistent with the underlying concepts in Vygotskian theory and has yet to be explored experimentally. But there is some evidence that infants begin using their index finger to examine objects before they begin pointing communicatively (Bates, Benigni, Bretherton, Camaioni, & Volterra, 1979). More generally, Franco and Butterworth (1996, p. 330) claim that their results, described above, "suggest that pointing originates independently of imperative gestures such as reaching." They argue instead that even when pointing is emerging at 10 months it is already serving a declarative communicative function. It is also possible that two of the functions of pointing – imperative and declarative – may develop somewhat independently, with protoimperatives emerging from reaching gestures and protodeclaratives from manual explorations. However, such possibilities are speculative.

Joint Attention and Theories of Infant Social Development

In this last section we return to some of the big issues with which we started the chapter. The first part revisits the debate over lean vs. rich interpretations of infant social development that has been the focus of this discussion. We analyze recent data and consider the transition to the child's first words in order to set this discussion into a wider context. In the second, we reflect upon the significance of joint attention for our understanding of major questions concerning the roles of genes and culture in the development of this ability. We end by returning briefly to the topic of autism to ask whether joint attention problems are central to this syndrome.

The rich–lean debate: recent evidence and the transition to language

What does our review of the evidence on pointing and gaze following imply for two of the main theories in this area discussed in this chapter? As mentioned above, Tomasello's (1995a) central hypothesis concerning joint attention is that these various skills are "all manifestations of infants' emerging understanding of other persons as intentional agents whose attention and behavior to outside objects and events may be shared, followed into, and directed in various ways" (Carpenter et al., 1998, p. 118). Support for the rich view would come from a study in which different joint attention skills correlated highly at any one point in time. Such relationships were found in Carpenter et al.'s (1998) longitudinal study of 24 infants assessed monthly between 9 and 15 months with nine different measures of joint attention including gaze following, point following, and use of imperative and declarative gestures. Tomasello (1999a, p. 64) has argued that the evidence reported by Carpenter et al. (1998), namely that "for virtually all infants the whole panoply of joint attentional skills emerge in fairly close developmental synchrony, in moderately correlated fashion, with a highly consistent ordering pattern across children," supports his position. The ordering pattern found by Carpenter et al. was that infants first show the ability to share attention with others, then to follow attention, and finally to direct others' attention.

However, other research has produced conflicting results. Slaughter and McConnell's (2003) cross-sectional study of 60 infants between the ages of 8 and 14 months found no correlations between gaze following, social referencing, and imitation. Although these studies used different definitions of these skills, the inconsistency between them makes it hard to accept a rich interpretation without clear supportive evidence. Slaughter and McConnell (2003, p. 67) interpret their results as "better explained by the lean interpretation, in which developmental requirements of specific, independent skills are responsible for the development of joint attention."

Moore (1998) criticizes the nature of infant cognition that Tomasello must assume in order for the infant to understand others as intentional agents. Although infants' activity at 9 months can be described as intentional, in that means and ends are separated (i.e., they do things to achieve goals), the next step to infants' understanding of their own action as intentional is far more problematic. Moore and his colleagues (Barresi & Moore, 1996; Moore, 1996; Moore & Corkum, 1994) provide a lean interpretation of infants' joint attention skills. They set up the problem to be solved as how the infant, with different information from their first-person experience compared to their experience of other people, comes to recognize the equivalence of the psychological relations of self and other. They suggest that the infant could learn joint attention skills without making conceptual leaps in their understanding. For example, the idea that following an adult's head turns rewards the infant with interesting sights was demonstrated by Corkum and Moore (1998). They showed that from about 8 months of age infants, who do not yet respond spontaneously to another person's orientation to objects, could be conditioned to use head turns to follow a person's gaze when a toy dog lighted up and rotated as an experimenter turned her head to look at it. They conclude that within bouts of such interaction the infant gradually forms a representation of joint attention. The infant has available "both first-person and third-person information about the same psychological relation and at this point intermodal integration can provide a representation of these activities that spans the relation between agent and object" (Moore, 1996, p. 30). This is only possible, according to Barresi and Moore (1996), at the end of infancy "when the infant can imagine the first-person information for another or the third-person information for self and thereby truly be said to recognize the equivalence of self and other in psychological activity" (Moore, 1996, p. 30).

However, Tomasello and his colleagues are not consistently committed to the idea of one insight changing the infant's understanding of others. Elsewhere they state that their view "does not imply that understanding others as intentional agents is an all-or-nothing affair, all infants' interactions with others being totally transformed instantaneously" (Carpenter et al. (1998, pp. 118–119). Indeed they acknowledge some sympathy with Moore's view "in the sense that each of the social-cognitive skills that we have observed does indeed require some specific learning experiences" (p. 120). Furthermore, Tomasello (2003, pp. 33–34) acknowledges that "empirically we do not know whether infants learn to point via ritualization or imitative learning or whether some infants learn in one way (especially prior to their first birthdays) and some learn in the other." This overlap between the positions makes straightforward differences in empirical predictions difficult to make.

Clearly this debate between rich and lean views of infant social development has not been resolved. There will undoubtedly be further research and arguments advanced from both sides. Our own position on this matter is in favor of a lean view to begin with. That is, we expect that infants begin to engage in particular forms of joint attention for various reasons as suggested by Moore and his colleagues and within such interaction they develop further social understanding. Moore (1998, p. 172) proposes a sensorimotor account of early infant social knowledge:

> The way to think about triadic interactive behavior is in terms of the infant's attention to people's activity and to the world of objects becoming coordinated. Critically, one must allow that infants can participate in social interactive structures in which their attention to others' action is linked to their attention to other objects and events. From a Piagetian point of view, such linkages would be seen as the coordination of schemes.

Taking such an activity-based approach does not mean ignoring the rich details of the interpersonal engagement pointed out by Hobson (2002) and Reddy (e.g., 2003) in which infants are involved during their first year. Rather, we think it is important to be clear about what is meant by self–other awareness early in infancy. We suggest that this is a form of practical, lived, or sensorimotor knowledge in Piaget's sense. That is, at this age infants are developing expectations about their interactions with others. As Reddy notes, babies are learning how to play with the reactions of others. However, we are lean in the conceptual understanding we attribute to young infants; there are still important developments in self–other understanding during the beginning of the second year of life. We further outline our position in chapter 10.

On the connection between joint attention and language, however, we are squarely in agreement with Tomasello (e.g., 2003). Like others

(Bates, 1976; Budwig et al., 2000; Wittgenstein, 1968), Tomasello claims that meaning of words is tied up with how they are used in interaction. From this perspective "the child's understanding is not just a matter of recognizing a correspondence between the mother's words and reality, but of grasping her *referential intent* in that situation – knowing what one is *meant* to attend to in response to her words and gestures" (Chapman, 1999, p. 34, emphasis original). That is, "a word is one means by which adults attempt to induce children to attend to certain aspects of a shared social situation" (Tomasello, 2001, p. 112). From this perspective, the meaning of words is not the object they map onto. The research on how children come to learn words appears to show that their very early use of words is tied up with specific contexts and then slowly generalizes to others. For example, Harris, Barrett, Jones, and Brookes (1988) observed children's use of language over the second year of life. One child [James] started to use the word "duck" only when banging his toy duck on the side of the bath – not when his mother showed him the toy or if he saw a real duck or a photo. Only gradually did he generalize his use of this word.

Learning to use words takes place within the context of the flow of interaction between infants, others, and events in the environment. In discussing this issue, Baldwin (1995) made a case for the need to understand the child's role in figuring out what another person is referring to. She pointed out that if infants did not understand others' referential intent they would make certain characteristic mistakes, or "mapping" errors. So, when they hear a new word they might simply assume that it refers to whatever object they are currently paying attention to. Clearly this would result in many confusing mistakes. For example, Baldwin relates an anecdote about her son playing with a new toy while she and her husband watched the news. At one point her young son said, "No legal precedent," repeating a phrase from the news broadcast. However, he did not make the mistake that this phrase referred to his new toy. Infants rarely make such mistakes. Some parents who follow their infants' focus of attention and label objects the infant is engaged in do have infants who are advanced in early word learning (see Baldwin, 1995; Carpenter et al., 1998). But this cannot hold in all cases and in all cultures, and infants must have some way of learning words that does not simply depend on forming associations between new words they hear and objects they are focused on.

To examine this issue experimentally, Baldwin (1991, 1995) studied infants between the ages of 16 to 19 months in two word-learning conditions. In the "follow-in labeling" condition the experimenter provided a new word for a novel toy the infant was presented with. The infants learned the new word in this condition. In the more difficult "discrepant labeling" condition the experimenter used the new word to refer to a second novel toy that was not the focus of the infant's attention. The infants over the age of 18 months tended to learn the new word in this condition but 16- to 17-month-old infants did not. Even though 16- to 17-month-olds did not learn the new word at above chance levels, they did not make systematic errors by assuming that the new word referred to the object they were playing with. How do the infants do this? They must use cues to understand the adult's referential intent. That is, infants must figure out what the adult is talking about and this requires achieving joint attention. This is why joint attention is such an important ability and it seems to be required for learning language, the skill beyond all others that separates us from other primates.

In the discussion above we referred to how the child uses a specific context to utter the word "duck" – on a nightly basis while he caused his toy serious brain damage. Such examples of language learning in action present us with a subtle but important issue concerning the role of joint attention in word learning. This is "the distinction between meaning as *object* and meaning as *act*" (Bates, 1976, p. 8, emphasis in original). We turn in chapters 7 and 10 to explore a key issue in language development, which is that word learning is no simple matter. We do not simply map a new word to a concept or object (Montgomery, 2002). We will argue that one of the major feats of social understanding is that children have to come to use the same words in different contexts to mean subtly or even radically different things. The research on joint attention that we have presented in this chapter provides us with clues as to how this can possibly take place. Three conclusions can be drawn. First, the child constructs meaning her or himself – no parent would attempt to teach their child to say the word duck in one specific context. Secondly, as we saw in the examples of pointing and the coordination of shared gaze, the developmental process is a slow one – we make the case for such "gradualism" in the construction of social understanding throughout the rest of this book. Thirdly, joint attention does not take place in a social vacuum. The infant constructs an understanding of gestures and words, but these are stage-managed by more advanced members of the child's social network – parents, siblings, grandparents, and others. The process occurs within that rich tapestry which culture provides.

Summary and Conclusions

Joint attention in infancy such as following adults' attention in their gaze or gestures, or directing others' attention with gestures, is a core part of social development in infancy. Debate has centered around whether such examples of joint attention should be richly interpreted as revealing infants' understanding of others as intentional agents, or whether such early instances of coordinated attention would be better thought of from a leaner perspective as an essential context in which infants develop an understanding of others. We described two different epistemological frameworks or sets of starting assumptions that lead to very different views about development. Many theories of social development are based on the individualistic approach and this generally means relying on the analogical argument which has been severely criticized. An alternative framework is the relational approach. We present our position on this issue in chapter 10.

In spite of debates about the origins of joint attention there is general agreement about the fundamental importance of joint attention as an ability that allows children to engage in the kind of interpersonal interaction in which they can develop further levels of social understanding. Furthermore, lack of joint attention often signals serious problems in social development including autism. And the capacity to share attention seems to be required for language development and engaging in culture. Language then becomes a means through which children's social cognition is transformed, as we discuss in chapter 7. In addition, the capacity to achieve joint attention makes it possible for infants to engage in more complex relationships with others that lead to further social development. Although toward the end of this chapter we have mentioned the role of infants' emotional engagement with others (Hobson, 2002; Reddy, 2003), the primary focus in much research on joint attention is on the cognitive dimension. It is important to remember that joint attention always occurs within affectively charged interpersonal relationships.

As discussed in chapter 1, some researchers in the "theory of mind" tradition refer to work on joint attention in infancy in terms of "precursors" to children's later false belief understanding. However, Tomasello (1995a) has argued that the basic level of social understanding manifest in the capacity to engage in joint attention or triadic interaction is a fundamental human ability which allows infants to experience interaction and acquire language in which they will later develop more sophisticated understandings of the social world. The rest of social understanding is "icing on the cake" compared to the importance of joint attention in human cognition, and might be might be better thought of as a "post-cursor" to children's ability to engage in joint attention (Tomasello, 1999a). The capacity to develop joint attention makes human language and culture possible, and Tomasello (1999c) has argued that it is this capacity that is a human adaptation for culture.

Chapter 5

Domain General Approaches to Reasoning about the Mind

Introduction

Debate on the nature of the child's understanding of the mind widened during the 1990s. Some researchers began to wonder if young children's failure on false belief tasks was due to lack of development of general reasoning skills rather than specific difficulties with understanding mental states. That is, attention shifted from a very focused examination of the nature and origins of mental state understanding to heated exchanges over the issue of whether this understanding is domain specific (i.e., relatively self-contained in terms of its content and developmental progression) or domain general (i.e., based on a series of interrelated skills like language and memory that are involved in all areas of thought). This chapter examines the evidence for a link between "theory of mind" and domain general skills and the theories proposed to explain this link.

This debate originated from two clear sources. In the first place, research on autistic children's more general cognitive skills found that success on a battery of false belief tasks correlated with the ability to switch rules on a card sorting task and carry out a planned sequence of actions on the Tower of Hanoi, a test in which the child has to move a set of disks from one pole to two others to match an array presented by the experimenter without putting a disk on top of a smaller disk (Ozonoff, Pennington, & Rogers, 1991).

Secondly, researchers within the theory of mind tradition almost stumbled upon the connections between mental state understanding and more general cognitive skills. James Russell was initially concerned that younger preschoolers fail the standard false belief task because it places too many cognitive and linguistic demands upon children. He therefore developed a procedure in which children had to deceive an experimenter into selecting an empty box to open. In this task a first

Figure 5.1 The child's perspective on the windows task: In the first trials the child cannot see into the boxes, but when these are replaced with a transparent window s/he can see where the reward is when choosing which box the experimenter should open. (Photo: Geoff Rushforth and Gordon Johnston)

experimenter told the child that there would always be a chocolate in one of two boxes, but that neither the child nor the second experimenter playing the game would know which box it was hidden in. The child was told that all he or she had to do was to point to a box to tell the second experimenter where to look. The second experimenter kept what was in the box indicated by the child, and the child kept what was in the other box. This procedure was called the *windows task* (Figure 5.1) because after a warm-up period with four opaque walls, one wall is replaced with a transparent screen so that the child can see the reward through this "window." Given the ability of 2-year-olds to deceive another person (Chandler et al., 1989: see chapter 3), one prediction was that 3-year-olds would be able to select the empty box for the experimenter in order to keep the reward for him/herself. Yet, it transpired that 3-year-olds tended to choose the baited box and thus the experimenter got the reward (Russell, Mauthner, Sharpe, & Tidswell, 1991). Unlike the false belief task, which once learned cannot be repeated with the same experimental props, this new task could be repeated over a series of trials with the reward placed in one of two boxes at random. Russell et al. (1991) found that many 3-year-olds pointed to the baited box repeatedly over 20 trials, even when given the negative feedback of not receiving the reward. In addition older, but mental age-matched, children with autism failed in this task over repeated trials. Why did these two groups of children continue to fail the task even when receiving feedback by not getting the reward? Russell et al. came to the conclusion that a theory of mind explanation did not suffice, as children should be able to deceive relatively early in their development. Rather, they suggested that this type of perseverative behavior (i.e., the act of repeatedly making the same choice, even if it is the wrong one) may reflect an inability in younger children and those with autism to inhibit making a reference to the object's actual location. It was data like these that forced "theory of mind" researchers to consider the role of general cognitive skills in their theoretical debates.

Russell's work in the 1990s culminated with his books *Autism as an Executive Disorder* (1997) and *Agency* (1996). Both aimed in part to explore the role of executive skills in the child's developing understanding of mental states. Similarly, a collection of readings in 2000 by Peter Mitchell and Kevin Riggs was dedicated in large part to exploring the role of inferential skills in the development of an understanding of mind. The three sections of this chapter chart the development of a debate fueled initially by data similar to those collected in the windows task. The first section describes two experimental procedures analogous to false belief tasks in terms of their structure and which present similar difficulties to 3-year-olds, but do not involve mental state reasoning. On the strength of associations between children's understanding of belief and these related tests, it has been argued that the problems children face with false belief concern their ability to perform reasoning in general, not a specific problem in inferring mental states. The second section describes a recent debate between proponents of the view that "theory of mind" tasks or even an understanding of mind in general can be attributable to a range of skills which in terms of neurophysiology are located in the prefrontal cortex and in terms of psychological functioning involve the control of prepotent behavior – like blurting out the current location of the chocolate in the Maxi task, or erring in a game of "Simon says" by following instructions that should be ignored. The final section attempts to assess the current state of play within a heated debated over the relative contribution of domain general accounts to our theorization about mental state understanding. We contend that by themselves domain general approaches ask many searching questions about the validity of "theory of mind" accounts of social development, but they themselves lead us to ask further questions that we turn to in the following chapters.

Is the False Belief Problem just a Reasoning Task?

During the 1990s a rumbling of discontent was audible at many conferences on child development. It has been argued that children's problems with false belief tasks may be due to a more general difficulty in reasoning about situations in which one must set aside what is currently known about a situation (Harris, 1991, p. 293). This ability to reason about how the world might have been is called counterfactual reasoning, and it may be that reasoning about false beliefs is just one application of this more general ability to "imaginatively reason about inaccessible things" (Riggs & Peterson, 2000, p. 88). For example, a team at Birmingham University conducted a series of experiments in which children were given a variant on the Unexpected Transfer test (see chapter 3) which is of similar complexity, but which does not contain a false belief component. In one task children were told that Peter goes to bed because he is feeling unwell, while Sally goes to get him some medicine. While she is out Peter is phoned and asked to go and help put out a fire at the post office, which he does. The children are then asked two questions. The obvious false belief question (Where does Sally think Peter is?) is given to half the children first, whereas the rest are first asked a "*Counterfactual reasoning*" question, which is more complex in its structure (it uses conditional language rather than the present tense), but which contains the same type of reasoning, comparing one state of affairs with another (Riggs, Peterson, Robinson, & Mitchell, 1998). The question "If there had been no fire, where would Peter be?" contrasts current reality (Peter is helping to put the fire out) with a recently known fact (Peter was in bed before being called out). Riggs et al. found a remarkable consistency between children's responses to these two types of question. For example in one task only 12 percent gave different responses across the two conditions, whereas the rest of the children either failed or passed both. It could be the case that 3-year-olds fail the counterfactual reasoning question because they simply do not understand the complex language used (constructions like "If . . ." and verbal forms like "would be"), but their experiment included some checks to control for this simple explanation. Riggs and Peterson (2000, p. 90) offer an alternative account:

the ability to ascribe false beliefs is part of a more general imaginative capacity to make known to be false adjustments to one's own knowledgebase in reasoning conditionally to a new conclusion. This general imaginative reasoning ability is used to make inferences about many inaccessible things, other people's beliefs being just one of many applications.

A difficulty with this claim, that false belief reasoning is just a special case of counterfactual reasoning, is the evidence that 3- and 4-year-olds can reason counterfactually (Harris, German, & Mills, 1996). In examining the conflict between Harris et al.'s research, demonstrating an early ability in counterfactual reasoning, and Riggs et al.'s study showing that this ability develops later, Harris and Leevers (2000, pp. 83–84) point out that "Harris et al. (1996) created stories in which an initially ordinary or unblemished state was transformed into a negative state by some mishap. For example, a clean floor was dirtied by muddy footprints, a tower of bricks was knocked down by a stick, or a finger was pricked by a pin." They suggest that such situations involving negative transformations are likely to optimize counterfactual reasoning because children may have spontaneously considered ways to avoid the regrettable outcome. By contrast, in the neutral situations used by Riggs and his colleagues (1998) counterfactual thinking may not have occurred because the children were not aware of the need to think about the problem in this way. The experimenter's question came too late to allow them to do this, Harris and Leevers argue.

Another difference, however, between the two experiments is that with the stories used by Harris et al., the child hardly needs to know or remember the details of the plot. That is, general knowledge is enough to answer questions about floors getting dirty, whereas in the Riggs et al. stories the child needs to understand and keep track of the movements of people and objects in order to answer the questions correctly (cf. Perner, Sprung, & Steinkogler, 2004). Thus, one possibility is that the tasks differ in how much information must be held in mind and coordinated to reach a conclusion. This factor relates to the possible role that executive functioning may have in false belief reasoning. We return to consider this possibility later in this chapter. But first we review the work of another group that has made related claims about the relationship between false belief understanding and reasoning skills.

From a different theoretical orientation Douglas Frye and Philip Zelazo examined the domain specificity of the false belief task by comparing it with a task which requires the child to shift from one rule set to another within the same procedure. They tested the claim that children find false

Figure 5.2 In the Dimensional Change Cart Sort procedure the child sorts by shape (color) first and then has to sort by color (shape). These materials were made by Shimmon (2004). Reproduced with permission

belief tasks difficult because these tasks require the comparison of two embedded propositions (Maxi thinks the chocolate is in one location, while his mother has moved it and the child research participant knows it to be in another). They developed a task that has been used extensively (Figure 5.2). Frye, Zelazo, and Palfai (1995) asked children to sort cards showing blue rabbits and red boats into two trays. Above each tray was a target card, a blue boat above one and a red rabbit above the other. The child is told that they are going to play the "shape game" and they happily place the rabbits face down into the tray beneath the rabbit and the boats in the other tray beneath the boat. After sorting five cards, the child is told that they are now going to play a different game, the color game, and their task is to put the red cards into the red tray and the blue cards into the blue tray. Of course now the child has to place cards in the opposite tray and disregard the shape of the object. For half the participants the color game is played first – order does not matter. Almost 90 percent of children appear to follow one of two patterns, either using the first or the second rule when sorting the second set of five cards. Significantly more 3-year-olds continued to sort by shape even when clearly told to "Put the blue ones here; put the red ones here." In addition, success on a false belief task correlated with an ability to make the switch from one rule to another during the card sort.

Variations on this task, known as the Dimensional Change Card Sort (DCCS), yield some interesting findings. Children still make the perseverative error when there is a single pre-switch trial, when the pictures on the boxes were replaced by familiar TV characters and the rule is "If it's red then you have to put it into Ernie's [or 'Big Bird's] box" and when children simply have to say where the card should go (Zelazo, Frye, & Rapus, 1996). The most surprising feature of these tasks is that children answer specific questions about the rules correctly. So when asked "Where do the rabbits go in the shape game?" they can answer correctly, even though they then go on to make perseverative sorting errors, in this instance by color rather than shape. Zelazo et al. suggest that 3-year-olds tend to make "abulic" errors, that is, they articulate the rule but appear not to be able to act on it. In their recent work this group of researchers has shown that this pattern of performance cannot simply be a result of a failure in related skills, like memory capacity or the number of rules that the child has to recall (Zelazo, Müller, Frye, & Marcovitch, 2004). Their experiments suggest that the problem for the child centers around the fact that tasks like the card sort rely upon the child's ability to construct higher order rules that make the two rule systems (e.g., the shape and color rule sets) accessible to conscious control.

Such data led Frye and Zelazo to construct a more general account of the ability to embed two contradictory rules, known as the Cognitive Complexity and Control (CCC) theory (see, e.g., Zelazo, 2000). According to CCC theory, the crucial error that younger children tend to make on the false belief task occurs because children ignore the setting condition (shape, or color) and make their judgments based on simpler if–then rules. Children thus pass through a number of developmental transitions, or stages, which identify the degree to which they can reflect on their plans (see, e.g., Frye et al., 1995; Zelazo et al., 1996; Zelazo, 2000). Plans involve setting conditions and rules, and children are faced with increasingly complex rule structures in developing them. Zelazo and Frye (1998) claim that the way in which children compare lower-level rules is by embedding them into a superordinate rule structure. Two-year-olds can represent a single rule (i.e., "If red, then here") and act accordingly. By 3 the child can represent a pair of rules simultaneously ("If red, here. If blue, here."). When children reach their fifth birthday, they can represent embedded rules, or rules within rules ("If this is the color game, then if red car, then here; but if it is the shape game, then if red car, then here."). Such a rule system requires a basic embedded structure in which the rules for each game are subordinate to the rule concerning which game is being played.

Perhaps the most crucial finding for our analysis of the child's understanding of the mind is that false belief test performance is correlated in many studies with a particular level of complexity of sorting, in which children sort by one of two dimensions (using an if–if–then structure), rather than just one, or two simultaneously (see Frye et al., 1995, experiment 3). Frye et al. (1995) claim that such a rule structure can be applied equally to both executive and false belief tests, and this probably explains the significant correlations found between the two types of task. They argue that the if–if–then structure required for the DCCS task (e.g., if shape game, and if blue rabbit, then place with red rabbit) requires the same skills as do false belief tests. Frye (1999) suggests that this account may explain the connection between tasks involving mental states and those not doing so. For example, John Flavell and his colleagues (1983, 1986) designed the "sponge-rock" appearance-reality test, in which the child is shown an object that looks just like a rock. When asked to squeeze it he or she is asked "When you look at this with your eyes right now, does it *look like* a rock or does it *look like* a sponge." There is a 3–4 shift in this task, in that younger children deny that the object now looks like a rock, even though some seconds before they had identified it as such. Another approach focusing on the levels of task complexity has been proposed by Andrews, Halford, Bunch, Bowden, and Jones (2003). Their theory and experimental evidence support the position that level of structural complexity of the inferences required is a factor in false belief task performance.

CCC theory has been criticized both in terms of its theoretical coherence and in terms of the relationship between theory and the data from the card sort task. Perner (2000) claims that the embedded rules required for success on the card sort task do not necessarily have to be applied to the traditional false belief task. He argues that the Maxi task could alternatively be described in terms of two simple conditions that should pose no problem even to 3-year-olds, such as: if I am looking for the chocolate then there; if Maxi is looking for the chocolate then here. He therefore maintains his original position, that "the belief task . . . capture(s) a deeper understanding that allows behavioral predictions without knowledge of behavioral regularities in specific situations" (Perner, Stummer, & Lang, 1999, p. 137).

It is hard to evaluate the impact of this research that treats an understanding of mental states as exemplars of more general reasoning and the embeddedness of rules. The counterfactual task, for example, is not completely the same as the false belief test and might simply show a relationship between "mindreading" and language ability, a point we return to in chapter 7. The card sort test has also received much critical scrutiny and there is controversy over what it shows. Towse, Redbond, Houston-Price, and Cook (2000) conducted a series of experiments in which they explored whether an elaborately connected rule system was required to explain the shift in the card sort task. In each manipulation children's performance was supported to ensure that they could remember the rules. For example, the children were asked about the rules and reminded about the salient one before each sort, or the correct action was demonstrated before the child sorted the cards. In these cases children demonstrated greater levels of success, and Towse et al. suggested that the card sort task is difficult, not because the child has to understand embedded rules, but because the first sorting strategy becomes cognitively salient to him or her. However, it is possible that these manipulations might just help shift the child to the other branch of the CCC tree without the child needing to reason in terms of embedded rules and thus would not be inconsistent with CCC theory (Müller, personal communication).

Similar caution about the card sort task has been raised by Kirkham, Cruess, and Diamond (2003). They performed two manipulations. In the first they got children to label the cards before they sorted them and found that almost 80 percent of 3-year-olds now sorted correctly. This labeling effect was not, however, replicated in a study by Lurye and Müller (2003). In a second task Kirkham et al. simply modified the procedure so that children sorted the cards face up, rather than face down as in Frye et al.'s (1995) procedure. They found that this led to a greater preponderance of perseverative errors, presumably because seeing the wrong card in the sort tray is sufficient to induce a perpetuation of the initial rule. At the same time Shimmon, Lewis, and Francis (2003) conducted an almost identical manipulation, except that they removed the cards from the trays before the second rule was introduced. They found that this slight change led to greater success than the Frye et al. procedure. A recent experiment that employed the "traditional" (i.e., Frye et al.), Kirkham et al., and Shimmon et al. procedures in the same design produced results that fitted these patterns. The Kirkham procedure led to greater failure than the standard condition and the Shimmon et al. manipulation led to greater success (Warburton, 2004).

These manipulations of the card sort task make it hard to interpret the rule-use explanations of mental state understanding. For Zelazo et al. (2004) the results of such modifications do not undermine the CCC theory, although their later work does not look at the relationships with tasks like false belief. Kirkham et al. (2003) attribute the child's perseveration to a problem of attending to novel procedures once a pattern of response has been established – children cannot resist performing the first rule because they do not have the ability to suppress or inhibit it. Zelazo (Happaney & Zelazo, 2003) has interpreted Kirkham et al.'s results in terms of his own theory.

Not only is there debate about the relationship between card sort test performance and CCC, there is also controversy about their possible links with false belief understanding. Perner and Lang (2000) claim to provide empirical evidence for his criticisms of CCC theory. One of the tasks given involves understanding the involuntary nature of the knee-jerk reflex. In this task, the experimenter elicits the knee-jerk reflex from the child and then asks the child whether he or she did it on purpose. Three-year-olds have previously been found to have problems with this task (Shultz, Wells, & Sarda, 1980) and, as Perner, Lang, and Stummer (1998; discussed in Perner & Lang, 2000) point out, the task does not involve any obvious conditional reasoning requirements. At the same time Perner et al. gave children a test of inhibitory control known as Luria's hand game. Here the child has to copy one of two gestures (a fist or finger point) for a few trials and then to do the opposite (e.g., to point if the experimenter holds up a fist). Children performed similarly on all four tasks (DCCS; false belief; Luria's hand game; knee-jerk reflex), with approximately half of the children passing each. More importantly, the reflex task explained more than 50 percent of the total variance of false belief performance, with age and verbal intelligence taken into account; substantially more than the variance explained by the DCCS and Luria tasks. Such data need an explanation and many researchers, including Zelazo, have turned to the construct of "executive function" to explain them. It is this topic that we turn to next, with the conclusion to this section that the tests of reasoning which correlate with false belief understanding may tell us more about the complexity of tests than the relationship between underlying constructs like "theory of mind" or "counterfactual reasoning."

Is the False Belief Test simply a Measure of Executive Function?

The research described thus far in this chapter – the windows task, the counterfactual reasoning experiment, and the card sort – have crystallized into the claim that the child's understanding of mind is part of a wider problem of the control of higher-level skills – under the banner "executive function" (for a recent analysis see Schneider, Schumann-Hengsteler, & Sodian, 2005). Russell concluded that 3-year-olds fail the windows task on repeated trials because they cannot inhibit the compulsion to blurt out where the reward is. Likewise Kirkham et al. (2003) attribute perseveration to the inertia set up in the pre-switch trials. This line of research ties in with earlier developments in the study of executive control in typically developing children and those with autism. For example, Bruce Pennington and his colleagues' work on children with autism (Ozonoff et al., 1991) was complemented by research on typically developing children. In an early study they administered a wide battery of complex tasks to children over the school years. Welsh, Pennington, and Grossier (1991) conducted a factor analysis on this battery and identified three clusters of variables, measuring "fluid and speeded responses," "hypothesis testing and impulse control," and "planning."

Research since has concentrated on three differently labeled skills in preschoolers – inhibitory control, attentional flexibility, and working memory (Hughes, 1998a). *Attentional flexibility* is the skill involved in shifting from one rule to another and is characterized by the card sort task, described in the previous section. *Inhibitory control* is the ability to suppress a prepotent response, as exemplified in the compulsion to point to the baited box in the windows task or to copy the hand gesture in Luria's hand game (we examine this issue below). *Working memory* refers to the ability to hold information in mind and manipulate it. One view is that this construct describes how short-term storage feeds into longer-term storage. It consists of two slave systems, the articulatory loop and visual spatial scratchpad, that momentarily hold information before a higher-order structure, the "central executive," commits the items to longer-term store (Baddeley & Hitch, 1974; see Gathercole, 1999 for a review of the developmental literature).

The label "executive function" has gained popularity and has been used to explain various forms of task performance from infancy through childhood. In this section we explore current analyses of the relationship between mental state understanding and executive skills. The framework we adopt comes from Josef Perner and Birgit Lang's (e.g., 1999,

2000) evaluation of the range of explanations that have been proposed to explain the relationship between mental state understanding and executive control. Two of these views have already been discussed. The first is the idea that mental state understanding and executive skills are driven by the same brain area, like those shown in Figure 1.4. For our purposes such neurological links tell us little about the developmental psychological relationship between the two skills. Although it is the case that children with autism appear to perform badly on procedures like the windows task and also on false belief tasks, this might not reveal a complete physiological interdependence of these abilities. Indeed there is neuropsychological evidence that the two sets of skills are dissociable. For example, in a case study of a patient with left amygdala damage, Fine, Lumsden, and Blair (2001) provide a clear dissociation between executive and mental state tasks. Their patient, called "B.M.," showed severe impairments on false belief tests, but sailed through comparable executive tasks. However, from the perspective of CCC theory it is the level of complexity of the tasks that is important and this was not controlled (Müller, personal communication). Secondly, Perner and Lang analyze the claim that false belief understanding is the product of advances in the child's ability to perform tasks involving conditional reasoning. This view was discussed in the first section of the chapter, in which it was concluded that there is still controversy surrounding just what tasks like the card sort reveal about the nature of reasoning. Thus, it is difficult to draw firm conclusions about the claim that false belief is just one example of a range of skills, some of which do not involve an understanding of mental states.

We turn our attention here to three remaining hypotheses raised by Perner and Lang. The first of these is that developing an understanding of the mind, especially the metarepresentational skill described in Perner's theory (chapter 2), is a prerequisite for gaining control over one's actions. The second is that executive control is a precursor to mental state understanding, whereas the third is that the two are intertwined, because understanding the mind requires the components of executive skills, notably holding in mind the actions of the protagonists and inhibiting prepotent responses.

"Theory of mind" development improves self-control

Perner's own account of the relationship between executive and mental state skills (Perner & Lang, 1999, 2000) was first put forward by his collaborator, Heinz Wimmer. It holds that developing a "theory of mind" gives children more control over their mental processes. According to Perner and Lang (2000), the child comes to construct "action schemas" (e.g., Maxi putting his chocolate into the red cupboard) as mental representations. Coordinating groups of representations requires mental control in the false belief task. The child has to maintain that action schema while holding in mind more recent ones (Maxi's mother moving the chocolate and its current location) that are required for inhibition of competing action schemas. For Perner, Kain, and Barchfeld (2002, p. 143) the major cognitive achievement in the later preschool years is "improved self-insight due to a better theory of mind which enables greater self-control." It is not the content of our minds that is important, but an understanding that "mental states are based on representations (vehicles) that have causal force and make people do things" (Perner & Lang, 2000, p. 153). In consequence, it is this representational understanding required for "theory of mind" that forms the basis of the skills required for the inhibition of action schemas in executive tests.

Which empirical evidence might support Perner's theoretical position? As with the two other perspectives outlined below, Perner (1998) expects that the emergence of false belief and executive skills should occur at the same time. He also cites the data (e.g., Russell's windows task described above) that children with autism show problems in both sets of tasks (Perner & Lang, 2000). Perner's recent work (Lang & Perner, 2002; Perner, 1998; Perner, Lang, & Kloo, 2002; Perner, Kain, & Barchfeld, 2002) has examined the relative performance of preschoolers on executive function tasks, false belief tasks and an understanding of reflexive actions, as described in the last section. For example, Lang and Perner (2002) found that understanding reflex movements as unintentional was related to success in false belief and executive function after controlling for the effects of age and verbal intelligence. This supports their claim that children come to understand that mental representations (beliefs, actions, and intentions) are causally responsible for their actions.

There is another explanation for the associations found by Lang and Perner. It could be the case that the three tasks they examine have the same underlying complexity and/or require similar reasoning capabilities. Thus the jury is still out on Perner's theory about the idea that theory of mind underpins executive skills. Certainly the theory cannot account for the neuropsychological dissociations described above in the patient B.M. who passed executive tests but failed false belief (Fine et al., 2001). Baron-Cohen and Robertson (1995) reported the same results in a case study of a child with autism. Perner and Lang argue that single case studies do not necessarily provide an "existence proof" of the dissociation between tasks – they might simply show that tasks are of different difficulty. However, the same argument might be used to criticize the data that support any theory in this area.

Theory of mind tasks are really executive measures

This is a view that emerged largely because of the findings on the windows task, described at the start of the chapter. Russell et al. (1991) used the failure of 3-year-olds and children with autism over repeated trials to argue that in this procedure, as in false belief, failure is caused by a more general executive problem: both tasks "require subjects to inhibit reference to a salient object" (p. 341). The salience hypothesis (also called the reality masking hypothesis; Mitchell, 1996) holds that preschoolers lack executive control over their actions, so that physical reality has a hold over the child that overrides any understanding of mental states. In chapter 3 we summarized data from modified false belief tasks that appear to show that if the procedure is simplified children's performance improves, citing Zaitchik's (1991) task in which children were merely told about the transfer of the object, and Lacohée's (Mitchell & Lacohée, 1991; Freeman & Lacohée, 1995) experiment in which they posted a picture of the item they expected to be in the deceptive box. Such manipulations can be explained by the salience hypothesis, as they suggest that failing the traditional task may be caused by the way in which the current state of affairs lures the child into simply stating what is there without drawing upon any knowledge of the protagonist's actions. As Mitchell and Lacohée (1991, p. 122) write: "young children are capable of understanding that the mind is representational, but are biased to base judgements about beliefs and perhaps other representations on a known physically enduring reality."

Further evidence for the importance of executive skills within an understanding of "theory of mind" comes from manipulations of executive tests. James Russell, for example, has explored the windows task further. In a second experiment (Russell, Jarrold, & Potel, 1994) he made a simple modification of taking the competitive element out of the task. Instead of having a competitor whom the child has to direct to the empty box, the participant simply had to point to the empty box in order to obtain the reward from the full one for her/himself. However, children still make the same error of pointing to the baited box.

The windows task is not without its detractors. One replication of the experiment failed to find the expected difference between 3- and 4-year-olds that matched false belief performance (Samuels, Brooks, & Frye, 1996) and subsequent experimentation has suggested that children as young as $3^{1}/_{2}$ pass the test (e.g., Moore, Barresi, & Thompson, 1998). Furthermore, Simpson, Riggs, and Simon (2004) argue that children's difficulty with the windows task is due to having to infer the rule "point to the empty box," not to problems with using this rule. However, explicitly giving the child the rule, as Simpson et al. did, may help the child to overcome the social norm to point to where objects actually are. All of this just shows the complexity and social embeddedness of inhibition. Hala and Russell (2001) argued that 3-year-olds demonstrate similar problems in both the first windows trial and perseveration over a series because the act of pointing may lure the child to the baited box – we usually point to indicate objects, not their absence. They tested this assumption in a variation in which children had to show their choice of box using a less social form of response. They had to mark the box by placing a cardboard star or pointing hand on it. Such a response mode led to great improvements in 3-year-olds' performance. In a design that explored the roles of competition and more general social inter-actional demands, Russell, Hala, and Hill (2003) presented children with an automated version of the task in which the box dispensed the reward to the child once s/he pressed a button below the empty container. They found slightly better performance in the automated task and in a joint version where the child works with an adult but does not deceive her. As a result they suggest that two forms of inhibition are in evidence: "inhibiting reference to a salient state of affairs" as in the communicative task and "inhibiting means-end action near a goal object," as seen in the automated version of the task (Russell et al., 2003, p. 130).

Do these experiments show that tasks assessing an understanding of mental states simply place too many executive demands upon 3-year-olds? Such a conclusion is a bit premature. Take the false belief test in which the child does not see the object. Perner (1995) provides an alternative explanation. In one version of this test the object disappears – for example, Maxi's mother grates the chocolate to make a chocolate cake (Wimmer & Perner, 1983). In such cases the executive demands are reduced as the reality bias is taken away. But an alternative explanation is that the chocolate has only been in one location. Perner and Lang (2000) cite two further pieces of evidence which cannot be explained by the claim that false belief tasks are really tests of inhibition and working memory. First, in a study mentioned in the previous section the association between the child's understanding of the knee-jerk reflex and false belief overrides any link between the latter and inhibitory control. Secondly, there are studies that do not show an association between executive and theory of mind tasks (e.g., Hughes, 1998a). Although such studies exist, a sufficiently large corpus of data does highlight the link. It is to these studies that we turn in the next section.

Individual skills underpin mental state understanding: the working memory explanation

This is a perspective that has received increasing attention over the past few years. This is really a range of accounts that analyze individual executive components identified under the umbrella "executive function." Thus it has been argued that each of the constituent skills might be responsible for the acquisition of mental state understanding. This account can be distinguished from the idea that false belief tasks place executive demands on the child on the grounds that it is more clearly argued that individual skills are required before the child can grasp mental state concepts. We have already explored the idea that set shifting is important in the section on rule usage, so here we look at the child's ability to retain information in working memory, as we will turn again to the problem of inhibiting a prepotent or salient response in the next section.

The claim that false belief understanding cannot be grasped until the child acquires sufficient information processing skills was made by Robbie Case in 1989, in a conference paper that to our knowledge was never published. As a result, several researchers attempted to show that the ability to compare a protagonist's belief state with an updated state of affairs is intricately linked with the child's understanding of events in time. The theoretical construct of working memory presents an obvious explanation of how executive skills might be used to hold sufficient information in mind to perform the reasoning skills required for an understanding of mental states. According to Case's model, the development of this cognitive capacity unfolds over the preschool years. Susan Gathercole (1999) argued that two forms of long-term memory can be distinguished: a store which simply reflects our ability to recall events termed memory capacity, and information that is manipulated by the central executive is true "working memory." To test the relationship between working memory and "theory of mind," Davis and Pratt (1995) compared false belief performance with two subtests taken from traditional IQ tests: forward digit span, a memory capacity task in which the participant has to recall strings of numbers, and backward digit-span in which the numbers have to be recalled in reverse order. The trials start with two digits and increase in number as long as the child succeeds in recalling them. So, in a backward digit-span task, if the experimenter says 3–9–5, the child has to respond with 5–9–3, demonstrating that the working memory system has manipulated the database. Davis and Pratt found that backward digit-span performance was significantly related to a measure of false belief understanding and concluded that working memory may well be a necessary requirement for mental state awareness.

This relationship was replicated and extended by Keenan, Olson, and Marini (1998) with a different measure of working memory and additional tests of false belief understanding. These authors suggested, on this basis, that working memory is perhaps a mechanism partially responsible for the shift in mental state understanding at the age of 4. In a later study, Keenan (2000) examined the performance of preschoolers on working memory, inhibitory control, and speed of processing. Again working memory was a significant predictor of false belief, accounting for 7 percent of the variance even after the effects of age, language, and speed of processing had been statistically removed. Keenan suggested that there is a small but consistent role for working memory in the child's acquisition of false belief understanding.

In Keenan's earlier study working memory accounted for 7 percent of the variance in the false belief performance. This still leaves 93 percent of the variance to be explained and shows the weakness of the reported effect. There are other problems for the working memory account. To begin with, close examination of the data collected in the original study by Davis and Pratt shows that the 3- and 4-year-olds were almost at floor on the backward digit-span test – they find it very difficult to recall even two digits. There are two interpretative problems that arise from these data. First, if large numbers of the sample score zero and only a few get one trial correct, then this raises serious questions about whether backward digit span is an adequate or sufficient measure of working memory for young children. Secondly, even if the measure is adequate the distribution of scores does not provide enough variance with which to associate variability in false belief. So, it is not surprising perhaps that two other studies fail to find any association between working memory and false belief, once the age of the child and language ability are taken into account (Hughes, 1998b; Jenkins & Astington, 1996).

The case of working memory is typical as an example of a construct that seems to relate to mental state understanding, in that some studies show a weak relationship, whereas others do not. Thus the claim that executive skills drive "theory of mind" is not fully borne out when we examine individual components of such skill. More precisely, working memory and mental state understanding do appear to be somewhat separate activities. Recent analyses of brain functions using fMRI scans suggest that the areas of the brain activated when each skill is engaged in are distinct (Kain & Perner, 2005). Kain and Perner point out that while still obviously separate, mental state understanding is more closely associated with inhibitory control – an issue to which we return in the next main section of the chapter.

Issues in Understanding the Link between Mental State Understanding and Executive Function

Given the somewhat sparse data linking individual executive skills and false belief understanding, it is important to identify why so much attention has been paid to it. In this section we describe the exciting associations that have been found between the two sets of skills in children with different types of developmental problems, the studies which have attempted to combine executive skills, and, thirdly, the potential for theoretical developments in this area.

Mental state understanding, executive function and developmental psychopathology

In chapters 1 and 3 we described the use of "theory of mind" research in the 1980s in an attempt to understand autism. The debate in the 1990s developed into an examination of the link between such skills and executive abilities, initially in children with autism (e.g., Hughes, 1996; Ozonoff, Pennington, & Rogers, 1991; Russell, Saltmarsh, & Hill, 1999; for a recent review see Hill, 2004). Autism has long been linked to problems in frontal lobe functioning (Damasio & Maurer, 1978). The study by Ozonoff et al. (1991) found that children with autism seemed more impaired on a task of planning, the Tower of Hanoi, in which the child has to coordinate working memory and inhibitory skills, than they appeared to be in "theory of mind" tasks. Their sample had a wide range of IQs, but most of the children were within the normal range. This led to the claim that the problem common to autism may well be in executive functioning, not in "theory of mind." This fits with the idea that tasks like false belief necessarily require the use of inhibitory skills as well as a need to hold information in mind and manipulate such a memory store.

At the same time, data from Russell et al. (1991) on the windows task (mentioned at the start of this chapter) found that children with autism were as impaired on the task as 3-year-olds. This finding was replicated in a later study which examined the performance of children with autism and learning disabled children as controls on the windows task and a measure of inhibitory control: the detour-reaching task (Hughes & Russell, 1993), in which a child has to either turn a knob or press a switch on the side of a box before retrieving a sweet within it – if they did not do so, their hand broke an infrared beam, making the sweet disappear down a trapdoor. In the original experiment, Hughes and Russell found that children with autism had difficulty with the windows task, even when the opponent had been removed. However, Russell et al. (2003) failed to replicate this finding: children with autism seemed to perform the automated version of the windows task without an opponent as well as a control group matched for IQ but without autism. They attribute such success to the possibility that the task is not highly practiced, presumably implying that the inhibitory demands might be reduced. Some support for this comes from the fact that Hughes and Russell's (1993) detour-reaching task was failed by much more cognitively advanced children. Their mental ages were around the age of 10, whereas Russell's team have produced successful performance on this task in typically developing 2-year-olds (Bíró, 2001, cited in Russell et al., 2003).

What explains the poor performance of children with autism on executive tests? Russell claims that early executive impairments shown by children with autism appear to limit subsequent acquisition of a "theory of mind" (Russell, 1997). He argues that such children do not develop a skill that is characteristic of typically developing children as they acquire a "theory of mind." It follows that in any population with problems in executive skills, we should also find a disordered conception of mentality. Perner and Lang (1999, 2000) cast doubt on this claim. Some groups of individuals with executive impairments appear to be unimpaired in their acquisition of mental state understanding. Children with Prader-Willi syndrome (a rare genetic disorder), for example, have been found to fail executive tasks but pass false belief tests (Tager-Flusberg, Sullivan, & Boshart, 1997), as do children at risk of attention deficit disorder with hyperactivity (ADHD) (Perner, Kain, &

Barchfeld, 2002; though Sodian & Hülsken (2005) report specific problems in mental state understanding associated with ADHD) and individuals with Tourette's syndrome (a psychological condition in which the sufferer has multiple tics) (Baron-Cohen et al., 1997). Thus when the range of children with known problems in executive skills are studied, the evidence for Russell's claim is not complete.

The executive function–mental state understanding link is more complex

We reviewed evidence above that working memory is a predictor of mental state understanding, but when considered by itself the association is statistically significant but weak. The same can be said for other individual executive skills. For example, Keenan (2000) demonstrated no link between inhibitory control and false belief, whereas Carlson et al. (1998) found that performance on a task involving deception improved when the inhibitory demands were reduced. This study will be discussed in more detail in the final part of this section, when the nature of executive demands in "theory of mind" tests will be addressed. It is important because it marks a shift in research over the past few years. It explored the links between different individual skills, particularly the combination of inhibition and working memory.

In keeping with this shift, Carlson and Moses (2001) examined the relationship between inhibitory control and "theory of mind" in 3- and 4-year-old children. They gave 107 children a large battery of tests involving different mental state inferences (including appearance-reality and deceptive pointing). They tested the idea that executive control is necessary before the acquisition of concepts of mental representation, in line with Russell's theoretical position. A factor analysis revealed that the measures of inhibition were responded to similarly by children, including measures involving inhibition of conflicting responses in a game like "Simon says" and delay inhibition in a task requiring the child to wait before grabbing a reward. The "theory of mind" tasks were found to correlate strongly with these inhibition measures. The raw correlation was .66, which means that just under half the variability in one measure was predicted by the other (this is calculated by squaring r: $R^2 = .66^2 = .44$). Although reduced after controlling for a number of intelligence and demographic variables including verbal age and family size, the relationship remained highly significant ($r = .41$). "Theory of mind" did not, however, relate to a motor sequencing task, a measure of executive competence that does not require inhibition. This research suggests that specific relationships between executive skills and false belief can be identified.

One of the major strengths of this study is that Carlson and Moses examined two types of inhibitory test: delay and conflict. *Delay tasks* are less demanding. They simply require the ability to delay or suppress an impulsive response like peeking at a present that is being wrapped for them or grabbing for a promised snack before their allotted time (following Kochanska et al., 1996). *Conflict tasks* require the child to produce a novel response against a highly salient conflicting option. For example, in the day/night task, children are required to say "night" when a card with a picture of the sun is presented and "day" to a picture of the moon (Gerstadt, Hong, & Diamond, 1994). In Carlson and Moses' (2001) study, the two categories were found to be differentially related to the "theory of mind" measures. The conflict tasks were better predictors of "theory of mind" performance than the delay tasks. They suggested that working memory might account for the strength of this relationship because the working memory demands are greater in conflict tasks – the child has to keep in mind the rule to suppress the prepotent response to say "day" when the sun picture is presented.

Carlson and Moses claimed that their interpretation was consistent with Roberts and Pennington's (1996) model, which stresses the interactive nature of working memory and inhibitory control. In most accounts until the late 1990s, the relationships between component skills were overlooked. Roberts and Pennington (1996) carried out a detailed analysis of the tasks then used to measure prefrontal processes and proposed the hypothesis that successful responding on any executive task requires both inhibitory control and working memory. Accordingly, working memory is required for generating and keeping in mind a correct response, whereas inhibitory control is responsible for suppressing an incorrect response that is prompted by an environmental cue. Successful performance is a balance between the two and if, for example, the working memory demands of a task are increased, the ability to inhibit a prepotent response may also decrease. Roberts and Pennington called for studies that systematically manipulate and vary the processing demands of different neuropsychological tests.

One such study was conducted by Hala, Hug, and Henderson (2003). They administered a battery of inhibitory control, working memory, and false belief tasks to a group of 3- and 4-year-olds. As with previous studies (Carlson et al., 2002; Perner, Lang, & Kloo, 2002), they found that inhibitory control (IC) alone did not explain mental state understanding. However, when combined with working memory (WM) the link with false belief was significant, even after the child's age and verbal skills were taken into account. Hala et al. (2003, p. 292) conclude: "Specifically, the strong predictive value of the dual executive demand tasks points to a unique contribution of the interaction of WM and IC. These findings are also consistent with the proposal put forward by Diamond and her colleagues (Diamond et al., 1997; Gerstadt et al., 1994) wherein prefrontal involvement is claimed to be required for tasks where information must be held in memory while inhibiting an interfering response. Theory of mind tasks can also be regarded as prefrontal tasks in that they also combine these two executive demands."

Current theoretical and methodological issues

The quotation from Hala et al.'s paper above neatly summarizes a strength of the "executive" account of "theory of mind," in the links that are consistently found between the two types of measures, but it also underlines a series of problems with such an account. First, the studies tend to show a moderate, but by no means perfect relationship between the two types of task, given correlations of around .45 between individual executive measures and false belief. As Hala et al. do not present the actual figures in their multiple regression analyses, let us assume that the overall R^2 in their model is around .3, then this would leave 70 percent of the variability in false belief scores to be explained by other factors. Furthermore, correlation does not lead to causation here. Secondly, even if reasoning about beliefs involves executive functions, there is still much left unexplained. Carlson and Moses' (2001) data, described above, show that not all inhibitory tests are good predictors of tests of mental state understanding, so we must not oversimplify the construct "inhibition" and overstress its importance. As Moses and Carlson (2004, p. 142) point out: "A fully functioning executive/regulatory system could never, by itself, deliver concepts of mental life." Furthermore, Zelazo and Müller (2002, p. 453) state that "the construct of inhibition fails to address how one decides what is to be inhibited."

There are two implications of this conclusion. First, we must be aware that the measures we develop to assess constructs like "inhibitory control" do not necessarily pinpoint a unitary underlying psychological construct. So, to perform a test like the day/night task involves working memory and possibly set shifting as well as its intended focus, inhibitory control. Such "task impurity" has been discussed in the literature on executive functions (e.g., Gerstadt, Hong, & Diamond, 1994; Roberts

& Pennington, 1996), but has been somewhat overlooked in research which links this work to "theory of mind." A recent examination of such task impurity by Karen Shimmon (2004) shows that even small manipulations to executive tests give rise to significant differences in the performance of children. Such findings make it difficult conceptually to link the constructs.

The second implication is that any theoretical account of the link between executive functions and mental state understanding must attempt to explain the psychological processes which underlie these connections. As one recent review put it: "much more work is needed to elucidate the nature of the relation between ToM and EF" (Zelazo, Qu, & Müller, 2005, p. 87). One feature of all the work discussed in the chapter so far is that it falls short of such an account. An exception is the theory of James Russell (1996). He attempts to situate the child's developing understanding of mental states within a more general develop-mental framework in which self-knowledge is a central core. For Russell, a major problem with the "theory of mind" tradition is that it pays very little attention to the issue of what it is to have a mind that synthesizes everyday experiences: "any account of what it takes to have a mind that ignores the unity of experience, the self-ascription of experi-ences to this unitary self and the central contribution of agency to both is just false" (Russell, 1996, p. 180). By agency he does not imply that we have a little person in our heads controlling our actions (the homunculus problem). Rather "in being self aware, we, as subjects, take ourselves as the objects of our reflections" (p. 171). Borrowing from theory theory (see chapter 2), he suggests that we need somehow to make sense of our own reactions to the world, and from simulation theory he argues that first-person experience is vital. Nevertheless, he contends that such skills develop with the emergence of our executive capacities, without which self-reflection is not possible: ". . . under-4s fail tasks with this structure [mentalizing tasks] because they have inad-equate strategic control over their mental processes, specifically over the items of information that must be held in mind when answering the relevant questions. This is an *executive* as opposed to a *theoretical* failure, something that reveals inadequate executive control" (Russell, 1996: p. 210, emphasis in original). Russell's ideas are difficult to sum-marize in a paragraph and his book *Agency* has been studiously avoided by most researchers in the field because, in its attempts to show how we need a phenomenological account of executive and theory of mind skills, it is very complex. For our purposes, it shows how the simple categor-ization of terms like "working memory" and "inhibitory control" and the tests we devise to measure such constructs only scratch the surface of deep theoretical issues.

Some attempts to delve into the complexities of this relationship have been made by Moses and Carlson (2005; Moses, Carlson, & Sabbagh, 2005). They suggest that the link between executive function skills and understanding mental states might take two forms – "expression" accounts in which executive skills are depicted as influencing children's ability to utilize existing skills in task performance, and "emergence" accounts in which executive functions are crucial in the development of "theory of mind" capabilities. In an argument with Russell, they argue that the evidence favors the latter, "emergence," account. The evidence for this view comes from the indeterminate results of a training study in which training on executive skills or mental state tasks led to improvements in the skill not trained (Kloo & Perner, 2003). Longitudinal data, however, seem to show that executive skills predict later "theory of mind" performance in 3-year-olds whereas the reverse is not the case (Carlson, Mandell, & Williams, 2004). Nevertheless, such evidence scratches at the surface of the theoretical analysis presented by James Russell.

Conclusion: Getting the Point of the Links between Executive Functions and Mental State Understanding

So, is an understanding of the mind simply the by-product of the child's capacity to perform mental operations involving the embedding of rules or to retain information in mind and override the impulse to say what is true? The issues we have discussed in this chapter reflect a shift in thinking away from the idea that mental state understanding is a specific evolutionary inheritance (see chapter 1), in favor of accounts which suggest that both "theory of mind" and executive skills are more general and intertwined cognitive skills (Bjorklund, Cormier, & Rosenberg, 2005). The evidence shows that the child performs a range of executive and conditional reasoning tasks at around the same age as she or he passes the false belief test. Nevertheless, we have attempted to show that any causal sequence behind such associations is hard to demonstrate. Developmental psychologists have been reluctant to conduct longitudinal analyses of the development of these skills and the results from existing research are not as clear as they might be in that they show only a few connections between some executive and "theory of mind" tests (Hughes, 1998b; Shimmon, 2004). In conceptual terms we feel that only analyses like that of James Russell (1996) can capture the interweaving of "executive" and "mindreading" skills. It is not just the case that the jury is out over the existing data but, rather, we need to be more theoretically sophisticated about these data. Russell suggests that we need a more grounded account of how the child constructs such knowledge and he bases his approach within the account of development put forward by Piaget. Similarly, we draw on Piaget in our account presented in chapter 10.

One reason why the research in this chapter has failed to demonstrate that one of these skills depends on the other is that both are intertwined. The same holds for our methods. Although they often pay lip service to the work of the theoretician who promoted the term executive function, Alexander Luria (1961), contemporary researchers neglect the fact that Luria was attempting to set executive skills within a social framework in which the child acquires cultural symbols. Some research suggests a need for the broader perspective suggested by Luria. For a start, some neglected research by Ignatius Toner (Toner, Moore, & Emmons, 1980; Toner & Smith, 1977) showed that if children were told that the experimenter had heard that they were good at an executive skill, they would perform significantly better at a task assessing that skill than children told that the experimenter had heard that they had lots of friends in the preschool. Such social conditions work with 3-year-olds in tests of inhibition and set shifting (Lewis, Harrison, & Warburton, in progress). They suggest we should look more closely at the dynamics of tests of executive functioning. To do so we can return to the windows task that has been discussed throughout this chapter.

The windows procedure is both a measure of executive control [pointing to an empty location to receive a reward] and strategic deception [in most experiments a second experimenter is involved and the focus of attention is the child's interaction with another]. It is important here to revisit some of the findings discussed above. Recall that if the child uses a marker [either a pointing hand or a star] to identify which box the experimenter should open, he or she finds the task much easier. Indeed after a few trials 12 out of 15 children were at ceiling when using a star to mark which box an experimenter should open (Hala & Russell, 2001, experiment 3). As Carlson, Moses, and Hix (1998) suggest, in tasks involving deceptive pointing young children appear to be intimidated, perhaps fearing punishment for "lying" to adults. In a neat series of experiments, Hala and Russell show that 3-year-olds also come to succeed at this task if they take part in a game in which they are in allegiance with the second experimenter (both child and adult obtain a reward if the child selects the empty box), or if the child uses a pointer (a pointing hand) for a first experimenter when the second one is either out of the room or present. Why do children succeed in these tasks when using an artificial medium like a pointing hand or a star? Hala and Russell suggest that pointing is "natural" and combines the goal and response, whereas a "pointer" or "marker" is a "nonnatural, symbolic mode of responding" (Hala & Russell, 2001, p. 131), which distances the child from the actions he or she performs:

> The psychological significance of this distinction, we claim, is that natural meaning can be something nearer to an unthinking reflex, more closely akin to an expression of emotion or orienting than to expressing a judgement. Nonnatural meaning however, given its conventional nature, requires the more or less deliberate adoption of one mode of communication among the many that are possible and so in that sense there is not a one-to-one mapping between referent (the treat in box) and mode of referring (the point).

In short, Hala and Russell reveal that there is something about the child's learning of cultural symbol systems that helps them to perform an act of deception. The conclusion to this chapter is that the effect of using a symbol in the windows task reveals how interconnected domain general skills and false belief skills are with the child's social and communicative skills. We return to the most poignant form of symbolic communication, language, in chapter 7. Zelazo et al. (2004, p. 111), in their revised CCC theory, point out the importance of the environment in general and parent–child interaction, particularly in the development of executive functions. In chapter 6 we examine the role of social interaction in the development of social understanding.

Chapter 6

Social Interaction and the Development of Social Understanding: The Role of Relationships in Social Cognitive Development

To hold that social life acts at every level of development is to say something as obvious, but also just as vague, as to attribute a continuing influence to the external physical environment.

(Piaget, 1977/1995, p. 278)

As previous chapters have indicated, there is now clear evidence that children's social experience is associated with their social understanding (Hughes & Leekam, 2004). The key question addressed in this chapter concerns the relationship between the child's daily social interactions and the development of social understanding. There are many possible explanations for these links: they may occur independently of one another, one might "cause" changes in the other, or both might be determined by other skills, like executive function as we discussed in chapter 5. One of the key assumptions in the previous chapter, which stemmed from the discussion in chapters 2 and 3, was that research with false belief tasks has tended to focus on the average age at which children pass traditional versions or subtle manipulations of these. But averages may conceal important variability. Although children tend to pass false belief tasks on average at 4 years of age, in fact, some children pass at 3 and others not until the age of 5 or later. One trend in the data, for instance, concerns a slight advantage of girls over boys in some studies (Charman, Ruffman, & Clements, 2002; Hughes & Dunn, 1998) even when general skills like language level are taken into consideration. However, these slight differences are not evident in most studies. We describe other, more predictive, individual differences here.

An immediate question is what is it about those children who pass early or late? Some, like Jenkins and Oatley (2004, pp. 112–113), dismiss such age of acquisition effects as trivial: "Variation with family and cultural experience becomes irrelevant: the false belief switch gets turned on anyway." However, other researchers, whom we focus upon here, have closely explored the idea that individual differences in the age at which children pass false belief and related tests give clear indication of the effects of different types of social experience on their development. It was this approach to social experience and individual differences in children that Judy Dunn and her colleagues took in a series of pioneering longitudinal studies. In this chapter we review these and other studies on the possible role of social interaction in social development. The question now is how might these family factors influence social cognitive development (Cutting & Dunn, 1999)? The analysis divides into two parts. In the first we describe the evidence that has been collected to show which social factors correlate with the development of social understanding. This is sufficient to suggest that Jenkins and Oatley are incorrect in dismissing individual differences. The longer "half" of the chapter takes this evidence and attempts to analyze just what the connection implies for theories of social development. While followers of the mainstream traditions that we summarized in chapter 2 have argued that social data can easily be incorporated into traditional accounts, many others are not so sure. This chapter addresses Piaget's challenge, quoted above, to see if we can understand the social data in a way that pinpoints the obvious without being vague. That is, if it is recognized that social life influences development, it is important to go beyond this observation to explain how various forms of social interaction may differentially influence social cognitive development. As the chapter will indicate, accounting for the evidence that social interaction influences social development within the existing theories presents a challenge.

Evidence for the Influence of Social Life on Social Knowledge

The earliest and most consistent source of interest in the intimate links between children's social lives and their developing social knowledge comes from Judy Dunn's research on family interaction (for a summary of this work see Astington, 2003). Dunn extended her earlier research on siblings (reviewed in Dunn & Kendrick, 1982) and emotional development (e.g., Dunn & Munn, 1987) into the "theory of mind" area with a first influential article published in 1991. In this paper Dunn and her colleagues (Dunn, Brown, Slomkowski, Tesla, & Youngblade, 1991) reported a longitudinal study in which they visited families in their homes and observed their daily interactions as well as assessed the target child's understanding of beliefs and emotions. At the first visit when the child being focused on was 33 months old, they assessed various aspects of the family interaction such as talk about emotions, desires, and psychological causality (e.g., "You broke my glass . . . and that makes me sad," p. 1356). They found that families in which there were more frequent conversations about feelings and causality had children who, when assessed 7 months later at 40 months of age, were better able to explain story characters' actions in terms of false beliefs. In large measure Dunn sets standards of research in the area which casts a shadow over many of the studies from within the "theory of mind" tradition, mainly because she relies upon close observations of children in social settings within a longitudinal design. Other researchers have relied on the quick fix of the cross-sectional study (i.e., inferring developmental change from the *differences* between age groups) in which social factors are assessed by questionnaires administered to parents or teachers. Nevertheless, we now review six areas of research which suggest that Dunn's earlier work pinpoints several issues about the importance of social interaction in social development.

The "sibling effect"

The first spin-off from Dunn's research involving the connection between relationships and social development was a group of studies showing that children with siblings were more advanced in false belief understanding than were children with no brothers or sisters. A first study by Perner, Ruffman, and Leekam (1994) found that this effect was substantial – that is, the difference between having or not having siblings was as large as the difference between 3- and 4-year-olds. They continued this strand of research with a series of larger studies both in the UK and Japan showing that having older rather than younger siblings is the cause of the sibling effect (Ruffman, Perner, Naito, Parkin, & Clements, 1998). Other studies confirmed either a general effect or simply an older sibling association with false belief. However, they also complicated the picture. For a start, the age of the sibling seems to be a factor. Peterson (2000) reported two experiments with large groups of children in which children with a sibling between 12 months and 12 years of age performed significantly better than children with no sibling. However, having an infant or adolescent sibling was not linked to advanced false belief understanding. Further, children with a twin but no other siblings were not advanced in false belief understanding compared to children with no siblings (Cassidy, Fineberg, Brown, & Perkins, 2005). Secondly, Jenkins and Astington (1996, p. 76) found that "[f]amily size has a very small effect on false belief understanding when children's language ability is high, and a stronger association with performance when language ability is low." Thirdly, Lewis, Freeman, Kyriakidou, Maridaki-Kassotaki, and Berridge (1996) replicated the association between number of siblings and performance on false belief tests, but explored whether the sibling effect was unique as a predictor of false belief performance. In one study participants reported the number of cousins, uncles, and aunts living within walking distance, as is the custom in many parts of Greece and Cyprus, while in a second parents were asked to recall the numbers of family members the child interacted with on a particular day. A consistent effect of the presence of older siblings and older kin on the level of false belief understanding was found and Lewis et al. argued that the preschooler has to serve an apprenticeship with more proficient members of a culture in order to pick up the skills required for false belief understanding.

Thus, there is now evidence from studies in Australia, Canada, England, Greece, and Japan that having brothers or sisters is related to advanced social understanding, at least as manifest on false belief tasks. However, these studies do not reveal what it is about having siblings that facilitates social development. There are a number of possibilities, from just an increase in the quantity of social experience available, to cooperative play with siblings, to, in contrast, conflict with siblings. Furthermore, having siblings may simply be a marker for a change in the nature of the parent–child interaction experienced by children. Interestingly, there have also been a number of studies published that have not found this "sibling effect" (Cole & Mitchell, 2000; Cutting & Dunn, 1999; Peterson & Slaughter, 2003), suggesting that the sibling effect may be less important than other influences. One important point that can be drawn from this research on siblings is that social interaction is important in some way. However, it is not just a matter of having a lot of bodies around in the house, but rather what may be important for social development is the nature of the relationships children experience. An interesting difference associated with siblings is that in one study 4-year-old children with a sibling heard more talk about thoughts, memories, or knowledge than children without a sibling (Jenkins, Turrell, Kogushi, Lollis, & Ross, 2003). The role of language in social development will be taken up in the next chapter.

One particular sibling relationship, twins, has been studied in order to examine more closely the role of interactions and genetic influences on the development of social understanding. While siblings and fraternal twins share on average 50 percent of their genetic make-up, identical twins share 100 percent. Thus studies over the past few years have attempted to tease apart the amount of genetic similarity that monozygous (one egg) and dizygous (two eggs: fraternal twins) share in relation to shared and unshared environmental influences. In a first study Hughes and Cutting (1999) published some data that suggested a key inherited influence on the age at which children acquire the ability to pass a battery of eight false belief tests and two deception tasks. They compared the relative influence of heredity and environment and their analyses suggested that while the latter was nonsignificant, heredity accounted for 67 percent of the variance in 119 children's test performance at 42 months. If this study were replicated, it would provide strong support for an innate account of theory of mind understanding. However, Hughes (Hughes, Jaffee, Happé, Taylor, Caspi, & Moffitt, 2005) recently conducted a much larger study of 1,116 twin pairs. They administered six tasks, including two belief–desire reasoning tasks, two first-order false belief and two second-order tasks. No differences were found between monozygous and dizygous twins, but they reported that some effects of shared and nonshared environmental factors were important. Why were there such differences between the two studies? First, the sample in the second study was ten times the size of the first. Secondly, the sample in the larger study contained a higher proportion of low SES children. Thirdly, in the second study the children were 6 years old, some 18 months older. Given that the second study is consistent with other recent data with twins (Deneault, Morin, Morin, Ricard, Décarie, & Quintal, 2003), we may conclude that the evidence is stronger in favor of environmental than genetic influences.

Parenting

Many of the studies reviewed above indicate that there is something about children's experience of family interaction that influences the development of their social understanding. One approach to studying the role of families is through assessing style of parenting. Several studies on the relations between parenting and false belief understanding have now been published, although their findings are not straightforward. In one of the early studies exploring the possible connections between parenting and false belief understanding, Ruffman, Perner, and Parkin (1999) asked parents to fill out a questionnaire in which they were presented with five disciplinary situations and asked what they had done or would do in such situations. Those parents who reported that they would ask their children to reflect on the feelings of the other people involved had children who were more advanced in false belief performance. We also discuss this study in chapter 7 because it focuses on the role of language in development.

Hughes, Deater-Deckard, and Cutting (1999) conducted another study on parenting that used observation rating as well as self-reported parenting practices. Two dimensions of parenting strategies were investigated: parental warmth and disciplinary style. The assessments of parental warmth as well as positive and negative disciplinary strategies were based on observer ratings of videotaped parent–child interaction, consisting of 10 minutes of free play and 10 minutes of a structured task that required collaboration. Hughes et al. found that in a sample of twins and their parents, aspects of parents' interaction with their children were related to their child's performance on false belief and deception tasks, but the relations were different for boys and girls. For girls, parental warmth was positively linked to their advanced false belief understanding. For boys, on the other hand, strictness and severity of discipline including physical punishment was, unexpectedly, associated with advanced false belief understanding. Hughes et al. (1999, p. 156) speculate about this unexpected finding: "Do boys use their developing (but still inexpert) awareness of mental states to find new ways of getting into trouble?" However, this finding needs to be replicated and further examined in other studies. There is also the additional complication that another measure of negative disciplinary control (e.g., "criticism or physical control of child" [p. 149]) was negatively associated with performance on the false belief and deception tasks.

Given the findings reported above that various family background factors as well as aspects of parenting strategies are related to false belief understanding, Pears and Moses (2003) set out to explore the relations among these sets of factors in a group of 3- to 5-year-old children and their parents. In contrast to Hughes et al.'s finding of a positive association between power assertion and belief understanding for boys, Pears and Moses found a negative association with power assertive techniques such as yelling and spanking; that is, parents who reported using such techniques had children who were less advanced in understanding beliefs. It is important to remember that this is a correlation and although it may be that such ways of interacting with children have a negative effect on social development, another explanation is also possible. Pears and Moses point out that for children who are less advanced in understanding others, parents may tend to use power assertive techniques. Such techniques might work for these children, whereas more positive parenting strategies may be effective with more socially mature children. However, if this idea that parents use more positive strategies with more mature children is correct, it would be expected that the use of positive strategies would be linked to children's increasing age. But this was not found, suggesting that the use of such parenting strategies is not simply linked to the child's maturity, and may instead facilitate social development.

These few studies on parenting have produced complex results, and Pears and Moses acknowledge that the measures of parenting strategies explained only a small amount of variability in children's social understanding. Thus there are many factors that are not being fully captured here. Furthermore, there are the issues of what aspects of parent–child interaction are focused on as well has how it is assessed (i.e., self-report versus observation). Hughes et al. (1999, p. 156) conclude that "attempts to identify universal relations between parenting and children's socio-cognitive development are doomed to fail, since the salient proximal processes in parent–child interactions can, and do, vary dramatically according to sex of child and family culture." However, another way of viewing these studies is that these results should be taken as encouragement to look much more closely at the nature of the social interaction children experience within their families. Furthermore, a theoretical framework is needed for making sense of this evidence.

Peer relationships, pretend play and the direction of causality

The threads of evidence that suggest a link between factors within family relationships and social understanding are matched with data from outside the family. Judy Dunn extended her work to involve close observations of friendships and peer relationships (Dunn, 2004; Slomkowski & Dunn, 1996). For example, Dunn and Cutting (1999) found that 4-year-old children's false belief performance, as measured on a battery of tasks, was positively related to the frequency of pretend play and the total amount of talk between friends and negatively related to the amount of conflict and failed bids of communication between them. These data are consistent with other research. First, studies rating social competence with teacher reports have found that false belief performance is related to a greater likelihood that teachers will assess the child as able to engage in shared pretence and cooperative play with their peers (Lalonde & Chandler, 1995; see also Astington, 2003). Secondly, studies which use peer nomination techniques to assess peer popularity find that popular children score higher on false belief batteries (Peterson & Siegal, 2002), at least for children over the age of five (Slaughter, Dennis, & Pritchard, 2002). We return to these studies in chapter 9 where we also consider the broader issues of peer relationships in terms of more extreme issues like bullying and "Machiavellian intelligence."

How can the link between peer relationships and the child's mental state understanding be explained? As Astington (2003) points out, "theory of mind" skills could determine the sophistication of the child's interactions – the ability to "read" others' gestures and respond more appropriately – or the opposite might be the case. That is, the data from peer interactions and sibling relationships suggest that there might be something about the give and take of children's everyday negotiations with other children that prompts social development. Given that pretence has been theorized to be a precursor to false belief (see chapter 3) and that peer and sibling pretend play correlate with the child's mental state understanding, it could be that the former is an important context, or even a driving force, for developing an understanding of the psychological world. Using Vygotsky's terminology, some have argued that play acts as a "zone of proximal development" (Lillard, 1993a) for social understanding. By this term Vygotsky hypothesizes that more competent individuals help the child to operate at a level that is above their level of individual competence. It is in such interaction that individual competence gradually emerges. Pretence, by its very detachment from reality, is an ideal opportunity for such joint involvement to take place. However, peer relationships will differ depending on the characteristics of the other child; pretend play may be an important part of some relationships but not others (Dunn, 2004; Dunn & Brophy, 2005).

So, can we identify a role of pretence with siblings and peers in the child's developing understanding of mind? There is some evidence for the hypothesis that pretence comes first. For example, young children's

tendency to enact roles in play was found to predict false belief understanding some seven months later (Youngblade & Dunn, 1995). However, the picture is more complicated and there are strong grounds for
assuming that any direction of causality would be far more complex. To
begin with, it might not be the case that pretence is the driving force –
it might simply be a marker for another causal influence. In their close
observations of sibling interactions, Nina Howe and her colleagues (Howe
et al., 1998, 2002) and indeed Youngblade and Dunn (1995) found that
the frequency of pretend play between siblings is correlated with the use
of internal mental state language in the observation sessions. Longitudinal research also casts further doubt on a simple pattern. In Astington
and Jenkins' (1995) cross-sectional analysis there were concurrent associations between false belief and two features of the interactions that
the child engages in during shared pretence: making joint plans and the
allocation of roles. However, in their longitudinal research (Jenkins &
Astington, 2000) not only did the two interaction measures not predict
later false belief understanding, but also the opposite pattern was significant – false belief understanding predicted later role assignment and
joint plans seven months later. Other research suggests similar patterns
over longer time periods. For example, early false belief predicts greater
communication between friends at age 4 (Slomkowski & Dunn, 1996)
and pretence between friends at age 6 (Maguire & Dunn, 1997). Such
directional patterns do not rule out the importance of relationships and
interactions, but they do raise sufficient serious doubts about the direction of causality for Astington (2003) to explore the idea that false
belief understanding underpins competence in social interaction. She
argues cogently that a grasp of false belief is "sometimes necessary" for
individual differences in social behavior but is "never sufficient" for
these. It is important to examine research which goes more deeply into
the link and we now turn to explore the range of social factors that
have been thought to enhance false belief understanding.

Sensory loss: deafness and blindness

An alternative way of studying the role of social interactions in the
development of social understanding has been to explore the effects of
deafness and blindness on social understanding. The research that we
discussed in chapters 1 and 3 shows that children with autism show
profound problems in understanding mental states, suggesting a specific
problem in reading minds or a more general deficit in social interaction

skills. Over the past decade studies of deaf children in particular have come to the fore because children with sensory loss do not usually have other disabilities, whereas most children with autism have severe learning problems. They thus help us to explore the claim that social interaction plays a role in social development in a novel way. The first evidence was presented by Peterson and Siegal (1995) who found that deaf children aged between 8 and 13 performed much worse on false belief tests than a comparison group of hearing children aged 4 to 5. A follow-up study suggested that deaf children might pass standard false belief in the age range of 13 to 16 years (Russell, Hosie, Hunter, Banks, & Macaulay, 1997). Similar delays have been noted in children with congenital blindness (Minter, Hobson, & Bishop, 1998), with success on false belief apparent at age 12 (Peterson, Peterson, & Webb, 2000).

This evidence from both deaf and blind children suggests a delay in social understanding and subsequent research with deaf children has explored a possible reason for this. We must be slightly cautious about the use of the false belief task as a litmus test for an understanding of the mind. Research on children's understanding of stories told by deaf children over the age of 9 suggest that they attribute mental states to people (Marshark, Green, Hindmarsh, & Walker, 2000), so there may be a specific problem with the standard tests like those described in chapter 3. Nevertheless, it is still important to understand why children with sensory loss find these so difficult. Deaf children whose parents are also deaf, and thus fluent in sign language, do not seem to be delayed in social understanding in a modified false belief task in picture form, whereas their counterparts with hearing parents who are not native signers are delayed (e.g., P. de Villiers, 2005; Peterson & Siegal, 2000; Woolfe, Want, & Siegal, 2002). There are a number of possible explanations for this striking finding, but they all are related to the possible difference in social interaction and conversation experienced by these children. The issues to do with language will be taken up in the next chapter, but the conclusion here is that deaf children with hearing parents, who are not generally fluent in sign language, experience language and interaction that may differ in ways that hinder social development, whereas deaf children with deaf parents are exposed to complex language and interaction just like hearing children.

Social understanding and forms of attachment

One important approach to studying the role of social relations in social development has been with attachment theory. Freud argued that the emotional exchange within early social relationships forms the basis of social understanding and his ideas were taken up by his followers, including John Bowlby (1969). Early work found close links between parent–infant communication and attachments (Bretherton, Bates, Benigni, Camaioni, & Volterra, 1979), and more research since the mid-1990s has examined such connections in preschoolers. In a cross-sectional study Fonagy, Redfern, and Charman (1997) used the Separation Anxiety Test (SAT), a projective measure of attachment, to classify 3- to 6-year-old children as either securely or insecurely attached. This test involves presenting children with a series of pictures depicting various social situations involving separation and asking a series of questions to elicit emotional narratives that are assumed to reflect the child's own feelings about separation. This provides an indirect measure of the child's form of attachment with his or her own parents. Fonagy et al. found that securely attached children were more advanced on a belief-dependent emotion task. A positive association between 5-year-olds' attachment security and belief understanding has also been found with a Q-sort measure of attachment (Symons & Clark, 2000). This is a set of 90 specific infant behaviors related to attachment that are used by a rater to describe the observed child. As well as rating the attachment behaviors of the child, the mother's sensitivity toward the child was also rated, that is, "a mother's ability to perceive, identify, and respond consistently and accurately to signals from her child" (Symons & Clark, 2000, p. 9). In this study security of attachment assessed at age 2 was not related to performance on standard false belief tests at age 5. But this might have been because most of the children did very well on these standard tasks. However, the children were also given a version of the false belief task that involves a character's false belief about the location of a mother-character rather than an object. There was more variability on this task and performance was related to the measure of the mother's sensitivity assessed when the child was 2 years old. This contributes further evidence of the connection between the child's relationship history with caregivers and the child's social understanding.

In another longitudinal study Meins, Fernyhough, Russell, and Clark-Carter (1998) assessed the attachment security of 33 infants with the strange situation procedure at either 11 or 13 months of age. The strange situation procedure is often referred to as "the" infant attachment procedure. It is a series of separations and reunions between mother and child designed to promote sufficient stress in the infant to activate his or her attachment system. It allows the observation of the form of attachment the infant has developed with his or her caregiver. Meins et al. found the following set of links between security of attachment and social development:

(a) children who received a secure attachment classification in infancy were better able to incorporate the pretence suggestions of an experimenter into their play sequences at 31 months, despite no group differences in the level of sophistication of play *before* the experimenter intervened: (b) mothers of securely attached children adopted more sensitive tutoring strategies on a collaborative task at age 3; (c) mothers of securely attached children were more likely to describe their children in terms of their mental characteristics, rather than their physical or behavioural qualities; (d) children who were securely attached in infancy were more likely to pass a version of the unexpected transfer task at age 4; and (e) when assessed at age 5, securely attached children were more likely than their insecurely attached counterparts to give the maximum number of correct answers on a task requiring an understanding of informational access." (pp. 18–19, emphasis in original)

Interestingly, the link between belief understanding and attachment was not replicated by Meins, Fernyhough, Wainwright, Das Gupta, Fradley, and Tuckey (2002). But they did find that maternal "mind-mindedness," that is, "the proclivity to treat one's infant as an individual with a mind, capable of intentional behavior" (p. 1716), was positively associated with advanced social understanding. We will take up the issue of mind-mindedness in the second half of the chapter.

The role of culture and family background in social development

Yet another factor to consider that may contribute to differences in parent–child interaction is culture. In the studies across the world there have been wide differences in the age at which children acquire a proficiency in the standard false belief test. Wellman et al. (2001, pp. 667–668) report that "If at 44 months of age children in the United States are 50% correct, then children in Australia are 69% correct and children in Japan are 40% correct." Two strands of research are apparent. First, there are differences within a particular culture which suggest that factors like social class may be important. These studies have explored the finding that family background is related to false belief understanding. Cutting and Dunn (1999) found that mothers with more education and both parents' occupational status predicted more advanced performance by preschoolers on false belief tests. Consistent with this,

Holmes, Black, and Miller (1996) found that false belief understanding was delayed in children from families in lower socioeconomic circumstances. Such data suggest that there may be different social interactional styles which promote or delay the development of social understanding, although they do not allow us to pinpoint just why such differences arise. A second strand of studies has explored the much greater differences between members of societies that are very different from Western cultures. Some research finds patterns of data that are roughly consistent with those in the West (Avis & Harris, 1991). However, Penny Vinden (1996) reported that false belief test performance in the Junín Quechuan people of Peru appeared to lag behind Western children by at least three years [and possibly much longer]. She selected this group because their language appears not to refer directly to mental states. Her next study was conducted with four cultural groups. A sample of Western children and three non-Western cultures: the Mofu of Cameroon, and the Tolai and the Tainae of Papua, New Guinea. In this sample, Vinden found some delays in false belief understanding and she also reported that "almost all children from non-Western cultures . . . had difficulty predicting an emotion based on a false belief about the world" (Vinden, 1999, p. 19).

Vinden (2001) next studied the relations between parenting and social development in order to explore possible practices linked to different cultural groups that might explain such differences. She found that authoritarian parenting was negatively related to social understanding, but only in European-American families, not in Korean-American families. Clearly something about the nature of family relationships and the child's history of social experience is important in social cognitive development, but the nature of the relationship that goes along with endorsing authoritarian parenting seems to differ across cultures. We do not want to reify culture. It is not an entity independent of the relations between people. One way in which culture may influence child development is through parents' beliefs about how a child should be developing and how parents should interact with their children. Such patterns need to be identified before we can fully explore the link between the patterns of social interaction that are shared by a society or subgroup (e.g., a social class group) and the influences on children's developing social understanding. However, we may conclude this brief analysis with the observation that the demonstrated social class and cultural differences lend support to the claim made by Tomasello, Kruger, and Ratner (1993) that social understanding cannot simply be wired into our genetic make-ups. The practices devised by cultural groups serve to channel whatever is inherited into further developments. Angeline Lillard (1998) takes this argument further to suggest that while all children go through similar processes in developing a "theory of mind" (i.e., false belief understanding), culture channels this basic insight into diverse adult systems of folk psychology.

How Can We Incorporate Social Interactions into a Theory of Social Understanding?

The evidence that we presented in the first half of this chapter is compelling in that it comes from a wide variety of areas and each shows strong correlates with tests of social understanding. The questions that underlie these data concern the direction of causality – does social interaction affect the development of social understanding or does social understanding make social interaction possible? In this second half of the chapter we explore three lines of theoretical analysis that have been raised by the literature we have described above. We first consider attempts by the dominant theories discussed in chapter 3 to account for this evidence. The second section examines some of the issues that arise as a result of the demonstrated links between early attachments and later performance in theory of mind. Recent findings have necessitated the development of more sophisticated analyses of the child's developing social understanding. This leads to other recent accounts that have attempted to analyze the role of social interaction from a perspective that is consistent with Vygotsky's theory.

Traditional interpretations of the social data

The variability across cultures and social groups in the development of social understanding or the subtle effects of a preschooler having an older sibling might be taken as evidence for a social account of children's development that is at odds with the ones presented in chapter 3. In response to early research showing links between social interactions and false belief understanding, representatives of the dominant perspectives, particularly theory theory (see chapter 2), defended their position on two counts. First, they described a position that holds that all social understanding can be put down to the learning of social rules as an "enculturation" view. The contrast between such a position and the theory theory is clear:

theories always develop with reference to the outside world; put very simply, a theory former wants to get closer to the truth. Cultural practices, on the other hand, are, at least largely, self-constitutive: they make themselves the case. Theories are true or false, cultural practices are right or wrong. (Astington & Gopnik, 1991, p. 20)

Development from this latter view "would be socialization or enculturation – children would learn how to psychologize appropriately in the way that they learn to dress properly or eat politely" (Astington & Gopnik, 1991, pp. 19–20) or learn social conventions such as "forks go on the left" (Gopnik, 1993, p. 3).

We are not wholly convinced that this enculturation position has ever been endorsed within the "theories of mind" literature. Astington and Gopnik attribute it to the philosopher Ludwig Wittgenstein and to Jerome Bruner in his 1990 book, which criticizes the "theory of mind" for being too cognitive. However, as we suggest in chapter 2, close inspection of that book indicates that Bruner does not deny the importance of psychological processes, as implied in the criticisms above. We also discuss a different view of Wittgenstein in chapters 7 and 10. While the enculturation view might be a straw person, in that no one holds it in the "theories of mind" area, it is clear that Astington and Gopnik's view is correct – we need to do more than describe social conventions without attempting to understand how the child comes to understand mental state terms and this brings us to the second point made by theory theorists.

The second issue to be raised by the dominant account of theory of mind is that the child may need to engage in social interactions in order to develop a "theory of mind" (Gopnik & Wellman, 1994). Thus according to theory theory, social experience may be important for the child to realize the discrepancy between their current "theory" and their observations of how actors behave, and is thus important for theory change. According to the traditional perspective the shift is a sudden one – the child suddenly realizes that their theory has been wrong. However, recent analyses from this perspective appear not to have the same confidence in the child as theoretician, perhaps because of the weight of the social evidence described above. For example, Karen Bartsch (2002; Bartsch & Estes, 2004) takes a theory-theory perspective on the role of such social experience, but she is aware of a need to articulate the role of experience more clearly. Bartsch and Estes (2004, p. 99) state that

According to theory-theory, experience drives conceptual development; if experience concerning false belief occurs (in this important sense) only in social encounters, then it seems to us that theory-theory necessarily accords an important role to such encounters. Perhaps theory-theorists have not yet offered sufficiently extensive analyses of how experience (social or otherwise) translates into conceptual development, but that does not mean that such experience is any less than the primary engine of development on this account.

Ted Ruffman (2004, p. 120) also argues that theory theory is not at odds with the evidence reviewed in this chapter. However, he too is less convinced by the idea of sudden paradigm shifts and he states that the theory theory

is based on the idea that children form theories about the mind that are in some ways similar to scientific theories. Scientific theories are often the result of years or decades of hard work, sometimes with many scientists from different laboratories contributing. Thus, scientific theories, the very basis for [theory theory], are typically constructed both gradually and as the result of a community (social) effort.

Interestingly, this approach differs from the more typical theory-theory position according to which, despite social influences, theory change is essentially endogenous. That is, the individual child-theorist forms and tests hypotheses. For example, Bartsch (2002) describes the role of social interaction in providing experience that is inconsistent with the child's current theory, promoting theory change, and more social experience just provides more data for the child-theorist to work with. However, Bartch (2002, p. 151) notes that: "Of course, it is known that merely being talked to about more advanced concepts does not necessarily change a person's theory, but a good deal of science education appears to assume that lecturing might have some benefit. In this regard, the noted relationships between others' talk and children's theory of mind are consistent with a theory-theory perspective."

We have spelled out these recent statements from two leading theory theorists because we feel that there has been a shift from a firm theory-theory view, which recognizes the need for the child-theorist to collect social data but not the role of social processes in influencing change. Bartsch recognizes the possible role of instruction in the "lecturing" a child receives and Ruffman acknowledges that theories are the result of social collaboration and can be passed on from previous generations. To our minds this suggests that enculturation is now a part of the theory-theory view.

Similar issues emerge with reference to the innate module position. These theoreticians also have argued that the social data are wholly compatible with their approach. For example, German and Leslie (2004, p. 106) claim that "[t]heories that propose a modular basis for developing a 'theory of mind' have no problem accommodating social interaction or social environment factors into either the learning process or into the genotypes underlying the growth of the neurocognitive modules." They go on to state that "Maturation of hardwired mechanisms enables the child to make appropriate sense of social inputs and *hence* to learn about the social and mental worlds" (p. 107, emphasis in original). It is not wholly clear what German and Leslie mean by "into the genotypes," but they may be referring to the effect of heredity because they cite the Hughes and Cutting (1999) article discussed above. However, as we have noted, Hughes et al.'s (2005) more recent research contradicts the earlier small study and shows the strong influence of environmental factors. Like the theory-theory approaches described above, the social data are not wholly incompatible with the innate module account but statements like those we have cited make it difficult to discern how either perspective can ever be tested. We now turn to more specific explanations for the relations reported above between the history of social interaction children experience with their caregivers and the child's developing understanding of beliefs and emotions.

Explanations emerging from the data on attachments and social understanding

Having reviewed evidence above showing a link between security of attachment and social cognitive development, we now consider the theoretical analyses that have been proposed to explain the connection. These have led to important developments in theory regarding the social influences on the development of an understanding of mind. In a landmark review of this area Fonagy and Target (1997) pointed out that there are both trivial and substantive explanations for the associations between attachment security and social understanding. They note that the association would be trivial if it "was due to an as yet unknown and unmeasured third factor, such as temperament" (p. 687). Hughes and Leekam (2004, p. 600) point out that some studies have "shown that attachment security is closely related to child characteristics such as temperament." However, Elizabeth Meins (1999) has argued that temperament does not adequately account for attachment security because "difficult" infants are just as likely to be securely attached as "easy" infants. Moreover, the same infant may form different types of attachment with different caregivers, suggesting that temperament or other aspects of the child's personality cannot be a complete explanation for the form of attachment that infants develop with their caregivers. A more plausible but still trivial explanation would be that "the facilitative effect of secure attachment is due to a more relaxed, task-oriented attitude, a general facility to engage in a cognitively demanding task, to relate to an adult experimenter in a playful, exploratory way and so on" (Fonagy & Target, 1997, p. 687). That is, attachment security may affect just the child's performance on false belief tasks and not their general cognitive competence with false beliefs. This account is hard to refute, but given that so many of the studies that we review in these chapters employ measures of general social or intellectual development to control for such a general explanation, we can consider it unlikely.

Fonagy and Target (1997) then consider two sets of more substantive explanations. The first is that secure attachment might facilitate a child's engagement in forms of interaction that would help in social development. A central assumption of Bowlby's (1969) theory is that securely attached children react less to everyday separations from their parents and have more time to explore their environment, and engage in more interactions. Thus security would allow children to engage in more shared pretense, conversations about feelings and thoughts, and peer group interaction. According to this account, attachment security might be a great boost to the development of mental state understanding but it would not explain much more than the individual differences at any age. As an alternative, which marks a move toward a more cognitive developmental interpretation, Fonagy and Target propose that security of attachment may be an indicator of the "quality of infant–caregiver relationship which generates psychological understanding. In this second model, the social processes which accelerate the mentalizing quality of self-organization are the very same as those which ensure security of attachment" (Fonagy & Target, 1997, p. 687). In other words, caregivers who are sensitive to their infant will respond in ways that facilitate the formation of a secure attachment but they will also talk to their infant in psychological terms which may facilitate the child's understanding of the psychological world. It is this latter model that represents most current thinking on the association between attachment and later mental state understanding.

Indeed there are reasons why the field has moved on from the notion of attachment that we referred to in the section on attachment in the first half of the chapter. Recall that Elizabeth Meins (1999) tested the idea that security of attachment provides a window into children's social understanding through her notion of maternal "mind-mindedness" – "the proclivity to treat their infants as individuals with minds, rather than merely entities with needs that must be met" (p. 332). That "mind-mindedness" was a stronger predictor of false belief understanding three years later than was the child–mother attachment relationship (Meins et al., 2002) provides clear support for her claim that it is what mothers do within attachment relationships that appears to be crucial. "Mind-minded" mothers tend to "focus upon *mental* attributes, rather than physical or behavioral characteristics, when given an open-ended invitation to describe their children" (Meins, 1999, p. 332, emphasis in original). According to Meins, this way of thinking about infants in terms of their thoughts and feelings results in mothers responding to their infants in sensitive and appropriate ways and thus their infants form secure attachments.

How does this work exactly? Meins et al. (2002, p. 1724) propose that the reason that mothers' mentalistic comments on their child's behavior are linked to social development is that "exposure to such language from the earliest months of life provides children with an opportunity to integrate their own behavior with an external comment that makes reference to the mental states underlying that behavior. Such comments thus offer a scaffolding context within which infants can begin to make sense of their own behavior in terms of its underlying mental states." The word "scaffold" was first used by Jerome Bruner in the 1970s to refer to Vygotsky's account of the part played by a more skillful interactant in helping a child to develop a skill. Such support was evident in Meins et al.'s study. For example, some mothers talked to their 6-month-old babies in the following sorts of ways: "You recognize this, don't you?" or "Are you thinking?" It is not clear how this form of talk can be helpful when infants are only 6 months of age and would have little understanding of such words, but there may be continuity with later parent–child interaction.

Some researchers have argued that sensitive patterns of parent–infant interaction are vital in helping the infant to orient to social stimuli. For example, Hobson (2002) suggests that the ways mothers interact with infants result in secure attachment and provide a form of interpersonal engagement that facilitates the development of thinking about the social world. In keeping with Bowlby's ideas about the infant's developing internal working models of self in relationships, Fonagy (2004) has argued for the role of attachment in the regulation of emotions and attention to social interactions. Yet Meins' data may simply demonstrate influences that take a long time to germinate. Infants' close relationships show a continuity into the preschool years, as do their internal working models (Thompson, 2000). Meins et al.'s data tie in neatly with those of Judy Dunn, mentioned at the start of the chapter, which suggest that maternal talk about mental states in the third year of life predicts earlier understanding of the false belief test. We know little of the mental state references of other interactants like fathers (Howe, 2004) or exactly how such talk may facilitate social development. We return to this topic in chapter 7.

The conclusion from the research on attachment is that we need to go beyond simple claims that secure babies will develop earlier insights into the mind. Research like that of Meins and Dunn suggests that we need to look at the processes which may convey meaning to the child. Although most studies have found that sensitive parenting is correlated with better social understanding, this could be because of the measures of mental state understanding that are used. Howard Steele (2004) has argued cogently that different types of adult–child relationship might facilitate different types of social understanding in the child. In one of his studies good performance on mental state understanding tests was found in securely attached children, but it was also found in those who were most anxious and disorganized in their attachments (Fonagy, Steele, Steele, & Holder, 1997). Such data remind us that research has only scratched the surface of the complexity of early relationships and their possible influences on the child's developing social understanding.

The Vygotskian perspective

The data from attachment research raise many interesting questions about how to explain the influence of social factors on development. Since the mid-1990s several researchers have taken a stance against the cognitivist and individualist focus of the dominant theories that we discussed in chapter 2. These researchers consider the issue of how, in general, should the relations between development and social experience be thought about (Astington, 1996; Fernyhough, 1996, 2004; Garfield, Peterson, & Perry, 2001; Raver & Leadbeater, 1993; Symons, 2004)? These perspectives highlighted important tensions and a possible solution to these tensions.

As we stated in chapter 2, one of the leading proponents of the view that traditional approaches are too individualistic has been Janet Astington (e.g., Astington, 1996). She has long been concerned with how individuals' "theory construction," the province of "theory of mind," might relate to the range of social processes that we described in the first half of this chapter: "The contrast is between autonomous individual development which is facilitated by the social world, and interdependent activity within a communal world" (Astington, 1996, p. 188). In this chapter we have underlined how difficult it is to pinpoint the links here. Astington draws upon Vygotsky's idea that mental functions are first social and then later individual. As she points out, Vygotsky uses Marxist theory because it places history and culture at the heart of an understanding of the individual's functioning within social interactions – the child's development cannot be abstracted out of his or her experience within relationships. Central to Vygotsky's theory are two processes, mediation and internalization. Cultural tools like language and other symbol systems are used in forms of thought that appear first between the child and adult as a social process and are then internalized. Thus the theory predicts the very variations between individuals, social groups, and cultures that have been shown in this chapter.

Astington's Vygotskian perspective would be supported by data which show the influence of social mediation on developing understanding. There are many possible examples and we cite two here. First, researchers are now looking for relationships between theory of mind test performance and real-world activities. In one of these studies Peskin and Ardino (2003) explored the links between two types of false belief task, unexpected transfer and the deceptive box tasks (see chapter 3), and two common social activities – playing hide-and-seek and keeping a secret. They found a correlation between particular tasks and activities. Their multivariate analysis showed some interesting links between particular activities and tests. Over and above the effects of age, the unexpected transfer test, which involves the movement of an object from one hidden location to another, was predicted by children's understanding of hide-and-seek. On the other hand, deceptive box test performance was predicted not by hide-and-seek, but by the child's ability to keep a secret – that there was a present for the second experimenter that the child was not supposed to mention. We take these connections to be due to the similarities between the social activities and the tasks. Such associations between each real-world activity and particular tasks suggest that the uniformity found in the meta-analysis described in chapter 3 (Wellman et al., 2001) may in fact conceal links between particular skills developed in social interaction and particular abilities as measured in standard tests of social development. Such data do not appear to fit well with theory theory, which holds that the child should apply his or her theory across all settings.

The second area of research that seems to support the Vygotskian perspective (in addition to all the data presented in the first half of the chapter) concerns attempts to train mental state understanding in preschoolers. If children can be trained to pass false belief tests then the social processes utilized in such training might indicate the typical process of development. This approach has yielded some success (e.g., Slaughter & Gopnik, 1996). For example, Appleton and Reddy (1996) examined the effects of a training regime in which children were encouraged to converse about their responses in the false belief task. They watched a video of someone acquiring a false belief and were asked questions such as, "Why did the first child look in the original place for the object?" (p. 281). They found that such conversational training led to improvement on similar and novel tests of mental state understanding. The most striking result was that 18 out of 23 in the training group were successful on an unexpected transfer test, while only 1 of 23 in a control group passed. Such training data are interesting and appear to suggest that training has clear effects on social understanding. However, we must be cautious about assuming that the link between children's everyday actions and their social understanding will be easy to pinpoint: it could be the case that the training helps children to pass the false belief test without necessarily developing a full understanding.

The research reviewed in this section and throughout this chapter points to an important role for social interaction in social development. This evidence, however, is in need of an explanation. Vygotsky's (1978, 1986) general view of development is that higher mental functions appear first in interaction between the child and an adult or more expert peer and these mental functions are then internalized. This gives an essential role to the process of internalization. However, Duveen (1997, p. 78) notes that

> the process is described only through the briefest sketch of its contours which rarely provide a sense of detail in the way in which the process operates. What is provocative in Vygotsky's formulation is that it suggests a simple solution to what is a complex problem, the relations between social and cognitive processes, so that it seems to dissolve the mysteries of the socialisation of cognitive functions and thereby to offer a resolution of some of the deepest problems of developmental psychology.

Furthermore, Vygotsky (1978, p. 57) in writing about internalization acknowledges that "[a]s yet, the barest outline of this process is known." There are two main views of the process of internalization (Lawrence &

Valsiner, 1993): passive or transformational. Passive or transmission models "assume some degree of match between the original and any copy" (Smith, 1996, p. 258). An example of this would be the enculturation model described at the beginning of this chapter. In contrast, transformation models assume that the process of internalization involves a transformation rather than simply a passive copying. Most theorists reject a transmission model (e.g., Astington, 2004; Symons, 2004) but it is still difficult to provide the details of a transformation model.

There are, however, limitations to many interpretations of Vygotsky. For example, the metaphor that often arises is of an apprenticeship. Yet Duveen (1997, p. 82) notes that if all the child does is to learn the rules of his or her culture "[o]ne can legitimately ask how social change can be brought about through a process of apprenticeship." This point echoes Piaget's classic criticism of socialization accounts; that is, they do not explain the development of new knowledge, nor how the child develops to the point at which he or she can assimilate socially available knowledge (e.g., Chapman, 1988). Here we also raise the question of what form of knowledge would arise from a Vygotskian process. In particular, could a "theory of mind" in the sense of a set of principles or laws develop through such a process? Research within the "theory of mind" tradition has been very clear in showing how children's understanding is radically different from that of adults and goes through successive changes. It is unclear how such changes can be explained by a model which simply stresses the role of tutelage by older siblings and adults. Fernyhough (1996, 1997, 2004) draws upon Vygotskian theory in proposing quite a different view of what an understanding of the psychological world is really like. He argues that Vygotsky's theory is important because it focuses upon a transformational approach to the social processes. The crucial issue is the "triadic" relationship between self, other, and the mediational system of language. He offers us a way of using Vygotsky's theory that we take up later, in chapter 10:

In a now-familiar set of arguments, Vygotsky proposed that higher mental functions such as mediated memory and self-regulatory inner speech are formed through the progressive internalization and transformation of semiotically mediated interpersonal exchanges (Vygotsky, 1934/1987, Ch. 4). In internalizing dialogue with others, the child internally reconstructs the dynamics of that dialogue with, crucially, all of its triadic intentional relations intact. The essential thing about dialogue, for our purposes, is that it involves a simultaneous unity of different perspectives

(Holquist, 1990) on the element of reality to which the dialogue is intentionally related. (Fernyhough, 2004, p. 105)

Summary and Conclusion

We have covered a lot of ground in this chapter. Many studies in many areas have been described and still we have had to be selective in this coverage. A wide variety of social influences correlate with individual differences in performance on standardized tests of social development. We have reviewed evidence of the influence of siblings, forms of infant attachment, parenting style, family background, culture, and sensory loss on children's social development. And yet, in the second half of the chapter we have attempted to show that interpreting such data is no easy business. Traditional accounts of "theory of mind" attempt to bolt a social perspective onto their theory, although the sheer weight of social data makes this difficult to accommodate. The findings on attachment have given rise to an interpretation of "theory of mind" connections in keeping with a fundamental principle of attachment, that the child's internal working models of such relationships are vital influences upon how they construct models of themselves and their social experience. Recent concepts like "mind-mindedness" lead to accounts of mental state understanding in which the child's developing understanding has to be conceptualized within a social and interpretive framework. Many contemporary theoreticians have chosen Vygotsky's theory as a guide to this framework. We feel that in order to understand the complexities of data like those presented in this chapter we need to join together the ideas of Vygotsky with an account that examines the dynamic between individual psychological functioning and mediational processes more closely. To do this we turn to Piaget. We started the chapter with an incisive remark from him about the influence of social factors: that they are pervasive but require an explanation. This chapter has served to illustrate how difficult it is to conceptualize how social interactions and relationships might be incorporated into an understanding of the mind. We will need the whole of chapter 10 to undertake such a task.

The focus of this chapter has been on exploring the possible roles that social relationships may have in social cognitive development. However, "a *relationship* involves two people" (Dunn, 2004, p. 129, emphasis in original). Parent–child relationships will be influenced by the child's characteristics as well as the parents' characteristics. But the role of "child effects" has, so far, attracted less attention in the "theory of mind" literature. A child's relationships with siblings and peers will also be influenced by the characteristics of their siblings and peers (Dunn, 2004). Furthermore, in considering the relations between social interaction and social understanding we should also consider the potential for children's social cognitive development to transform their social relations (Hughes & Leekam, 2004). We turn to this issue in chapter 9.

Chapter 7

Language and Social Understanding

The evidence of the relations between children's social experience and their social understanding reviewed in the previous chapter leads us to ask what it is about social interaction that is important in social development. This directs our attention to the relations between language and social understanding. Several studies have reported correlations between false belief understanding and various measures of language ability, in both cross-sectional (Cutting & Dunn, 1999; Happé, 1995; Jenkins & Astington, 1996; Milligan & Astington, 2005) and longitudinal designs (Astington & Jenkins, 1999; Watson, Painter, & Bornstein, 2001). Now that there is sufficient evidence the question is why? There is considerable debate about the nature of this relationship (Astington & Baird, 2005). The topic raises broader issues about the relations between language and thought, or more particularly about language as a route for psychologists to understanding the nature of thinking.

The relation between language and social understanding can be thought about in different ways and the chapter divides into three sections. The first considers commonly held assumptions about what language tells us about the mind. There are two views. Some research takes the view that language can be thought of as a window on development and a tool for researchers to use in revealing young children's early social understanding. At the same time it has also been argued that language may be an important context for development (Budwig, 2000). The second section reviews research testing four different hypotheses regarding the possible role that language may play in facilitating the development of belief understanding. The data presented reveal the complexities of the possible links between the two skills. Thus the final section of the chapter presents what we feel are crucial issues to do with the nature of language itself. We critically consider the view of language that is endorsed in the "theory of mind" literature, particularly assumptions about how children learn the meaning of mental state terms. We conclude by drawing upon recent theoretical analyses which suggest that the key to understanding language is not in focusing on individual words, like "think." Rather it is in how we *use* language in our everyday activities.

Language and Theory of Mind: Two Models

Two clear assumptions are apparent in the theory of mind literature. First, the language that children use is a strong clue to the way in which they construct an understanding of the mind. Secondly, a recent wave of research has explored the transmission of "theory of mind" skills from parent to child. We explore each of these themes in turn.

Language as a window on development

One reason for interest in the link between language and social understanding is that young children's language might be an empirical "window" to their early social understanding. This well-used analogy was originally applied to the study of children's drawings (Luquet, 1913). The idea is that observing young children's naturally occurring speech provides vital clues to their early social understanding that cannot be derived from interviews with children. A number of observational studies have documented the emergence of young children's use of internal state words.

In one of these early studies, Bretherton, McNew, and Beeghly-Smith (1981) examined children's use of internal state terms beginning at 20 months of age, including the categories of perceptual, physiological, emotional (e.g., happy, sad), and moral (e.g., good, bad). They suggested that children's use of such internal state language indicates the development of their "*explicit, verbally expressible* theory of mind that begins to emerge at the end of the second year" (p. 356, emphasis in original). Bretherton and Beeghly (1982) extended this study by collecting mothers' reports of their 28-month-old children's use of internal state terms and added the additional category of cognition, including words such as "know," "think," and "remember." They found that children begin using mental state terms in the second year, but this use increases greatly in the third year.

In further study of young children's naturally occurring speech to determine the earliest uses of mental verbs, Shatz, Wellman, and Silber

(1983) pointed out that we should not be too hasty in assuming that children have a "theory of mind" based on their utterance of specific terms. Adults use mental verbs to serve many different functions in conversation and not always to refer to mental states. Therefore, it is not enough just to count mental state terms. It is important to look at the function that such words play in young children's interaction. Shatz et al. examined the function of such words in children's utterances to distinguish "conversational" usage from actual "mental reference." Based on their contexts, Shatz et al. (1983, pp. 307–309) coded the utterances of a small group of preschoolers using categories such as: *mental state* (e.g., "She doesn't know all this"), *modulation of assertion*, i.e., expressing degree of certainty ("I think this is a lamb"), *directing the interaction* (e.g., "It's a hat, you know," or "I guess I'll go for a ride"), *clarification* ("I mean that one"), and *expression of desire* ("I hope we have popcorn"). The phrase "I don't know" was coded as a separate category because these researchers viewed it as merely an idiomatic negative expression. In addition, *contrastives* (e.g., "Before I thought this was a crocodile; now I know it's an alligator") were considered especially good evidence of mental state understanding. Shatz et al. reported that children begin using mental verbs during their third year but at first just for conversational functions to direct interaction; only later, beginning at 2 years 8 months, did children use such words in ways these researchers categorized as referring to mental states.

Many other researchers have also used children's natural speech as a window on their developing social understanding (e.g., Dunn, Bretherton, & Munn, 1987; Shatz, 1994). Here we turn to Bartsch and Wellman's (1995, p. 3; Wellman & Bartsch, 1994) work as a good example of very detailed research of this type based on the premise that "children's talk about the mind reveals their thoughts about this intriguing subject." They used the Child Language Data Exchange System (CHILDES) database consisting of computerized transcripts from a number of researchers. The data for their project were based on transcripts from ten children, although transcripts from four children provided the majority of the data. In looking for evidence relevant to these children's understanding of desires and beliefs they searched the database for the following list of belief and desire terms: want, hope, wish, care (about), afraid (that), think, know, believe, expect, wonder, and dream (note that all possible variants of a term were included in the search, e.g., wanna, etc.). Before about the age of $2^1/_2$ years Bartsch and Wellman found a large use of desire terms with little or no use of belief terms. From about that age onward the children's use of belief terms increased to become equal to, and at about 4 years of age to often exceed, their use of desire terms. This was taken to mean that children acquire the concept of desire before the concept of belief, and this fits with their theory that an understanding of belief builds onto a "theory" of desire within a belief–desire framework.

In addition to examining the children's general use of desire and belief terms, Bartsch and Wellman (1995) note that some types of utterances appear to be especially convincing as indicators of children's understanding of the psychological world. In particular, utterances that explicitly contrast a psychological state and the real world, those labeled as "contrastives" above, are important in their potential for revealing children's mentalistic understanding. For example, Adam, at 3 years and 3 months, said, "It's a bus; I thought a taxi" (p. 206). Examples such as this seem to suggest an understanding of mental states as different from reality.

Bartsch and Wellman's (1995) analyses were, however, based on transcripts from a relatively small sample and the parents of several of these children were language researchers. Sabbagh and Callanan (1998) extended one aspect of Bartsch and Wellman's approach by studying young children's use of epistemic terms (e.g., think and know) in a more representative sample. They found that very few 3-year-olds used contrastive statements such as the one from Adam, above. These sorts of utterances, which provide clear evidence of a representational understanding of belief, were more common in 4- and 5-year-olds.

Sabbagh and Callanan (1998) were also interested in the way that parents responded to various forms of their child's mental state utterances. This leads to a second reason for the interest in language and social understanding; that is, the possibility that language may be a beneficial context for the development of social knowledge. The research reviewed in this section shows that language may be useful in revealing children's social understanding. We now turn to research on language as a context for social development, focusing in particular upon the nature of talk in families and its possible influence on the child's developing understanding of the mind.

Language in families as a context for social development

Does the language used to preschool children influence their understanding of social relationships? As mentioned in chapter 6, Ruffman et al. (1999) found that the way parents talk to their children about disciplinary situations is associated with the development of social understanding. Specifically, in the context of disciplinary situations, parents who report that they would talk to their children about how the other people involved might feel have children who are more advanced in false belief understanding. This type of approach has been extended by Peterson and Slaughter (2003) by developing a more extensive questionnaire that goes beyond just disciplinary situations to include more everyday sorts of events. They found that mothers who reported being in favor of discussing and elaborating on mental states in their conversations with their young children tended to have children who were advanced in false belief understanding.

One reason for caution in interpreting correlational studies is, of course, that it is not possible to be certain concerning the causal direction of the influence. It could be that it is the way that mothers talk that influences the child's social cognitive development. However, the converse direction of influence is also possible. It could be that mothers of children who are advanced in their social understanding somehow pick up on this, perhaps from the child's language, and thus talk more about mental states than other mothers. And of course a third factor could be involved, such as IQ: brighter children might produce more language about mental states and elicit such language from their parents. For these reasons researchers have been cautious about inferring from these correlations that mothers' talk "causes" their children's social development.

One way to attempt to tease apart cause and effect is to design longitudinal research in which the relative influence of each factor on the other can be examined at discreet time intervals. There have been several longitudinal studies on the relations between family talk and children's later social understanding. In one of the first of these studies Judy Dunn and her colleagues (Dunn, Brown, Slomkowski, Tesla, & Youngblade, 1991) followed a sample of 50 children and their families with in-home observations of family interaction beginning when the children were 33 months of age. The children were given tests to assess their understanding of belief and emotions when they were 40 months old. In this ground-breaking study, Dunn et al. found that families in which there was more talk about feelings and more use of causal mental state language had children who were more advanced in understanding beliefs when they were tested seven months later.

In another study following children longitudinally, Furrow, Moore, Davidge, and Chiasson (1992) addressed the question of how children acquire mental state understanding by examining the relations between mothers' and their children's use of mental state terms. They collected samples of parent–child talk at 2 and at 3 years of age. The coding system they used was adapted from Shatz et al. (see above) with the exception that Furrow et al. argued that the category "modulation of assertion" (that is, the use of mental state terms such as "think" to express degree of certainty) requires mentalistic understanding and they therefore considered this category to indicate an understanding of mental states. Furrow et al. found a large increase of mothers' use of mental state terms between the two time points. The children's use of these words was rare at 2 years of age, but there was an even larger increase in their children's use of mental state terms over this year. They found that mothers' use of mental state terms when their child was 2 years old was correlated with their child's use of such words, and also with their child's used of mental state words one year later when their child was 3. Like Shatz et al., Furrow et al. found that young children often use mental state terms in utterances that have "conversational" functions, as part of "directing the interaction." These results suggest that mothers influence their child's acquisition of these terms, although other possibilities cannot be ruled out.

Moore, Furrow, Chiasson, and Patriquin (1994) extended the Furrow et al. (1992) study by examining the relations between mothers' use of belief terms and their children's later understanding of such terms. In a longitudinal project with 14 families visited when the children were 2, 3, and 4 years of age, Moore et al. found that mothers' use of belief terms was correlated with their children's use of such words at all of the three time points. Furthermore, children's comprehension of the distinctions between "think," "know," and "guess" was also correlated with mothers' use of belief terms at age 2. It is interesting to note that children had been using the terms think, know, and guess for about one year but were still only at the age of 4 beginning to appreciate the differences between these words in degree of certainty expressed. These results suggest that mothers' language influences the development of their children's social understanding.

A similar pattern of results has been found concerning the relations between parents' talk about emotions and their child's later talk about, and understanding of, emotions. Dunn, Bretherton, and Munn (1987) studied family talk about emotions over a six-month period and found that the amount of talk about emotions from mothers and other siblings when the target child was 18 months was associated with that child's own talk about emotions when they were 24 months of age. Dunn, Brown, and Beardsall (1991) identified differences in conversations between 3-year-old children and their mothers in the diversity of emotions discussed, the causes and consequences of emotions, the frequency of these discussions, as well as whether the discussion involved a dispute about the action, intentions, or beliefs of another. And they also found that such differences were positively related to these children's ability to recognize emotions later at age 6 (see also Denham, Zoller, & Couchoud, 1994).

One of the consistent findings in the literature is that boys and girls appear to acquire an understanding of mental states at the same age. Any differences are minor (Charman, Ruffman, & Clements, 2002). However, there is evidence of some differences in the talk about emotions used between parents and their sons versus daughters. Kuebli, Butler, and Fivush (1995) found gender differences in a longitudinal study. They reported that when talking to their daughters compared to their sons both mothers and fathers used more and greater variety of emotion words. Although the boys and girls did not differ at the beginning of the study in their use of emotion words, by the end of the longitudinal study girls were using more and a greater variety of emotion words than boys.

What is it about parental speech that might influence the child's developing understanding? One way of formulating this is Elizabeth Meins's (1997) notion of "mindmindedness": "the proclivity to treat one's infant as an individual with a mind, rather than merely an entity with needs that must be satisfied" (Meins, Fernyhough, Wainwright, Clark-Carter, Das Gupta, Fradley, & Tuckey, 2003, p. 1194). Meins and her colleagues (1998) found that mothers who describe their 3-year-old children in mentalistic terms rather than physical appearance or behavioral tendencies had children who later at the age of 4 performed better on a false belief task. Mothers' mindmindedness has also been found to be linked with advanced performance on tasks requiring an understanding that emotions depend on beliefs (Rosnay, Pons, Harris, & Morrell, 2004). Such data seem to suggest that there is a link between the particular style the mother adopts and what her child picks up in an understanding of the mind.

However, the authors of these longitudinal studies still suggest caution in drawing causal conclusions regarding the role of family talk in social development. Ruffman, Slade, and Crowe (2002) point out that although longitudinal studies are better than single time point studies and are suggestive of a causal role played by family talk in social cognitive development, they do not conclusively reveal causality. These studies used a single measure at time one, generally some form of maternal intervention such as amount of mental state talk, and a second measure at time two, usually the child's performance on false belief tasks. Among the possible explanations for the correlations found is the possibility that children's precocity in social understanding, as revealed in their use of mental state language (Brown, Donelan-McCall, & Dunn, 1996), might elicit their mothers' talk about psychological matters (Ruffman et al., 2002).

Ruffman et al.'s (2002) study was designed to overcome such limitations of earlier research. They assessed children's linguistic competence and social understanding (with a series of false beliefs tasks and tests of children's understanding of emotion), as well as the mother's tendency to talk about mental states (assessed in a discussion of a series of pictures with her child). These three measures were taken three times over the course of one year. Ruffman et al. found that the mothers' mental state language at earlier time points predicted their children's social understanding at later points even after accounting for the child's prior language ability and level of social understanding within their statistical analyses. The converse relation between earlier social under-standing and the mothers' mental state talk did not hold. Ruffman et al. (2002) also found that mothers' talk about mental states had an effect on social development beyond the effect of the child's earlier linguistic ability. Furthermore, they concluded that the effect was due to general talk about mental states rather than a particular type of talk.

Meins et al. (2002), however, found that not all mental state talk was helpful – that is, correlated with later false belief understanding. Mothers' mentalistic comments regarding their 6-month-old infants that were judged to be inappropriate were not significantly (and in fact negatively) correlated with the child's later false belief understanding. This is in contrast to appropriate mind-minded comments which focused upon the mother's interpretation of the child's perspective on events. These were significantly and positively correlated with false belief under-standing some three years later ($r = .34$). Meins et al. also did not replicate earlier findings that attachment security was related to social understanding, suggesting that mindmindedness has a pride of place in the child's developing understanding.

Talking and Thinking

We have now considered young children's early language use as a useful empirical window onto their developing social understanding. We have also reviewed research showing that the amount of talk about the psychological world that young children are exposed to is positively related to their later social understanding and apparently plays a causal role in the development of such understanding. That is, children who hear more talk about the psychological world become more advanced in their social understanding. Is there a link between the child's own language skills and her or his understanding of the mind? Several studies have reported that various measures of the child's linguistic ability are correlated with false belief understanding both in cross-sectional (Cutting & Dunn, 1999; Happé, 1995; Jenkins & Astington, 1996) and longitudinal studies (Astington & Jenkins, 1999; Ruffman, Slade, Rowlandson, Rumsey, & Garnham, 2003; Watson, Painter, & Bornstein, 2001). Watson, Painter, and Bornstein (2001) assessed individual differences in children's language at 24 months with both a structured language assessment and maternal reports. They found that early language competence was associated with children's advanced performance on false belief tasks at 48 months.

Now the question is what do these correlations mean? These findings raise the issue of the nature of the relation or relations between language and thought, or talking and thinking. With these correlations between language and social understanding we have, of course, three logical groups of possibilities. Social understanding may depend on language, language may depend on social understanding, or some third factor may be involved that may be required for both. In addition, there are various versions of each possibility (Astington & Jenkins, 1999).

First, the idea that language depends on social understanding may be a default assumption in psychology. This is probably the most common view of the relation between language and thought. That is, conceptual development underlies language development. In other words, children first acquire concepts such as false belief understanding and then later acquire the language to express the concept.

The converse possibility, that social understanding depends on language, comes in a number of versions of varying strength. According to a weak version of this position linguistic ability is required to pass false belief tasks – the procedures are fairly verbal and simplifying them does help, but that is not the same as removing language. Supposedly "nonverbal" tasks may be somewhat easier for 3-year-olds, as we reported in chapter 3. A stronger version of this position is that language is essential in social cognitive development. A final group of possibilities is that language and social understanding might be indirectly related through a third factor. For example, children who are more advanced linguistically may also be more social and so may be exposed to more social experience (Dunn & Brophy, 2005; Jacques & Zelazo, 2005). Alternatively, various executive functions, like working memory, might be required for the development of language and social understanding (Astington & Jenkins, 1999). Language also may play a role in the development of executive functions. Jacques and Zelazo (2005) argue that the use of language for labeling relevant stimuli results in increased cognitive flexibility, and this in turn is important for social cognitive perspective-taking tasks. The role of executive functions in the development of social understanding was more extensively considered in chapter 5.

Longitudinal evidence relevant to this debate suggests that it is early linguistic ability that leads to "theory of mind" development, defined as false belief understanding (Astington & Jenkins, 1999). Earlier language ability was found to be associated with more advanced false belief understanding measured at two later points over a seven-month period, but early false belief understanding was not associated with later language development (Astington & Jenkins, 1999). This suggests that language ability facilitates the development of social understanding. Ruffman et al. (2003) also found a longitudinal relationship between language development and later false belief understanding over a 2.5-year period.

In interpreting this evidence we have to keep in mind that both social understanding and language are very complex phenomena. For a start, here "theory of mind" is defined predominantly as false belief understanding. In addition, it is important to think about language in all its complexity. In chapter 4 the argument that joint attention is essential in learning language was presented. If we think about earlier forms of social understanding in infancy required for joint attention skills then this earlier ability to coordinate attention with others would clearly be important in language development. Most of the tests of "language" presented refer to the child's understanding of individual words or the structure of sentences. As a communicative system, other aspects of language development such as understanding politeness and even forms of humor that turn on multiple meanings of words may necessarily require some level of social understanding and may, in fact, overlap to a significant degree with sophisticated social understanding. That is, we could talk about aspects of pragmatics either in terms of language ability or in terms of social understanding. This shows just how much language and social understanding are intertwined. In this section we focus upon more narrow definitions, but in the final part of the chapter we broaden our attention to reflect upon just what "language" entails. Here we examine four currently debated accounts of the relationship between language and social understanding.

Three general theoretical explanations of the relations between language and social understanding

Given the current general agreement that language is related to social cognitive development (Astington & Baird, 2005), there are now several suggested theoretical explanations for this relation ranging from the role of syntax to the role of conversation. Lohmann and Tomasello (2003) suggest that there are four global hypotheses regarding the relation between language and social understanding. In this subsection we will mention the first three of these, while the fourth will take up the next subsection as much recent attention has been paid to it. The first position considered by Lohmann and Tomasello is that, in fact, there is no special relation between language and social understanding. Rather, any source of evidence, including linguistic evidence, is important for the child in forming a theory about the mind. Lohmann and Tomasello acknowledge that it is not clear that any theorist is currently advocating such a strong position but it does follow from the theory theory. Perhaps this is close to what Bartsch (2002) has recently argued for in presenting a theory theory view of evidence that social interaction is related to social understanding (see also Bartsch & Estes, 2004). Language is important but only in providing evidence for the child theoretician of mind to construct a theory.

The second hypothesis is that what is important about language is learning mental state terms such as "think" and "know," which helps children learn the concepts by learning the referents of the terms. Olson (1988, p. 420) proposed that when children learn this language they "acquire the cognitive machinery that makes intentional state ascription literally true of them. . . . Thus the behaviorists may be correct in deny-ing the reality of beliefs and desires to infants, while the intentionalists may be correct in claiming the reality of beliefs and desires in older, linguistic children and adults" (see also Astington, 2000).

The third general hypothesis, proposed by Harris (1996, 2005), is that language is related to social development because in conversation, conceived as a means for the transmission of information, we are constantly reminded that others have different beliefs, desires, and intentions. Mental state terms might be used in conversation, but the importance of language is that conversation is a means through which others' perspectives are conveyed (Harris, 2005). A count of mental state terms is a useful correlate of maternal input, but this, according to Harris, is not the essential aspect of language. He argues that it is the mother's pragmatic intent in introducing alternative points of view in the conversation that is the important factor in social development. But Harris acknowledges that semantic and syntactic factors will co-vary, making it difficult to determine the essential factor.

All of the above theoretical positions are equally plausible. However, the data required to test each of them are not yet available, nor indeed easy to obtain. We turn now to the final perspective, which has received close attention in recent research.

Are beliefs hard to comprehend because belief terms involve complementation?

The final hypothesis discussed by Lohmann and Tomasello (2003) focuses upon the way the language is structured. Jill and Peter de Villiers (2000; de Villiers, 2000) have proposed that children's understanding of mental state terms like beliefs is tied up with their grasp of the structure of sentences. It is the syntax of complementation that is required by children as a representational format for dealing with false beliefs. In English mental verbs require the special syntax of complementation. For example, consider the statement "Sarah thought *the earth was flat*" (de Villiers & Pyers, 2002, p. 1038, emphasis in original). The child has to understand that "the overall sentence can be true, though the embedded complement can refer to a proposition that is false" (de Villiers & de Villiers, 2000, p. 196). The de Villiers' position is supported by a cor-relational study (de Villiers & de Villiers, 2000) in which children's understanding of belief was shown to relate to their grasp of nonmental verbs (e.g., *say* and *tell*) that also take complements.

Hale and Tager-Flusberg (2003) explored the role of the syntax of complementation with a training study and found that children who were trained on sentential complementation significantly increased their scores on a range of false belief tasks. This finding supports de Villiers' view that a particular aspect of syntax, that is, sentential comple-mentation, is required for false belief understanding.

A key question that needs to be answered is whether the link here is a specific one as suggested by the de Villiers or a more general one as found in the many studies cited above. In a longitudinal study Astington and Jenkins (1999) reported that it was the child's general grasp of syntax that was related to later false belief understanding. However, Astington and Jenkins acknowledge that they did not directly address the issue of complementation because their measure of language develop-ment did not have any syntactic items that included instances of object complementation. They question whether the syntax of complementation is the essential factor since young children seem to understand the use of such syntax when referring to pretending before false beliefs (Custer, 1996).

However, Ruffman, Slade, Rowlandson, Rumsey, and Garnham (2003) critique Astington and Jenkins' (1999) conclusion concerning the im-portance of syntax. They point out that Astington and Jenkins used the syntax items from the Test of Early Language Development (TELD) and "performance on the items meant to tap syntax in the TELD is heavily dependent on semantic knowledge and it is quite possibly this rather than syntax that correlates with [false belief understanding]" (Ruffman et al., 2003, p. 141). Thus, Ruffman et al. (2003) argued that syntax and semantics (the meaning of words) are intertwined in typical develop-ment and they report two experiments showing that false belief under-standing is related to general language ability. In the first experiment children's semantic ability at age 3, but not their syntactic ability, predicted later belief understanding over a 2.5-year period. In a second experiment Ruffman et al. (2003, p. 153) did find that children's performance on syntax tests was related to false belief understanding but they also note that "the composite measure (syntax + semantics) accounted for considerably more variance than syntax on its own" (see also Milligan & Astington, 2005).

Furthermore, Hale and Tager-Flusberg (2003) acknowledge that in their study they did not completely separate syntactic from semantic features because their complementation training always involved what are termed false complements. For example, in one story used in the sentential complements training, a boy is shown to kiss Big Bird and then the child was told "The boy says, 'I kissed Grover'" (Hale & Tager-Flusberg, 2003, p. 357). This is an example of how the commun-ication verb, "say," takes sentential complements, just as verbs of mental states do, such as "thought." That is, the main clause may be true whether or not the embedded clause is true. Whether the child is correct or not in being able to say what the boy said they are reminded that in fact the boy kissed Big Bird not Grover. The children may be learning something from these false statements that contrast with the event they have just observed. They thus can use information beyond the syntactic aspect of the statement made to them. Furthermore, Hale and Tager-Flusberg (2003, p. 355, emphasis in original) acknowledge that their "data argue against the claim that the acquisition of sentential complements is a *necessary* prerequisite for the development of a representational understanding of mind." This is because children who were trained on false beliefs showed equivalent improvement on the subsequent false belief tasks with no improvement on a post-test of their skills in general sentential complementation.

In response to Ruffman et al.'s (2003) argument against the role of syntax it should be noted that de Villiers' position is not for syntax in general but rather for a particular aspect of syntax, i.e., complementation. Furthermore, de Villiers and Pyers (2002, p. 1038) acknowledge that "there is an intimate connection between the syntax and semantics of mental verbs and their arguments." In addition, de Villiers and Pyers' (2002, p. 1040) specific hypothesis concerning the development of false belief understanding is that it "rests on the child's mastery of the grammar (semantics and syntax) of complementation." They assessed this position in a longitudinal study of 28 children followed over one year. Their results are consistent with their position but do not conclusively rule out other views. They found that children's understanding of false beliefs was best predicted by their mastery of complement structures and that this was not just a matter of overall language ability. De Villiers and Pyers acknowledge that there are many aspect of social understanding that would not be related to such sophisticated grammatical understanding such as joint attention and understanding desires. But they propose that the mastery of complementation is a "keystone" that connects an emerging understanding of others' behavior and the ability to talk about this behavior, even allowing for the possibility that change might be theoretical in its nature (p. 1058). What are we to make of the current state of conflicting evidence regarding the role of a specific aspect of language (i.e., complementation) versus general language ability? We can say that increases in the complexity of the ways in which children can talk about human activity – in this case the grammar (or both semantics and syntax) of complementation – is likely to be related to further social development. However, at this point we should be cautious about assuming a causal role for specific aspects of language.

The hypothesis proposed by de Villiers and de Villiers (2000) also provides an explanation for why children develop an understanding of desire before belief. This is because in English the syntax concerning desire is simpler and does not involve such complementation. This explanation can be evaluated with cross-language research with languages having different complement structures. Tardiff and Wellman (2000) tested this claim with Mandarin- and Cantonese-speaking children. These languages provide an opportunity to assess the de Villiers' idea because it is possible to talk about both beliefs and desires with the same relatively simple grammatical construction. If the de Villiers are correct then in these Chinese languages children should learn to use belief terms at about the same age as they do desire terms. Tardiff and Wellman's (2000) results did not, however, support the de Villiers because the Mandarin- and Cantonese-speaking children participating in their study talked about desire earlier than belief, similar to English-speaking children. Research with Austrian children is also relevant for the de Villiers' hypothesis because in German the grammatical requirements are the same for talking about wanting, saying, and thinking (Perner, Sprung, Zauner, & Haider, 2003). The prediction that appears to follow from the de Villiers' position is that German-speaking children should be delayed in talking about desires. However, this is not what Perner et al. (2003) found. Instead they found that children's performance with desire statements was better than their performance with say and think statements.

A third cross-language study was conducted by Cheung, Hsuan-Chih, Creed, Ng, Wang, and Mo (2004) with Cantonese-speaking children. Cantonese is an interesting test case because it provides alternative ways of talking about lies and mistakes other than with complements. Cheung et al. found that although the children's understanding of complex complements was correlated with their false belief performance, this relation was mostly accounted for by the children's general language ability. Thus, general language ability seems to be most important. However, Cheung et al. (2004, p. 1168) do acknowledge that "because complementation and general language were themselves highly correlated, it might be difficult to tease apart and evaluate their independent effects by statistical means." In general, the evidence from the cross-language studies conducted by Cheung et al. (2004), Perner et al. (2003), and Tardiff and Wellman (2000) suggest that mastering particular grammatical structures may not be what determines children's grasp of false belief understanding. Instead Perner et al. (2003) argue that development in false belief understanding is better explained in terms of conceptual progress. And Cheung et al. (2004, p. 1168) claim that "language in its totality provides a way to think and talk about other minds."

Training studies

How else can we explore the connection between language and social understanding? In addition to the correlational data that we have described above there are now several training studies, like the one by Hale and Tager-Flusberg (2003) that we cite above. In this section we will focus on two such studies which attempt to explore language in its complexity. Lohmann and Tomasello's (2003) language training study was designed to evaluate the four contrasting hypotheses that we described in the two previous subsections. Their four training conditions involving exposing the children to 16 objects, 12 of them being deceptive in the sense that they appeared to be one thing, such as a flower, but when looked at more closely they turned out to have a different function, such as a writing pen. In the *full training* condition the experimenter talked about the deceptive nature of the objects using either mental state terms (think, know) or communication verbs (say) within sentential complement constructions. In the *discourse only training* the experimenter highlighted the deceptive nature of the objects but without using sentential complement constructions. For example, instead of asking, "What do you think this is?" children were asked, "What is this?" (p. 1134). In the *no language training* condition the deceptive nature of the objects was also highlighted but the experimenter "did this basically nonverbally. Thus, children were first shown an object and the experimenter said, 'Look!' and then their attention was drawn to the real function by showing it and saying 'But now look!'" (p. 1134). Finally, in the *sentential complement only training* condition the deceptive nature of the objects was not pointed out and the experimenter "simply talked about them as normal objects using mental verbs or communication verbs and sentential complements" (p. 1134) in the context of short stories.

After three training sessions Lohmann and Tomasello found significant effects for training in the syntax of complementation, supporting the de Villiers, but they also found significant improvement in the discourse only condition, supporting Harris. In addition, the full training condition, involving both perspective-shifting discourse and training in the syntax of complementation, resulted in significantly greater improvement in false belief performance than either of the two conditions separately, suggesting that both may play a role in social development.

This study does not support Olson's (1988) position that what is important is the learning of mental state terms such as "think" and "know." Lohmann and Tomasello (2003) found no difference between two versions of the full training condition, one using mental state terms such as "think" and "know," and the other using communication verbs such as "say" and "tell." This suggests that it is not just mental state terms themselves that are essential. However, Lohmann and Tomasello (2003) acknowledge that in the syntax training condition sentential complement sentences did contain mental state terms and, thus, these may have played a role in the training effect. Perhaps especially in this case semantics and syntax are closely related (de Villiers & de Villiers, 2000; Lohmann & Tomasello, 2003), and even in this carefully designed study it is not straightforward to separate them completely.

Jill de Villiers (2005) has further clarified, or elaborated, her hypothesis but this issue is not resolved and debate continues (Perner, Zauner, & Sprung, 2005). Lohmann, Tomasello, and Meyer (2005), however, suggest that there is no conflict between the view that discourse is important in the development of false belief understanding through confronting children with different perspectives and that the syntax of complementation is also important. They argue that what is of "greatest importance is reflective discourse in which the adult and child comment on the ideas contained in the discourse turn of the other (or the self)" (p. 262). This reflective process has simply become part of the grammar of sentential complement constructions and "so looser discourse interactions and tighter syntactic constructions are all a part of the same process" (p. 262).

The second training study that we raise here was on the role of metacognitive terms in mental state understanding and was conducted by Peskin and Astington (2004). These terms include words like know, think, guess, wonder, and figure out. In this study the experimental group of 4-year-olds was read story-books with these explicit metacognitive terms, whereas the story text for the control group lacked these words. After 4 weeks of training the children in the experimental group used more metacognitive terms than the control group, but they showed no improvement in comprehension of these words. Furthermore, the control group performed better than the experimental group on the false belief explanation tasks given to the children at the end of the study. Thus, hearing mental state terms does not by itself result in social cognitive development.

Peskin and Astington's results pinpoint important issues about "language." The fact that their control group performed better on false belief tests has to be explained. The stories that this group heard did not contain specific reference to the act of thinking, but they did contain simpler words such as "hide" and "look." Not only are such words simpler in terms of their grammatical construction, they also involve some understanding of how people know things, and how people can be prevented from knowing things (Turnbull & Carpendale, 1999a, 1999b; see also Russell, 1992, regarding words like "because"). It is highly possible that the results reflect the fact that in using such terms children understand the relevant events and learn how to talk about them, which may or may not be correlated with the use of mental state terms. Thus the use of such terms is merely a likely indicator of such psychological talk, but this is not a necessary relationship. We turn to an analysis of this issue in the next section.

The Role(s) of Language in Social Cognitive Development

In this final section of the chapter we examine recent moves in the study of language and mental state understanding. Our aim is in part to explain why the relationship between language and social understanding is so hard to pin down. Astington (2001, p. 686) has suggested that language plays two crucial roles in the development of false belief understanding: "It provides a means for representing false belief in contradistinction to the evidence given in reality, and it is also a means by which children become aware of beliefs, both content and attitude." She goes on to add that "it is important that the two not be treated as competing hypotheses but rather as complementary accounts." We return to consider research on the use of mental state terms in order to examine and critique the assumptions about the nature of language and mental states on which this research is based.

Issues with counting mental state terms

The literature on counting the uses of mental state terms that we described in the first section of this chapter has produced some interesting results. However, there are a number of issues with this approach that are worth considering. In Shatz, Wellman, and Silber's (1983) words, "It is essential . . . to go beyond a tally of the mere production of particular words" (p. 317). As we asserted in the previous section, the psychological world can be referred to without using mental state terms and mental state terms themselves can be used in different ways. In fact, such words are often used when not talking about mental states at all.

For example, the statement, "It will rain, I think," is generally used to express some degree of uncertainty, not to refer to one's own mind. Researchers attempt to deal with the multiple ways in which words are used by coding the *use* of such terms. However, difficulties still remain. For example, the expression "I don't know" has been coded as conversational (i.e., a turn of phrase to keep the conversation going) by some researchers, as in our children's stock response to the question of who left the top off the marmalade: "Dunno." But how do we know for sure? Would we automatically code it this way if uttered by a philosopher engaged in reflecting upon the nature of knowledge? Not all uses of "I don't know" are simply conversational. Furthermore, the more fundamental issue of what exactly is meant by conversational use of mental state terms will be considered below.

We do not wish to detract from the important contribution that research of this type has made, but it is worthwhile to consider some difficulties with coding categories. For example, Ruffman et al. (2002) use the categories from Bartsch and Wellman (1995) and in the category of "modulations of assertion" they include such words as "might," "perhaps," and "must." However, as we suggested above, "think" can also be used to express degree of certainty (e.g., it's raining, I think). However, Ruffman et al. followed Bartsch and Wellman and coded "think" in the "think and know" category. There is also debate about whether or not use of words to serve the function of "modulation of assertion" requires some degree of mentalistic understanding. Moore and Furrow (1991) argued that such use of mental state terms to express degree of uncertainty does require some level of mentalistic understanding. And, in fact, Ruffman et al. (2002) reported positive correlations between this category and children's false belief understanding. This claim was also supported by Hughes and Dunn's (1998, p. 36) finding that "'conversational' and 'genuine' uses of mental state talk were both associated with theory-of-mind task performance." Words like "think" and "know" are not the only ones that can be open to complex interpretations. For example, Ruffman et al.'s category of "physical state" terms includes words such as "laugh." The authors note that such terms have "strong links to emotions, but were coded separately because they described physical manifestations, whereas an emotion term such as 'happy' could also refer to an internal experience" (p. 741). However, it could be argued that physical manifestations may be important, especially for young children.

The data and theoretical analysis presented in the previous section suggest that it is possible to talk about the psychological world without using mental state words. This raises an additional difficulty with inferring children's level of social understanding based on the mental state terms they use. That is, young children may, and in fact generally do, begin using words without a full understanding of the words' meanings. Thus, in addition to such observational studies of children's natural language, experimental studies are useful in determining how children understand mental state words (e.g., Moore, Bryant, & Furrow, 1989). For example, Moore et al. (1989) found that before about 4 years of age children had difficulty distinguishing the differences in degree of certainty expressed by the terms, "know," "think," and "guess." As Katherine Nelson (1996, 1997, 2004) suggests, children often begin using words when supported by the context. Nelson refers to this as "use without meaning." That is, children begin using words with only a partial or incomplete understanding of their full adult meaning.

Another difficulty with stopping our analysis with counting mental state terms is that we might assume that parents and their children use such terms in similar ways. Nancy Budwig (2002), however, showed that this is not the case and, in fact, caregivers and their children often use the same mental state term to convey different meanings. Budwig focused on the term "want" in a four-month longitudinal study of six children ranging in age from 18 months to 36 months. She found that the children were using this term from the beginning of the study, caregivers and their children used the term approximately the same amount, and both tended to use the term to refer to the child's desires. However, caregivers and their children differed in the pragmatic function (i.e., the use of language in context) that the term served in their utterances. Children tended to use the term "want" when asserting what they wanted, sometimes in conjunction with actions to fulfill their desire. In contrast, for caregivers this was a small percentage of their use, and they tended to use "want" in inquiries or clarification regarding their child's desires.

There were also interesting developmental changes. Before 2 years of age children used "want" to refer to their own desires for objects and their caregiver was usually the one who acted to fulfill the child's desires. Thus many of the children's assertions at this age functioned as requests. However, this changed over the period of the longitudinal study. At later time points children could act to achieve their own desires, so although they still used the word to refer to their own desires, they now used these utterances to seek permission, thus demonstrating the development of some understanding of the other's perspective on the interaction. These developmental changes and the differences between caregivers and their children in the ways a term such as "want" actually functions would tend to be overlooked if researchers just focused on the earliest usage or the frequency of use of mental state terms instead of also looking at how the utterance functions in particular situations. Budwig (2002) also argues that taking this indexical approach (studying the *use* of words across different contexts) need not be restricted to mental state terms. She argues that we should also pay attention to other aspects of language such as children's use of pronouns and active versus passive voice as means of understanding their grasp of mental states. Rather than focusing on words that explicitly refer to mental states Budwig (2004) suggests that we should rely on a usage-based unit of analysis (Budwig, 1998; Tomasello, 1998).

A further problem with focusing on mental state terms turns on a critique of the idea introduced above that there is a distinction between "referential" and "non-referential" or "conversational" uses of mental state terms. In the following section we consider this issue and the implications raised for how we think about language and the mind.

Psychological talk and social understanding

Data like those from Budwig presented in the previous section make the relationship between a word and its referent more complex than many traditional accounts of language would suggest. As noted above, these "coding" approaches assume that mental verbs simply refer to mental states, and so language use is important in revealing children's acquisition of this mapping of word to mental entity. From this perspective the problem the child faces is figuring out the referent for mental state terms when these are assumed to be private internal events or states. This is the way that the problem of how social understanding develops is set up within the many official versions of the "theory of mind" tradition that we described in chapter 2. This view that learning the meaning of a word involves forming word–referent relations or figuring out the word-to-world "mapping" is what Montgomery (2002) referred to as the "ostension paradigm."

Montgomery (1997, 2002, 2004, 2005) provides a critique of the ostension paradigm that mental state terms refer to inner mental entities by drawing on the private language arguments from the philosopher Ludwig Wittgenstein (see also Carpendale & Lewis, 2004a; Chapman, 1987; Racine, 2004; Racine & Carpendale, in press; Sharrock & Coulter, 2004). According to this position, there are a number of difficulties with the idea that learning the meaning of words involves mapping mental state terms to private inner sensations. One difficulty with the idea that learning the meaning of mental state terms involves mapping from word to inner sensation is that it is not possible for a listener to know if a speaker is correctly mapping a word to a referent because the referent is private. Furthermore, for the child to match a current sensation to a previous sensation puts the child in the position of being "jury and defendant. The private linguist is imagining the criterion for correctness and imagining whether it has been satisfied; consequently that person cannot distinguish following the rule from seeming to follow it" (Montgomery, 2002, p. 363). But even if this difficulty could be overcome, meaning would still not consist of a connection to a mentalistic referent because two people could have different referents for the same word. Wittgenstein (1968, para. 293) shows this with his beetle box story.

> Suppose everyone had a box with something in it: we call it a "beetle." No one can look into anyone else's box, and everyone says he knows what a beetle is only by looking at his beetle. – Here it would be quite possible for everyone to have something quite different in his box. One might even imagine such a thing constantly changing. – But suppose the word "beetle" had a use in these people's language? – If so it would not be used as the name of a thing. The thing in the box has no place in the language-game at all; not even as a something: for the box might even be empty. – No, one can "divide through" by the thing in the box; it cancels, whatever it is.

The beetle box story can be used to show that the idea of mental state terms as naming inner states collapses. Instead, Montgomery argues on the basis of Wittgenstein's work that knowing the meaning of a word is related to knowing how to use it in particular situations, not what it refers to. Some scholars suggest that Wittgenstein was denying that we have inner mental processes. Olson (1988, p. 415) wrote that Wittgenstein "cast doubt on the idea that mental terms simply referred to what are now called psychologically real events." Wittgenstein (1968, para. 308) anticipated and blocked this interpretation when he wrote: "And now it looks as if we had denied mental processes. And naturally we don't want to deny them." Wittgenstein's goal was to eradicate a misconception that is embedded in our language. In Hacker's (1996, p. 132) words: "If one thinks of words as names one will be prone to think of psychological expressions as names of psychological objects, events, processes or states." Wittgenstein was not denying mental processes but rather a particular way of thinking that our language leads us into. It is this way of thinking that misleads, or "bewitches," us (Chapman, 1987; Montgomery, 1997, 2002, 2004, 2005; Williams, 1999. See Sokol and Lalonde [2004] for a similar point from John Dewey).

Mark Bickhard (2001, 2004) has added to the Wittgensteinian argument that learning the meaning of mental verbs cannot be learning an association between a name and a referent. What Bickhard draws from this issue is the problem that when one begins to think of all the beliefs one could be said to have, the number is simply unbounded and could not be learned in a reasonable time. Bickhard's example is that it could be said that most of us believe that stepping in front of an oncoming truck is bad for our health but we also believe the same thing about striped trucks or polka dotted trucks, and this list could go on and on. The point is that there can be no simple individuated matter of fact for belief talk to be about.

Thus learning to talk about belief cannot be a naming game. From a Wittgensteinian perspective, by contrast, the problem of learning the meaning of mental state verbs is turned upside down. Children's hunger, pain, tiredness, or reactions of joy, interest, and their goals are obvious to adults. Adults talk about the situation and the child learns new behavior – i.e., talk – that is grafted onto to the prelinguistic actions and reactions (Hacker, 1997). The child does not learn the meaning of words referring to inner experience through introspection (as shown in Wittgenstein's private language argument), but rather through learning what has been termed the *public criteria* for the use of such words. The circumstances surrounding the use of psychological words become the criteria for their use (Malcolm, 1991; Canfield, 1993, 1995). All psychological terms "either redescribe or else presuppose, *ways of acting*. It is these ways of acting that provide the foundation for the psychological concepts" (Malcolm, 1991, p. 46, emphasis in original). It is these more primitive ways of acting that psychological terms are grafted onto. For example, words such as "see" and "look" may be grafted onto earlier joint attention behaviors and used to direct attention (Racine & Carpendale, in press).

Words derive their meaning from the role they play in patterns of human action and interaction. This is a constructive process; children do not directly acquire concepts from the social world. Rather, they slowly learn the criteria for the correct use of mental state terms (Montgomery, 1997). The word "look" can also be used in other ways such as to convey intentions, as in the test question on the unexpected transfer task, when the child is asked where Maxi will look for his chocolate. If we link this discussion to the issues we raised in chapter 4, the criteria for linguistic terms can be seen to develop from earlier nonverbal interaction. For example, the pointing gesture can be used in several different language games – to direct others' attention, or to make a request. The ability to talk about the mental world – acquired interpersonally – then provides an intrapersonal resource for children to reflect on their experience and to reason about others' action (see Carpendale & Lewis, 2004a; Fernyhough, 1996; Lewis & Carpendale, 2002; Turnbull & Carpendale, 2001). This approach is based on a particular conception of language; that is, language viewed as activity (Budwig, 2000).

To begin with, once infants have developed an initial level of social understanding, manifest in forms of joint attention, they have developed the capacity to coordinate attention with others and thus to infer what others are talking about. This capacity is involved in beginning to learn language (e.g., Baldwin & Moses, 1994; Tomasello, 2003). Language then provides a context for further social cognitive development (Lohmann, Tomasello, & Meyer, 2005). Infants now start to use actions and words to talk about other things and activities. That is, infants indicate what they mean the adult to attend to and are also able to determine adults' referential intent. At this point, "words begin to mediate children's sensorimotor acquaintance with reality. Children no longer know reality solely in terms of what they could *do* with it, but also in terms of what they could potentially say (or hear) *about it*" (Chapman, 1999, p. 34, emphasis in original). Language then becomes a means through which social development is transformed.

Summary and Conclusions

In this chapter we have discussed work explicitly on language, or language viewed as linguistic competence, but if language is more broadly defined and viewed as social action then we find it popping up in several other chapters. Language has already made its appearance in chapter 4 on infancy. There we addressed the prerequisite form of interaction on which language is based. And some specific aspects of language in use, or pragmatics, such as irony and sarcasm will be discussed in chapter 9. Also in chapter 9 we return to consider the overlap between social understanding and competence in social interaction (i.e., language broadly defined).

It has been evident in this chapter that, as one might expect, how the relations between language and social understanding are understood depends a great deal on how each is conceptualized. There are two main ways of thinking about language. One aspect of the most common approach in psycholinguistics is to think of how children learn meanings as a problem of reference. That is, a matter of figuring out how words "map" onto the world. An alternative view of language is to consider the meanings of words as tied up with the purposes for which they are used. This has been referred to as the social pragmatic view of language (Tomasello, 2003; Turnbull, 2003), and it also has older roots (Bühler, 1934/1990) and connections to philosophical views regarding meaning as non-mechanistic (Wittgenstein, 1968).

By analyzing the existing research in the "theory of mind" literature, we have attempted to show that language is more complex than current formulations within that tradition suggest. It is important to think about what aspect of language is being considered. It seems that just about any way that researchers measure language (e.g., semantics, syntax, or a combination) it is related to children's performance on false belief tasks. To complicate matters further we should also keep in mind the possibility of bi-directional and transactional effects. That is, early forms of social understanding manifest themselves in forms of joint attention and may be required in order to participate in language. Then language provides a means that builds upon and transforms this earlier practical or lived understanding of others.

Another aspect to this issue is that even to ask the question of whether language and social understanding are related is based on the logically prior assumption that they are separable. Alternatively they may be intertwined and not so easy to separate clearly, that is, they may be different aspects of the same thing. In other words, it is necessary to step back even further in considering preconceived assumptions concerning what is meant by language, and to consider models of language or social interaction. We return to these questions in later chapters, particularly chapter 10.

Chapter 8

Beyond (False) Belief: What Do Preschoolers and Older Children Still Have to Learn about the Mind?

Recall the anecdote in chapter 1 in which a 4-year-old boy who wants to take a cookie asks his father to leave the kitchen so that his father will not know about the pilfered cookie. This shows that young children may understand that false beliefs are possible but may still not grasp many of the resulting implications such as, in this case, suspicion. Understanding how suspicion might arise involves thinking about what other people might think. The occasion of buying presents provides another example of the need to think about others' thoughts and desires. Does the purchaser buy what he or she really wants or think about what the other person might want? This example makes it clear that some people are better at this than others even in adulthood, but research has focused on the basic abilities that develop in childhood.

Consider another anecdote involving choosing a birthday present: When Max's friend, Jacob, invited Max and several other friends to his birthday party, Jacob told them all what he wanted as a birthday present. When going out to buy a present for Jacob, Max and his sister, Hannah, started talking and Max said that Jacob had told everyone the same thing (i.e., what present he wanted), so they started thinking that everyone might buy him the same present. They then thought that maybe everyone would realize this, and so no one would get him the present he asked for. In fact, at the party it turned out that no one gave him that particular present. However, if younger children had been involved perhaps everyone would have brought the same present, assuming that their parents did not intervene. This example involves children's ability to think about thinking, or engage in "recursive thinking" – which we define and discuss below.

Our reason for presenting these examples is that researchers in the "theories of mind" tradition initially focused only on young children's understanding that beliefs can be mistaken – making it appear that they felt able to do without research participants older than 4 (Chandler & Carpendale, 1998). This was not true of the earlier literature on perspective taking, which explored transitions in social understanding through adolescence (e.g., Selman, 1980). However, there is now more interest in what it is that 5-year-olds still have to learn about the mind (Flavell et al., 1995). The point is that just because children understand false beliefs this does not necessary mean that they will see the many interconnections between the possibility of mistaken beliefs and other aspects of their young social lives or be able to make use of this insight to draw inferences.

In this chapter we review some of the developments in children's social understanding that occur after they have mastered the false belief task. It divides into two main sections. In the first we reexamine the consequence of the concentration of attention upon false belief as a key cognitive transition. This focus may have been due to the assumption that other achievements are less important or to the tendency to explore later skills only in relation to the ability to represent beliefs that are discrepant with reality. We analyze this idea in three ways. We start by setting recent discussion into a historical context that has been conveniently forgotten by contemporary accounts of "theory of mind." Then we consider whether children who understand false belief can also grasp the implications of belief understanding for making inferences and for thinking about other people's thinking. The second section considers the possibility that there may be other important transitions in understanding knowledge beyond false belief understanding. It explores the point that social understanding is often about issues over which people interpret the same event in different ways. Understanding the development of children's ability to grasp such differing perspectives leads us to explore issues that draw from the history of developmental psychology that we start with. In particular, in this chapter we discuss the development of the capacity to draw inferences, children's understanding of thinking about thinking, and we focus on the development of children's early understanding of the interpretive nature of knowledge. In a short, final section, we consider developments in understanding the nature of knowledge beyond childhood.

Is There Developmental Life after False Belief Understanding?

In earlier chapters we explored the possibility that young children may have some early understanding of false belief before being able to pass the standard task, as suggested by naturalistic observation (e.g., Newton et al., 2000). As we state above, in this chapter we consider developments that may occur after children have mastered the false belief task. If we think about the difference between 4-year-olds and adults it seems fairly clear that preschoolers have a long way to go to reach maturity in social competence. But one question is whether this just involves getting better at using the same concept, i.e., metarepresentation, or whether children develop different concepts.

Social understanding: a brief history of social developmental psychology

One reason for the focus on false belief understanding is the assumption that it is a major transition point after which children have acquired a "theory of mind" that is essentially equivalent to an adult's understanding of mind, although obviously they must get better at using it. That is, children have acquired a representational theory of mind (see chapter 2). Chandler (1988) has referred to this position as a "one miracle" approach to children's epistemic development, involving only one major watershed at the age of 4. In contrast, Chandler argues that some understanding of false beliefs emerges earlier, but this is not equivalent to an understanding of the interpretive nature of knowledge, which is an insight that occurs later than 4. In Chandler and Hala's (1994, p. 403) words:

> Flooding the market of current claims concerning children's earliest theories of mind is a cluster of aggressively promoted, and still widely subscribed "one miracle" views – a stern and withholding family of heavily inbred accounts, according to which the years both before and after four are largely dismissed as wastrel years; slack times seen to make no real substantive contributions to the supposedly singular, stand-alone insight that minds, by their very nature, are representational. . . . In the place of all such scant and increasingly outmoded one-miracle views, this chapter aims at substituting an alternative and, we hope, less withholding vision that sees children's progress toward a mature conception of mind as altogether more spread out, as starting sooner, as going on longer, and

as marked by more in the way of qualitative transformations than has been widely supposed.

More recently, researchers in the "theory of mind" tradition have turned attention to infancy and later developments such as second-order false belief. At this point some historical reflection is needed as an antidote to the tendency to reduce development to one major transition point. Here we discuss a methodological and conceptual lesson from the history of research on social development to remind readers that it is important to think in terms of a progression of forms of knowledge in development. As mentioned in chapter 1, the work on social development that preceded the current "theories of mind" enterprise was referred to as perspective taking or role taking. This literature from the 1970s was largely inspired by Piaget and Inhelder's (1948/1967) research on the development of visual perspective taking. Piaget and Inhelder used a task, now known as the "three mountains task," in which children from 4 to 12 years of age were presented with a model of three mountains and were asked a series of questions about the visual perspectives of other people who viewed the scene from different sides. For example, in various conditions the child had to select the view held by a doll placed opposite to or at 90° from the child. The child chose from a group of ten pictures of the mountains from different perspectives. These pictures included the child's own view and the correct perspective of the doll, plus other pictures depicting different views of the array. Piaget and Inhelder described a series of stages in the development of visual perspective taking. The younger children tended to choose their own view, suggesting that they have difficulty in understanding that others see the world from different perspectives. Even when children understood that others' perspectives do differ in some way from one's own, it was not until they were about 9 years old that they had mastered the task of transforming the internal relations among the three mountains in order to reliably select the picture of the other's viewpoint, thus signaling an ability to "decenter" from their own perspective.

Piaget and Inhelder's research served as a springboard, inspiring researchers to transplant notions of perspective taking from visual perspective taking to social perspective taking (Chandler & Boyes, 1982). The key research question concerned when can children take the perspective of others? The idea was that children's increasing ability to take the perspectives of other people could be explained by a decline in egocentrism. One of the lines of research was to modify tasks to see if younger children could pass them. For example, Borke (1971) presented child participants with stories such as a child story character who has lost a coin down a hole and asked them how this unfortunate child in the story would feel. Even preschoolers were competent in knowing that the story character would feel sad. Thus it seems that 3-year-olds can take the story character's perspective in such situations.

Does this mean that 3-year-olds can take another's perspective in all situations? Chandler and Greenspan (1972) demonstrated that it might be too hasty to jump to this conclusion. In the bystander task employed by Chandler and Greenspan (1972) the simple story line used by Borke was presented first and then the plot thickens because the young boy's friend arrives after the coin has been lost down the hole. This late-arriving bystander sees his friend sitting forlornly on the curb but knows nothing about the preceding event. The child participant hearing this story is then asked why the friend thinks the boy is sad. On this task even the majority of the 6-year-olds made the egocentric error of attributing their own knowledge to the uninformed bystander. In order to answer this question correctly the child must take the bystander's perspective – the perspective of someone whose thoughts and feelings are different from their own. Therefore they had to set aside their own knowledge in order to be able to answer the questions correctly. By the age of 13 almost all the children could do this. This is a more complex form of perspective taking than that assessed by Borke. She examined some early and simple forms of perspective taking, but not the more sophisticated skill required to understand others' perspective on the world.

There are two lessons to draw from these studies. First, researchers should carefully analyze what it is that particular tests assess and not just modify tests with the goal of getting younger children to pass them. Instead, researchers should think about how children pass the tests; that is, what form of reasoning is being used. Some researchers have succeeded so well in simplifying tasks that they "ended up measuring something else entirely" (Chandler, 2001, p. 46). A second and related point is that we should think about gradual development (a central focus of chapter 10). That is, there are different forms of social understanding or role taking – not just one miraculous transition. We now apply these points to the development of children's understanding of the process of knowledge acquisition – how it is that we come to know things about the world.

Understanding inference as a source of knowledge

Understanding false beliefs involves realizing not only that knowledge can be acquired through direct experience, but also that much can be learned through inference. For example, if it is known that a child has taken something from a bag that contains only blue balls it can be inferred that the child is now the proud owner of a blue ball. Drawing such a conclusion is not, however, an automatic result of achieving an understanding that false beliefs are possible. Young children's understanding of how knowledge can be derived from inference seems to involve a further step in understanding the nature of knowledge acquisition. When do children understand that inference is a source of knowledge in addition to direct perception?

Some of the early research on inference was conducted by Sodian and Wimmer (1987) using tasks from which the example of inferring the color of the ball above is taken. Although many of the 4- to 6-year-old children in this study could correctly draw the conclusion about the color of the removed ball, they were less accurate in realizing that others could also use inferences. Thus this research suggested that children do not recognize the role of inference in acquiring knowledge until they are about 6 years old. Keenan, Ruffman, and Olson (1994) attempted to simplify these tasks by making the information very salient for the children. They concluded that "a fledging understanding of inference as a source of knowledge begins to develop sometime around 4 years of age." But they go on to note that although "a substantial number of 4-year-olds do show an understanding that another person could know a fact by logical inference, this understanding is far from perfect and lags behind false-belief understanding" (p. 349).

Young children understand that if someone has looked in a box they will know what is in it. However, imagine now that there are two boxes, one with a red pen and the other containing a green pen, and you or a friend are allowed to peek into one of these. Adults would understand that if they look in only one box it is straightforward to infer the contents of the remaining box, but not to make the same inference if someone else looks – to admit one's ignorance. However, performance in 4–5-year-old children was far more patchy (Varouxaki, Freeman, Peters, & Lewis, 1999). About one-quarter of this age group passed with flying colors over a succession of trials both when asked to infer another's ignorance on the basis of their own knowledge and their own ignorance on the basis of the other's knowledge. The rest appeared to be unable to apply their knowledge of perceptual access and knowledge. Two-thirds treated the other's mind as similar to their own mind, attributing knowledge to the other child only if they had seen into their box. Furthermore, one-quarter of the children both incorrectly attributed knowledge to the other when they had looked into their own box and to themselves when the other looked. Such patterns show that applying a "seeing = knowing" rule is complex, as it depends upon who does the seeing. Children have to learn to integrate their own and another's knowledge into a framework in which one's own and the other's perspectives are understood to be related to one another.

Pillow (2002) has further explored this topic by studying children's understanding of the relative certainty of inferences versus guesses. He found that 4- to 6-year-old children did not view deductive inferences as more certain than mere guesses. But by the age of 8 to 9 years children were aware that claims based on inference are more certain than guesses. The conclusion to be drawn from the research on inference is that there is much to be learned about how we judge others' actions and knowledge that does not immediately follow from understanding false beliefs. We turn now to analyze whether such complementary skills are simply built onto false belief understanding.

The case of referential opacity: is second-order false belief the key to understanding inference?

As well as inference there is a further understanding of the implications of beliefs that young children still have difficulty with. For example, in a task used by Russell (1987), a story character's watch is stolen while he is asleep by a man with curly red hair. Children understand that when the character wakes up it can be said that he may be thinking he must find the person who stole his watch. However, young children who have passed false belief tasks still have difficulty realizing that it *cannot* be said that the character would be thinking he must find the man with curly red hair who stole his watch. This issue is referred to as children's handling of "referential opacity" (Apperly & Robinson, 1998, 2001; Robinson & Apperly, 2001) – that is, knowledge that is unavailable to others because they do not have access to it. This is an aspect of children's understanding of belief that children seem to find more difficult than false belief understanding. When we add such a problem to the data on inference reported in the previous section, this suggests that children do not acquire an understanding of belief at some point that immediately generalizes to all aspects of belief. The traditional way of explaining these new developments is that there are additional aspects to the notion of belief that are gradually acquired after false belief understanding. These rely upon the notion of recursion.

Recursive thinking is the form of thinking exemplified in the example at the beginning of the chapter about buying a birthday present. It is the ability to look at a problem from at least two perspectives. This is thinking about what someone else is thinking, so false belief is an example. However, there are more complex types of recursion than false belief understanding and these form important aspects of human thought about social matters. Let us consider the form of thinking required in the game "rock, paper, scissors." Winning this game depends, in skilled players, on attempting to guess one's opponent's strategy – a game that some adults apparently find engrossing enough to have a world championship! This form of thinking can get very complex. The player has to predict the other's next move on the basis of both partici-pants' recent moves. The fact that some people seem to excel at this game suggests that thinking about another person's thoughts about the possible action to take can be highly predictive and involves your thoughts about what the other thinks you are thinking about what you and they are going to do. In more complex games like chess, good players think several possible moves ahead by both players. Indeed, most of us think about such possibilities in everyday activities on a daily basis. Hannah and Max's deliberations about the birthday present are by no means unique in older children. Indeed teenagers spend many hours on the telephone attempting to solve such problems. We would not consider someone to have achieved an adult understanding of other people it they did not understand the recursive nature of thought.

Children's understanding of recursive thinking has been studied by Flavell and his colleagues (1968). In one of the experimental tasks the participants played a game of strategy that allowed for sophisticated cognition about thoughts – children had to think about what another person would think. The game involved two cups placed upside down on a table. One cup had a nickel stuck on it and the other cup had two nickels stuck on it. The participants were told that this was meant to indicate how many nickels were under the cup. They were then told that another person would shortly enter the room, choose one of the two cups, and get to keep any money that might be hidden under it. The experimenter explained that the task was to fool the other person by guessing which one he would choose and taking the money from under that cup. The participants were also told that the other person knew that the goal was to fool him. (This research was done in 1968 when a nickel was still worth something.) The key outcome of interest was which cup the child took the money from and their reasons for choosing that cup. The participants were from 7 to 17 years of age and many of the 7- to 10-year-olds assumed that the other person would just choose the cup with the two nickels. From 11 years, the children started using strategies involving thinking about the other person's thoughts (e.g., "he's gonna know we're gonna fool him – or try to fool him – and so he might think that we're gonna take the most money out so I took the small one (the one nickel cup)" (Flavell et al., 1968, p. 47)).

The notion of recursive thinking, or thinking about others' beliefs, has also been explored from the perspective of the theories of mind tradition. Perner and Wimmer (1985) designed a "second-order" false belief task based on extending the first-order false belief task. This task involves a story about John and Mary and an ice-cream van. Both John and Mary see an ice-cream van at the park where they are playing. Mary goes home to get money to buy some ice cream. But on his way home John discovers that the ice-cream van has moved to the church. He does not know, however, that Mary has, independently, also been told that the van has moved to the church. John is then told that Mary has gone to buy ice cream and the child participants were asked where John would think that Mary has gone. Many of the 6- to 7-year-olds passed by saying that John would look for Mary at the park. But the younger children failed by thinking that John would assume that Mary had gone to the church. This suggests that there may be a two-year lag between false belief understanding on a typical first-order belief task and second-order belief understanding involving beliefs about some one else's beliefs.

More recently, however, Sullivan, Zaitchik, and Tager-Flusberg (1994) simplified the second-order task. They were concerned that information processing demands might be making the tasks more difficult than necessary. They questioned whether a conceptual advance is involved or if what is required for passing the tests is just more complex information processing. If the difficulty was information processing then reducing the demands on the second-order task should enable younger children to pass. They approached the issue of reducing the information processing demands in several ways: by shortening Perner and Wimmer's (1985) standard stories, having them presented by an experimenter rather than a tape recorder, adding a memory aid, and, to make sure that the child was actively processing the stories, additional probe questions were added. Furthermore, they added new stories that were shorter and simpler, involving fewer characters and locations and also deception. For example, in one of these stories "a mother deliberately misinforms her son about what he will receive for his birthday, because she wants to surprise him. Unbeknownst to his mother, the child actually discovers the true birthday present. Later, when speaking to the child's grandmother, the mother is asked whether the child knows what he is getting for his birthday . . . and then what the child thinks he is getting" (Sullivan et al., 1994, p. 397).

Sullivan et al. (1994) found that even with conservative criteria for passing, over 90 percent of the $5^{1}/_{2}$-year-old children passed these second-order false belief tasks and that even 40 percent of the 4-year-old preschoolers passed the tasks. The children's performance was good on the new stories and also was improved on the simplified standard stories from Perner and Wimmer (1985). The finding that some preschoolers can reason about second-order beliefs supports Sullivan et al.'s position that such reasoning does not involve further conceptual development but rather the recursive application of the same insight. However, second-order tasks, even simple ones, are still more complex than standard false belief tasks and, therefore, there should still be some lag in when children can pass them if social understanding were reducible to the skill assessed in the false belief task. If recursive thinking does not involve a qualitative change in children's thinking about the mind, are there other developments that do amount to a qualitative change? We explore this possibility in the next section.

Social Understanding Goes to the Movies: False Belief vs. Interpretation

To illustrate that our understanding of knowledge is tied up with our understanding of everyday social situations, consider the following situation. Imagine that two people watch the same movie but at a critical moment in the film one of them goes out of the theater to buy popcorn. This situation is similar to the false belief task where one individual lacks key information. A child with a false belief understanding will be able to appreciate that these two people may reach different conclusions and will have different beliefs regarding the movie because one of them lacks some important information due to being out of the room at a critical moment. But social understanding is more complex. Adults know that if both people watch the entire movie they may still arrive at different conclusions. To explain a case in which two people differently interpret the very same object or event, false belief understanding alone would not be adequate. Instead this requires an "interpretive" understanding of mind (Carpendale & Chandler, 1996; Chandler

& Carpendale, 1998). That is, a mature adult understanding of mind must also include a commonsense understanding that knowledge is interpretive and that the mind itself influences how the world is experienced. An interpretive or constructive understanding of the knowing process involves the insight that there is a two-way street between the mind and the world, and the mind influences how the world is experienced.

Before understanding the interpretive or constructive nature of knowledge children seem to understand knowledge as simply objectively given in the world. Chandler and Boyes (1982, p. 391) describe this "copy theory" which is based on the assumption that knowledge is simply a copy of reality. It holds that knowledge has its "origins in the thing known and not in the persons who know them." Furthermore, "such children seem to proceed as though they believe objects to transmit, in a direct-line-of-sight fashion, faint copies of themselves, which actively assault and impress themselves upon anyone who happens in the path of such 'objective' knowledge." According to such a copy theory, "becoming knowledgeable is the direct result of passive visitation and is taken as the epistemological equivalent of having been mugged by the facts" (Chandler, 1988, pp. 407–408). The shift from this way of understanding knowledge to some insight into interpretation involves an understanding of the source of knowledge as shifting "from *objects* to *subjects*, and knowing begins to be recognized as a constructive, meaning-generating, human activity" (Chandler & Boyes, 1982, p. 395).

Competing views on the nature of interpretation

The question, therefore, is when do children begin to develop some early understanding of the interpretive nature of knowledge? There are competing claims about when children first begin to understand interpretation. According to Meltzoff and Gopnik (1993, p. 335), "by five years old, children seem to know that people have internal mental states such as beliefs, desires, intentions, and emotions. Moreover, they understand that a person's beliefs about the world are not just recordings of objects and events stamped upon the mind, but are active interpretations or construals of them from a given perspective." Similarly, Wellman (1990, p. 244) claimed that at about this age children have "an interpretational or constructive understanding of representations." Perner (1991, p. 275, emphasis in original) also argued that "around 4 years children begin to understand knowledge as representation, with all its essential characteristics. One such characteristic is *interpretation*." Perner and Davies (1991, p. 65, emphasis original) do go on to acknowledge that this is "nascent *interpretive theory* of mind."

These researchers have assumed that passing a false belief test reveals an interpretive understanding of knowledge, because it demonstrates an understanding that the same situation can be represented in different ways by Maxi and the child participant. That is, Maxi believes that the chocolate is in one cupboard whereas the preschooler knows the chocolate is in another cupboard – they represent the same situation in different ways. But the story has been set up to ensure that Maxi and the child have access to different information and so experience different situations. Maxi is out of the room and so ignorant about the fact, known to the child watching the show, that the location of his candy has been changed. Thus, this task assesses the understanding that different information will lead to different beliefs, but not the more complex insight that even after experiencing the same event people may still come away with differing interpretations (Carpendale & Chandler, 1996).

One issue in this debate is that there are different definitions of the word "interpretation." Most dictionaries list two general meanings. The first concerns clarifying something that is obscure. For example, if the question is "Can you interpret an aerial photograph?" then this means "Is there enough information available to make out what it really is?" On the other hand, the second definition of interpretation is to construe something in a particular way, as in an interpretation of *Hamlet*. This second definition implies that the task is not simply determining what it, in fact, really is. Instead, multiple interpretations can legitimately be arrived at. It is this second and more complex view of interpretation that has been studied by a number of researchers (Carpendale & Chandler, 1996). If false belief tests do not assess all aspects of interpretation then some independent procedure was needed to measure the concept.

Understanding biased interpretation

One line of research in moving from false belief understanding to interpretation is Bradford Pillow's (1991) work on young children's understanding of the role of preexisting biases in people's interpretation of ambiguous events. In one study children were presented with stories involving an ambiguous event that was observed by two characters who differed in their biases or knowledge of the actor's intentions. For example, in one of the stories a character, Joan, is seen holding a doll in front of a donation box containing toys for poor children. This is observed by Cathy, who likes Joan, and also by Sarah, who does not like Joan. The children were asked about how Cathy and Sarah might interpret this ambiguous situation. That is, would they understand that because of Cathy's preexisting biases she would likely think that Joan was helpfully donating a doll for the poor children? But, in contrast, because Sarah does not like Joan and believes that Joan is a trouble-maker, Sarah would instead probably think that Joan was stealing a doll from the toys destined for the poor children's Christmas. The results depended somewhat on the questions asked and the complexity of the stories presented, but generally this ability to recognize the influences of previous biases on how people will understand ambiguous events develops between 5 and 8 years of age. Pillow (1991) found than even the 5- to 6-year-old children in kindergarten showed some understanding that prior beliefs and expectations can influence interpretations of ambiguous events, but 7–8-year-olds could adequately explain their answers.

These situations of biased interpretation are likely to be important in children's social lives, and this is a step beyond false belief understanding. However, it deals with only an aspect of interpretation. That is, it deals with how individuals might arrive at the particular interpretations that they espouse, through considering individuals' past experience. However, it is also important to consider a second issue concerning interpretation and that is when children understand that interpretation is possible at all. In other words, one question concerns whether interpretation is possible; that is, is it reasonable to have more than one legitimate interpretation, or must one of them be wrong? Then, if so, a second question is how do individuals, based on their past histories, arrive at the particular interpretations they propose? It is children's beginning understanding of this second question that Pillow has addressed in his research program (see also Pillow & Mash, 1999). It is the first question that we turn to now.

Methods for studying interpretation: visual ambiguity

We now move on to consider studies that more directly examine young children's understanding that different people may encounter the very same event yet go away from it with sharply differing interpretations, regardless of their particular likes, dislikes, or biases. To do so requires a consideration of methodology. Two general approaches have been taken. One is to employ truly ambiguous stimuli such as Rorschach inkblots and ask children how these might be interpreted by different individuals. Such stimuli are so without definite form that it would

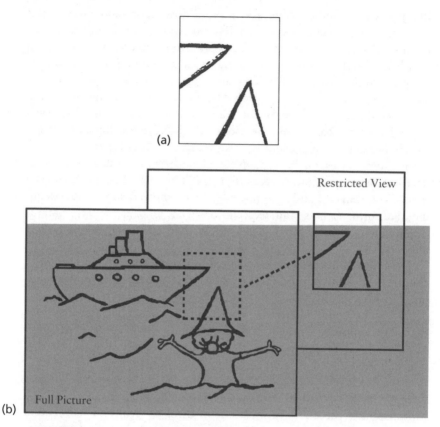

Figure 8.1 (a) Droodle labeled "A ship arriving too late to save a drowning witch"; (b) the Ship–Witch droodle. *Source*: Lalonde & Chandler (2002). Reprinted from *New Ideas in Psychology*, vol. 20, L. E. Lalonde, M. J. Chandler, Children's understanding of interpretation, pp. 163–198, © 2002, with permission from Elsevier

be extremely unlikely that two individuals would arrive at the same interpretation. In taking this approach, the stimuli selected by Lalonde and Chandler (2002; Chandler & Lalonde, 1996; also used by Chandler & Helm, 1984) are based on pictures called "droodles" popularized by Roger Price. Droodles are small portions of larger drawings that are intentionally restricted in order to leave the keyhole view ambiguous regarding the nature of the full picture. One example from Lalonde and Chandler's research is of two triangles, one protruding from the left side edge and the second rising from the bottom, captioned by Roger Price as "a ship arriving too late to save a drowning witch" (Figure 8.1). When children have seen the larger drawing this procedure also provides a test of false belief understanding because the restricted keyhole view does not provide sufficient information to be able to guess the contents of the full picture. That is, having just seen the two triangles no one could guess that it actually is "a ship arriving too late to save a drowning witch." The children are asked what first one and then a second puppet character as naïve observers would think that the picture fragment was. If children claimed that the puppet would say a ship and a witch they failed the false belief portion of this task. However, most of the 5- to 8-year-old children in this series of studies had little trouble coming up with something other than a ship and witch that the observer would think and, thus, successfully passing the false belief question. The 5- to 6-year-old children, however, had much more difficulty in coming up with another interpretation for a second naïve observer of the picture fragment that differed from the first observer's interpretation. This reveals a lack of understanding that given ambiguous stimuli it is extremely unlikely that two independent naïve observers will interpret it in the same way. The 7- to 8-year-olds, in contrast, demonstrated an understanding of interpretation by providing differing interpretations from the two observers.

It should be noted that this same methodology, as any other procedure, can be employed with different questions asked of the children to produce sharply differing results. Perner and Davies (1991), in an attempt at replication of the Chandler and Helm (1984) droodle procedure, presented children with droodles but asked them if the doll used would know what the small circle in the picture fragment was (i.e., "does Peter know that this (points to circle) is the sun?" p. 60). This question simply requires a yes or no response and thus changes the nature of the understanding of interpretation that is being assessed. This fits with the first meaning of interpretation described above; that is, is there enough information available to make out what this really is, or, in other words, is this interpretable? Perner and Davies (1991, p. 51) report that children as young as 4 years of age have an understanding of "the mind as an active information processor" in the sense that these children "understand that incoming verbal information is evaluated in view of previous experience" (p. 64). Similarly, research on children's understanding of ambiguity (Ruffman, Olson, & Astington, 1991; Sodian, 1990) has been viewed as a demonstration that false belief understanding allows children to understand interpretation. This research concerns children's understanding of whether or not sufficient information is available to disambiguate the identity of an object. It could be argued that this involves interpretation in the first sense described above; however, this is not the same meaning of interpretation that has been investigated by other researchers. The droodle procedure was used by Lalonde and Chandler (2002) and Chandler and Helm (1984) to assess children's understanding of interpretation in the second and more complex sense; that is, given an ambiguous stimulus, do children understand that there are many different ways it could legitimately be construed?

Methods for Studying Interpretation: Humor, Message Ambiguity and Perspective

We now move on to a second methodology used to assess young children's understanding of interpretation, which makes use of a special class of ambiguous stimuli that afford evidence of two equally likely interpretations. Children can then be presented with these two contrasting interpretations and asked to make sense of this situation. Furthermore, children can be asked about the likely interpretation of an additional individual (Carpendale & Chandler, 1996).

There is converging evidence from research on ambiguity and from other areas of research such as humor and referential communication that it is not until about 7 or 8 years of age that children begin to appreciate the possibility of multiple meanings. This is about the age at which children start to get jokes based on one word having multiple meanings. In the study of humor, McGhee (1979) has described a series of stages in the development of children's sense of humor. It is at McGhee's fourth stage that children's humor begins to resemble the humor of adults, much of which is based on ambiguity in meanings. According to McGhee, children reach this fourth stage at about 7 or 8 years of age, because it is at this time that they first begin to appreciate multiple meanings. Puns are a classic example of humor that is based on a key word having more than one meaning. Consider, for example, the following classic joke: "Hey, did you take a bath?" "No. Why, is one missing?" (McGhee, 1979, p. 76). Similarly, the following jokes turn on an appreciation of lexical ambiguity:

Question: What has 4 wheels and flies?
Answer: A garbage truck.
Question: What has 18 legs and catches flies?
Answer: A baseball team.

These are the sort of jokes that preschoolers don't get but children in their early school years do understand. Understanding riddles like these requires that the children cope simultaneously with two or more meanings for a single word. Although preschoolers do understand both meanings of the words, they just cannot put it together to appreciate the humor. Shultz's research on the development of changes in the appreciation of riddles (Shultz, 1974) and the ability to detect linguistic ambiguity (Shultz & Pilon, 1973) is generally supportive of McGhee's claims about humor. Because humor typically involves contrasting a normal situation with an alternative, incongruous situation it does not tend to offer equally compelling evidence for two alternative interpretations, and thus, may not be the most appropriate situation to begin assessing young children's early understanding of interpretation. However, examples can be drawn from this literature on linguistic ambiguity in which a word or a message could be interpreted as having two possible meanings that are equally likely.

Research on children's understanding of referential communication offers a further example of an area that involves children's understanding of ambiguity. It has been shown in a number of studies that young children of 5 to 6 years of age often fail to recognize that ambiguous messages do not give enough information to correctly identify the referent. Much of this research has employed variations of referential communication tasks in which children are given directions for making a block building, selecting an item from an array, or finding a hidden object. In a typical referential communication task a speaker must describe a referent object such as a doll and the task of the listener is to correctly select the referent from among a group of other dolls. If the message is ambiguous (e.g., "choose the doll with the hat" when more than one doll has a hat on) then two or more objects may fit the speaker's description equally well. Of course, older children notice this ambiguity and either ask for further description or else blame the speaker's inadequate message for the failure to choose the correct object. However, children younger than 5 or 6 years old seem relatively unaware of the inadequacies of ambiguous messages and they tend to blame the listener rather than the speaker if a mistake is made because of an ambiguous message. However, those children that judge an ambiguous message to be adequate may still display some verbal or nonverbal signs of uncertainty (Flavell, Speer, Green, & August, 1981).

Even when children were made aware of the two possible interpretations of ambiguous referential communication, because they had to make these interpretations for puppets, they still tended to be confident that they themselves had made the correct interpretation (Robinson & Robinson, 1983). These results from research on children's understanding of communication are generally consistent with the view that it is not until 7 or 8 years that children acquire the understanding that the same message can have two meanings. Young children overlook problems with messages and assume that if the message is received the listener should possess the speaker's knowledge. It is not until they are about 7 or 8 years old that children seem consciously to recognize ambiguity in messages – i.e., messages can have more than one interpretation. This insight involves recognizing that knowledge is not simply the result of a direct transmission of information from one's environment. Instead, since messages can have more than one meaning, the person must have some role in interpreting or deciding on that meaning. This insight involves a shift in one's understanding of the source of knowledge from the environment to a recognition of the complementary role of the mind in the acquisition of knowledge.

These lines of research can be used to draw stimulus events that afford two different interpretations that are equally likely (Carpendale & Chandler, 1996). Children's early understanding of interpretation can be assessed with situations in which two people interpret the very same stimulus event in different ways. Problems were drawn by Carpendale and Chandler (1996) from three areas: ambiguous figures; lexical ambiguity; and ambiguous referential communication. All these areas seem to involve an underlying conception of the interpretive nature of knowledge.

To use pictorial ambiguity as an example, two puppets were made to offer different interpretations of the same ambiguous stimulus, in this case, Jastrow's (1900) well-known "duck-rabbit" figure (Figure 8.2). One puppet said that an ambiguous figure was a rabbit while the other puppet insisted it was a duck. After making sure that the child could see both the duck and the rabbit the experimenter asked two types of question. First, the children were asked to explain the disagreement. Children passed the explanation questions simply by saying something like, "It looks like a duck and a rabbit." Children who failed the explanation questions did not seem to be able to accept the idea that one and the same thing could afford more than one legitimate interpretation. Even though they saw both the duck and the rabbit, they insisted that one of the puppets was right and the other one was wrong. The second type of question involved asking the child participants about their ability to predict how someone else would interpret the picture. Children passed this question by refusing to make a prediction and saying something like, "I don't know, because they could say it's a duck or a rabbit." This shows a recognition that given an ambiguous stimulus it is not possible to predict with certainty how someone else will interpret

Figure 8.2 Duck–rabbit. *Source*: From Jastrow (1900)

it. Children who did not understand this implication of ambiguity failed the question by making a firm prediction about what the puppet character would say.

Two examples of lexical ambiguity were also used by Carpendale and Chandler (1996) (i.e., the word "ring" and the word "pair/pear"). In addition, two examples of ambiguous messages were used. A sticker was hidden under one of three cards, each with a drawing of a block on it. There was one large blue block, one large red block, and one small red block. The puppets were told, for example, that the sticker was under the card with the "big block." The problem was that this message is ambiguous because there were two big blocks, and one puppet chose one and the other puppet chose the other big block (adapted from Sodian, 1990). Five to 8-year-old children participated in this research and the results clearly show that whereas the 5-year-old participants easily passed the false belief test, children generally do not develop competence with tests of interpretation until two to three years later. These results are consistent with the idea that the understanding that knowledge is interpretive in nature is not equivalent to the understanding of false beliefs. In other words, understanding interpretation is a more complex and significantly later-arriving understanding of knowledge and the mind than is implied by the insight that persons who are differently informed may hold different beliefs. The understanding of interpretation is also distinct from the apparently similar issue of differences in taste, which develops much earlier (Carpendale & Chandler, 1996).

This type of task requires that children articulate their understanding of interpretation and it might be thought that this would be too difficult for children at 5 years of age. However, Carpendale and Chandler (1996) matched the explanation questions on the false belief tasks and the interpretation tasks and even the 5-year-old children had no difficulty in explaining the source of false beliefs on the false belief task. The fact that these young children could provide lengthy explanations about the source of false beliefs but were not able to come up with the few words required to demonstrate an understanding of interpretation suggests a problem with understanding interpretation rather than a general difficulty with providing explanations (Carpendale & Chandler, 1996).

Beyond Interpretation? More Miracles?

An understanding that the mind plays a role in interpreting or construing experience means that children who have developed this insight have acquired a more active conception of mental life than that involved in false belief understanding (Sokol & Chandler, 2003). The fact that the 8-year-old participants in these studies had fairly competently mastered these simple problems of interpretation does not, however, imply that these children have a mature adult understanding of the complex issue of interpretation. Even though the 8-year-old children in these studies were competent at explaining differences in interpretation on these very simple tasks, they were still not equally competent at drawing the implication that it is difficult to predict how another person will interpret an ambiguous stimulus. The competence demonstrated in this research indicates only an initial insight into the interpretative nature of knowledge and the mind that continues to develop through adolescence and probably early adulthood as well.

Lalonde and Chandler (2002; Chandler, 2001) clarify that they are not proposing a "two-miracle" view in place of a one-miracle view. Eight-year-old children still do not have a complete understanding of interpretation – this is just a beginning. Instead, children's implicit or commonsense epistemology – i.e., their understanding of how knowledge can be acquired – continues to develop through childhood and beyond (Hallett, Chandler, & Krettenauer, 2002; Mansfield & Clinchy, 2002). A next step in epistemic development may be Chandler's (1988) distinction between case-specific or "retail" doubt, and generalized or "wholesale" doubt. When children first begin to understand that knowledge claims can be open to doubt, these early insights are restricted to specific cases. That is, such small-scale or "retail" doubts about the certainty of knowledge are safely constrained to particular issues. Gradually, however, children and adolescents begin to realize that more and more of what they had previously taken to be absolutely certain is, in fact, open to doubt and thus no longer certain. Their initial "case-specific" or "retail" insight now becomes a "wholesale" realization about the subjective and interpretive nature of knowledge in general.

Epistemic development continues through adolescence with the beginning of adolescent relativistic thinking (Chandler, 1987). This research concerns the question of how children and then adolescents and finally young adults grapple with the fact that people may differ in their beliefs. Perry (1970) did the pioneering work in this area of research on the development of an understanding of diversity of belief with longitudinal studies of college students going to Harvard in the 1950s and 1960s. His full theory includes nine steps in students' understanding of knowledge but the basic story line can be described as students beginning with the realist position that there is only one right answer – that is, their professor's views – and then moving to the relativistic position that it is all just a matter of opinion and anyone's opinion is as good as any other. Finally, students move on to the position that even in the face of uncertainty some views are better argued and grounded in evidence than others. Other researchers have extended this line of research to work with adolescents and have described these general transitions in epistemological thinking in slightly different ways, although preserving the general story plan (e.g., Boyes & Chandler, 1992; Chandler, 1987; Kuhn, 2000; Kuhn, Amsel, & O'Laughlin, 1988; Kuhn, Cheney, & Weinstock, 2000; King & Kitchener, 1994).

When the topics of the differing views are less complex than those dealt with by Perry's Harvard students, Mansfield and Clinchy (2002) found the same general pattern in a longitudinal study with children at age 10, 13, and 16. In addition, Mansfield and Clinchy varied the issues from questions of fact to matters of personal taste. Similarly, other

researchers have also explored the development of epistemic understanding within different domains of thought. Kuhn, Cheney, and
Weinstock (2000) explored the development of epistemological understanding within different domains of thought including personal taste,
aesthetic value, and truth. The general finding across these studies is
that children and adolescents first recognize the subjective nature of the
individual regarding matters of personal taste and only later concerning
more objective facts. Furthermore, Hallett, Chandler, and Krettenauer
(2002) argue that even within the domain of facts it seems that not all
facts are created equal. Actually, the point that facts are created at all
may be evident earlier in development for some types of facts before
others. Hallett, Chandler and Krettenauer (2002) describe a knowledge
continuum from more social constituted facts to more objective facts.
Their research participants found it easier to acknowledge the subjective
role of interpretation in the situations involving socially constituted or
"institutional" facts in contrast to more physical or "brute" facts.

Summary and Conclusion

We have reviewed the development of children's understanding of how
beliefs are acquired after false belief understanding. It appears that
passing a false belief task does not mean that children will immediately
understand all aspects of belief such as referential opacity and the implications for holding beliefs such as making inferences. Furthermore, things
can get still more complicated when children must deal with beliefs
about beliefs. However, this step to recursive thinking or second-order
false belief understanding may turn more on the complexity of integrating the many story elements in such a scenario than on further conceptual development. A next step in children's understanding of the process
of knowledge acquisition may be when they begin to understand interpretation. Such an interpretive understanding of the role of the mind in
making sense of experience is part of a mature adult understanding of
mind. There is some debate about just when this happens and some of
this controversy may turn, in part, on different means of interpretation.
In any case, there seems to be considerable development in children's
social understanding after achieving false belief understanding. In addition, such understanding of belief and mind should be interrelated with
other aspects of children's social development such as the understanding
of emotions that depend on beliefs. We turn to these topics in the next
chapter.

Chapter 9

Social Understanding and Children's Social Lives

We now turn to the "so what?" question. Of what relevance is social cognition for the rest of children's social lives? The development of social understanding has been the focus throughout this book, but one important reason for the great interest in this area of research is the common assumption that social understanding should be related to other important aspects of children's social lives. We assume that social understanding should matter in some real-world sense; there should be important connections between children's social understanding and the rest of their young social lives. In Dunn and Cutting's (1999, p. 201) words: "Children's capacities for empathy, for understanding how to comfort or to frustrate, for sharing imaginative worlds, for deceiving and teasing, and for negotiation and compromise in conflict are all linked to their growing understanding of the connections between what people want or believe and their behavior" (see also Dunn, 2004).

Although this research topic has yet to live up to its full potential, there are a number of interesting areas of research exploring such possible connections. We will discuss topics such as the relations between children's understanding of mind and emotions, social understanding and social skills, bullying and forms of aggression in relation to levels of social understanding, relations between competence in social interaction and social understanding, and, finally, we consider morality and social understanding. Some of these research topics are more developed than others and our coverage of potentially related topics is certainly not exhaustive. However, we hope to move in the direction of broadening the definition of social understanding and setting children's developing social understanding more firmly in the context of their complex social lives.

We should point out that in some ways this chapter is the inverse of chapter 6. That is, in chapter 6 we also reviewed studies on the relations between social understanding and aspects of children's social experience. But the emphasis in that research was on the potential for social interaction to act as a context facilitating the development of social understanding. In contrast, the current chapter reviews studies in which the underlying assumption is often that levels of social insight may influence children's social interaction. Clearly a sharp division here would be artificial. Some topics, such as pretense, may show up in both categories. Rather than assuming separate causal directions, we may find transactional and bidirectional effects. For example, children's developing understanding of the mind may result in increased competence in social interaction, which in turn may give children the kind of social experience that will be helpful in further social development. In the historical development of the "theories of mind" literature, one of the first connections with social development discussed was the case of children with autism. This disorder has been discussed throughout this book. As children with autism have severe problems in displaying and "reading" social skills it might be expected that children who are advanced in social understanding might be advanced in social competence. This is the issue we turn to in the first section. We consider whether an acute grasp of social relationships is necessarily a good thing – it might lead children into the sorts of coercive approach to interactions that are the hallmark of the bully. In the second section we compare an understanding of belief with a grasp of emotions, concluding that the relationship between these two aspects of social cognition is far more complex than meets the eye. This leads into the third section in which we briefly reflect upon the massive literature on children's understanding of moral principles. We discuss ways in which children's moral development is related to and may be intertwined with social understanding as we have explored it in the rest of this book. This conclusion leads into the final section in which we reflect upon the nature of communication itself. If in everyday interaction a speaker has to appreciate her or his listener's perspective on events, then this could be the seat of much social learning. This is an area of research ripe for further exploration.

Social Understanding and Social Competence: Social Skills and Peer Relations

Perhaps the most obvious potential connection between social understanding and other aspects of social development is with competence in social interaction. That is, it would be expectable that children who are advanced in social understanding might also be advanced in social skills. In considering how thinking about the social world may have evolved, one factor that comes to mind is the adaptive significance of such thinking for manipulating social situations to one's own advantage, and such thinking has been referred to as "Machiavellian intelligence" (Byrne & Whiten, 1988). This implies that social understanding might be used in the social manipulation of others in competitive situations. Levinson (1995, p. 227), however, has argued that cooperative interaction is even more complex than competitive social interaction. In any case, interacting with other people presents very complex problems. Thus it seems to follow that advanced social understanding would facilitate social interaction, raising the question: Is social understanding helpful in getting along with one's mates?

Preschoolers' social understanding and social skills

It seems logical to expect connections between social understanding and competence in social interaction and several studies have explored this possibility. Lalonde and Chandler (1995) found that 4-year-olds' performance on a series of false belief tests was positively correlated with some aspects of teachers' reports on the children's social activity but not others. In particular, false belief understanding was positively correlated with skills that seem to require some level of understanding others, such as the ability to play cooperatively with other children and to follow rules in simple games. In contrast, false belief understanding was negatively correlated with routine, formulaic social conventions, such as saying please and thank-you, that do not seem to require much in the way of social understanding. This general finding was replicated by Astington (2003) while controlling for age and language ability, although with some disagreement about which items on Lalonde and Chandler's teacher report measure involved following social conventions. Watson, Nixon, Wilson, and Capagne (1999) also reported positive correlations between young children's false belief understanding and their social interaction skills as rated by their teachers.

This link between social understanding and social skills has also been found in research with pairs of friends. Dunn and Cutting (1999) found that children who were relatively advanced in understanding beliefs and emotions also experienced low frequencies of conflict with a friend and increased cooperative pretend play. Astington and

Jenkins (1995) also found that children who were more advanced in false belief understanding were more likely to engage in two aspects of pretend play: making proposals about what they both should do within the pretend play and explicitly assigning a role to themselves or the other child.

Children's social competence can be thought of as having positive and negative dimensions. In a longitudinal study Astington (2003) formed a composite scale counting prosocial items on a teacher report as positive and items concerning aggressive, disruptive, or withdrawn behavior as negative. Children's teacher-reported social competence on this scale at the end of the second year of this study was predicted by the children's performance on false belief tasks when they were 4 to 5 years of age, independent of age and language ability. In a regression analysis age and language ability accounted for 10 percent of the variance, but beyond this, false belief understanding accounted for an additional unique 8 percent of the variance in the teacher ratings of social competence (Astington, 2003). Another factor that accounted for an additional 10 percent of the variance was children's spontaneous production of metacognitive terms (e.g., think, know, remember) in a story retelling task. A further question addressed by Astington (2003) concerns the longer-term effects of individual differences in false belief understanding. That is, since it is expected that all children do acquire false belief understanding at some point, does it make any difference in children's lives if they acquired it earlier than their age-mates? In fact, Astington (2003) found that, independent of age and language ability, early competence on false belief tasks did account for 9 percent of the variance in teacher ratings of social competence which was assessed 20 months later when all the children considered had completely mastered the false belief tasks. There are a number of possibilities raised by this finding. It could be that those children who were advanced in false belief tasks early on are also ahead of their age-mates in social understanding later on.

In related research, Foote and Holmes-Lonergan (2003) examined the relations between children's false belief understanding and their ways of dealing with conflict with a sibling. Three- to five-year-old children's interaction during conflict episodes was coded as no argument (e.g., "give it to me," or "I want that," self-oriented argument (e.g., "I need the blue block for my laser," or "I chose the horse first") and other-oriented argument (e.g., "I'll give you all these [building blocks] if you give me that one [a block with wheels on it]," or "She said we have to play together. Let's finish the building, then we'll play with that").

They found that using no arguments in conflicts was negatively associated with false belief understanding, whereas the use of other-oriented arguments was positively associated with false belief understanding, after controlling for age and general language ability.

Developments into the school years

It is expectable that the issue of the relations between social understanding and social competence would continue throughout development, but the nature of these two components likely changes as children grow up. Social competence has also been related to second-order false belief understanding – that is, an understanding of beliefs about beliefs. Baird and Astington (2004) reported significant correlations between second-order false belief understanding and teachers' rating of the children's prosocial behavior (e.g., "shares with others") and peer competence (e.g., "seeks other children to play with").

As discussed in chapter 8, an issue that begins to become important at around the age of 7 or 8 is an early understanding of ambiguity and interpretation. It would seem that this type of insight might be importantly related to children's social competence (Ross, Recchia, & Carpendale, 2005). Some of the conflicts that children experience with their siblings and peers may be due to differences in interpretations of ambiguous events or utterances. Ross et al. compared children's judgments on general interpretive tasks (Carpendale & Chandler, 1996, see chapter 8) with their understanding of sibling conflicts arising because of multiple yet legitimate interpretations. In a group of 4- to 9-year-olds there was an increase across this age range in these children's understanding of the role of interpretation in both of these tasks. It was particularly from about 7 to 8 years of age that interpretation made sense for these children. Children's judgments over which multiple interpretations were legitimate were correlated across the two tasks. However, the children's explanations for the conflicting interpretations were more sophisticated on the sibling conflict interpretation task than on the general interpretation task, perhaps because children tend to have more experience with such conflicts than with the ambiguous figures, words, and utterances used in the general interpretation task.

The relation between social understanding and social competence also seems to hold in preadolescence. At the age of 11 to 12 years, false belief understanding is far too simple. Instead Bosacki and Astington (1999) explored this issue by assessing preadolescents' social understanding with an interview about two ambiguous social events. For example, one of the stories presented to children was as follows:

> Nancy and Margie are watching the children in the playground. Without saying a word, Nancy nudges Margie and looks across the playground at the new girl swinging on the swingset. Then Nancy looks back at Margie and smiles. Margie nods, and the two of them start off towards the girl at the swingset. The new girl sees the strange girls walk toward her. She'd seen them nudging and smiling at each other. Although they are in her class, she has never spoken to them before. The new girl wonders what they could want. (p. 255)

Bosacki and Astington (1999) asked children a series of questions about this and another ambiguous story. They found that preadolescents' understanding of the possible interpretations and associated emotions involved in these ambiguous social situations was correlated with peers' ratings of these children's ability to deal with social situations. And what seemed especially important in this relationship was children's ability to understand others' emotions in the ambiguous situations. But, in contrast to other research, they found no links between social understanding and teachers' ratings of social skills. Along with the differences between studies in the way teachers' ratings are obtained, Bosacki and Astington (1999) also suggest that at this age peers may be more important in children's social lives than teachers. Social understanding was also linked to popularity, but not when children's performance on a vocabulary task was taken into account.

Social competence can be conceptualized in various ways, including popularity with peers. In investigating the relationship between peer popularity and social understanding, Slaughter, Dennis, and Pritchard (2002) found that for children older than 5 years of age popular children were advanced in their understanding of false beliefs and emotions compared to rejected children. In children younger than 5, popularity was linked with prosocial and non-aggressive behavior. This general finding held in a second study with just false belief tasks, but further analyses suggested that verbal ability played an important role in the relationship. These findings suggest that friendship in children over 5 is related to their ability to understand others' thoughts, and furthermore that language is closely involved in the connections between social understanding and social relations. Peterson and Siegal (2002) also reported that in 4- to 5-year-olds popular children were more advanced in false belief understanding than rejected peers but they did not report differences in the relation for children older and younger than 5. Furthermore, Peterson and Siegal (2002) found that rejected individuals who had a stable mutual friendship were more advanced that those rejected children who did not. The link with friendship was also evident for popular preschoolers; that is, having a friendship was associated with more advanced false belief understanding. This raises the issue of the causal direction in this finding. Is it that children who are advanced in social understanding are popular and other children want to be their friends, or is it that the experience of having friends and experiencing cooperative social interaction results in further social development? Further, popularity in a large peer group is not necessarily the same thing as having friends. Children who might not be classified as popular may still have one or more close friendships (Dunn, 2004; Rubin, Bukowski, & Parker, 1998). The role of social interaction in facilitating social development was discussed in chapter 6 but it is likely that there is a bidirectional influence.

Much of the research reviewed above has been based on the assumption that there would be a positive relationship between social understanding and social competence. However, when we introduced this section we raised the issue of Machiavellian intelligence and the potential use of social understanding to manipulate the beliefs of others. The possibility that the personality characteristic referred to as Machiavellianism (i.e., the view that other people can be manipulated to achieve one's personal goals) might be associated with superior levels of social understanding, or alternatively with the use of an understanding of others to achieve personal and manipulative ends, was explored by Repacholi, Slaughter, Pritchard, and Gibbs (2003). In a first study these researchers found no relation between teacher reports of Machiavellianism in 4- to 6-year-old children and false belief understanding. In a second study with 9- to 12-year-old children using a self-report measure of Machiavellianism they again found no significant differences in social understanding between the children who were high and low on this scale. There were, however, differences in how the children viewed the ambiguous social situations used to assess their level of social understanding. When asked about the actors' intentions and the likely outcome of the situations, high Machiavellian children were more likely to "report that the other person's behavior involved trickery, selfishness, or rejection" and more likely to "predict that these social situations would lead to negative outcomes (e.g., arguments, termination of the friendship)" (Repacholi et al., 2003, p. 90). There is currently no direct evidence that Machiavellianism is associated with higher levels of social understanding. However, these findings show that it may be linked to differences in the use of such understanding which are related to differences in values and concern for others or differences in ways of justifying acting in one's own interest.

In another strand of research, Hughes, Dunn, and White (1998) found that "hard-to-manage" 4-year-olds were slightly delayed on tasks assessing an understanding of false beliefs and emotions compared to typical preschoolers. There were also some differences in their pattern of development compared to typical children. Specifically, the hard-to-manage children showed better performance on "nasty" compared to "nice" surprises. This is opposite to the pattern found with typically developing children and it is some support for Happé and Frith's (1996) idea that some children might develop a "theory of nasty minds." However, Hughes et al. (1998, p. 992) note that "it is possible that the 'bias' in hard-to-manage preschoolers' understanding of intentions actually provides an accurate reflection of their social environments," that is, as characterized by hostility.

Aggression, bullying, and social understanding

Extending the idea of Machiavellianism it is possible to consider relations between social understanding and aggression and bullying. Bullying is, unfortunately, a very serious issue in children's lives. One view about bullies is that they are physically powerful yet lacking in social skills and they bully others because they lack an understanding of the harmful effect they cause. In contrast to this stereotype of a socially incompetent oaf, Sutton, Smith, and Swettenham (1999a, 1999b, p. 435) argued instead that "the bully may be a cold, manipulative expert in social situations, organizing gangs and using subtle, indirect methods." These researchers explored this possibility that bullies may be skilled manipulators. In a large group of 7- to 10-year-olds Sutton et al. found positive correlations between children's tendency to bully and their social cognition score. In contrast, they found a negative correlation between social cognition and the tendency to be a victim of bullying.

Bullying, however, is one particular type of aggression. It is generally considered to be proactive or "cold-blooded" aggression. Proactive aggression is planned and instrumental, controlled and motivated by external rewards; "proactive-aggressive children are likely to view aggression as an effective and viable means for obtaining social goals" (Crick & Dodge, 1996, p. 998). In contrast, reactive or "hot-headed"

aggression is impulsive in nature (Crick & Dodge, 1996, 1999). React-
ively aggressive children are more likely to interpret an ambiguous
event such as getting hit on the back of the head as being a hostile act
rather than an accident. There is some evidence that only reactive and
not proactive aggression is associated with lower social understanding
(Jones & Carpendale, 2002).

This debate has certain implications for intervention in bullying. For
example, it suggests that social skills training may not be effective and
may in fact backfire for some types of bullies and aggressive children
who are already socially skilled, in effect creating a "school for scoun-
drels" (Chandler, 1973). Instead, the family backgrounds of bullies
may need to be considered (Bowers, Smith, & Binney, 1992) and interventions should consider change of school culture (Sutton, Smith, &
Swettenham, 2001). The role of peers in supporting aggression and
bullying must also be considered in the complex social context of
aggression, as well as the potential role of peers in interventions
(Vaillancourt & Hymel, 2004).

This evidence of a link between some forms of bullying and social
cognition may now seem to contradict what we reported in an earlier
section regarding the correlation between social understanding and
social skills. How can social understanding be positively correlated with
social skills and at the same time with bullying? The bullies in the
Sutton et al. study, however, did not differ in social cognition from
children who were not involved in bullying in either the roles of bully,
victim, assistant, or reinforcer. Displaying competence in passing "theory
of mind" tasks "says nothing about how that knowledge will be
utilized" (Arsenio & Lemerise, 2001, p. 62). That is, one's action does
not just depend on one's abilities but rather how one uses them [as
Dumbledore told Harry Potter, who was concerned because he shared
characteristics with his arch enemy, Lord Voldemort]. It seems that
bullying cannot be explained through a lack of social understanding.
But bullying also cannot be explained simply in terms of advanced
social understanding. Other factors, such as empathy and the child's
values, must be involved (Sutton et al., 1999b; Arsenio & Lemerise,
2001), and the role of emotions and morality in children's thinking
about social matters also must be considered (Arsenio & Lemerise,
2001).

A question that now arises is whether we have to add dimensions
such as empathy and values to social understanding – conceived of as
understanding belief and emotions – or whether, in fact, we should be
broadening our definition of social understanding. Is bullying only an

apparently successful, but short-sighted strategy that is rejected by those children taking a longer view of the social landscape and their place in it? Now we have entered controversial terrain and we will find no general consensus, yet it is an important issue when we consider the place of the "theories of mind" research program more broadly within the larger context of social cognitive development, including moral development. Furthermore, it reminds us that we cannot simply focus on beliefs and neglect emotions. We need to seriously consider the role of emotions (Dunn, 1996; Harris, 1989).

Relations between Children's Understanding of Belief and Emotions

There is currently no clear consensus on what should and should not be included in the notion of social understanding, or "theory of mind." Although many studies focus on false belief tasks, and a battery of such procedures is now generally used, other studies also combine tests of children's understanding of emotions in an overall measure sometimes referred to as "theory of mind understanding" (e.g., Ruffman et al., 2002). As discussed in most of this book, the focus of the literature on social cognitive development has been on children's developing understanding of belief, particularly false beliefs. There is also a body of research on children's grasp of emotion, but these two aspects of children's social understanding have generally been investigated separately. A number of authors have criticized the "theories of mind" literature for neglecting emotions and have argued for the importance of emotions in the development of social understanding (e.g., Banerjee, 2004; Dunn, 1996; Hobson, 2002, 2004; Thompson & Raikes, 2004). We suggest that understanding the mind and emotions are two interrelated aspects of children's social development. An understanding of both beliefs and emotions would be required in making sense of many social situations. That is, "understanding the nature and causes of emotions is part and parcel of acquiring a theory of mind and understanding internal states of mind is part and parcel of acquiring an understanding of emotion" (Wellman & Banerjee, 1991, p. 191).

One issue concerns how these two aspects of social understanding might be related in children's development. Studies that have examined the relations between children's understanding of belief and their understanding of emotion have reported mixed results. Judy Dunn and her colleagues (Dunn, 1995; Cutting & Dunn, 1999; Hughes & Dunn,

1998) are the primary researchers examining this issue and they have suggested the possibility that children's understanding of mind and emotions may be separate domains. In a first study on this issue, Dunn et al. (1991a) reported, somewhat counter-intuitively, that in a sample of 50 forty-month-old children the correlation between understanding belief and emotions was not significant (r (50) = .25, n.s.). However, in the same study the correlation between the number of children's utterances referring to emotions and their belief understanding, although only moderate and not much larger, was significant (r (50) = .31, $p < .05$). In a longitudinal study following 46 of these same children into their eighth year Dunn (1995) found that early competence in these two areas was related to different dimensions of later school adjustment. Early understanding of belief was related to negative initial perceptions of school in kindergarten and to sensitivity to teacher criticism, whereas early understanding of emotions was related to children's positive perception of their peer experiences and to their moral sensibility (Dunn, 1995). These results, as Dunn acknowledges, are based on a small sample and therefore need to be replicated.

In contrast to this apparent lack of a relationship between understanding belief and emotions, Hughes and Dunn (1998) found significant correlations between children's understanding of belief and emotions in a one-year longitudinal study with 50 four-year-old children. They note that "these results suggest close links between children's understanding of feelings and their understanding of belief" (Hughes & Dunn, 1998, p. 1035). They consider two possible explanations for the discrepancy between their results and those in Dunn (1995). First, Hughes and Dunn used a series of false belief tasks, whereas Dunn et al. (1991) used only one task. The second possibility considered by Hughes and Dunn was that the different sequelae of understanding mind and emotion may take longer to develop. The Hughes and Dunn study was a 13-month longitudinal study, whereas the Dunn (1995) study covered 30 months. This possibility remains to be tested.

Similarly, in a cross-sectional study, Cutting and Dunn (1999) found that in a sample of 128 four-year-olds, children's understandings of mind and emotions were positively correlated. They went on, however, to argue that since language was highly correlated with children's understanding of both belief and emotions, it should be partialled out before looking at the correlation between them. When they statistically removed the effect of language the correlation between children's understanding of beliefs and emotions dropped and was fairly low but was still significant. Cutting and Dunn then conducted regression analyses (which take into account all the explanatory variables simultaneously and extract the partial correlations between them) and showed that when the shared variance with other factors was accounted for these two domains of children's understanding of the psychological world appeared no longer to be related, suggesting that the correlation between children's understanding of belief and emotions may just be due to the shared influence from other factors like the child's language skills and family background. Although at times Dunn has made broad claims about the relations between emotions and beliefs, elsewhere she is more cautious (Dunn, 1999) and Cutting and Dunn qualified their claim by suggesting that the link between belief and emotion understanding may be restricted to 4-year-olds and to basic emotions.

In the case of more complex emotions it would seem logical to expect that there should be connections with understanding belief. For example, it seems that a grasp of surprise would involve understanding false beliefs, inferring regret would depend on being able to think about counter-factual beliefs, and self-conscious emotions such as embarrassment, guilt, and shame must involve some understanding of others' perspective on the self (Tangney & Fischer, 1995).

However, even so-called basic emotions can be embedded in complex situations that make understanding such emotions more difficult. Belief-dependent emotions are one case of such situated complexity of emotions. For example, for children to know that Little Red Riding Hood would not be afraid when she sees the wolf dressed up as her grandmother they would need to realize that Little Red Riding Hood would have a false belief (Bradmetz & Schneider, 1999). In belief-dependent emotion tasks children have to realize that duped story characters would feel happy when they, for example, see a Smarties box on the table because they do not know that they have been tricked by a mischievous monkey who has replaced their favorite candy with stones (Harris, Johnson, Hutton, Andrews, & Cooke, 1989).

A more complex task is Chandler's (Chandler & Greenspan, 1972) bystander experiment, mentioned in chapter 8, which illustrates the interconnections between beliefs and emotions. In this procedure children have to understand that although getting a present usually makes children happy, this is not always the case. In one scenario, a little girl who is feeling sad because her father has just left in an airplane then feels happy when she receives a present delivered by a mail carrier. But when the girl discovers that the present contains a toy airplane, this reminds the child of her father having just left on an airplane and the memory makes the girl sad. Furthermore, the mail carrier delivering the present knows nothing about the previous sequence of events and therefore might derive a different explanation for the young girl's sadness. Understanding that getting presents makes children happy may be an early developing ability, but an appreciation of the more indirect connection between the toy airplane, the father's absence, and the child's sadness is more complex. An even higher level of analysis is the realization that the bystander would lack knowledge of all of this and therefore would view the child's emotions differently. This is an example of apparently basic emotions, happiness and sadness, being set within complex situations, which thus require a complexity of understanding of beliefs and thoughts, each nested within one another.

Surprise is an example of an emotion that, at least for a mature understanding, seems to require an understanding of beliefs. The idea that children's understanding of surprise may be constrained by their grasp of false beliefs, on which surprise is based, was supported by research showing a developmental lag between children's success on false belief tasks and their later mastery of surprise (Hadwin & Perner, 1991; Ruffman & Keenan, 1996). Wellman and Banerjee (1991), however, report that when told that a character is surprised, for example, because his grandmother's house is painted purple, 3- and 4-year-old children's explanations reveal their understanding "that the reaction of surprise depends on the actor's prior beliefs" (p. 208). This difference between prediction and explanation tasks returns us to the debate about appropriate methodologies and the early development of an understanding of emotions and beliefs. A theme through this book has been to encourage a developmental approach in which we explore various forms of understanding.

Further development in children's understanding of complex emotions include the idea of mixed emotions – that is, situations in which someone might feel two emotions of opposite valence at the same time, such as a child feeling excited but also worried when riding a bicycle for the first time. Such mixed emotions can necessarily involve basic feelings such as being happy or sad. But it is a more complex and later-developing insight to understand that in some situations these emotions can be experienced at the same time (Dunn, 1995).

As well as assessing children's performance on tests of emotion understanding using hypothetical stories, it is also important to study children's real-life understanding of emotions in particular close relationships. Dunn and Hughes (1998) studied 4-year-old children's understanding of what makes themselves, their friends, and their mothers happy, sad, angry, and afraid. They found that children develop an understanding of particular emotions within particular relationships. For example, children provided reasons for their mothers' happiness and anger, but many children could not say what made their mother sad or afraid. In contrast, the children did not know what caused their friends' anger.

Self-conscious emotions and children's understanding of self-presentation

It seems intuitively clear that some emotions are tied up with thinking about others' views of the self, and therefore would seem to be closely connected to children's social understanding, even by definition. This would seem to apply in particular to self-conscious emotions such as embarrassment and guilt (Bennett & Matthews, 2000; Tangney & Fischer, 1995). Bennett and Matthews (2000) found that in a group of 4- to 7-year-olds the children who passed a second-order false belief task were much more likely to refer to social emotions such as shame and humiliation when they were asked to imagine how they would feel in various social situations such as, for example, unintentionally going to a store in their pajamas. However, these researchers note that a sophisticated understanding of belief was not by itself sufficient to predict children's reference to these feelings. Only about half of the children passing the second-order tasks did go on to talk about social emotions. Thus these researchers caution that although the cognitive ability to take the other's perspective on the self may be required for thinking about social emotions, children, as well as adults, may differ in the extent to which they are sensitive to this dimension of their social life.

This idea that second-order reasoning abilities are prerequisite skills but are not sufficient to explain children's awareness of social emotions was further explored by Banerjee (2002a) in two studies with children ranging in age from 6 to 11. Banerjee studied the relations between children's awareness of self-presentational concerns (Goffman, 1959) and their spontaneous awareness of embarrassment. Managing the impression one makes on others is a concern that children become increasingly aware of during childhood and this would seem to require an understanding of others' perspectives on the self. Second-order belief understanding seems to be required for understanding embarrassment and self-presentational behavior but by itself does not seem to be sufficient to explain this understanding (Bennett & Matthews, 2000; Banerjee, 2002b). Among children who are able to pass tests requiring an understanding of someone's beliefs about another person's beliefs, there is still variability in whether or not they are spontaneously aware of embarrassment and self-presentation. Thus motivational factors must be considered as well as cognitive abilities in accounting for children's emerging competence in adult forms of social interaction (Banerjee, 2002b).

The costs of understanding: sensitivity to criticism

Most of the research we have reviewed above is based on the assumption that advanced social understanding is advantageous. However, it is possible that there are costs associated with such developments. For example, a sophisticated understanding of others' perspectives on the self might result in increased social anxiety. There is some evidence that sensitivity to criticism is associated with early social understanding. In a longitudinal study, Dunn (1995) found that children who were advanced in false belief understanding relative to their peers reported more negative experience in kindergarten when they were followed up on two years later, and these children were more sensitive to criticism from their teachers because they took such criticism into account when evaluating their own work. This finding was replicated by Cutting and Dunn (2002) with a larger group of 5-year-olds in their first year of school. Cutting and Dunn also found that children who are advanced in social understanding, as assessed with first- and second-order false belief tasks, were more sensitive to teachers' criticism, as assessed with two puppet scenarios in which a teacher puppet criticizes errors in the work of a puppet given the child's name. After each scenario the children were asked how they felt (i.e., happy, sad, or angry) and how they rated their own ability as "good or not good." It was especially early false belief understanding assessed the year before these children started kindergarten that predicted sensitivity to criticism. We should note that it was the children's appraisal of their ability at the task after criticism that was associated with belief understanding and not children's rating of emotional reactions to teacher criticism. Furthermore, there was also a tendency for children who were advanced in false belief understanding to rate their ability as "not good" even after scenarios in which there was a mistake in the work done by the puppet character with their name but no criticism from the teacher. Also, this relationship accounted for about 10 percent of the variance, meaning that other factors are also involved in explaining children's reactions to criticism (Cutting & Dunn, 2002).

Social Understanding and Morality

An important topic to address in this chapter is how moral development may be related to social understanding. This has been particularly neglected, even though it has been argued that morality is an aspect of social cognition (for exceptions see Chandler, Sokol, & Hallett, 2001; Chandler, Sokol, & Wainryb, 2000; Dunn, 1995; Dunn et al., 1995; and the articles in Baird & Sokol, 2004). There is some evidence that children's social understanding is linked with their grasp of morality. Dunn, Cutting, and Demetriou (2000) found that 4-year-olds' understanding of beliefs and emotions was positively correlated with their explanations of why a moral transgression against a friend such as "name-calling, taking a toy from a friend and excluding a friend from play" (p. 163) was or was not permissible. Children who justified their views about transgressions involving friends in terms of feelings and psychological or interpersonal issues were more advanced in their understanding of beliefs and emotions than children whose justifications referred to external punishment or rules. In related work, Baird and Astington (2004) reported that 5-year-olds' evaluation of acts in terms of the underlying moral motivation was positively correlated with their performance on false belief tasks. The same relationship was found for 7-year-olds and their understanding of second-order false beliefs. One aspect of children's moral action that may be closely related to false belief understanding is lying.

Lying and deception

A topic of research at the interface of social understanding and morality that has been of interest, beginning with Piaget's (1932/1965) early work on moral development, is children's understanding of lying. It seems that lying should require false belief understanding. That is, the whole point in lying is to instill a false belief in another person. Therefore, it would seem that in order to lie a child must at least be able to understand that false beliefs are, in fact, possible (Sodian, 1994). Thus, engaging in deception and attempting to trick others may be a marker of an early understanding of beliefs (Chandler, Fritz, & Hala, 1989; Hala, Chandler, & Fritz, 1991). And lying may be a skill at which children improve (Chandler & Afifi, 1996), with early attempts such as "I didn't break the lamp and I won't do it again" being less convincing (Vasek, 1986).

Young children, however, appear to engage in various acts of deception months or even years before they can pass a standard false belief task (Newton, Reddy, & Bull, 2000). What may underlie this apparent paradox is that in carefully designed laboratory experiments children cannot get away without some understanding of false beliefs. However, in their everyday home life things are different. That is, there is far more support from the context that may enable a young child to engage in deception with as yet only a partial understanding of what is going on. For example, in Newton et al.'s (2000) diary study of deception in 3- to 4-year-old children they found no relationship between children's false belief understanding, as assessed with standard tests, and their deceptive acts. These deceptive acts included cases such as a child being caught red handed by his mother after just smashing an egg, but when asked "Did you smash the egg?" the child relied "No." They also report a case study with a child who at $2^{1}/_{2}$ failed most false belief tasks yet claimed "Daddy says I could have it," in an attempt to get a biscuit he wanted. Although we tend to be inclined to interpret such observations richly and assume that the child understood that he was instilling a false belief, leaner interpretations are possible. There are many instances of forms of deception in nature that do not depend on understanding others' beliefs and intentions. For example, evolved body characteristics such as camouflage or misleading eye-spots, or behaviors such as the killdeer's attempts to lead potential predators away from its ground-based nest do not emerge because the individual makes a decision to hide from or deceive others. Many of the examples from the Newton et al. study may not be based on a mature understanding of deception. These sorts of situations are still likely to be the forms of interaction in which young children do develop a more sophisticated understanding of deception.

Peterson and Siegal (2002) explored the relations between children's false belief task performance and their understanding of the distinction between mistakes and lies in popular and rejected children. These researchers found that although understanding lies and false beliefs were correlated, there was no independent contribution of false belief performance to moral awareness independent of age, verbal ability, and peer popularity.

Clearly, the topic of lying in moral development does not stop with learning how to lie effectively. Rather, in the moral domain children should develop some conception of when they should or should not lie, and the reasons for doing so. In Piaget's (1932/1965) interviews with children about lying, young children operating within

the morality of constraint imposed by relationships of unilateral respect with adults equated the naughtiness of the lie with the likelihood
of being caught out and punished. That is, telling one's mother that
you saw a dog as big as a cow is naughtier than telling her that you
got a good mark at school because she will not believe the first lie but
is likely to believe the second one. This also means that these children
thought that it was worse to lie to an adult than a child because you
are much more likely to be caught and punished. In contrast, slightly
older children thought that although it was sometimes necessary to lie
to grownups, lying to one's mates would be really despicable because
it would violate the trust on which friendships are based. This
thinking reveals a shift to a morality of cooperation based on mutual
respect.

Since the 1960s Kohlberg's (e.g., Colby & Kohlberg, 1987) system of
stages has been considered as the gold standard of assessments of moral
reasoning. It holds that there is much to be learned in adolescence and
even early adulthood. According to this system, reasons for not lying at
Stage 1 would involve simple obedience to authority, at Stage 2 to avoid
punishment, and at Stage 3 because of the mutual trust on which relationships are based. Moral development also involves the realization
that there may be some situations in which telling the truth might
endanger someone's life, and then the morally correct thing to do would
be to lie. Lying might also be appropriate in many less dramatic situations. Children have to learn about situations in which politeness
demands white lies or restraining the tendency to blurt out the truth as
in "You're fat!" (Talwar & Lee, 2002). We will return to the issue of
politeness but we first turn to research more centrally within the field of
moral development.

Moral reasoning

With these correlations between children's social and moral understanding it behooves us to explore theoretical explanations for such
links. The possible relations between social understanding and moral
development depend on how we think about moral reasoning. One
possibility is that understanding others' perspectives, which depends on
social understanding, is required in thinking about moral conflicts. The
assumption within this approach is that development in social cognition
is necessary but not sufficient for moral development. Within the
Kohlbergian approach, moral reasoning is assessed with dilemmas

requiring a decision about what to do in situations in which moral rules are in conflict. The structure of individuals' reasoning to resolve these dilemmas is used to classify their responses in terms of Kohlberg's stages of progressively more adequate forms of moral reasoning. Kohlberg viewed the development of moral reasoning as the ability to grasp increasingly complex forms of reasoning. The principles that define the various stages through which individuals develop are then applied by individuals to reason about and resolve moral conflicts. However, Kohlberg also viewed moral reasoning as ideal perspective taking. If we think of moral reasoning as the ability to understand and coordinate conflicting perspectives, then social understanding would clearly be very important in this process (Carpendale, 2000).

An issue faced by those taking Kohlberg's approach is to explain the transition from moral reasoning to moral action. That is, whether people's action is based on their moral reasoning. Yet it is clearly moral action that is of concern. Chris Moore and his colleagues have addressed this issue by exploring the relations between preschoolers' altruism and prudence, that is, their ability to delay receiving a reward. Both altruism and prudence involve action that is motivated by goals that are not in the immediate interest of the self. Altruism involves the interest and goals of others whereas prudence involves future goals for the self in contrast to present goals of the self. Moore and his colleagues reasoned that these are two forms of complex social behavior and that "theory of mind," that is "the ability to explain and predict behavior by attributing mental states to agents is functional in the organization of social behavior" (Moore & Macgillivray, 2004, p. 52). Moore and his colleagues presented children with various situations in which they had to choose, for example, between one sticker immediately or two stickers later. There were also various conditions involving sharing such as deciding between one sticker for the self now or one sticker each for self and their partner later. They found that 4-year-olds' sharing of rewards in a delay situation was positively correlated with their false belief understanding (Moore, Barresi, & Thompson, 1998; Moore & Macgillivray, 2004). However, by the age of $4^{1}/_{2}$ years there was no relation between sharing and false belief understanding. A difficulty with just focusing on the reasoning process is that we neglect the issue of moral motivation (Moore & Macgillivray, 2004). People have to care about others' differing perspectives, and give them equal weight in reaching a solution; that is, some notion such as caring or valuing others' perspectives must be considered. Astington and Jenkins (1995) found that peer nominations of children's empathetic concern were not related to performance on false belief tasks. In arguing for the importance of caring about others' perspectives, Wright (1982, p. 211) stated that "the universe of moral discourse is not one that I can be logically compelled to enter, but must, so to speak, step into voluntarily." Wright (1982), in interpreting Piaget (1932/1965), argued that a sense of moral obligation is rooted in close personal relationships.

Another way to bridge morality and understanding the mind is to examine how children's judgments of moral responsibility depend on their developing conceptions of knowledge. Chandler, Sokol, and Hallett (2001) investigated this issue by using a series of scenes from the "Highly Moral Drama of Punch and Judy." In one scene Punch sees Judy fall into a box and, seizing on the opportunity to rid himself of her, he plans to push the box off the stage. But unbeknownst to him she had slipped out of the box while he was off stage looking for a rope to tie it shut. In contrast to this unsuccessful attempted murder, other scenes involve unintentional manslaughter. For example, in one scene Punch is clearing the stage of boxes and accidentally pushes Judy off in a box that he thought was empty. What further complicates matters is when some ambiguity is introduced rather than simple ignorance. For example, in a further scene Judy falls into a green box and calling for help says, "check the green one." Unfortunately, Punch thinks she means a second box on the stage with a large green numeral "1" stamped on it. Punch, only wishing to help, quickly clears the stage of the green-colored box, and in doing so again commits accidental manslaughter.

Children's ratings of these acts on a "badness meter" depended on whether they had developed an understanding of interpretation. Those with a false belief understanding but no understanding of interpretation rated these two forms of manslaughter as equally bad as they understood both to be based on simple ignorance. However, children who had acquired an understanding of interpretation, and thus an understanding of active process of knowledge construction, rated the second case of manslaughter, which involved misinterpretation, as worse than the first case, which was due to simple ignorance. This research reveals the role of children's understanding of how knowledge is acquired in their evaluation of moral events. Noninterpretive children did not assign moral responsibility in the cases of misinterpretation because they view the process of knowledge acquisition in a passive sense. In contrast, children with an interpretive understanding have an active conception of mental life from which it follows that agents have some responsibility for how they interpret ambiguous events or utterances (Sokol, Chandler, & Jones, 2004).

Morality as foundational for social interaction

What can we conclude about the relationship between moral reasoning and social understanding? Following the groundbreaking work of Kohlberg, the study of moral development has tended to focus on large life-and-death moral dilemmas. However, the evidence on much younger children suggests that there is more to moral reasoning than the ability to justify such crucial decisions. We draw from the work cited above, like that of Moore and his colleagues, that much more elementary social interaction like prudence or altruism can be conceived of as a form of morality on a small scale. Here moral action has to be understood at the level of interpersonal face-to-face interaction. This leads to the view that almost all interaction involves concern for others' feelings and well-being. Thus, in a sense the "theory of mind" tradition may already have been studying morality without realizing it. Rather than needing to build a bridge between two separate domains we may instead find that the very foundations of interactional competence are moral in nature.

Such a view is not new. In Winch's (1972, pp. 60–61, emphasis in original) words: "The social conditions of a language and rationality must also carry with them certain fundamental *moral* conceptions." Furthermore, "the existence of a norm of truth-telling is a *moral* condition of language" (Winch, 1972, p. 63, emphasis in original). Holiday (1988) also derived a similar position from the philosopher Wittgenstein. That is, human interaction and language are not possible without a norm like truth-telling. Such a norm must be presupposed as a prerequisite for interaction. It constitutes interaction, and is also constituted by interaction. It is required for language to get off the ground. Only with such a norm is it possible to deceive. Children may well develop an understanding of moral principles in the course of their everyday social interactions. The potential for morality – for treating others with equal respect – is rooted in the conditions for social interaction and is not just an externally imposed culturally specific concept. This approach is one way of making sense of Piaget's (1932/1965, p. 404) insightful but somewhat cryptic remark that "logic is the morality of thought just as morality is the logic of action." That is, there is a form of morality in the logic or the structure of interaction – the necessary preconditions that make social interaction possible.

Broadening the Conception of Social Understanding: Building Bridges or Negotiating Border Disputes?

This chapter is devoted to a discussion of connections, of building bridges between social understanding and other aspects of children's social development. But we should now consider the broader question of whether it is a matter of building bridges between separate domains or of recognizing that we may be talking about different aspects of the same thing, perhaps seen from different theoretical perspectives. When we use terms like social understanding or social cognition, this indicates that we are concerned with children's thinking about social matters. It then follows that we could study the relations between such thinking and children's social activity, for example. Children's social understanding is often assessed with false belief tasks but it may be broader in nature. Perhaps competence in social interaction should be considered as a form of social understanding. People who are skilled in interaction are considered to have tact or poise. But this is different from the form of understanding assessed with false belief tasks.

We now turn to exploring connections to other parallel literatures which also are concerned in some way with social competence. The competence required to engage in, and make sense of, social interaction has been discussed by the philosopher Paul Grice. Grice (1975) outlined the knowledge he claimed is needed in order to infer what people mean from what they say. This includes the cooperative principle, which is defined as "Make our conversational contribution such as required, at the stage at which it occurs, by the accepted purpose or direction of the talk-exchange in which you are engaged" (Grice, 1975, p. 5). In addition to the cooperative principle, Grice's four conversational maxims are the maxims of quality ("say what is true; don't say what's false"), quantity ("say enough and no more"), relation "be relevant"), and manner ("be clear, concise, and to the point") (Turnbull, 2003, p. 83). The idea is that the knowledge of these maxims is required to draw additional meaning from utterances; that is, to fill in information that was not actually provided. This is what Grice labeled "conversational implicatures." For example, if in response to the question "how did Smith do in court the other day?" the answer given is "he got a fine," the clear expectation is that a fine is all that he received. This is because it is assumed that the speaker is cooperating and providing the appropriate amount of information. Listeners would be surprised and shocked if it was later discovered that Smith also got a life sentence as well as the fine. In fact, it would be generally considered that the speaker was not cooperating and by not volunteering enough information was actually misleading the listener. As another example consider Inspector Clouseau, played by Peter Sellers in the Pink Panther movies, who asks a Swiss hotel clerk if his dog bites. When the clerk answers that his dog does not bite, Clouseau goes ahead and pats the dog sitting beside the clerk and is promptly bitten. Clouseau reacts by saying, "I thought you said your dog doesn't bite!" and the clerk replies calmly, "That is not my dog, monsieur" (Turnbull, 2003, pp. 94–95). The humor derives from the clerk's non-Gricean response, which clearly does not contain the appropriate information in this context.

Grice also pointed out that these maxims can be used in an additional way in a second form of conversational implicature that involves blatantly flouting a maxim. In these situations the speaker is obviously failing to follow one of the maxims, but listeners assume that the speaker is still cooperating in some way and so draw additional inferences. Irony and metaphor are examples of flouting the maxim of quality (i.e., be truthful) yet speakers still convey meaning. An example of flouting the maxim of quality is when Eeyore says to Winnie the Pooh, "You're a fine friend," when he clearly means the opposite. Grice (1975) argued that this approach applies not just to conversation but to cooperative interaction in general. Daniela O'Neill (2005) refers to Grice in her discussion of the connections between young children's understanding of mind and their conversation. For example, it seems that 2-year-olds already vary the amount of information they provide in a request depending on the other person's knowledge.

A criticism of Grice's (1975) approach is that he focused on the most efficient way to communicate information and neglected the interpersonal concerns involved in social interaction. Many other things are accomplished in talk beyond the exchange of information such as "apologizing, appealing, complimenting, emoting, empathizing, esteeming, excusing, expressing affection, greeting, hedging, justifying, prefacing, stalling, showing support, sympathizing, and thanking" (Turnbull, 2003, p. 106). Grice did conclude his essay by acknowledging that other maxims might be required such as "be polite." Others theorists, however, have gone further in this direction.

To address the interpersonal dimension we turn to Brown and Levinson's (1987) politeness model. This theory is not just concerned with politeness in the formulaic sense of saying please and thank-you. Rather it is a general theory of social activity. Brown and Levinson claim to be outlining knowledge that is necessary in order to engage competently in social interaction – that is, to understand others' contributions to interaction and to respond appropriately. For example, consider the situation of accepting versus declining an invitation. Accepting is usually simple, short, and sweet. Declining, on the other hand, is often preceded by a pause, is usually much longer, and will generally contain excuses or justifications and may not even contain the word "no." This example reminds us of how important the interpersonal dimension is in structuring our talk (Turnbull, 2003). An implication is that people require an understanding of this interpersonal dimension to engage competently in social interaction and understand others' contributions to that interaction.

Furthermore, consider the everyday yet highly important act of making requests. Adults intuitively know that there are important differences in the way we make requests depending on the level of imposition involved. For example, compare asking for small change to make a phone call with asking to borrow someone's car. Whom one is asking also makes a big difference – compare asking someone of high versus low power, or a friend versus a stranger. For example, consider your expectations for politeness and indirectness of a request for a private asking a general to open a door versus a general asking a private. Having tea with the Queen might be an occasion for a high level of politeness as indicated by very indirect requests but if the same level of politeness was used with one's mother the request would appear overly polite and thus sarcastic and even rude (Turnbull, 2003).

Many of these structures used in conversation and related to politeness are concerned with maintaining self-image and dignity and avoiding embarrassment and humiliation. This is referred to as "face," and situations that potentially threaten face require "face work" (Brown & Levinson, 1987; Goffman, 1959). All of this "face work" is fairly obvious to adults when it is explicitly pointed out. But how do children develop competence in this area? There is very little research on the development of children's interactional competence (Goldbeck, Turnbull, & Carpendale, 2003). However, some aspects of an early understanding of sequential expectations seem to be already observable in the different ways in which very young children make requests (Wootton, 1997).

Children's understanding of the non-literal nature of language is ripe for further exploration in the research literature. The early research suggested that such a skill is slow to emerge in children. Let us look briefly at the example of sarcasm, the most blatant form of irony in language. Early analyses of the ability to understand that a remark might mean the opposite of what was said (see the example from Eeyore above) suggest that even in their teens individuals show an imperfect grasp of sarcasm (e.g., Demorest et al., 1984). More recent studies show some understanding in the early school years (Dews et al., 1996). Some appear to suggest that a speaker might use an ironical remark to "mute" or soften their criticism. However, some very recent research has attempted to explore the fundamental problem in irony, that what is said does not convey the speaker's intention – the say–mean distinction (Yasui & Lewis, 2005). In a series of experiments Yasui and Lewis acted out a story with dolls in which Miaow the cat puts salt into Teddy's cake-mix, thus ruining it. In various manipulations he does so inadvertently or as an act of malice, but these do not influence children's performance. In each case Teddy says "Oh great, you've really helped me now!" Previous studies would lead to the prediction that school-age children should find such a statement relatively hard to fathom. Yet, 3-year-olds were way above chance when responding to questions requiring an understanding of the distinction between what Teddy said and what he meant, even though they failed false belief tasks both within the same procedure and outside it. These data lead us to reflect upon how children are exposed to key issues to do with speakers' intentions long before they can pass the false belief test. They may even provide an insight into the role of such knowledge in later belief understanding.

Conclusion

We have discussed various interconnections between social understanding and children's social lives, the relations of each with social competence, aggression and bullying, the development of an understanding of emotions of varying degrees of complexity, and moral development. We have surveyed various areas of research but we acknowledge that there are other possible connections between children's social understanding and other aspects of their social development that are only beginning to be explored. For example, consider the development of children's teaching of younger children. To teach someone else a new skill competently would appear to require something in the way of an understanding of one's pupil's level of understanding. That is, an understanding of what knowledge the other lacks as well as ways in which to teach something new. Or perhaps more sophisticated levels of social understanding make more complex forms of teaching possible. Thus we might expect to see forms of children's teaching that would be related to their level of social understanding (Maynard, 2002; Strauss, Ziv, & Stein, 2002; Tomasello, Kruger, & Ratner, 1993). In studying children's understanding of teaching, Ziv and Frye (2004, p. 469, emphasis in original) found that "five- and six-year-olds, who performed well on a standard false belief task, further understood that it was the *awareness* of the knowledge difference that would actually govern whether teaching would take place."

Furthermore, social understanding broadly conceived should include children's developing conceptions of persons, and such conceptions would be expected to differ across cultures and between different social groups. We know, for example, that very early in the preschool years children's social understanding (Kujawski & Bower, 1993) and relationships (Smith, 1986) are divided into same-sex allegiances. It is not surprising that Richner and Nicolopoulou (2001) found that preschoolers' conceptions of persons as revealed in their narratives were gender related. Another angle on this issue is the development of children's understanding of personality traits, which also would be expected to vary across cultures since adults' views of traits do (Yuill, 1997).

In much of the research exploring the connections between children's social understanding and other aspects of their social lives, an implicit assumption seems to be that children's understanding would be expected to influence their social interaction. Although this certainly is a possibility to explore, we should not lose sight of the alternative possibility that children's experience in particular types of interaction may facilitate or hinder their social cognitive development. This point returns us to the discussion in chapter 6 regarding the role of relationships in social development. As already mentioned, much of the research discussed in chapter 6 was motivated by an interest in the possible role of aspects of social experience in the development of social understanding. The converse assumption is implicit in the present chapter. That is, the assumption that social understanding may influence children's social interaction. Of course, both possibilities may be true to varying extents and it is likely that there are bidirectional and transactional effects. However, notice that there is an underlying assumption here, that we can separate these aspects of child development. In some cases this may be a useful approach but at other times we should think about whether, when considering social action and social understanding, we are in fact looking at different sides of the same coin.

Chapter 10

Constructing an Understanding of Mind

We started this book with the question of how thinking arises from a collection of cells. The part of this complex and vast question that we have grappled with is how children become aware of themselves and others in a social world. The chapters in this book have reviewed a recent but massive literature in developmental psychology that has attempted to address this fundamental issue, collectively known as the "theory of mind." In this final chapter we hope to draw together the main threads in our analysis so far and put forward a theoretical position which we feel overcomes some of the problems which we have raised (for a full account see Carpendale & Lewis, 2004a). To do this we divide the discussion into four sections. In the first we briefly summarize the issues raised in previous chapters that we feel are necessary for a full account of the child's developing social understanding. This prepares the ground for the second section in which we outline what we feel has been missing in the "theory of mind" literature and present a constructivist account that draws from three major scholars: Piaget and Vygotsky in developmental psychology and the philosophy of Ludwig Wittgenstein. The third section develops this argument by considering what this theoretical position would predict about the way in which social understanding develops. Finally we consider the criticisms that have been made against this position and our responses to these (Carpendale & Lewis, 2004b).

The Story So Far

As the many recent references that we have cited show, "theory of mind" research and scholarship has been lively. In chapters 1 and 2 we attempted to describe just how diverse recent theorization has been, but yet how none of the existing accounts gives a complete explanation of how social understanding develops. You might have wondered why there is a need to account for the development of such skills. Humans live in complex social networks and evolution rarely leaves anything to chance – therefore, some theorists argue that there is likely to be a set of genes dedicated to social understanding. In chapter 1 we discussed one type of biological approach. According to this account humans have evolved a set of modules dedicated to understanding the social world by computing mental states. It is certainly the case that humans develop much more sophisticated forms of social understanding than chimpanzees and therefore we should think about the biological adaptations that make this possible. As we have emphasized, it is essential to base our theories on evolutionary theory. However, the modular approach is only one application of evolutionary theory. We have pointed out problems with the modular approach and we note that taking evolution seriously does not compel us to endorse modularity. It may be that human infants are biologically attuned to operate in a "shared intersubjective space" (Gallese, 2003). But even if this is so we still need to explain what happens to the basic selectivity and responsivity of nerve cells in the brain. Like Prinz (2003), we argue that we need to go much further than what may be a basic "simulation" skill. Although investigation of the neurological basis for thinking is clearly important, it by itself will not explain how children develop an understanding of meaningful human conduct (Bennett & Hacker, 2003; Mead, 1934).

To remind ourselves of the importance of others in an account of social development, consider the following example proposed by Chris Moore (personal communication) at a recent conference. Suppose you put a baby on a desert island, or anywhere where no social interaction takes place, and ensure that he or she gets nourishment without social interaction. Would this baby develop a mature "theory of mind" or, indeed, the general cognitive skills discussed in chapter 5? His, and our, answer would be a resounding "No." There is something about human interaction that is necessary for social development.

The main perspective in this area of scholarship, the theory theory, has been highly influential in directing research in this area and has provided key insights into the child's understanding. Its proponents have developed the main experimental technique in the area, the false belief task, and the main bulk of evidence suggests that there is a shift in performance on this task between the ages of 3 and 4. However, we have discussed criticisms of this position (see chapter 2) and noted that the evidence has been taken to support other perspectives (see chapter 3). We are left keeping an open mind about Josef Perner's (1991) claim that there is a basic shift at age 4 in children's ability to see two perspectives simultaneously which allows us to understand, for example, that beliefs or desires do not necessarily match what we know to be true. Wellman's notion of a framework theory explains how reasoning in the domain of psychology might be insulated from other areas of knowledge, but we point out several problems with a strong version of his account, that the developments displayed in the preschool period are equivalent to the changes in scientific revolutions (see chapter 2). At the same time, the weak version is something of a truism – areas of knowledge relate to one another. Our more fundamental critique of the "theory of mind" tradition, as discussed in chapter 7, concerns the view of language and the mind assumed by most approaches; that is, that the problem faced by the child in learning the meaning of mental state terms involves mapping words onto inner mental entities.

Chapters 5 and 6 summarize two different sub-areas of research that have developed in recent years. The large numbers of social correlates with the development of mental state understanding (chapter 6) present us with a quandary: How can we fully explain why there are so many connections between aspects of children's social experience and their social understanding? We charted some interesting contenders for an explanation, like attachment theory and the concept of "mind-mindedness," but concluded that none of these really identifies the processes involved in the development of social understanding – they show that social interactions and relationships are important in social development but not why or how. It is possible for traditional accounts to accommodate such data in that social interaction might help the theoretician of mind collect sufficient data to change his or her theory or it might help switch on the appropriate modules. However, we feel this evidence exposes problems with the individualist basis of contemporary theories and thus there is a need to consider the child's social relationships centrally in an explanation of how social development occurs.

A similar analysis can be made of the literature on general cognitive skills, under the banner of "executive functions" (chapter 5). Children's working memory, their ability to switch rules or inhibit a prepotent response all show key developments at the same time as children pass the false belief test. However, the longitudinal evidence is far from conclusive about any causal patterns between the two sets of skills and we finished chapter 5 by pointing out that we do not have a complete grasp of how executive skills themselves develop. Some evidence suggests that these skills, too, originate within social interaction (e.g., Landry et al., 2002).

A second set of contemporary issues was explored in chapters 8 and 9. In the first of these we discussed the place of the false belief test in the framework of developing social understanding. Although the focus on false belief understanding may make it appear that the only shift of importance occurs at the age of 4, other developments in the child's grasp of the social world are also worthy of study. Not only does the research on the development of second-order belief understanding and an interpretative understanding of knowledge show developments in the primary school years, there are further discernible shifts into preadolescence and the teenage years. The findings presented in chapter 8 thus point toward an account of development in which the child learns about the social world in a gradual, step-by-step way. In chapter 9 we reviewed a complementary literature which shows that the achievements in children's understanding of beliefs have to be understood in relation to a wide range of issues concerning other aspects of development, like moral reasoning and understanding emotions as well as real-world interaction involved in social competence and even forms of aggression such as bullying. We concluded chapter 9 by drawing attention to children's conversational skills as a vital clue to understanding their gradual entry into the complexities of the social world.

For the development of our theoretical position, two chapters of this book are crucial and have already spelled out some of the basic issues that we need to develop. In chapter 4 we described the debate between two different perspectives on social development in infancy. Many accounts assume that babies easily contrast "self" with "other" and that the infant starts with self-knowledge. The step to understanding others then involves transferring this understanding of self to others through analogical reasoning. Such approaches to infant social development are individualistic in the basic epistemological assumptions on which they are based. In chapter 4 we noted problems with these assumptions, such as the difficulty concerning how infants could understand their own intentional activity before using such experience to understand others, as well as the point that the analogical argument assumes the infant's understanding of self as distinct from others but does not explain the development of this insight.

We suggested that a more viable alternative is the relational perspective, according to which infants' understanding of self and other is differentiated out of activity (e.g., Piaget, 1936/1963; Hobson, 2002). We draw three interrelated conclusions from this research. First, infants' abilities develop within rich forms of interaction in which infants engage already during the first year of life. Secondly, infants begin to enter into forms of coordinated attention but these interactions are not yet manifestations of a general insight of others as intentional agents. As Astington (1993) points out, this richness of social interaction rituals does not necessarily imply deep understanding of the social world. Thirdly, the evidence that we presented on gaze following and the use of pointing gestures suggests that social development does not make a single dramatic appearance. The overall point is that various forms of social understanding need to be distinguished. We could describe earlier forms of social knowledge as practical, lived, or sensorimotor knowledge. In Hobson's (2002) terms, infants' understanding is first in feeling or action, not yet in thinking. These earlier forms only gradually become later-developing skills which demonstrate more explicit social knowledge.

Such a relational approach was further developed in chapter 7, in which we considered the possible causal connections between the development of language and social understanding. We concluded that there are various ways of viewing the relations between language and social understanding raised by considering broader definitions of both. In particular, early forms of social understanding manifest in joint attention (chapter 4) seem to be required for learning language, and language may then facilitate further social development. Furthermore, the pragmatic aspects of language and competence in conversation show how social understanding and language are intertwined. Some researchers have viewed language, in particular the child's use of mental state terms, as a window revealing the child's developing understanding of the psychological world. Although this approach has yielded interesting evidence, there are a number of issues that should be kept in mind when interpreting this research. Indeed the evidence suggests that children may use particular mental state terms with only partial understanding of their meaning (Nelson, 1996) and both children and adults may use the same mental state terms to perform different social acts (Budwig, 2002). Furthermore, it is also possible to talk about the psychological world without using mental state terms (Turnbull & Carpendale, 1999b). Thus, we have to be careful about using language as a social window. A difficult issue concerning mental state terms that most of these theories must address is the problem of how children learn the meanings of words about the psychological world. In keeping with authors like Montgomery (2002, 2004) and Bickhard (2004), whom we discussed in chapter 7, we take a different position on this issue that we outline below.

A Social-Constructivist Account of Social Understanding

Any account of social understanding must start with early interaction in infancy and explain the emergence, from earlier dyadic engagement between parents and infants, of triadic interaction between infant, adult, and objects in the environment. What does a model of such understanding require? Here we sketch out such developments in terms of the theoretical model that is based upon the work of three scholars who are not usually linked with one another: Piaget, Vygotsky, and Wittgenstein.

The epistemic triangle: Piaget, Vygotsky and Wittgenstein

Our approach is based on Michael Chapman's (1991, 1999) reworking of two key theories: Piaget's and Vygotsky's. Although Piaget is now known for his emphasis on children's interaction with the physical world in the construction of knowledge, Chapman pointed out that in his early work (e.g., Piaget, 1924/1928) as well as throughout his career (Piaget, 1977/1995), Piaget was also concerned with the social dimension to development (see also, Lourenço & Machado, 1996). Vygotsky (e.g., 1978), on the other hand, is well known for his concern with the role of social interaction in the development of "higher mental functions," which are mental activities that are channeled through cultural conventions and activities. Chapman proposed integrating these dimensions of development. How individuals interact with objects depends upon how their cultures define them. So, when one of us (CL) sees a ball he is influenced by his culture's obsession with kicking it, "heading" it, and his own lifelong obsession with Tottenham Hotspur Association Football (i.e., soccer) Club. The reader will doubtless have a different set of "understandings" of this term. Such an example shows how important cultural processes are in the way in which simple objects like balls are defined and observed. Children and adults gain access to such definitions within a framework of social interaction. This structure is what Chapman (1991, p. 211) termed the "epistemic triangle . . . consisting of an active subject, the object of knowledge, and a (real or implicit) interlocutor, together with their mutual relations" (see Figure 10.1). Thus, according to this approach, we have to take into account the way in which objects of knowledge are interpreted, or mediated, through culture in order to grasp how thinking develops. The epistemic triangle can be used to theorize the development of children's social

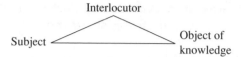

Figure 10.1   The epistemic triangle. *Source*: Chapman (1991). Reprinted by permission of Lawrence Erlbaum Associates Ltd.

understanding as well as the development of knowledge about the physical world. As we suggest later, others like Hobson (2002) use a similar theoretical framework emphasizing affective engagement in infancy.

The fundamental point of Chapman's approach is that understanding the development of "cognitive" skills is inseparable from an understanding of how such skills are constructed in social interaction. Within everyday interactions children constantly negotiate with others who may have different beliefs or perspectives. Such negotiations might involve issues like the location or identity of objects, but may also involve social or moral issues, like whether the child should get another cookie for good behavior. Children construct an understanding of how they and other people acquire knowledge of the world and they may achieve comparable levels of development at similar ages because of commonalities in their experience, not because a module is switched on or because the child suddenly realizes that the mind is a representational device.

Our contention is that social understanding in particular requires us to theorize about how children discover the world through their interactions with others. An examination of the child's negotiations leads us to look at the way in which words acquire meaning. In chapter 7 we did this by describing Wittgenstein's analysis of language use, especially his private language argument, which we used as a critique of a psychology based upon the assumption that the problem children face is how to label their internal mental states (remember the beetle box example?). To our minds, the addition of Wittgenstein to Chapman's interpretation of Vygotsky and Piaget has clear advantages because it highlights fundamental issues that we must overcome in understanding how children may come to understand the words used to talk about the psychological world. Wittgenstein's analysis gives us further justification for the validity of the epistemic triangle, in that it underlines the point that all our "internal" thoughts must be drawn from public conversation. In order to give this analysis a more concrete foundation (we realize that it is conceptually difficult to grasp), we turn to two areas of research to explore the development of the epistemic triangle and further development within this form of interaction.

Two areas of research: social development in infancy and talking about the mind

Social development in infancy

We first have to explain how infants develop the capacity to engage in triadic interaction. That is, how the epistemic triangle develops. From the relational perspective that we take (see chapter 4), the starting point in development is a position of relative non-differentiation between self, other, and the world (following Baldwin, 1906; Hobson, 1993, 2002; Merleau-Ponty, 1964; Piaget, 1936/1963; Vygotsky, 1998; Werner & Kaplan, 1963). It is through social interactions that infants develop a succession of differentiations between inner and outer, subject and object, and self and other (Müller & Runions, 2003). Within the perspective adopted by Piaget (1937/1971), such interactions are vital for infants to develop sensorimotor action schemes, which embody knowledge because they are modified as a function of the differences between what is anticipated and what the infant actually experiences (Chapman, 1999). Our position is that the early forms of coordinated attention in which infants begin to engage are not yet manifestations of a general insight of others as intentional agents. Rather, infants learn about particular joint attention events. We take a lean theoretical perspective but this does not mean that we ignore the rich forms of interaction in which infants engage already during the first year of life (e.g., Reddy, 2003). Instead we view this as an early form of practical, lived, or sensorimotor knowledge, which is not the same thing as later-developing forms of more explicit social knowledge.

In taking a lean view of infant social development, within an activity-based constructive view of knowledge that underlies Piagetian theory, how do we explain the development of concepts? At 9 to 12 months infants' interaction with others can be described as involving an understanding of others as intentional agents. But this is not a concept that drives their behavior. Rather, they have acquired patterns of interaction with others, or ways of engaging with and responding to others. Such skills begin during the first year of life, as we see in infants' ability to respond to and play with others' reactions to the self (Reddy, 2003). But it is essential to be clear that this is a sensorimotor understanding of others in that it is embedded within everyday actions. Infants have learned to respond to others' directedness toward objects and to the self. Such abilities to use gestures and respond to others' gestures and gaze are all forms of knowledge of other people. However, at first these sets of expectations about other people are not combined. They may develop separately within the infant's experience of interaction in different situations such as following others' gaze or directing others' attention. All of these various interactional schemes or patterns of responding to others begin to be combined, or reciprocally assimilated, because they all concern other people. This happens in the same manner as an infant develops knowledge about an object such as a ball. The baby develops various action schemes about what he or she can do with the object, such as grasping, dropping, and sucking. These schemes are combined, or reciprocally assimilated, and this process results in a separation from the infant's own action. When all of this is combined, then we can talk about the infant as having a concept, but it has developed through activity. The same process occurs with early knowledge of other people. This knowledge is at first manifest in infants' action; that is, they know what they can do in certain situations. They have expectations about what will happen. These are similar to a fundamental pattern in attachment theory; that infants develop internal working models, or sets of expectations about interactions with caregivers.

At this point infants and their caregivers have developed shared practices – routines in which the infant knows what to expect, including interaction involving joint attention such as pointing gestures. This is a form of social interaction that is sometimes referred to as prelinguistic because it is before words are used yet it is the basic form of interaction on which language is built. It involves directing others' attention to aspects of shared situations. At this point words can be added to the practices and the child begins to use these words. It follows from our position and the concept of the epistemic triangle that this process of learning about human activity is intertwined with learning to talk about such activity.

Language and social development

Language is based on earlier forms of triadic interaction and it also makes more complex forms of social understanding possible through the development of the ability to talk about the psychological world. As we discussed in chapter 7, there is considerable research on the relations between language and social understanding, and in particular on children's exposure to mental state terms. On the issue of how children learn the meaning of mental state terms, our approach differs in a fundamental way from most other theories. We will rehearse the central issue in chapter 7 here. One common view of language is that words are like names of things and so learning word meanings involves "mapping" a new word onto its referent. This also entails a code model of language, according to which communication is accomplished by words encoding meaning that is transmitted to others who decode the message (for a critique of such a view see Turnbull, 2003). On this view of language as based on word–object mappings, learning the meaning of mental state terms would involve linking mental state terms to inner mental entities. The meaning of a word is based on its connection to the referent, in this case a mental state. It is this view of language that is assumed in much of the "theory of mind" literature. The majority of accounts of mental state understanding in the "theories of mind" literature assume a view of mental states as inner mental entities that are causally related to behavior. Thus children must learn about them through inference or introspection.

However, there are a number of important critiques of this view of language from Wittgenstein (1968) and others (e.g., Budwig, 2000; Montgomery, 2002; Tomasello, 2003; Turnbull, 2003). Chapter 7 presented Wittgenstein's private language argument against the idea that beliefs and intentions are inner mental entities that cause behavior and can be introspected upon in order to learn the meanings of mental state words. From this perspective there is no inner mental entity that belief talk could refer to. Instead, talk about mental states refers to *activity*. How does the notion of activity fit into the notion of the epistemic triangle? It helps us to understand why there is a need to stress the role of social interaction in learning about words as objects of knowledge. Ways of acting provide the foundation for learning the meaning of psychological terms (Chapman, 1987; Malcolm, 1991; Racine, 2004; Racine & Carpendale, in press). For example, children's competence in the practices involved in joint attention such as following and directing others' attention usually provides the foundation for learning the use of words such as "look" and "see." Although these words would not be classified as mental state terms, they do refer to the psychological world. Learning how to talk about the psychological world involves learning the criteria for the use of such words. Much of Wittgenstein's discussion focused on sensation words. And as Chapman (1987, p. 105) noted,

the criteria for the correct use of sensation-words must be publicly available, otherwise we could never agree when we were using them correctly and communication on such matters would be impossible. But if the significance of sensation-words is based on public agreement, the same is true of psychological words such as "thinking," "feeling," "intending," "believing," and so on. The significance of these terms is not known to us only from our own subjective experience, rather we come to know them by learning the appropriate contexts in which they are used.

As Wittgenstein (1968, §580) stated, "An 'inner process' stands in need of outward criteria." Chapman (1987, p. 105) went on to define criteria as "the characteristic circumstances, behavior, or expressive reactions which by convention justify the use of terms denoting particular subjective states or processes. Indeed, if these 'external' tokens of 'internal' processes did not exist, we could never have learned how to use the respective psychological words in the first place."

It might seem that the position we are describing entails an enculturation approach according to which children passively adopt culturally specific concepts that are free to vary across language communities. We reject this approach for two reasons. First, although there are cultural differences in forms of social understanding (Lillard, 1998), at the basic level we are concerned with here we argue that there are universal and necessary aspects of human forms of life. Human infants are at first helpless and need to be cared for, which results in the need to share attention and make requests. There are universal patterns of human activity and experience due to our similar experiences. For example, as Canfield (1993) has argued, although cultures may differ in how they talk about intentions, it is likely that all cultures will need some way to talk about intentions. Second, from our perspective the process of children learning the meaning of mental state terms – that is, learning the criteria for the use of such terms – is constructive. That is, children will at first acquire a partial set of criteria, or a partial understanding of the correct context of use for mental state terms. And gradually, through interaction in the epistemic triangle sense, they will come to a more complete understanding of the meaning of such terms (Carpendale & Lewis, 2004a). For example, Lillard (1993b) found that when young children first use the word "pretend" they have a partial understanding of it as referring to an action being performed rather than also involving knowledge and intentions (see chapter 3).

Once children can begin to talk about the psychological world they can understand others' talk about such aspects of human activity in terms of the criteria for the use of such words. For example, if we talk about whether someone is happy or sad, or has seen something, children understand the meaning of these words in terms of the reactions or activity on which they are based. This understanding then gives children the ability to reflect upon the psychological world (Fernyhough, 2004).

What Do We Predict about the
Nature of Development?

If the child constructs an understanding of the social world within daily interactions, what should we predict about the development of these skills? How different is this theoretical perspective from traditional accounts, notably the "theory theory" approach described in chapter 2 that has dominated discussion over the past 20 years? We present here what we feel are the two main characteristics of development which follow from our theoretical argument, outlined above: gradualism and the role of social interaction.

Gradualism

If we look back at the evidence of social skills in infancy, no matter which example you choose, the evidence, we argue, is that babies learn the skills of coordinating attention and using gestures in a very piecemeal way determined by their own skills and the skills employed by adults to scaffold their activities. Chapter 4 details the slow emergence of infant social skills. Such *gradualism* is central to our position. We are not the first to make this claim about development. For example, it has been used to explain the very protracted development of language by Katherine Nelson (1997) and the nature of change within the child's developing understanding of the mind (Russell, 1996; Woodfield, 1996). We contend that such gradualism extends beyond infant development. Indeed preschoolers' capabilities have over the past decade been described in terms of more subtle shifts than the dramatic acquisition of false beliefs suggested by Wellman et al.'s (2001) interpretation of their meta-analysis.

Let's revisit two examples of research summarized in chapter 3. In the early 1990s a debate took place over the nature of pretend play. Attempts were made by Perner et al. (1994) to describe achievements in pretense that have similar complexity but do not, they claimed, involve mental state understanding, with the term "prelief." Similar differentiations have been made with reference to 2- to 3-year-olds' looks at the correct location in the unexpected transfer test (see chapter 3) before they fail the false belief test question by identifying the incorrect (i.e., true) location. Ruffman (2000, p. 263) has suggested that the child develops a succession of "rudimentary prototheories," while Clements and Perner (1994) suggest that an "implicit theory of mind" is replaced by an explicit one. However, we feel that this way of describing the child's developing skill is problematic for two reasons. First, it only goes so far in describing change. Terms like "implicit" false belief understanding carry with them much theoretical baggage, that presupposes that we have an understanding of the phenomenon. We contend that such a presupposition may actually mislead us rather than clarify subtle shifts in development. Secondly, they might distract us from looking for the other aspects of change. There is a tendency in developmental psychology to refer to major transitions, thus collapsing complex series of shifts (Chandler, 2001). A bias that for the past 30 years Michael Chandler has attempted to steer the field away from is the tendency to sensationalize development into one or two miraculous developments, like the demise of egocentrism at about age 7 or the acquisition of false belief understanding in the fifth year of life.

So why do there appear to be general developments like the acquisition of false belief understanding (Wellman et al., 2001)? From our theoretical position, they may simply show that 4- to 5-year-old children across a variety of cultures have engaged in sufficient interaction with others and how they can sometimes be mistaken, to enable them and not their younger counterparts to pass the false belief test (a similar argument is put by Scholl & Leslie, 2001). The constructivist view makes different predictions to the theory theory, by assuming that the child's acquisition of knowledge within a domain will vary according to subtle changes in the interactions in which they engage. For example, Wellman et al. found that if the protagonist's motive is made explicit or if the child actively participates in the procedure (we cited Chandler & Hala, 1994; Hala & Chandler, 1996, in chapter 3), then more preschoolers pass the test. Similar effects are produced when the child acts out the protagonist's search pattern by taking one doll to search for another in a game of hide-and-seek (Freeman, Lewis, & Doherty, 1991). Given that such improvements occurred only when the protagonist had a reason for searching in the wrong place (there was a control condition when one protagonist was casually looking for another), it seems that children in the hide-and-seek condition were more successful because they were actively supported both by a combination of the social interaction with the experimenter and the game they were playing. Such contrasts in findings provide a glimpse of how mental state understanding develops. That is, children's attention and motivation may at first be supported by interacting with others which facilitates their understanding of the implications of the comings and goings in situations involving false belief.

Other recent research provides further support for gradualism in that it demonstrates the influence of the social context of the assessment procedure on the child's performance. For example, some inconsistency between laboratory-based assessment procedures – standard false belief tests – and naturalistic observation of young children has been reported. Although children usually pass standard false belief tests after their fourth birthdays, parents report observing their $2^1/_2$- or young 3-year-olds apparently demonstrating an understanding of false belief at home (Astington, 2000; Newton, Reddy, & Bull, 2000). In Newton et al.'s (2000) diary study parents reported many incidents in which their young children were involved in deception, even though these children clearly failed false belief tasks. Although such data can be interpreted to reveal low competence in the child (Astington, 2003), Newton et al. put forward an argument in favor of gradualism: Young children engage in deceptive acts with only partial understanding and such experience is the context for learning about deception. The variability in performance across different tests is usually explained in terms of performance factors that mask the child's competence. Yet, if an individual has developed a particular competence, why do they demonstrate it in some situations but not others?

As Chapman (1987) pointed out, teasing apart performance factors from an underlying competence is no easy matter. It assumes that there is one competence which is presumed to arrive all in one piece, like a theory or a set of rules, and is what Chapman (1987) referred to as the "measurement model." He suggested an alternative, the "membership model," which describes varying degrees of understanding that are assessed with different procedures. This model appears to account for the child's gradual acquisition of knowledge about social relationships – what Judy Dunn (1996) calls "understanding-in-action" and what Vygotsky referred to as the driving force of development. The notion of gradualism can be applied to phases of development beyond the single "miracle" of false belief understanding. In chapter 8 we described research which suggests that after age 5 children attain further achievements in understanding. Thus, 5-year-olds find it hard to apply their simple false belief knowledge to understand their own and others' ignorance or inferential skill (Varouxaki et al., 1999). An interpretive understanding of the mind (Carpendale & Chandler, 1996) is then a step toward a more mature understanding of mind, but even during adolescence and adulthood further developments must take place (e.g., Chandler, Hallett, & Sokol, 2001). The dominant theories that we described in chapter 2 have been less clear about what happens in development after the child's fifth birthday.

The centrality of relationships in social development

In chapter 6 we charted the many social factors that appear to correlate with the development of skills like false belief understanding. However, we concluded that the currently dominant theories of social understanding have failed fully to account for the wealth of social data, which will undoubtedly be added to over the coming years. We return to these social factors here. Any account of how the child achieves social understanding must explain why tests of the child's understanding of the psychological world are significantly correlated with factors in their social environment, like attachments, the number of siblings, parenting styles, and parent–child communication. We suggest that these factors are important because they indicate the role of social processes in the child's development (following Dunn, 1996, 2004). We feel that the epistemic triangle is an important conceptual framework for explaining how these social processes might influence the child's developing social understanding. As we have stated above, it is based on the assumption that a grasp of any object of knowledge (social or indeed non-social) must be mediated through our negotiations with other people. The coordination of another person's differing perspectives with the child's own perspective allows access to greater insights into how the social world works. Accordingly, children develop an understanding of mind through such interaction, and in confronting others' often differing beliefs about the world children gradually construct a more complete understanding that increasingly coordinates their own experience with that of other people. As such interactions are the very stuff of social development, we would expect that differences in the amount and nature of the social interaction experienced would be related to individual differences in infants' early social understanding and to young children's further developing mentalistic understanding. Where do we see the importance of such relationships?

An aspect of relationships to begin with concerns the role of attachment in social understanding. In chapter 6 we pointed out that both the child's early attachment (e.g., Meins, 1997) and the mother's use of language referring to the child's beliefs, desires, and intentions (e.g., Meins et al., 2002) seem to be predictors of later social understanding. Although there is controversy over the mechanisms of change in the child, these two sets of evidence place centrally on the agenda the issue of the importance of close relationships in fostering the child's ability to make sense of social experience. Not only do close attachments increase the likelihood of young children being more likely to experience talk about the psychological world, they also lead us toward a social explanation of how these skills emerge and, more importantly, an analysis of how "affect" and "cognition" can be understood in relation to one another or as part of the same process. Bowlby's (1969) analysis of internal working models involves the assumption that attachment security is based on a parent's way of relating to the infant, which in turn may influence the infant's ability to engage with others. Within infants' everyday interactions, their developing internal working models consist of knowledge of other people and their expectations about relationships in general (Baldwin & Moses, 1996). This definition of internal working models converges with Piagetian ideas about development being rooted in the development of knowledge in interaction. Piaget (1945/1962) described the "affective schemes" (pp. 188–189) and "personal schemes" (pp. 206–207) that infants develop as "modes of feeling and reacting" to people in ways that sound like internal working models, that is, the set of expectations infants build up about other people and how they will act. This is early "sensorimotor" understanding: it is lived, practical knowledge about people based on expectations acquired through experience of how particular people respond.

This analysis of the infant's internal working models fits into the framework of our general developmental theory, which describes a gradual emergence of social knowledge within social interaction and relationships. The link with attachment is important because it identifies that "cognitive" processes, like mental state understanding, do not develop in an emotional vacuum. Hobson (1994, 2002) suggests that it is early affective engagement that provides the essential ingredients for the establishment of shared attention. At about 8 months a "relatedness triangle" is established in which it is the very intensity of affective exchange that facilitates this ability: "infants not only relate to another person and the nonpersonal world of objects and events, but they also relate to the *other person's* relatedness towards the world and towards themselves – the relatedness triangle among self, other, and the environment" (Hobson, 1994, p. 75, italics in original). Hobson's analysis shows how, even in infancy, we need to conceptualize the individual's construction of events within the "relatedness" between the self, the other, and the items to which each refers. Indeed it is the very fact that the infant comes to know that the world is "sharable" (p. 78) that drives him or her gradually to understand that others have unique perspectives on that world.

It is analyses like Hobson's that underpin why we dedicated a chapter of this book to the issues of how infants come to share attention with others – this extraordinary feature of human communication is the basis of so many of the skills that we regard as vital in social development. Research on the development of affective exchange in infancy has greatly illuminated key issues in infant development. The detailed examples in chapter 4 are convincing in showing the importance of gradual change in social relatedness. It is more difficult to pinpoint how these influences continue once the child acquires language and other symbolic systems of thought and communication. However, we have attempted to show some of these links in the data presented in chapters 6–9. For a start, the correlations between early exchanges and tests of later mental state understanding suggest that we need to understand the child's social cognition within a broad explanatory framework. In addition we need to explain factors like the link between parenting style and social cognitive development (Astington, 1996; Hughes, Deater-Deckard, & Cutting, 1999; Pears & Moses, 2003; Vinden, 2001). Why is it that cooperative sibling (Dunn et al., 1991) and peer interactions (Brown et al., 1996), or parental disciplinary styles that ask the child to reflect on the other's feelings (Ruffman et al., 1999), relate to the child's developing social understanding?

To address these connections we contend that we need to understand what Piaget termed "cooperative" relationships, which naturally extend from the embeddedness and mutual understanding within attachment relationships. When describing the epistemic triangle, Michael Chapman (1991, 1999) argued that it is in the act of coordinating other people's perspectives with one's own (a crucial part of the epistemic triangle) that children develop social understanding. Although "cognitive conflict" is often thought to be the major impetus for change in Piaget's theory, in his work on moral judgment Piaget (1932/1965, 1977/1995) suggests that it is cooperation that is important in such developments. Cooperation does not necessarily refer to harmonious interaction but rather to inter-action among equals who therefore feel obliged to explain their positions and understand other people's views. It is this form of interaction that Piaget argued is most likely to lead to mutual understanding and thus to the development of knowledge. Such cooperative interaction among equals stands in contrast to relationships of constraint in which, due to an imbalance of power, one person can simply impose his or her position without attempting to reach mutual understanding. In our terms, if social cognition is gradually constructed by the child within triadic interaction, then it follows that the extent and nature of cooperation between the child and others should facilitate the child's understanding of social situations and thus the development of social knowledge.

The data presented in chapters 6 and 7 show how varied are the types of interaction which need to be accommodated into a theory of the social influences on social understanding. How do we explain the roles of experiences in activities as various as cooperative peer interaction, shared pretense, and the different forms of talk? Of course, such correlations do not allow us to draw causal conclusions. Almost 40 years ago R. Q. Bell (1968) pointed out that the parent-child relationship is a system, in which interactions are influenced by contributions by both the child and the parents. So, although parents' beliefs about parenting or child rearing (e.g., Baumrind, 1991; Goodnow & Collins, 1991) may be important, many other factors influence their everyday parenting styles. For example, parents' skills are influenced by their levels of stress, the amount of support they feel they receive, their economic circumstances, and their other commitments, particularly those at work. At the same time, the amount of parental support of the child's reasoning will both partly depend on, and interact with, the characteristics of the child, like her temperament and her developmental level.

How can our claims about the centrality of the role of relationships in the child's construction of social understanding be tested empirically? Given the richness of factors that contribute to these relationships, no single causal explanation is possible. However, we feel that there are sufficient types of evidence that enable us to single out the general, yet important, influence of relationships. The most compelling comes from children with disabilities in interacting with other people, an area we discussed in chapter 6. Most research has been conducted on children with autism. While some have argued that the primary problem for children with autism lies in their lack of ability to engage in social interaction, and thus benefit from cooperative and supportive relationships (Hobson, 2002), other theoreticians have presented accounts which center on more complex skills like a deficiency in general cognitive skills (Hill & Frith, 2004; Russell, 1997) or "theory of mind" (Baron-Cohen et al., 2000). The research on children with sensory loss is more convincing because their problems are not usually compounded by learning disability and severe social problems. The performance of different subgroups of deaf children pinpoints important likely influences. Both deafness and blindness necessarily make joint attention more difficult to achieve and these children's general problems in mental state understanding have been used to demonstrate the link between social interaction and "theory of mind" (e.g.,

Minter et al., 1998; Peterson et al., 2000). Moreover, the more typical developmental pathways of deaf children with signing parents (Woolfe et al., 2002) allows us to be more confident about the centrality of factors like conversation in how the child develops social understanding.

To conclude this section: We feel that the evidence is compelling for gradualism in the child's unfolding grasp of the psychological world. This is shown clearly in the skills that combine as babies and toddlers come to master joint attention, and we feel there is also sufficient evidence for gradualism in the development of older children's social knowledge. The issue of joint attention is also vital as a means of showing the roles of relationships, communication, and cooperative interaction in the development of these skills. We cannot specify particular "mechanisms" of social influence because social relationships are complex and transactional – both parties contribute to the interactions in a dynamic way over time (Sameroff & Chandler, 1975). However, research like that on children with sensory loss points to the importance of social engagement in the development of these important skills. We agree with Peter Hobson (2002) that such factors reveal the centrality of the child's ability to engage in "interpersonal relatedness," to use daily interactions as a means of coming to see different perspectives and gain knowledge of the self in interaction.

What's Wrong with Our Analysis?

We have been fortunate to have received close critical scrutiny for the theoretical position that we have developed in this chapter, since the article in which we presented our case (Carpendale & Lewis, 2004a) was followed by 38 peer commentaries. We have addressed many of these criticisms through the book. In this section we rehearse the main points made in these analyses and our response to such criticisms (Carpendale & Lewis, 2004b). We identified three major criticisms within the commentaries. First, a group argued, from very different theoretical positions, that the theory does not make a new contribution to the literature on social understanding. A second theme concerns whether we can account adequately for particular milestones and issues in development. The third refers to whether we have gone far enough in embedding children's social understanding within a social framework. We will address each of these issues in two sections, combining the final two.

Is there a need for a *social*-constructivist theory?

Some commentators on our theoretical article claimed that we simply employ classic theories and there is nothing new in our approach (Lourenço, 2004) or that the social perspective has already been taken into consideration (e.g., Astington, 2004; Fernyhough, 2004; Meins, 2004; Steele, 2004). Clearly we do draw on the theories of Piaget and Vygotsky. However, these ideas cannot simply be used off the shelf and must be applied to the problem of how children develop social understanding. Furthermore, there are various interpretations of Piaget's and Vygotsky's theories. It is correct that several authors have discussed Vygotsky's theory in relation to the evidence of links between social interaction and social development. But as we discussed in chapter 6, there is still some distance to go in making sense of the notion of internalization.

The bonus of having had so many commentators reflect upon the position that we have summarized above is that collectively they have examined it from a diversity of theoretical angles. In psychology, as in other sciences, the interpretations that are given to the "facts" are as important as the "facts" themselves. Indeed we apply the epistemic triangle to adult thinking as much as we do to children developing knowledge. All our thoughts about events and concepts are mediated by our interactions with others, past and present, even if those "others" are hypothetical. As we have shown so often in this book, the data on infant social-cognitive development, general cognitive skills, the social correlates with "theory of mind" skill, language, and the panoply of other skills the child develops each can be interpreted in a diversity of ways. Our position has been reflected upon critically in such ways. To theory theorists (e.g., Bartsch & Estes, 2004; Ruffman, 2004) the social data that we have summarized are seen as unproblematic. According to them the young child theoretician needs evidence in order to construct a "theory of mind" – more, or perhaps more challenging, data increase the discrepancies that the child faces and are likely to force a change in their current theory.

Similarly, modularity theorists also claim to be able to account for the wealth of social evidence (German & Leslie, 2004). We have considered the theoretical problems associated with the theory theory and modularity views in chapter 2, so will not repeat these here. However, we reiterate our fundamental disagreement with the theory theory and modularity perspectives by citing another commentator. As Montgomery

(2004) pointed out, the fault line between our position and others concerns views about how children learn the meaning of mental state terms. He would agree with our analysis in chapter 7 and above, regarding views of mental states assumed in most approaches. In the approaches outlined in chapter 2 that have dominated discussion on social understanding over the past 20 years it is assumed that the mental state terms refer to inner mental states that causally influence behavior. And the problem the child faces is learning about such inner mental entities. In contrast, we have argued that the meaning of mental state terms is based on human activity (see also Sharrock & Coulter, 2004).

Did we go far enough?

A number of commentators argued that we did not go far enough and they have suggested ways to elaborate and extend our approach. One possible weakness in our approach is that it can be taken to suggest that social understanding begins when the child acquires the ability to engage in triadic interaction, while there is much that occurs during the first year (Wilson-Brune & Woodward, 2004). We were at pains to discuss in chapter 4 the work of Hobson and Reddy who place great emphasis upon dyadic exchanges between young infants and their caregivers. Nevertheless we could have gone further to explore the developments that take place during the first year when dyadic interaction is the main form of social interaction. For example, had space permitted here we would have developed this point to explore recent claims, like Hobson's, that autism is a disorder centered on problems in this early affective engagement (for a discussion see Leekam, 2005).

In reflecting on a potential problem from a Vygotskian perspective, Fernyhough (2004) questions whether the notion of the epistemic triangle is just a context for development or whether this structure also plays a role in children's reasoning about the mind. We (Carpendale & Lewis, 2004b) pointed out that the position from Chapman (1991, p. 219) that we draw on is that "interiorized communicative exchange between the subject and the interiorized interlocutor is the origin of reflective awareness." This is consistent with Fernyhough's (2004) use of Vygotskian theory in arguing that the epistemic triangle is internalized and this provides the ability for children to think about the psychological world. Further, because this form of thinking has its basis in social interaction this approach is naturally consistent with the evidence of social influences on social development.

Our analysis is social in its orientation, but we realize that in this book we have had to address a literature that has for 20 years focused upon somewhat "dry" mental states, like beliefs, as if children are small armchair philosophers. It was clear from many responses to our 2004 paper that there is a strong need to extend the "theory of mind" field to include a wider and more passionate list of topics. A common view was that we had not sufficiently included the role of emotions in our account (Banerjee, 2004; Fonagy, 2004; Hobson, 2004; Izard, 2004; Thompson & Raikes, 2004). We agree and in this book we have paid more attention to the role of emotions than we did in the article that they were discussing (see especially chapters 4 and 9). Other commentators pointed out that we did not spend enough time talking about other social factors in development such as the role of siblings, friendships, pretend play (Howe, 2004), peer interaction (Banerjee, 2004; Howe, 2004; Zerwas, Balaraman, & Brownell, 2004), the role of conflict (Howe, 2004; Thompson & Raikes, 2004), as well as the role of culture (Nelson, 2004; Vinden, 2004) and conversation (Astington, 2004; Nelson, 2004; Siegal, 2004; Thompson & Raikes, 2004; Walker-Andrews & Hudson, 2004). We agree and we feel that many such factors as well as executive functions (Hala, 2004) can be included in the general theoretical framework we have proposed. As we state earlier, the epistemic triangle which we have described has been applied to affective engagement in Hobson's (1994) "relatedness triangle." Still other commentators suggested broadening the definition of social understanding in various ways such as considering later developments after false belief understanding, including the understanding of more complex emotions (Banerjee, 2004). Here again we agree and in this book we have devoted chapters to exploring these issues and a broader view of social understanding.

Conclusion

How children become social beings and develop an understanding of their social worlds is the problem we have addressed in this chapter and through the book. It is important to remember that the way in which humans are social is very different from other social species such as social insects. We have argued that children's understanding of the social and psychological world develops within their interaction with others. Clearly we must explore the biological adaptations that make this development possible. However, such adaptations do not *constitute* social knowledge but rather concern the conditions which make it possible for such knowledge to develop. Why is it that such knowledge could not be pre-prepared and innately given? Why do we argue that the mind cannot be studied simply by studying the brain? Although we emphasize the importance of investigation at the neurological level, we point out that this does not solve the problem of how we make the leap from causal neurological processes to meaningful human conduct. It is somewhat paradoxical to use the computer as a model for the mind and to view thinking as based on algorithms because computers do not know anything or understand anything, yet it is knowledge and understanding that we are trying to explain. In some sense it could be claimed that computers contain and process information. But this is in the same sense that train schedules contain information – neither the computer nor the train schedule knows anything (Carpendale & Lewis, 2004b; Kenny, 1991; Müller et al., 1998a, 1998b).

We have argued that the forms of thinking we are investigating in this book are necessarily social and therefore cannot have evolved as algorithms embedded in evolved neurological circuitry. Instead we have proposed that human forms of cognition are built on the capacity to engage with other people's attention. This provides the foundation for language and forms of cognition resulting from the internalization of communicative interaction. It is important to be clear that this is not the common view of language as based on the transmission of encoded meaning. Instead, language is built on a process of directing others' attention (Mead, 1934; Tomasello, 2003; Tomasello et al. in press). Thus, it is necessarily indexical; that is, meaning depends on the sequence of ongoing interaction (Turnbull, 2003). Meaning is not fixed to words, but rather people use words to convey meaning. From this perspective, infants are not simply born with minds and have to learn how to communicate, but rather infants develop the capacity to communicate and this leads to the development of the mind and human forms of cognition (Mead, 1934).

When we apply this view of mind and meaning to social cognitive development we arrive at a picture of the human infant gradually forming and coordinating distinctions between his or her perspective and the perspectives of others. The ability to form expectations about shared activities provides the practices on which language is built. This then allows children to learn how to talk about the psychological world of human activity. And, in turn, the ability to talk about the psychological world can then be used to think about this dimension.

The preoccupation of developmental psychology over the past 20 years with the "theory of mind" account has been fascinating in its intellectual complexity and in the range of studies which it has inspired. However, we have questioned the philosophical basis of this enterprise and propose on the basis of the analysis in this chapter and the wealth of evidence presented in this book that it is time for the field to become more social and to pay more attention to the child as an emotional being who develops social understanding within the complexity of his or her relationships.

References

Abu-Akel, A. (2003). A neurobiological mapping of theory of mind. *Brain Research Reviews*, *43*, 29–40.

Adamson, L. B., & Frick, J. E. (2003). The still face: A history of a shared experimental paradigm. *Infancy*, *4*, 451–473.

American Psychiatric Association. (1994). *Diagnostic and statistical manual of mental disorders* (4th ed.). Washington, DC: American Psychiatric Association.

Amsel, E., & Smalley, J. D. (2000). Beyond really and truly: Children's counterfactual thinking about pretend and possible worlds. In P. Mitchell & K. J. Riggs (Eds.), *Children's reasoning and the mind* (pp. 121–148). Hove: Psychology Press.

Andrews, G., Halford, G. S., Bunch, K. M., Bowden, D., & Jones, T. (2003). Theory of mind and relational complexity. *Child Development*, *74*, 1476–1499.

Anisfeld, M. (1991). Neonatal imitation. *Developmental Review*, *11*, 60–97.

Anisfeld, M. (1996). Only tongue protrusion modeling is matched by neonates. *Developmental Review*, *16*, 149–161.

Anisfeld, M., Turkewitz, G., & Rose, S. (2001). No compelling evidence that newborns imitate oral gestures. *Infancy*, *2*, 111–122.

Apperly, I. A., & Robinson, E. J. (1998). Children's mental representations of referential relations. *Cognition*, *67*, 287–309.

Apperly, I. A., & Robinson, E. J. (2001). Children's difficulties handling dual identity. *Journal of Experimental Child Psychology*, *78*, 374–397.

Appleton, M., & Reddy, V. (1996). Teaching three year-olds to pass false belief tests: A conversational approach. *Social Development*, *5*, 275–291.

Arsenio, W. F., & Lemerise, E. A. (2001). Varieties of childhood bullying: Values, emotional processes and social competence. *Social Development*, *10*, 59–73.

Astington, J. W. (1990a). *Wishes and plans. Children's understanding of intentional causation.* Paper presented to the Annual Meeting of the Jean Piaget Society, Philadelphia, May.

Astington, J. W. (1990b). Narrative and the child's theory of mind. In B. K. Britton & A. D. Pellegrini (Eds.), *Narrative thought and narrative language* (pp. 151–171). Hillsdale, NJ: Lawrence Erlbaum Associates.

Astington, J. W. (1993). *The child's discovery of the mind.* Cambridge, MA: Harvard University Press.

Astington, J. W. (1996). What is theoretical about the child's understanding of mind?: A Vygotskian view of its development. In P. Carruthers & P. K. Smith, (Eds.), *Theories of theories of mind* (pp. 184–199). Cambridge: Cambridge University Press.

Astington, J. W. (2000). Language and metalanguage in children's understanding of mind. In J. W. Astington (Ed.), *Minds in the making: Essays in honor of David R. Olson* (pp. 267–284). Oxford: Blackwell.

Astington, J. W. (2001). The future of theory-of-mind research: Understanding motivational states, the role of language, and real-world consequences. *Child Development, 72,* 685–687.

Astington, J. W. (2003). Sometimes necessary, never sufficient: False belief understanding and social competence. In B. Repacholi & V. Slaughter (Eds.), *Individual differences in theory of mind: Implications for typical and atypical development* (pp. 13–38). New York: Psychology Press.

Astington, J. W. (2004). What's new about social construction? Distinct roles needed for language and communication. *Behavioral and Brain Sciences, 27,* 96–97.

Astington, J. W., & Baird, J. A. (Eds.) (2005). *Why language matters for theory of mind.* New York: Oxford University Press.

Astington, J. W., & Gopnik, A. (1988). Knowing you've changed your mind: Children's understanding of representational change. In J. W. Astington, P. L. Harris & D. R. Olson (Eds.), *Developing theories of mind* (pp. 193–206). Cambridge: Cambridge University Press.

Astington, J. W., & Gopnik, A. (1991). Theoretical explanations of children's understanding of mind. *British Journal of Developmental Psychology, 9,* 7–29.

Astington, J. W., & Jenkins, J. M. (1995). Theory of mind development and social understanding. *Cognition and Emotion, 9,* 151–165.

Astington, J. W., & Jenkins, J. M. (1999). A longitudinal study of the relations between language and theory-of-mind development. *Developmental Psychology, 35,* 1311–1320.

Astington, J. W., & Olson, D. R. (1995). The cognitive revolution in children's understanding of mind. *Human Development, 38,* 179–189.

Astington, J. W., Harris, P. L., & Olson, D. R. (Eds.) (1988). *Developing theories of mind.* New York: Cambridge University Press.

Avis, J., & Harris, P. L. (1991). Belief–desire reasoning among Baka children: Evidence for a universal conception of mind. *Child Development, 62,* 460–467.

Baddeley, A. D., & Hitch, G. J. (1974). Working memory. In G. Bower (Ed.), *The psychology of learning and motivation: Advances in research and theory* (pp. 47–89). London: Academic Press.

Baird, J. A., & Astington, J. W. (2004). The role of mental state understanding in the development of moral cognition and moral action. In J. A. Baird & B. W. Sokol (Eds.), *Connections between theory of mind and sociomoral development. New Directions for Child and Adolescent Development, 103,* 37–49. San Francisco: Jossey-Bass.

Baird, J. A., & Sokol, B. W. (Eds.). (2004). Connections between theory of mind and sociomoral development. *New Directions for Child and Adolescent Development, 103.* San Francisco: Jossey-Bass.

Bakeman, R., & Adamson, L. B. (1984). Coordinating attention to people and objects in mother–infant and peer–infant interaction. *Child Development, 55,* 1278–1289.

Baldwin, D. A. (1991). Infants' contributions to the achievement of joint reference. *Child Development, 62,* 875–890.

Baldwin, D. A. (1995). Understanding the link between joint attention and language. In C. Moore & P. J. Dunham (Eds.), *Joint attention: Its origins and role in development* (pp. 131–158). Hillsdale, NJ: Lawrence Erlbaum Associates.

Baldwin, D. A., & Moses, L. J. (1994). Early understanding of referential intent and attentional focus: Evidence from language and emotion. In C. Lewis & P. Mitchell (Eds.), *Children's early understanding of mind: Origins and development* (pp. 133–156). Hove, UK: Lawrence Erlbaum Associates.

Baldwin, D. A., & Moses, L. J. (1996). The ontogeny of social information gathering. *Child Development, 67,* 1915–1933.

Baldwin, J. M. (1906). *Thoughts and things, vol. 1: Functional logic.* New York: The MacMillan Company.

Banerjee, R. (2002a). Audience effects on self-presentation in childhood. *Social Development, 11,* 487–507.

Banerjee, R. (2002b). Children's understanding of self-presentational behavior: Links with mental-state reasoning and the attribution of embarrassment. *Merrill-Palmer Quarterly, 48,* 378–404.

Banerjee, R. (2004). The role of social experience in advanced social understanding. *Behavioral and Brain Sciences, 27,* 97–98.

Baron-Cohen, S. (1995). *Mindblindness: An essay on autism and theory of mind.* Cambridge, MA: MIT Press.

Baron-Cohen, S., & Robertson, M. (1995). Children with either autism, Gilles de la Tourette syndrome or both: Mapping cognition to specific syndromes. *Neurocase, 1,* 101–104.

Baron-Cohen, S., & Swettenham, J. (1996). The relationships between SAM and ToMM: Two hypotheses. In P. Carruthers & P. K. Smith (Eds.), *Theories of theories of mind* (pp. 158–168). Cambridge: Cambridge University Press.

Baron-Cohen, S. (1987). Autism and symbolic play. *British Journal of Developmental Psychology, 5,* 139–148.

Baron-Cohen, S. (2000). Theory of mind and autism: A fifteen year review. In S. Baron-Cohen, H. Tager-Flusberg, & D. J. Cohen (Eds.), *Understanding other minds* (pp. 3–20). Oxford: Oxford University Press.

Baron-Cohen, S., Allen, J., & Gillberg, C. (1992). Can autism be detected at 18 months? The needle, the haystack, and the CHAT. *British Journal of Psychiatry, 161,* 839–843.

Baron-Cohen, S., Cox, A., Baird, G., Swettenham, J., Nightingale, N., Morgan, K., Drew, A., & Charman, T. (1996). Psychological markers of autism at 18 months of age in a large population. *British Journal of Psychiatry, 168,* 158–163.

Baron-Cohen, S., Jolliffe, T., Mortimore, C., & Robertson, M. (1997). Another advanced test of theory of mind: Evidence from very high functioning adults with autism or Asperger syndrome. *Journal of Child Psychology and Psychiatry, 38,* 813–822.

Baron-Cohen, S., Leslie, A. M., & Frith, U. (1985). Does the autistic child have a "theory of mind"? *Cognition, 21,* 37–46.

Baron-Cohen, S., & Ring, H. (1994). A model of the mindreading system: Neuropsychological and neurobiological perspectives. In C. Lewis & P. Mitchell (Eds.), *Children's early understanding of mind: Origins and development.* Hove, UK: Lawrence Erlbaum Associates.

Baron-Cohen, S., Tager-Flusberg, H., & Cohen, D. J. (2000). *Understanding other minds.* Oxford: Blackwell.

Barreau, S., & Morton, J. (1999). Pulling smarties out of a bag: A headed records analysis of children's recall of their own past beliefs. *Cognition, 73,* 65–87.

Barresi, J., & Moore, C. (1996). Intentional relations and social understanding. *Behavioral and Brain Sciences, 19,* 107–154.

Bartsch, K. (2002). The role of experience in children's developing folk epistemology: Review and analysis from the theory-theory perspective. *New Ideas in Psychology, 20,* 145–161.

Bartsch, K., & Estes, D. (2004). Articulating the role of experience in mental state understanding: A challenge for theory-theory and other theories. *Behavioral and Brain Sciences, 27,* 99–100.

Bartsch, K., & Wellman, H. M. (1989). Young children's attribution of action to beliefs and desires. *Child Development, 60,* 946–964.

Bartsch, K., & Wellman, H. M. (1995). *Children talk about the mind.* Oxford: Oxford University Press.

Bates, E. (1976). *Language and context.* New York: Academic Press.

Bates, E. (1979). *The emergence of symbols: Cognition and communication in infancy.* New York: Academic Press.

Bates, E. (1984). Bioprograms and the innateness hypothesis. *Behavioral and Brain Sciences, 7,* 188–190.

Bates, E., Benigni, L., Bretherton, I., Camaioni, L., & Volterra, V. (1979). Cognition and communication from nine to thirteen months: Correlational findings. In E. Bates (Ed.), *The emergence of symbols: Cognition and communication in infancy* (pp. 69–140). New York: Academic Press.

Bates, E., Camaioni, L., & Volterra, V. (1975). The acquisition of performatives prior to speech. *Merrill-Palmer Quarterly, 21,* 205–226.

Bates, E., Camaioni, L., & Volterra, V. (1976). Sensorimotor performatives (pp. 49–71). In E. Bates (Ed.), *Language and context: The acquisition of pragmatics*. New York: Academic Press.

Baumrind, D. (1991). Parenting styles and adolescent development. In R. M. Lerner, A. C. Petersen, & J. Brooks-Gunn (Eds.), *Encyclopedia of adolescence* (vol. 2). New York: Garland.

Bell, R. Q. (1968). A reinterpretation of the direction of effects in studies of socialization. *Psychological Review*, 75, 81–95.

Bennett, M. R., & Hacker, P. M. S. (2003). *Philosophical foundations of neuroscience*. Oxford: Blackwell.

Bennett, M., & Matthews, L. (2000). The role of second-order belief-understanding and social context in children's self-attributions of social emotions. *Social Development*, 9, 126–130.

Bickhard, M. H. (2001). Why children don't have to solve the frame problems: Cognitive representations are not encodings. *Developmental Review*, 21, 224–262.

Bickhard, M. H. (2004). Why believe in beliefs? *Behavioral and Brain Sciences*, 27, 100–101.

Bjorklund, D. F., Cormier, C. A., & Rosenberg, J. S. (2005). The evolution of theory of mind: Big brains, social complexity and inhibition. In W. Schneider, R. Schumann-Hengsteler, & B. Sodian, B. (Eds.), *Young children's cognitive development: Interrelationships among executive functioning, working memory verbal ability and theory of mind* (pp. 147–174). Mahwah, NJ: Lawrence Erlbaum Associates.

Bloom, P., & German, T. P. (2000). Two reasons to abandon the false belief as a test of theory of mind. *Cognition*, 77, B25–B31.

Borke, H. (1971). Interpersonal perception of young children. *Developmental Psychology*, 5, 263–269.

Bosacki, S., & Astington, J. W. (1999). Theory of mind in preadolescence: Relations between social understanding and social competence. *Social Development*, 8, 237–255.

Bowers, L., Smith, P. K., & Binney, V. (1992). Cohesion and power in the families of children in bully/victim problems at school. *Journal of Family Therapy*, 14, 371–387.

Bowlby, J. (1969). *Attachment and loss. Vol. 1 Attachment*. Harmondsworth: Pelican.

Boyes, M., & Chandler, M. J. (1992). Cognitive development, epistemic doubt, and identity formation in adolescence. *Journal of Youth and Adolescence*, 21, 277–304.

Bradmetz, J., & Schneider, R. (1999). Is Little Red Riding Hood afraid of her grandmother? Cognitive vs. emotional response to a false belief. *British Journal of Developmental Psychology*, 17, 501–514.

Bretherton, I. (1991). Intentional communication and the development of an understanding of mind. In D. Frye & C. Moore (Eds.), *Children's theories of mind: Mental states and social understanding* (pp. 49–75). Hillsdale, NJ: Lawrence Erlbaum Associates.

Bretherton, I., Bates, E., Benigni, L., Camaioni, L., & Volterra, V. (1979). Relations between cognition, communication, and quality of attachment. In E. Bates (Ed.), *The emergence of symbols: Cognition and communication in infancy* (pp. 223–269). New York: Academic Press.

Bretherton, I., & Beeghly, M. (1982). Talking about internal states: The acquisition of an explicit theory of mind. *Developmental Psychology, 18*, 906–921.

Bretherton, I., McNew, S., & Beeghly-Smith, M. (1981). Early person knowledge as expressed in gestural and verbal communication: When do infants acquire a "theory of mind"? In M. E. Lamb & L. R. Sherrod (Eds.), *Infant social cognition: Empirical and theoretical considerations* (pp. 333–373). Hillsdale, NJ: Lawrence Erlbaum Associates.

Brown, J. R., Donelan-McCall, N., & Dunn, J. (1996). Why talk about mental states? The significance of children's conversations with friends, siblings, and mothers. *Child Development, 67*, 836–849.

Brown, P., & Levinson, S. (1987). *Politeness: Some universals in language usage*. Cambridge: Cambridge University Press.

Brown, T. (2003). Reductionism and the circle of sciences. In T. Brown & L. Smith (Eds.), *Reductionism and the development of knowledge* (pp. 3–26). Mahwah, NJ: Lawrence Erlbaum Associates.

Bruner, J. (1983). *Child's talk*. New York: Norton.

Bruner, J. (1986). *Actual minds, possible worlds*. Cambridge, MA: Harvard University Press.

Bruner, J. (1990). *Acts of meaning*. Cambridge, MA: Harvard University Press.

Bruner, J. (1995). From joint attention to the meeting of minds: An introduction. In C. Moore & P. J. Dunham (Eds.), *Joint attention: Its origins and role in development* (pp. 1–14). Hillsdale, NJ: Lawrence Erlbaum Associates.

Bruner, J., & Sherwood, V. (1976). Early rule structure: The case of "Peekaboo". In R. Harré (Ed.), *Life sentences: Aspects of the social role of language* (pp. 55–62). New York: Wiley.

Budwig, N. (1998). How far does a construction grammar approach to argument structure take us in understanding children's language development? *Journal of Child Language, 25*, 443–447.

Budwig, N. (2000). Language and the construction of the self. In N. Budwig, I. C. Uzgiris & J. V. Wertsch (Eds.), *Communication: An arena of development* (pp. 195–214). Stamford, CT: Ablex Publishing Corporation.

Budwig, N. (2002). A developmental-functionalist approach to mental state talk. In E. Amsel & J. P. Byrnes (Eds.), *Language, literacy, and cognitive development: The development and consequences of symbolic communication* (pp. 59–86). Mahwah, NJ: Lawrence Erlbaum Associates.

Budwig, N. (2004). The contributions of the interdisciplinary study of language to an understanding of mind. *Behavioral and Brain Sciences, 27*, 101–102.

Budwig, N., Wertsch, J. V., & Uzgiris, I. C. (2000). Communication, meaning, and development: Interdisciplinary perspectives. In N. Budwig, I. C. Uzgiris, & J. V. Wertsch (Eds.), *Communication: An arena of development* (pp. 1–14). Stamford, CT: Ablex Publishing Corporation.

Bühler, K. (1990). *Theory of language: The representational function of language*. Philadelphia: John Benjamins Publishing Co. (original work published 1934).

Butler, S. C., Caron, A. J., & Brooks, R. (2000). Infant understanding of the referential nature of looking. *Journal of Cognition and Development, 1*, 359–377.

Butterworth, G. (2001). Joint visual attention in infancy. In G. Bremner & A. Fogel (Eds.), *Blackwell handbook of infant development* (pp. 213–240). Oxford: Blackwell.

Butterworth, G. (2003). Pointing is the royal road to language for babies. In Sotaro Kita (Ed.), *Pointing: Where language, culture, and cognition meet* (pp. 9–33). Mahwah, NJ: Lawrence Erlbaum Associates.

Butterworth, G., & Jarrett, N. (1991). What minds have in common is space: Spatial mechanisms serving joint visual attention in infancy. *British Journal of Developmental Psychology, 9*, 55–72.

Butterworth, G. E. (1991). The ontogeny and phylogeny of joint visual attention. In A. Whiten (Ed.), *Natural theories of mind* (pp. 223–232). Oxford: Blackwell.

Butterworth, G. E. (1998). What is special about pointing in babies? In F. Simion & G. Butterworth (Eds.), *The development of sensory, motor and cognitive capacities in early infancy: From perception to cognition* (pp. 171–190). Hove, UK: Psychology Press.

Butterworth, G. E., Harris, P. L., Leslie, A. M., & Wellman, H. M. (Eds.) (1991). *Perspectives on the child's theory of mind*. Oxford: British Psychological Society/Oxford Science Publications.

Byrne, R., & Whiten, A. (1988). *Machiavellian intelligence*. Oxford: Oxford University Press.

Call, J. (2004). The use of social information in chimpanzees and dogs. In J. J. Rogers & G. Kaplan (Eds.), *Comparative vertebrate cognition*. New York: Kluwer Academic.

Call, J., & Tomasello, M. (1999). A nonverbal false belief task: The performance of children and great apes. *Child Development, 70*, 381–395.

Camaioni, L., Perucchini, P., Bellagamba, F., & Colonnesi, C. (2004). The role of declarative pointing in developing a theory of mind. *Infancy, 5*, 291–308.

Campbell, R. L., & Bickhard, M. H. (1993). Knowing levels and the child's understanding of mind. *Behavioral and Brain Sciences, 16*, 33–34.

Canfield, J. V. (1993). The living language: Wittgenstein and the empirical study of communication. *Language Sciences, 15*, 165–193.

Canfield, J. V. (1995). The rudiments of language. *Language and Communication, 15*, 195–211.

Carey, S. (1985a). *Conceptual change in childhood*. Cambridge, MA: MIT Press.

Carey, S. (1985b). Are children fundamentally different thinkers from adults? In I. S. F. Chipman, J. W. Segal, & E. R. Glaser (Eds.), *Thinking and learning skills* (vol. 2, pp. 485–517). Hillsdale, NJ: Lawrence Erlbaum Associates.

Carey, S. (1988). Conceptual differences between children and adults. *Mind and Language*, 3, 167–181.

Carlson, S. M., Mandell, D. J., & Williams, L. (2004). Executive function and theory of mind: Stability and prediction from ages 2 to 3. *Developmental Psychology*, 40, 1105–1122.

Carlson, S. M., & Moses, L. J. (2001). Individual differences in inhibitory control and children's theory of mind. *Child Development*, 72, 1032–1053.

Carlson, S. M., Moses, L. J., & Breton, C. (2002). How specific is the relation between executive function and theory of mind? Contribution of inhibitory control and working memory. *Infant and Child Development*, 11, 73–92.

Carlson, S. M., Moses, L. J., & Hix, H. R. (1998). The role of inhibitory control in young children's difficulties with deception and false belief. *Child Development*, 69, 672–691.

Caron, A. J., Kiel, E. J., Dayton, M., & Butler, S. C. (2002). Comprehension of the referential intent in looking and pointing between 12 and 15 months. *Journal of Cognition and Development*, 3, 445–464.

Carpendale, J. I. M. (2000). Kohlberg and Piaget on stages and moral reasoning. *Developmental Review*, 20, 181–205.

Carpendale, J. I. M., & Chandler, M. J. (1996). On the distinction between false belief understanding and subscribing to an interpretive theory of mind. *Child Development*, 67, 1686–1706.

Carpendale, J. I. M., & Lewis, C. (2004a). Constructing an understanding of mind: The development of children's social understanding within social interaction. *Behavioral and Brain Sciences*, 27, 79–96.

Carpendale, J. I. M., & Lewis, C. (2004b). Constructing understanding, with feeling. *Behavioral and Brain Sciences*, 27, 130–151.

Carpendale, J. I. M., Lewis, C., Müller, U., & Racine, T. (2005). Constructing perspectives in the social making of minds. *Interaction Studies*, 6, 341–358.

Carpenter, M., Nagell, K., & Tomasello, M. (1998). Social cognition, joint attention, and communicative competence from 9 to 15 months of age. *Monographs of the Society for Research in Child Development*, 63 (Serial No. 255).

Carruthers, P. (1996). Simulation and self-knowledge: A defense of theory-theory. In P. Carruthers & P. K. Smith (Eds.), *Theories of theories of mind* (pp. 22–38). Cambridge: Cambridge University Press.

Carruthers, P., & Smith, P. K. (Eds.) (1996). *Theories of theories of mind*. Cambridge: Cambridge University Press.

Cassidy, K. W., Fineberg, D. S., Brown, K., & Perkins, A. (2005). Theory of mind may be contagious, but you don't catch it from your twin. *Child Development*, 76, 97–106.

Chandler, M. J. (1973). Egocentrism and antisocial behavior: The assessment and training of social perspective-taking skills. *Developmental Psychology*, 9, 326–332.

Chandler, M. J. (1978). Social cognition: A selected review of current research. In H. Furth, W. Overton, & J. Gallagher (Eds.), *Knowledge and development: Yearbook of development epistemology* (pp. 93–147). New York: Plenum Press.

Chandler, M. J. (1987). The Othello effect: The emergence of skeptical doubt. *Human Development, 30,* 137–159.

Chandler, M. J. (1988). Doubt and developing theories of mind. In J. W. Astington, P. L. Harris, & D. R. Olson (Eds.), *Developing theories of mind* (pp. 387–413). New York: Cambridge University Press.

Chandler, M. J. (2001). Perspective taking in the aftermath of theory-theory and the collapse of the social role-taking literature. In A. Tryphon & J. Voneche (Eds.), *Working with Piaget: In memoriam – Barbel Inhelder* (pp. 39–63). Hove, UK: Psychology Press.

Chandler, M. J., & Afifi, J. (1996). On making a virtue out of telling lies. *Social Research, 63,* 731–762.

Chandler, M. J., & Boyes, M. (1982). Social-cognitive development. In B. B. Wolman (Ed.), *Handbook of developmental psychology* (pp. 387–402). Englewood Cliffs, NJ: Prentice-Hall.

Chandler, M. J., & Carpendale, J. I. M. (1998). Inching toward a mature theory of mind. In M. Ferrari & R. J. Sternberg (Eds.), *Self-awareness: Its nature and development* (pp. 148–190). New York: The Guilford Press.

Chandler, M. J., Fritz, A. S., & Hala, S. (1989). Small scale deceit: Deception as a marker of 2-, 3- and 4-year-olds' theories of mind. *Child Development, 60,* 1263–1277.

Chandler, M. J., & Greenspan, S. (1972). Ersatz egocentrism: A reply to Borke. *Developmental Psychology, 7,* 104–106.

Chandler, M. J., & Hala, S. (1994). The role of personal involvement in the assessment of early false belief skills. In C. Lewis & P. Mitchell (Eds.), *Children's early understanding of mind: Origins and development* (pp. 403–425). Hove, UK: Lawrence Erlbaum Associates.

Chandler, M. J., Hallett, D., & Sokol, B. (2001). Competing claims about competing knowledge claims. In B. K. Hofer & P. R. Pintrich (Eds.), *Personal epistemologies* (pp. 145–168). Mahwah, NJ: Lawrence Erlbaum Associates.

Chandler, M. J., & Helm, D. (1984). Developmental changes in the contribution of shared experiences to social role taking competence. *International Journal of Behavioral Development, 7,* 145–156.

Chandler, M. J., & Lalonde, C. (1996). Shifting to an interpretive theory of mind: 5- to 7-year-olds' changing conceptions of mental life. In A. Sameroff & M. Haith (Eds.), *Reason and responsibility: The passage through childhood* (pp. 111–139). Chicago: University of Chicago Press.

Chandler, M. J., Sokol, B. W., & Hallett, D. (2001). Moral responsibility and the interpretive turn: Children's changing conceptions of truth and rightness. In B. F. Malle, L. J. Moses, & D. A. Baldwin (Eds.), *Intentions and intentionality* (pp. 345–365). Cambridge, MA: The MIT Press.

Chandler, M. J., Sokol, B. W., & Wainryb, C. (2000). Beliefs about truth and beliefs about rightness. *Child Development, 71,* 91–97.

Chapman, M. (1987a). Inner processes and outward criteria: Wittgenstein's importance for psychology. In M. Chapman & R. A. Dixon (Eds.), *Meaning and the growth of understanding: Wittgenstein's significance for developmental psychology* (pp. 103–127). Berlin: Springer-Verlag.

Chapman, M. (1988). *Constructive evolution: Origins and development of Piaget's thought*. New York: Cambridge University Press.

Chapman, M. (1991). The epistemic triangle: Operative and communicative components of cognitive development. In M. Chandler & M. Chapman (Eds.), *Criteria for competence: Controversies in the conceptualization and assessment of children's abilities* (pp. 209–228). Hillsdale, NJ: Lawrence Erlbaum Associates.

Chapman, M. (1999). Constructivism and the problem of reality. *Journal of Applied Development Psychology, 20*, 31–43.

Charman, T., Baron-Cohen, S., Swettenham, J., Baird, G., Cox, A., & Drew, A. (2000). Testing joint attention, imitation, and play as infancy precursors to language and theory of mind. *Cognitive Development, 15*, 481–498.

Charman, T., Ruffman, T., & Clements, W. (2002). Is there a gender difference in false belief development? *Social Development, 11*, 1–10.

Cheung, H., Hsuan-Chih, C., Creed, N., Ng, L., Wang, S. P., & Mo, L. (2004). Relative roles of general and complementation language in theory-of-mind development: Evidence from Cantonese and English. *Child Development, 75*, 1155–1170.

Churchland, P. M. (1984). *Matter and consciousness*. Cambridge, MA: The MIT Press.

Churchland, P. M. (1995). *The engine of reason and the seat of the soul*. Cambridge, MA: MIT Press.

Clements, W. A., & Perner, J. (1994). Implicit understanding of belief. *Cognitive Development, 9*, 377–395.

Cohn, J. F. (2003). Additional components of the still-face effect: Commentary on Adamson and Frick. *Infancy, 4*, 493–497.

Colby, A., & Kohlberg L. (1987). *The measurement of moral judgment: Volume 1, Theoretical foundations and research validation*. New York: Cambridge University Press.

Cole, K., & Mitchell, P. (2000). Siblings in the development of executive control and a theory of mind. *British Journal of Developmental Psychology, 18*, 279–295.

Cole, M. (1992). Context, modularity, and the cultural constitution of development. In L. T. Winegar & J. Valsiner (Eds.), *Children's development within social context: Vol. 2, Research and methodology* (pp. 5–31). Hillsdale, NJ: Lawrence Erlbaum Associates.

Corkum, V., & Moore, V. (1995). Development of joint visual attention in infants. In C. Moore & P. Dunham (Eds.), *Joint attention: Its origins and role in development* (pp. 61–83). Hillsdale, NJ: Lawrence Erlbaum Associates.

Corkum, V., & Moore, V. (1998). The origins of joint visual attention in infants. *Developmental Psychology, 34*, 28–38.

Craig, A. P., & Barrett, L. (2004). I ain't got no body: Developmental psychology must be embodied and enactive as well as "social". *Behavioral and Brain Sciences*, 27, 103.

Crick, N. R., & Dodge, K. A. (1996). Social information processing mechanisms in reactive and proactive aggression. *Child Development*, 67, 993–1002.

Crick, N. R., & Dodge, K. A. (1999). "Superiority" is in the eye of the beholder: A comment on Sutton, Smith, and Swetteham. *Social Development*, 8, 128–131.

Custer, W. (1996). A comparison of young children's understanding of contradictory representations in pretense, memory, and belief. *Child Development*, 67, 678–688.

Cutting, A. L., & Dunn, J. (1999). Theory of mind, emotion understanding, language, and family background: Individual differences and interrelations. *Child Development*, 70, 853–865.

Cutting, A. L., & Dunn, J. (2002). The cost of understanding other people: Social cognition predicts young children's sensitivity to criticism. *Journal of Child Psychology and Psychiatry*, 43, 849–860.

D'Entremont, B. (2000). A perceptual-attentional explanation of gaze-following in 3- and 6-month-olds. *Developmental Science*, 3, 302–311.

Damasio, A. R., & Maurer, R. G. (1978). Neurological model for childhood autism. *Archives of Neurology*, 35, 777–786.

Davis, H. L., & Pratt, C. (1995). The development of theory of mind: The working memory explanation. *Australian Journal of Psychology*, 47, 25–31.

de Villiers, J. G. (2000). Language and theory of mind: What are the developmental relationships? In S. Baron-Cohen, H. Tager-Flusberg, & D. J. Cohen (Eds.), *Understanding of minds: Perspectives from developmental cognitive neuroscience* (pp. 83–123). New York: Oxford University Press.

de Villiers, J. G. (2005). Can language acquisition give children a point of view? In J. W. Astington & J. A. Baird (Eds.), *Why language matters for theory of mind* (pp. 186–219). New York: Oxford University Press.

de Villiers J. G., & de Villiers, P. A. (2000). Linguistic determinism and the understanding of false beliefs. In P. Mitchell & K. J. Riggs (Eds.), *Children's reasoning and the mind* (pp. 191–228). Hove, UK: Psychology Press.

de Villiers, J. G., & Pyers, J. E. (2002). Complements to cognition: A longitudinal study of the relationship between complex syntax and false-belief-understanding. *Cognitive Development*, 17, 1037–1060.

de Villiers, P. A. (2005). The role of language in theory-of-mind development: What deaf children can tell us. In J. W. Astington & J. A. Baird (Eds.), *Why language matters for theory of mind* (pp. 266–297). New York: Oxford University Press.

Demorest, A., Meyer, C., Phelps, E., Gardner, H., & Winner, E. (1984). Words speak louder than actions: Understanding deliberately false remarks. *Child Development*, 55, 1527–1534.

Deneault, J., Morin, P. L., Ricard, M., Décarie, T. G., & Quintal, G. (2003). *Understanding of mind in twins: Does zygosity make a difference?* Poster presented at the biennial conference of the Society for Research in Child Development, April, Tampa, Florida.

Denham, S. A., Zoller, D., & Couchoud, E. A. (1994). Socialization of preschoolers' emotion understanding. *Developmental Psychology, 30,* 928–993.

Dennett, D. C. (1978). Beliefs about beliefs. *Behavioral and Brain Sciences, 4,* 568–570.

Descartes, R. (1637). *A discourse on method* (trans. by John Veitch). London: Dent (published in 1962).

Desrochers, S., Morissette, P., & Ricard, M. (1995). Two perspectives on pointing in infancy. In C. Moore & P. J. Dunham (Eds.), *Joint attention: Its origins and role in development* (pp. 85–101). Hillsdale, NJ: Lawrence Erlbaum Associates.

Dews, S., Winner, E., Kaplan, J., Rosenblatt, E., Hunt, M., Lim, K., McGovern, A., Qualter, A., & Smarsh, B. (1996). Children's understanding of the meaning and functions of verbal irony. *Child Development, 67,* 3071–3085.

Diamond, A., Prevor, M. B., Callender, G., & Druin, D. P. (1997). Prefrontal cortex cognitive deficits in children treated early and continuously for PKU. *Monographs of the Society for Research in Child Development, 62* (4).

Donald, M. (2004). The virtues of rigorous interdisciplinarity. In J. M. Lucariello, J. A. Hudson, R. Fivush & P. J. Bauer (Eds.), *The development of the mediated mind* (pp. 245–256). Mahwah, NJ: Lawrence Erlbaum Associates.

Dunn, J. (1995). Children as psychologists: The later correlates of individual differences in understanding of emotions and other minds. *Cognition and Emotion, 9,* 187–201.

Dunn, J. (1996). Children's relationships: Bridging the divide between cognitive and social development. *Child Psychology and Psychiatry, 37,* 507–518.

Dunn, J. (1999). Introduction: New directions in research on children's relationships and understanding. *Social Development, 8,* 137–142.

Dunn, J. (2004). *Children's friendships: The beginnings of intimacy.* Oxford: Blackwell.

Dunn, J., Bretherton, I., & Munn, P. (1987). Conversations about feeling states between mothers and their young children. *Developmental Psychology, 23,* 132–139.

Dunn, J., & Brophy, M. (2005). Communication, relationships, and individual differences in children's understanding of mind. In J. W. Astington & J. A. Baird (Eds.), *Why language matters for theory of mind* (pp. 50–69). New York: Oxford University Press.

Dunn, J., Brown, J., & Beardsall, L. (1991). Family talk about feeling states and children's later understanding of others' emotions. *Developmental Psychology, 27,* 448–455.

Dunn, J., Brown, J. R., & Maguire, M. (1995). The development of children's moral sensibility: Individual differences and emotion understanding. *Developmental Psychology, 31,* 649–659.

Dunn, J., Brown, J., Slomkowski, C., Tesla, C., & Youngblade, L. (1991). Young children's understanding of other people's feelings and beliefs: Individual differences and their antecedents. *Child Development, 62,* 1352–1366.

Dunn, J., & Cutting, A. L. (1999). Understanding others, and individual differences in friendship interactions in young children. *Social Development, 8,* 201–219.

Dunn, J., Cutting, A. L., & Demetriou, H. (2000). Moral sensibility, understanding others, and children's friendship interactions in the preschool period. *British Journal of Developmental Psychology, 18,* 159–177.

Dunn, J., & Dale, N. (1984). I a daddy: Two-year-olds' joint collaboration in joint pretend play with sibling and mother. In I. Bretherton (Ed.), *Symbolic play: The development of social understanding* (pp. 131–158). London: Academic Press.

Dunn, J., & Hughes, C. (1998). Young children's understanding of emotions within close relationships. *Cognition and Emotion, 12,* 171–190.

Dunn, J., & Kendrick, C. (1982). *Siblings: Love, envy and understanding.* Oxford: Blackwell.

Dunn, J., & Munn, P. (1985). Becoming a family member: Family conflict and the development of social understanding in the second year. *Child Development, 56,* 764–774.

Dunn, J., & Munn, P. (1987). Development of justification in disputes with mother and sibling. *Developmental Psychology, 23,* 791–798.

Duveen, G. (1997). Psychological development as a social process. In L. Smith, J. Dockrell, & P. Tomlinson (Eds.), *Piaget, Vygotsky and beyond* (pp. 67–90). London: Routledge.

Eddy, T. J. (2004). Children, chimpanzees, and social understanding: Inter- or intra-specific? *Behavioral and Brain Sciences, 27,* 103–104.

Elias, N. (1978). *What is sociology?* New York: Columbia Press. (Original work published in 1970).

Feldman, C. F. (1992). The new theory of theory of mind. *Human Development, 35,* 107–117.

Fernyhough, C. (1996). The dialogic mind: A dialogic approach to the higher mental functions. *New Ideas in Psychology, 14,* 47–62.

Fernyhough, C. (1997). Vygotsky's sociocultural approach: Theoretical issues and implications for current research. In S. Hala (Ed.), *The development of social cognition* (pp. 65–93). Hove: Psychology Press.

Fernyhough, C. (2004). More than a context for learning? The epistemic triangle and the dialogic mind. *Behavioral and Brain Sciences, 27,* 104–105.

Feyerabend, P. (1975). *Against method: Outline of an anarchistic theory of knowledge.* London: Humanities Press.

Fine, C., Lumsden, J., & Blair, R. J. (2001). Dissociations between "theory of mind" and executive functions in a patient with early amygdala damage. *Brain, 124,* 287–298.

Flavell, J. H. (1974). The development of inferences about others. In Mischel, T. (Ed.), *Understanding other persons* (pp. 66–116). Oxford: Blackwell.

Flavell, J. H. (1992). Perspectives on perspective taking. In H. Beilin & P. B. Pufall (Eds.), *Piaget's theory: Prospects and possibilities* (pp. 107–139). Hillsdale, NJ: Lawrence Erlbaum Associates.

Flavell, J. H., Flavell, E. R., & Green, F. L. (1983). Development of the appearance–reality distinction. *Cognitive Psychology, 15,* 95–120.

Flavell, J. H., Fry, C., Wright, J., & Jarvis, P. (1968). *The development of role-taking and communication skills in children.* New York: John Wiley.

Flavell, J. H., Green, F. L., & Flavell, E. R. (1986). Development of knowledge about the appearance-reality distinction. *Monographs of the Society for Research in Child Development, 51.*

Flavell, J. H., Green, F. L., & Flavell, E. R. (1995). Young children's knowledge about thinking. *Monographs of the Society for Research in Child Development, 60* (1, Serial No. 243).

Flavell, J. H., Speer, J. R., Green, F. L., & August, D. L. (1981). The development of comprehension monitoring and knowledge about communication. *Monographs of the Society for Research in Child Development, 46,* 1–65.

Fodor, J. (1981). *Representations: Philosophical essays on the foundations of cognitive science.* Hemel Hempstead: Harvester.

Fodor, J. (1983). *The modularity of mind.* Cambridge, MA: The MIT Press.

Fodor, J. (1992). A theory of the child's theory of mind. *Cognition, 44,* 283–296.

Fogel, A. (1993). *Developing through relationships.* Hemel Hempstead: Harvester.

Fogel, A., & Hannan, T. E. (1985). Manual actions of nine- to fifteen-week old human infants during face-to-face interaction with their mothers. *Child Development, 56,* 1271–1279.

Fonagy, P. (2004). The roots of social understanding in the attachment relationship: An elaboration on the constructionist theory. *Behavioral and Brain Sciences, 27,* 105–106.

Fonagy, P., Redfern, S., & Charman, T. (1997). The relationship between belief–desire reasoning and a projective measure of attachment security (SAT). *British Journal of Developmental Psychology, 15,* 51–61.

Fonagy, P., Steele, H., Steele, M., & Holder, J. (1997). Attachment and theory of mind: Overlapping constructs? *Association for Child Psychology and Psychiatry Occasional Papers, 14,* 31–40.

Fonagy, P., & Target, M. (1997). Attachment and reflective function: Their role in self-organization. *Development and Psychopathology, 9,* 679–700.

Foote, R. C., & Holmes-Lonergan, H. A. (2003). Sibling conflict and theory of mind. *British Journal of Developmental Psychology, 21,* 45–58.

Forrester, M. (1992). *The development of young children's social-cognitive skills.* Hove: Lawrence Erlbaum Associates.

Franco, F., & Butterworth, G. E. (1996). Pointing and social awareness: Declaring and requesting in the second year. *Journal of Child Language, 23,* 307–336.

Freeman, N. H., & Lacohée, H. (1995). Making explicit 3-year-olds implicit competence with their own false beliefs. *Cognition*, *56*, 31–60.

Freeman, N. H., Lewis, C., & Doherty, M. (1991). Preschoolers' grasp of a desire for knowledge in false-belief reasoning: Practical intelligence and verbal report. *British Journal of Developmental Psychology*, *9*, 139–157.

Friedman, O., Griffin, R., Brownell, H., & Winner, E. (2003). Problems with the seeing equals knowing rule. *Developmental Science*, *6*, 505–513.

Frith, C. D., & Frith, U. (1999). Interacting minds – a biological basis. *Science*, *286*, 1692–1695.

Frith, C. D., & Frith, U. (2000). The physiological basis of theory of mind. In S. Baron-Cohen, H. Tager-Flusberg, & D. J. Cohen (Eds.), *Understanding other minds* (pp. 335–356). Cambridge: Cambridge University Press.

Frith, U. (2003). *Autism*. Oxford: Basil Blackwell.

Frith, U., & Frith, C. D. (2001). The biological basis of social interaction. *Current Directions in Psychological Science*, *10*, 151–155.

Frye, D. (1999). The development of intention. The relation of executive function to theory of mind. In P. D. Zelazo, J. W. Astington, & R. R. Olson (Eds.), *Developing theories of intention* (pp. 119–132). Mahwah, NJ: Lawrence Erlbaum Associates.

Frye, D., & Moore, C. (Eds.) (1991). *Children's theories of mind*. Hillsdale, NJ: Lawrence Erlbaum Associates.

Frye, D., Zelazo, P. D., & Palfai, T. (1995). Inference and action in early causal reasoning. *Cognitive Development*, *10*, 120–131.

Furrow, D., Moore, C., Davidge, J., & Chiasson, L. (1992). Mental terms in mothers' and children's speech: Similarities and relationships. *Journal of Child Language*, *19*, 617–631.

Gallagher, H. L., & Frith, C. D. (2003). Functional imaging of "theory of mind." *Trends in Cognitive Science*, *7*, 77–83.

Gallagher, H. L., Jack, A. I., Roepstorff, A., & Frith, C. D. (2002). Imaging the intentional stance in a competitive game. *Neuroimage*, *16*, 814–821.

Gallese, V. (2003). The manifold nature of interpersonal relations: The quest for a common mechanism. *Philosophical Transactions of the Royal Society of London* B, *358*, 517–528.

Gallese, V., Fadiga, L., Fogassi, L., & Rizzolatti, G. (1996). Action recognition in the premotor cortex. *Brain*, *119*, 593–609.

Garfield, J. L., Peterson, C. C., & Perry, T. (2001). Social cognition, language acquisition and the development of the theory of mind. *Mind and Language*, *16*, 494–541.

Gathercole, S. (1999). Cognitive approaches to the development of short-term memory. *Trends in Cognitive Science*, *3*, 410–419.

Gellatly, A. (1997). Why the young child has neither a theory of mind nor a theory of anything else. *Human Development*, *40*, 32–50.

Gergely, G. (2002). The development of understanding self and agency. In U. Goswami (Ed.), *Blackwell handbook of childhood cognitive development* (pp. 26–46). Oxford: Blackwell.

German, T. P., & Leslie, A. M. (2000). Attending to and learning about mental states. In P. Mitchell & K. J. Riggs (Eds.), *Children's reasoning and the mind* (pp. 229–252). Hove, UK: Psychology Press.

German, T. P., & Leslie, A. M. (2004). No (social) construction without (meta) representation: Modular mechanisms as a *basis* for the capacity to acquire an understanding of mind. *Behavioral and Brain Sciences, 27,* 106–107.

German, T. P., & Leslie, A. M. (2001). Children's inferences from "knowing" to "pretending" and "believing". *British Journal of Developmental Psychology, 19,* 59–83.

Gerstadt, C. L., Hong, Y. J., & Diamond, A. (1994). The relationship between cognition and action – performance of children 3 1/2–7 years old on a Stroop-like day–night test. *Cognition, 53,* 129–153.

Goffman, E. (1959). *The presentation of the self in everyday life.* New York: Anchor.

Goldbeck, D., Turnbull, W., & Carpendale, J. I. M. (2003, July). *Developmental changes in the response to and understanding of requests.* Paper presented at the 8th Biennial Convention of the International Pragmatics Association, Toronto.

Goldberg, B. (1991). Mechanism and meaning. In J. Hyman (Ed.), *Investigating psychology: Sciences of the mind after Wittgenstein* (pp. 48–66). London: Routledge.

Goldman, A. I. (1989). Interpretation psychologized. *Mind and Language, 4,* 161–185.

Goodnow, J., & Collins, A. (1991). *Development according to parents: The nature, sources, and consequences of parents' ideas.* London: Lawrence Erlbaum Associates.

Gopnik, A. (1993). How we know our minds: The illusion of first-person knowledge of intentionality. *Behavioral and Brain Sciences, 16,* 1–14.

Gopnik, A., & Graf, P. (1988). Knowing how you know: Young children's ability to remember the sources of their beliefs. *Child Development, 59,* 1366–1371.

Gopnik, A., & Wellman, H. M. (1992). Why the child's theory of mind really is a theory. *Mind and Language, 7,* 145–171.

Gopnik, A. (1996). Theories and modules; creation myths, developmental realities, and Neurath's boat. In P. Carruthers & P. K. Smith (Eds.), *Theories of theories of mind* (pp. 169–183). Cambridge: Cambridge University Press.

Gopnik, A., Capps, L., & Meltzoff, A. N. (2000). Early theories of mind: What the theory theory can tell us about autism. In S. Baron-Cohen, H. Tager-Flusberg, & D. J. Cohen (Eds.), *Understanding other minds* (pp. 50–72). Oxford: Oxford University Press.

Gopnik, A., & Wellman, H. M. (1994). The theory theory. In L. A. Hirschfeld & S. A. Gelman (Eds.), *Mapping the mind: Domain specificity in cognition and culture* (pp. 257–293). New York: Cambridge University Press.

Gordon, R. M. (1986). Folk psychology as simulation. *Mind and Language, 1,* 156–171.

Greenwood, J. D. (1991). *The future of folk psychology: Intentionality and cognitive science*. New York: Cambridge University Press.

Grice, H. P. (1975). Logic and conversation. In P. Cole & J. L. Morgan (Eds.), *Syntax and semantics. Vol. 3: Speech acts*. London: Academic Press.

Hacker, P. M. S. (1991). Seeing, representing and describing: An examination of David Marr's computational theory of vision. In J. Hyman (Ed.), *Investigating psychology: Sciences of the mind after Wittgenstein* (pp. 119–154). London: Routledge.

Hacker, P. M. S. (1996). *Wittgenstein's place in twentieth-century analytic philosophy*. Oxford: Blackwell.

Hacker, P. M. S. (1997). *Wittgenstein: On human nature*. London: Phoenix.

Hadwin, J., & Perner, J. (1991). Pleased and surprised: Children's cognitive theory of emotion. *British Journal of Developmental Psychology, 9*, 215–234.

Hala, S. (2004). The role of executive function in constructing an understanding of mind. *Behavior and Brain Sciences, 27*, 108–109.

Hala, S., & Chandler, M. J. (1996). The role of strategic planning in accessing false-belief understanding. *Child Development, 67*, 2948–2966.

Hala, S., Chandler, M. J., & Fritz, A. (1991). Fledgling theories of mind: Deception as a marker of 3-year-olds' understanding of false belief. *Child Development, 62*, 83–97.

Hala, S., Hug, S., & Henderson, A. (2003). Executive function and false belief understanding in preschool children: Two tasks are harder than one. *Journal of Cognition and Development, 4*, 275–298.

Hala, S., & Russell, J. (2001). Executive control within strategic deception: A window on early cognitive development? *Journal of Experimental Child Psychology, 80*, 112–141.

Hale, C. M., & Tager-Flusberg, H. (2003). The influence of language on theory of mind: A training study. *Developmental Science, 6*, 346–359.

Hallett, D., Chandler, M. J., & Krettenauer, T. (2002). Disentangling the course of epistemic development: Parsing knowledge by epistemic content. *New Ideas in Psychology, 20*, 285–307.

Happaney, K., & Zelazo, P. D. (2003). Inhibition as a problem in the psychology of behavior. *Developmental Science, 6*, 468–470.

Happé, F. G. E. (1995). The role of age and verbal ability in the theory of mind task performance of subjects with autism. *Child Development, 66*, 843–855.

Happé, F. G. E., & Frith, U. (1996). The neuropsychology of autism. *Brain, 119*, 1377–1400.

Hare, B., Brown, M., Williamson, C., & Tomasello, M. (2002). The domestication of social cognition in dogs. *Science, 298*, 1634–1636.

Harris, M., Barrett, M., Jones, D., & Brookes, S. (1988). Linguistic input and early word meaning. *Journal of Child Language, 15*, 77–94.

Harris, P. L. (1989). *Children and emotion: The development of psychological understanding*. Oxford: Blackwell.

Harris, P. L. (1991). The work of the imagination. In A. Whiten (Ed.), *Natural theories of mind* (pp. 283–304). Oxford: Blackwell.

Harris, P. L. (1992). From simulation to folk psychology: The case for development. *Mind and Language, 7,* 120–144.

Harris, P. L. (1996). Desires, beliefs, and language. In P. Carruthers & P. K. Smith (Eds.), *Theories of theories of mind* (pp. 200–220). Cambridge: Cambridge University Press.

Harris, P. L. (2005). Conversation, pretense, and theory of mind. In J. W. Astington & J. A. Baird (Eds.), *Why language matters for theory of mind* (pp. 70–83). New York: Oxford University Press.

Harris, P. L., German, T. P., & Mills, M. (1996). Children's use of counterfactual reasoning in causal reasoning. *Cognition, 61,* 283–304.

Harris, P. L., Johnson, C. N., Hutton, D., Andrews, G., & Cooke, T. (1989). Young children's theory of mind and emotion. *Cognition and Emotion, 3,* 379–400.

Harris, P. L., & Kavanaugh, R. D. (1993). Young children's understanding of pretense. *Monographs of the Society for Research in Child Development, 58.*

Harris, P. L., & Leevers, H. J. (2000). Reasoning from false premises. In P. Mitchell & K. J. Riggs (Eds.), *Children's reasoning and the mind* (pp. 67–86). Hove: Psychology Press.

Heal, J. (1986). Replication and functionalism. In J. Butterfield (Ed.), *Language, mind and logic* (pp. 135–150). Cambridge: Cambridge University Press.

Heider, F. (1958). *The psychology of interpersonal relations.* Chichester: Wiley.

Heyes, C. M. (1998). Theory of mind in nonhuman primates. *Behavioral and Brain Sciences, 21,* 101–148.

Hill, E. L. (2004). Executive dysfunction in autism. *Trends in Cognitive Sciences, 8,* 26–32.

Hill, E. L., & Frith, U. (2004). Understanding autism: Insights from mind and brain. In U. Frith & E. L. Hill, *Autism: Mind and brain* (pp. 1–19). Oxford: Oxford University Press.

Hobson, P. (2002). *The cradle of thought: Explorations of the origins of thinking.* Macmillan: London.

Hobson, R. P. (1991). Against the theory of "theory of mind." *British Journal of Developmental Psychology, 9,* 33–51.

Hobson, R. P. (1993). *Autism and the development of mind.* Hove, UK: Lawrence Erlbaum Associates Erlbaum.

Hobson, R. P. (1994). Perceiving attitudes, conceiving minds. In C. Lewis & P. Mitchell (Eds.), *Children's early understanding of mind: Origins and development* (pp. 71–93). Hove, UK: Lawrence Erlbaum Associates.

Hobson, R. P. (2004). Understanding self and other. *Behavioral and Brain Sciences, 27,* 109–110.

Hogrefe, G. J., Wimmer, H., & Perner, J. (1986). Ignorance versus false belief: A developmental lag in the acquisition of mental states. *Child Development, 57,* 567–582.

Holiday, A. (1988). *Moral powers: Normative necessity in language and history.* London: Routledge.

Holmes, H. A., Black, C., & Miller, S. A. (1996). A cross-task comparison of false-belief understanding in a Head Start population. *Journal of Experimental Child Psychology*, 63, 263–285.

Holquist, M. (1990). *Dialogism: Bakhtin and his world*. London: Routledge.

Howe, N. (2004). The sibling relationship as a context for the development of social understanding. *Behavioral and Brain Sciences*, 27, 110–111.

Howe, N., Petrakos, H., & Rinaldi, C. M. (1998). "All the sheeps are dead. He murdered them": Sibling pretense, negotiation, internal state language, and relationship quality. *Child Development*, 69, 182–191.

Howe, N., Rinaldi, C., Jennings, M., & N., & Petrakos, H. (2002). "No! The lambs can stay out because they got cosies": Constructive and destructive sibling conflict, pretend play, and social understanding. *Child Development*, 73, 14560–1473.

Hughes, C. (1996). Control of action and thought: Normal development and dysfunction in autism: A research note. *Journal of Child Psychology and Psychiatry*, 37, 229–236.

Hughes, C. (1998a). Executive function in preschoolers: Links with theory of mind and verbal ability. *British Journal of Developmental Psychology*, 16, 233–253.

Hughes, C. (1998b). Finding your marbles: Does preschoolers' strategic behavior predict later understanding of mind? *Developmental Psychology*, 34, 1326–1339.

Hughes, C., Adlam, A., Happé, F., Jackson, J., Taylor, A., & Caspi, A. (2001). Good test–retest reliability for standard and advanced false-belief tasks across a wide range of abilities. *Journal of Child Psychology and Psychiatry*, 41, 483–490.

Hughes, C., & Cutting, A. L. (1999). Nature, nurture, and individual differences in early understanding of mind. *Psychological Science*, 10, 429–432.

Hughes, C., Deater-Deckard, K., & Cutting, A. L. (1999). "Speak roughly to your little boy"? Sex differences in the relations between parenting and preschoolers' understanding of mind. *Social Development*, 8, 143–160.

Hughes, C., & Dunn, J. (1998). Understanding mind and emotions: Longitudinal associations with mental-state talk between young friends. *Developmental Psychology*, 34, 1026–1037.

Hughes, C., Dunn, J., & White, A. (1998). Trick or treat: Uneven understanding of mind and emotion and executive functioning among "hard to manage" preschoolers. *Journal of Child Psychology and Psychiatry*, 39, 981–994.

Hughes, C., Jaffee, S. R., Happé, F., Taylor, A., Caspi, A., & Moffitt, T. E. (2005). Origins of individual differences in theory of mind: From nature to nurture? *Child Development*, 76, 356–370.

Hughes, C., & Leekam, S. (2004). What are the links between theory of mind and social relations? Review, reflections and new directions for studies of typical and atypical development. *Social Development*, 13, 598–619.

Hughes, C., & Russell, J. (1993). Autistic children's difficulty with mental disengagement from an object – its implications for theories of autism. *Developmental Psychology, 29*, 498–510.

Iarocci, G. (2002, March). *Multisensory processing in autism: New directions in research.* Invited Address at the New Developments in Cognitive Research Conference at Cambridge University, Cambridge, England.

Izard, C. E. (2004). Emotions and emotion cognition contribute to the construction and understanding of mind. *Behavioral and Brain Sciences, 27*, 111–112.

Jacques, S., & Zelazo, P. D. (2005). Language and the development of cognitive flexibility: Implications for theory of mind. In J. W. Astington & J. A. Baird (Eds.), *Why language matters for theory of mind* (pp. 144–162). New York: Oxford University Press.

Jastrow, J. (1900). *Fact and fable in psychology.* Boston, MA: Houghton-Mifflin.

Jenkins, J. M., & Astington, J. W. (1996). Cognitive factors and family structure associated with theory of mind development in young children. *Developmental Psychology, 32*, 70–78.

Jenkins, J. M., & Astington, J. W. (2000). Theory of mind and social behavior: Causal models tested in a longitudinal study. *Merrill-Palmer Quarterly, 46*, 203–220.

Jenkins, J. M., & Oatley, K. (2004). The space in between: The development of joint thinking and planning. *Behavioral and Brain Sciences, 27*, 112–113.

Jenkins, J. M., Turrell, S. L., Kogushi, Y., Lollis, S., & Ross, H. S. (2003). A longitudinal investigation of the dynamics of mental state talk in families. *Child Development, 74*, 905–920.

Johnson, C. N. (1988). Theory of mind and the structure of conscious experience. In J. W. Astington, P. L. Harris, & D. R. Olson (Eds.), *Developing theories of mind* (pp. 47–63). New York: Cambridge University Press.

Johnson, S. N. (2003). Detecting agents. *Philosophical Transactions of the Royal Society of London*, Series B 358, 549–559.

Jones, C. P., & Carpendale, J. I. M. (2002, May). *Social understanding and subtypes of aggression in young children.* Poster presented at the Vancouver Conference on Aggression, Vancouver, BC.

Jones, S. S. (1996). Imitation or exploration? Young infants' matching of adults' oral gestures. *Child Development, 67*, 1952–1969.

Jopling, D. (1993). Cognitive science, other minds, and the philosophy of dialogue. In U. Neisser (Ed.), *The perceived self* (pp. 290–309). Cambridge, MA: MIT Press.

Kain, W., & Perner, J. (2005). What fMRI can tell us about the ToM–EF connection: False beliefs, working memory and inhibition. In W. Schneider, R. Schumann-Hengsteler, & B. Sodian, B. (Eds.), *Young children's cognitive development: Interrelationships among executive functioning, working memory verbal ability and theory of mind* (pp. 189–218). Mahwah, NJ: Lawrence Erlbaum Associates.

Kaminski, J., Riedel, J., Call, J., & Tomasello, M. (2005). Domestic goats, *Capra hircus*, follow gaze direction and use social cues in an object choice task. *Animal Behaviour, 69*, 11–18.

Kanner, L. (1943). Autistic disturbances of affective contact. *The Nervous Child, 2*, 217–250.

Karmiloff-Smith, A., & Inhelder, B. (1974). If you want to get ahead get a theory. *Cognition, 3*, 195–212.

Keenan, T. (2000). Working memory, "holding in mind", and the child's acquisition of a theory of mind. In J. W. Astington (Ed.), *Minds in the making: Essays in honour of David R. Olson* (pp. 233–249). Oxford: Blackwell.

Keenan, T., Olson, D. R., & Marini, Z. (1998). Working memory and children's developing understanding of mind. *Australian Journal of Psychology, 50*, 76–82.

Keenan, T., Ruffman, T., & Olson, D. R. (1994). When do children begin to understand logical inference as a source of knowledge?. *Cognitive Development, 9*, 331–35.

Kenny, A. (1991). The homunculus fallacy. In J. Hyman (Ed.), *Investigating psychology: Sciences of the mind after Wittgenstein* (pp. 155–165). London: Routledge.

King, P. M., & Kitchener, K. S. (1994). *Developing reflective judgment: Understanding and promoting intellectual growth and critical thinking in adolescents and adults*. San Francisco: Jossey-Bass.

Kirkham, N. Z., Cruess, L., & Diamond, A. (2003). Helping children apply their knowledge to their behavior on a dimension-switching task. *Developmental Science, 6*, 449–467.

Kloo, D., & Perner, J. (2003). Training transfer between card sorting and false belief understanding: Helping children apply conflicting descriptions. *Child Development, 74*, 1823–1839.

Kochanska, G., Murray, K., Jacques, T. Y., Koenig, A. L., & Vandegeest, K. A. (1996). Inhibitory control in young children and its role in emerging internalisation. *Child Development, 67*, 490–507.

Kohlberg, L. (1976). Moral stages and moralization: A cognitive-developmental approach. Chapter 2 in T. Lickona (Ed.), *Moral development and behavior* (pp. 31–53). New York: Holt, Rinehart & Winston.

Kohler, E., Keysers, C., Umiltà, M. A., Fogassi, L., Gallese, V., & Rizzolatti, G. (2002). Hearing sounds, understanding actions: Action representation in mirror neurons. *Science, 297*, 846–848.

Köhler, W. (1925). *The mentality of apes*. London: Kegan Paul, Trench, Trubner & Co., Ltd.

Kuebli, J., Butler, S., & Fivush, R. (1995). Mother–child talk about past emotions: Relations of maternal language and child gender over time. *Cognition and Emotion, 9*, 265–283.

Kuhn, D. (2000). Theory of mind, metacognition, and reasoning: A life-span perspective. In P. Mitchell & K. J. Riggs (Eds.), *Children's reasoning and the mind* (pp. 301–326). Hove: Psychology Press.

Kuhn, D., Amsel, E., & O'Laughlin, M. (1988). *The development of scientific thinking skills*. Orlando, FL: Academic Press.

Kuhn, D., Cheney, R., & Weinstock, M. (2000). The development of epistemological understanding. *Cognitive Development, 15,* 309–328.

Kuhn, T. S. (1962). *The structure of scientific revolutions*. Chicago: Chicago University Press.

Kujawski, J. H., & Bower, T. G. R. (1993). Same-sex preferential looking during infancy as a function of abstract representation, *British Journal of Developmental Psychology, 11,* 201–209.

Lakatos, I. (1970). Falsification and the methodology of scientific research programmes. In I. Lakatos & A. Musgrave (Eds.), *Criticism and the growth of knowledge* (pp. 91–196). New York: Cambridge University Press.

Lalonde, C. E., & Chandler, M. J. (1995). False belief understanding goes to school: On the social-emotional consequences of coming early or late to a first theory of mind. *Cognition and Emotion, 9,* 167–185.

Lalonde, C. E., & Chandler, M. J. (2002). Children's understanding of interpretation. *New Ideas in Psychology, 20,* 163–198.

Landry, S. H., Miller-Loncar, C. L., Smith, K. E., & Swank, P. R. (2002). The role of early parenting in children's development of executive processes. *Developmental Neuropsychology, 21,* 15–41.

Lang, B., & Perner, J. (2002). Understanding intention and false belief and the development of self control. *British Journal of Developmental Psychology, 20,* 67–76.

Lawrence, J. A., & Valsiner, J. (1993). Conceptual roots of internalization: From transmission to transformation. *Human Development, 36,* 150–167.

Leavens, D. A. (2002). On the public nature of communication. *Behavioral and Brain Sciences, 25,* 631–632.

Leavens, D. A., Hopkins, W. D., & Thomas, R. K. (2004). Referential communication by chimpanzees (*Pan troglodytes*). *Journal of Comparative Psychology, 118,* 48–57.

Leekam, S. (2005). Why do children with autism have a joint attention impairment? In N. Eilan, C. Hoerl, T. McCormack, & J. Roessler (Eds.), *Joint attention: Communication and other minds* (pp. 205–229). Oxford: Oxford University Press.

Leslie, A. M. (1987). Pretense and representation: The origins of "theory of mind." *Psychological Review, 94,* 412–426.

Leslie, A. M. (1988). Some implications of pretence for mechanisms underlying the child's theory of mind. In J. W. Astington, P. L. Harris, & D. R. Olson (Eds.), *Developing theories of mind* (pp. 19–46). Cambridge: Cambridge University Press.

Leslie, A. M. (1991). The theory of mind impairment in autism: Evidence for a modular mechanism of development? In A. Whiten (Ed.), *Natural theories of mind* (pp. 63–78). Oxford: Blackwell.

Leslie, A. M. (1994). Pretending and believing: Issues in the theory of ToM. *Cognition, 50,* 211–238.

Leslie, A. M., & Frith, U. (1988). Autistic children's understanding of seeing, knowing and believing. *British Journal of Developmental Psychology*, 6, 315–324.

Leslie, A. M., & Polizzi, P. (1998). Inhibitory processes in the false belief task: Two conjectures. *Developmental Science*, 1, 247–253.

Leudar, I., & Costall, A. (2004). On the persistence of the "problem of other minds" in psychology. *Theory and Psychology*, 14, 601–621.

Levinson, S. C. (1995). Interactional biases in human thinking. In E. N. Goody (Ed.), *Social intelligence and interaction* (pp. 221–260). Cambridge: Cambridge University Press.

Lewis, C., & Carpendale, J. I. M. (2002). Social cognition. In P. K. Smith & C. Hart (Eds.), *The handbook of social development* (375–393). Oxford: Blackwell.

Lewis, C., & Mitchell, P. (Eds.) (1994). *Children's early understanding of mind: Origins and development*. Hove, UK: Lawrence Erlbaum Associates.

Lewis, C., Freeman, N. H., Kyriakidou, C., Maridaki-Kassotaki, K., & Berridge, D. M. (1996). Social influences on false belief access: Specific sibling influences or general apprenticeship? *Child Development*, 67, 2930–2947.

Lewis, C., Freeman, N., Hagestadt, C., & Douglas, H. (1994). Narrative access and production in preschoolers' false belief reasoning. *Cognitive Development*, 9, 397–424.

Lewis, C., Harrison, A., & Warburton, K. Social factors in executive functions (in progress).

Lewis, C., & Osborne, A. (1990). Three-year-olds' problems with false belief: Conceptual deficit or linguistic artifact? *Child Development*, 61, 1514–1519.

Lewis, D. (1966). An argument for the identity theory. *Journal of Philosophy*, 63, 17–25.

Lewis, D. (1972). Psychophysical and theoretical identifications. *Australian Journal of Philosophy*, 50, 249–258.

Lillard, A. (1998). Ethnopsychologies: Cultural variations in theories of mind. *Psychological Bulletin*, 123, 3–32.

Lillard, A. S. (1993a). Pretend play skills and the child's theory of mind. *Child Development*, 64, 348–371.

Lillard, A. S. (1993b). Young children's conceptualization of pretense: Action or mental representational state? *Child Development*, 64, 372–386.

Lillard, A. S., & Flavell, J. H. (1992). Young children's understanding of different mental verbs. *Developmental Psychology*, 28, 626–634.

Liszkowski, U., Carpenter, M., Henning, A., Striano, T., & Tomasello, M. (2004). Twelve-month-olds point to share attention and interest. *Developmental Science*, 7, 297–307.

Liszkowski, U., Carpenter, M., Striano, T., & Tomasello, M. (in press). Twelve- and 18-month-olds point to provide information for others. *Journal of Cognition and Development*.

Lock, A., Young, A. W., Service, V., & Chandler, P. (1990). The origins of infant pointing gestures. In V. Volterra & C. J. Erting (Eds.), *From gesture to language in hearing and deaf children* (pp. 42–55). New York: Springer Verlag.

Lohmann, H., & Tomasello, M. (2003). The role of language in the development of false belief understanding: A training study. *Child Development, 74,* 1130–1144.

Lohmann, H., Tomasello, M., & Meyer, S. (2005). Linguistic communication and social understanding. In J. W. Astington & J. A. Baird (Eds.), *Why language matters for theory of mind* (pp. 245–265). New York: Oxford University Press.

Lourenço, O. (2004). Rich interpretations and poor theories. *Behavioral and Brain Sciences, 27,* 114–115.

Lourenço, O., & Machado, A. (1996). In defense of Piaget's theory: A reply to 10 common criticisms. *Psychological Review, 103,* 143–164.

Lunn, J., & Lewis, C. (2003). *Is language or social interaction a route into mental state understanding?* Paper presented at the International Society for the Study of Behavioral Development, July, Ghent.

Luquet, G.-H. (1913). Le dessin enfantin. Republished in 1927 and again in 2001. London: Free Association Books.

Luria, A. R. (1961). *The role of speech in the regulation of normal and abnormal behavior.* New York: Liveright Pub. Corp.

Lurye, L., & Müller, U. (2003, April). *The effect of labeling on the performance in the dimensional change card sort task.* Poster presented at the Society for Research in Child Development, Tampa, FL.

Maguire, M. C., & Dunn, J. (1997). Friendships in early childhood, and social understanding. *International Journal of Behavioral Development, 21,* 669–686.

Malcolm, N. (1991). The relation of language to instinctive behaviour. In J. Hyman (Ed.), *Investigating psychology: Sciences of the mind after Wittgenstein* (pp. 27–47). New York: Routledge.

Mansfield, A. F., & Clinchy, B. (2002). Toward the integration of objective and subjectivity: Epistemological development from 10 to 16. *New Ideas in Psychology, 20,* 225–262.

Marshark, M., Green, V., Hindmarsh, G., & Walker, S. (2000). Understanding theory of mind in children who are deaf. *Journal of Child Psychology and Psychiatry, 41,* 1067–1073.

Mayes, L. C., Klin, A., Tercyak, K. P., Cichetti, D. V., & Cohen, D. J. (1996). Test retest reliability for false belief tasks. *Journal of Child Psychology and Psychiatry, 41,* 313–319.

Maynard, A. E. (2002). Cultural teaching: The development of teaching skills in Maya sibling interactions. *Child Development, 73,* 969–982.

McGhee, P. E. (1979). *Humor: Its origin and development.* San Francisco: W. H. Freeman and Company.

Mead, G. H. (1934). *Mind, self and society.* Chicago: University of Chicago Press.

Meins, E. (1997). *Security of attachment and the social development of cognition*. Hove, UK: Psychology Press.

Meins, E. (1999). Sensitivity, security and internal working models: Bridging the transmission gap. *Attachment and Human Development*, 1, 325–342.

Meins, E. (2004). Infants' minds, mothers' minds, and other minds: How individual differences in caregivers affect the co-construction of mind. *Behavior and Brain Sciences*, 27, 116.

Meins, E., Fernyhough, C., Russell, J., & Clark-Carter, D. (1998). Security of attachment as a predictor of symbolic and mentalising abilities: A longitudinal study. *Social Development*, 7, 1–24.

Meins, E., Fernyhough, C., Wainwright, R., Clark-Carter, D., Das Gupta, M., Fradley, E., & Tuckey, M. (2003). Pathways to understanding the mind: Construct validity and predictive validity of maternal mind-mindedness. *Child Development*, 74, 1194–1211.

Meins, E., Fernyhough, C., Wainwright, R., Das Gupta, M., Fradley, E., & Tuckey, M. (2002). Maternal mind-mindedness and attachment security as predictors of theory of mind understanding. *Child Development*, 73, 1715–1726.

Meltzoff, A. N. (2002). Imitation as a mechanism of social cognition: Origins of empathy, theory of mind, and the representation of action. In U. Goswami (Ed.), *Blackwell handbook of childhood cognitive development* (pp. 6–25). Oxford: Blackwell.

Meltzoff, A. N., & Brooks, R. (2001). "Like me" as a building block for understanding other minds: Bodily acts, attention, and intention. In B. F. Malle, L. J. Moses, & D. A. Baldwin (Eds.), *Intentions and intentionality: Foundations of social cognition* (pp. 171–191). Cambridge, MA: The MIT Press.

Meltzoff, A. N., Gopnik, A., & Repacholi, B. M. (1999). Toddlers' understanding of intentions, desires, and emotions: Explorations of the dark ages. In P. D. Zelazo, J. W. Astington, & D. R. Olson (Eds.), *Developing theories of intention* (pp. 17–41). Mahwah, NJ: Lawrence Erlbaum Associates.

Meltzoff, A. N., & Moore, M. K. (1977). Imitation of facial and manual gestures by human neonates. *Science*, 198, 75–78.

Meltzoff, A., & Gopnik, A. (1993). The role of imitation in understanding persons and developing a theory of mind. In S. Baron-Cohen, H. Tager-Flusberrg, & D. J. Cohen (Eds.), *Understanding other minds: Perspectives from autism* (pp. 335–366). Oxford: Oxford University Press.

Merleau-Ponty, M. (1964). The child's relations with others. In M. Merleau-Ponty, *The primacy of perception* (pp. 96–155). Evanston, IL: Northwestern Press. (Original work published 1960).

Metzinger, T., & Gallese, V. (2003a). The emergence of a shared action ontology: Building blocks for a theory. *Consciousness and Cognition*, 12, 549–571.

Metzinger, T., & Gallese, V. (2003b). Of course they do. *Consciousness and Cognition*, 12, 574–576.

Milligan, K., & Astington, J. W. (2005, April). *The relations between language and false-belief understanding: A meta-analysis.* Paper presented at the biennial meeting of the Society for Research in Child Development, Atlanta.

Minter, M., Hobson, R. P., & Bishop, M. (1998). Congenital visual impairment and "theory of mind." *British Journal of Developmental Psychology, 16,* 183–196.

Mitchell, P. (1996). *Acquiring a conception of mind: A review of theory and research.* Hove, UK: Psychology Press.

Mitchell, P., & Lacohée, H. (1991). Children's early understanding of false belief. *Cognition, 39,* 107–127.

Mitchell, P., & Riggs, K. J. (Eds.) (2000). *Children's reasoning and the mind.* Hove, UK: Psychology Press.

Moll, H., & Tomasello, M. (2004). 12- and 18-month-old infants follow gaze to spaces behind barriers. *Developmental Science, 7,* F1–F9.

Montgomery, D. E. (1997). Wittgenstein's private language argument and children's understanding of mind. *Developmental Review, 17,* 291–320.

Montgomery, D. E. (2002). Mental verbs and semantic development. *Journal of Cognition and Development, 3,* 357–384.

Montgomery, D. E. (2004). Challenging theory-theory accounts of social understanding: Where is the social constructivist advantage? *Behavioral and Brain Sciences, 27,* 118–119.

Montgomery, D. E. (2005). The developmental origins of meaning for mental terms. In J. W. Astington & J. A. Baird (Eds.), *Why language matters for theory of mind* (pp. 106–122). New York: Oxford University Press.

Moore, C. (1996). Evolution and the modularity of mindreading. *Cognitive Development, 11,* 605–621.

Moore, C. (1998). Social cognition in infancy. In M. Carpenter, K. Nagell, & M. Tomasello, Social cognition, joint attention and communicative competence from 9 to 15 months of age. *Monographs of the Society for Research in Child Development, 63,* 167–174.

Moore, C. (1999). Intentional relations and triadic interaction. In P. D. Zelazo, J. W. Astington, & D. R. Olson (Eds.), *Developing theories of intention* (pp. 43–61). Mahwah, NJ: Lawrence Erlbaum Associates.

Moore, C., Barresi, J., & Thompson, C. (1998). The cognitive basis of future-oriented prosocial behavior. *Social Development, 7,* 198–218.

Moore, C., Bryant, C., & Furrow, D. (1989). Mental terms and the development of certainty. *Child Development, 60,* 167–171.

Moore, C., & Corkum, V. (1994). Social understanding at the end of the first year of life. *Developmental Review, 14,* 349–372.

Moore, C., & D'Entremont, B. (2001). Developmental changes in pointing as a function of parent's attentional focus. *Journal of Cognition and Development, 2,* 109–129.

Moore, C., & Dunham, P. (Eds.) (1995). *Joint attention: Its origins and role in development.* Hillsdale, NJ: Lawrence Erlbaum Associates.

Moore, C., & Furrow, D. (1991). The development of the language of belief: The expression of relative certainty. In D. Frye & C. Moore (Eds.), *Children's theories of mind: Mental states and social understanding* (pp. 173–193). Hillsdale, NJ: Lawrence Erlbaum Associates.

Moore, C., Furrow, D., Chiasson, L., & Patriquin, M. (1994). Developmental relationships between production and comprehension of mental terms. *First Language, 14,* 1–17.

Moore, C., Jarrold, C., Russell, J., Lumb, A., Sapp, F., & MacCallum, F. (1995). Conflicting desire and the child's theory of mind. *Cognitive Development, 10,* 467–482.

Moore, C., & Macgillivray, S. (2004). Altruism, prudence, and theory of mind in preschoolers. In J. A. Baird & B. W. Sokol (Eds.), Connections between theory of mind and sociomoral development. *New Directions for Child and Adolescent Development, 103,* 51–62. San Francisco: Jossey-Bass.

Morton, A. (1980). *Frames of mind: Constraints on the common-sense conception of the mental.* New York: Oxford University Press.

Moses, L., Carlson, S., & Sabbagh, M. (2005). On the specificity of the relation between executive function and theories of mind. In W. Schneider, W. R. Schumann-Hengsteler, & R. Sodian (Eds.), *Young children's cognitive development* (pp. 131–145). Mahwah, NJ: Lawrence Erlbaum Associates.

Moses, L. J. (2001). Executive accounts of theory-of-mind development. *Child Development, 72,* 688–690.

Moses, L. J., & Carlson, S. M. (2004). Self-regulation and children's theories of mind. In C. Lightfoot, C. Lalonde, & M. Chandler (Eds.), *Changing conceptions of psychological life* (pp. 127–146). Mahwah, NJ: Lawrence Erlbaum Associates.

Moses, L. J., & Flavell, J. H. (1990). Inferring false beliefs from actions and reactions. *Child Development, 61,* 929–945.

Muir, D., & Lee, K. (2003). The still-face effect: Methodological issues and new applications. *Infancy, 4,* 483–491.

Müller, U., & Carpendale, J. I. M. (2004). From joint activity to joint attention: A relational approach to social development in infancy. In J. I. M. Carpendale & U. Müller (Eds.), *Social interaction and the development of knowledge* pp. 215–238). Mahwah, NJ: Lawrence Erlbaum Associates.

Müller, U., & Runions, K. (2003). The origins of understanding of self and other: James Mark Baldwin's theory. *Developmental Review, 23,* 29–54.

Müller, U., Sokol, B., & Overton, W. F. (1998a). Constructivism and development: Reply to Smith's commentary. *Developmental Review, 18,* 228–236.

Müller, U., Sokol, B., & Overton, W. F. (1998b). Reframing a constructivist model of the development of mental representations: The role of higher-order operations. *Developmental Review, 18,* 155–201.

Müller, U., Zelazo, P. D., Frye, D., & Lieberman, D. (2002). *The developmental relations among perspective taking skills, language development, and cognitive flexibility in toddlers.* Paper presented at the Jean Piaget Society Conference, Philadelphia.

Mundy, P., & Sigman, M. (1989). The theoretical implications of joint attention deficits in autism. *Development and Psychopathology, 1*, 173–183.

Mundy, P., Sigman, M., & Kasari, C. (1994). Joint attention, developmental level and symptom presentation in autism. *Development and Psychopathology, 6*, 389–401.

Murphy, C. M., & Messer, D. J. (1977). Mothers, infants and pointing: A study of gesture. In H. R. Schaffer (Ed.), *Studies in mother–infant interaction* (pp. 325–354). London: Academic Press.

Nelson, K. (1996). *Language in cognitive development: The emergence of the mediated mind.* New York: Cambridge University Press.

Nelson, K. (1997). Cognitive change as collaborative construction. In E. Amsel & K. A. Renninger (Eds.), *Change and development: Issues of theory, method, and application* (pp. 99–115). Mahwah, NJ: Lawrence Erlbaum Associates.

Nelson, K. (2004). Toward a collaborative community of minds. *Behavioral and Brain Sciences, 27*, 119–120.

Nelson, K. (2005). Language pathways into the community of minds. In J. W. Astington & J. Baird (Eds.), *Why language matters for theory of mind* (pp. 26–49). Oxford: Oxford University Press.

Newson, J., & Newson, E. (1975). Intersubjectivity and the transmission of culture. *Bulletin of the British Psychological Society, 28*, 437–446.

Newton, P., Reddy, V., & Bull, R. (2000). Children's everyday deception and performance on false-belief tasks. *British Journal of Developmental Psychology, 18*, 297–317.

O'Neill, D. K. (2005). Talking about "new" information: The given/new distinction and children's developing theory of mind. In J. W. Astington & J. A. Baird (Eds.), *Why language matters for theory of mind* (pp. 84–105). New York: Oxford University Press.

Olson, D. R. (1988). On the origins of beliefs and other intentional states in children. In J. W. Astington, P. L. Harris, & D. R. Olson (Eds.), *Developing theories of mind* (pp. 414–426). New York: Cambridge University Press.

Oyama, S. (1999). Locating development: Locating developmental systems. In E. K. Scholnick, K. Nelson, S. A. Gelman, & P. H. Miller (Eds.), *Conceptual development: Piaget's legacy* (pp. 185–208). Mahwah, NJ: Lawrence Erlbaum Associates.

Ozonoff, S., Pennington, B. F., & Rogers, S. J. (1991). Executive function deficits in high-functioning autistic individuals – relationship to theory of mind. *Journal of Child Psychology and Psychiatry, 32*, 1081–1105.

Pears, K. C., & Moses, L. J. (2003). Demographics, parenting, and theory of mind in preschool children. *Social Development, 12*, 1–20.

Perner, J. (1988). Developing semantics for theories of mind: From propositional attitudes to mental representation. In J. W. Astington, P. L. Harris, & D. R. Olson (Eds.), *Developing theories of mind* (pp. 141–172). New York: Cambridge University Press.

Perner, J. (1991). *Understanding the representational mind.* Cambridge, MA: The MIT Press.

Perner, J. (1995). The many faces of belief: Reflections on Fodor's and the child's theory of mind. *Cognition*, *57*, 241–269.

Perner, J. (1996). Simulation as explication of predication – implicit knowledge of the mind. In P. Carruthers & P. K. Smith (Eds.), *Theories of theories of mind* (pp. 90–104). Cambridge: Cambridge University Press.

Perner, J. (1998). The meta-intentional nature of executive functions and theory of mind. In P. Carruthers and & J. Boucher (Eds.), *Language and thought* (pp. 270–283). Cambridge: Cambridge University Press.

Perner, J. (2000). About + belief + counterfactual. In P. Mitchell, & K. J. Riggs (Eds.), *Children's reasoning and the mind* (pp. 367–402). Hove, UK: Psychology Press.

Perner, J., Baker, S., & Hutton, D. (1994). Prelief: The conceptual origins of belief and pretence. In C. Lewis & P. Mitchell (Eds.), *Children's early understanding of mind: Origins and development* (pp. 261–286). Hove, UK: Lawrence Erlbaum Associates.

Perner, J., & Davies, G. (1991). Understanding the mind as an active information processor: Do young children have a "copy theory of mind?" *Cognition*, *39*, 51–69.

Perner, J., Kain, W., & Barchfeld, P. (2002). Executive control and higher-order theory of mind in children at risk of ADHD. *Infant and Child Development*, *11*, 141–158.

Perner, J., & Lang, B. (1999). Development of theory of mind and executive control. *Trends in Cognitive Sciences*, *3*, 337–344.

Perner, J., & Lang, B. (2000). Theory of mind and executive function: Is there a developmental relationship? In S. Baron-Cohen, H. Tager-Flusberg, & D. J. Cohen (Eds.), *Understanding other minds* (pp. 150–181). New York: Oxford University Press.

Perner, J., Lang, B., & Kloo, D. (2002). Theory of mind and self-control: More than a common problem of inhibition. *Child Development*, *73*, 752–767.

Perner, J., Leekam, S. R., & Wimmer, H. (1987). 3-year-olds difficulty with false belief – the case for a conceptual deficit. *British Journal of Developmental Psychology*, *5*, 125–137.

Perner, J., Ruffman, T., & Leekam, S. R. (1994). Theory of mind is contagious: You catch it from your sibs. *Child Development*, *65*, 1228–1238.

Perner, J., Sprung, M., & Steinkogler, B. (2004). Counterfactual conditionals and false belief: A developmental dissociation. *Cognitive Development*, *19*, 179–201.

Perner, J., Sprung, M., Zauner, P., & Haider, H. (2003). Want that is understood well before say that, think that, and false belief: A test of de Villiers's linguistic determinism on German-speaking children. *Child Development*, *74*, 179–188.

Perner, J., Stummer, S., & Lang, B. (1999). Executive functions and theory of mind: Cognitive complexity or functional dependence? In P. D. Zelazo, J. W. Astington, & D. R. Olson (Eds.). *Developing theories of intention* (pp. 133–152). Mahwah, NJ: Lawrence Erlbaum Associates.

Perner, J., & Wimmer, H. (1985). "John thinks that Mary thinks that . . .": Attribution of second-order beliefs by 5- to 10-year-old children. *Journal of Experimental Child Psychology, 39,* 437–471.

Perner, J., Zauner, P., & Sprung, M. (2005). What does "that" have to do with point of view? Conflicting desires and "want" in German. In J. W. Astington & J. A. Baird (Eds.), *Why language matters for theory of mind* (pp. 220–244). New York: Oxford University Press.

Perry, W. G. (1970). *Forms of intellectual and ethical development in the college years.* New York: Holt, Rinehart, & Winston.

Peskin, J., & Ardino, V. (2003). Representing the mental world in children's social behavior: Playing hide-and-seek and keeping a secret. *Social Development, 12,* 496–512.

Peskin, J., & Astington, J. W. (2004). The effects of adding metacognitive language to story texts. *Cognitive Development, 19,* 253–273.

Peterson, C., & Slaughter, V. (2003). Opening windows into the mind: Mothers' preferences for mental state explanations and children's theory of mind. *Cognitive Development, 18,* 399–429.

Peterson, C. C. (2000). Kindred spirits: Influences of siblings' perspectives on theory of mind. *Cognitive Development, 15,* 435–455.

Peterson, C. C., & Siegal, M. (1995). Deafness, conversation and theory of mind. *Journal of Child Psychology and Psychiatry, 36,* 459–474.

Peterson, C. C., & Siegal, M. (2000). Insights into theory of mind from deafness and autism. *Mind and Language, 15,* 123–145.

Peterson, C. C., & Siegal, M. (2002). Mindreading and moral awareness in popular and rejected preschoolers. *British Journal of Developmental Psychology, 20,* 205–224.

Peterson, C. C., Peterson, J. L., & Webb, J. (2000). Factors influencing the development of a theory of mind in blind children. *British Journal of Developmental Psychology, 18,* 431–447.

Piaget, J. (1924/1928). *Judgment and reasoning in the child.* London: Kegan. (Original work published 1924).

Piaget, J. (1954). *The construction of reality in the child.* New York: Basic Books. (Original work published 1937).

Piaget, J. (1962). *Play, dreams and imitation in childhood.* New York: W. W. Norton & Co. (Original work published 1945).

Piaget, J. (1963). *The origins of intelligence in children.* New York: Norton. (Original work published 1936).

Piaget, J. (1965). *The moral judgment of the child.* New York: The Free Press. (Original work published 1932).

Piaget, J. (1971). *The construction of reality in the child.* New York: Ballantine. (Original work published 1937).

Piaget, J. (1972). *The principles of genetic epistemology.* London: Routledge & Kegan Paul. (Original work published in 1970).

Piaget, J. (1995). *Sociological studies.* London: Routledge. (Original work published 1977).

Piaget, J., & Inhelder, B. (1967). *The child's conception of space.* New York: Norton. (Original work published 1948).

Pillow, B. H. (1991). Children's understanding of biased social cognition. *Developmental Psychology, 27,* 539–551.

Pillow, B. (2002). Children and adults' evaluation of the certainty of deductive inferences, inductive inferences, and guesses. *Child Development, 73,* 779–792.

Pillow, B., & Mash, C. (1999). Young children's understanding of interpretation, expectation and direct perception as sources of false belief. *British Journal of Developmental Psychology, 17,* 263–276.

Plaisted, K. C. (2000). Aspects of autism that theory of mind cannot explain. In S. Baron-Cohen, H. Tager-Flusberg, & D. J. Cohen (Eds.), *Understanding other minds: Perspectives from cognitive neuroscience* (pp. 222–250). Oxford: Oxford University Press.

Povinelli, D. J. (1999). Social understanding in chimpanzees: New evidence from a longitudinal approach. In P. D. Zelazo, J. W. Astington, & D. R. Olson (Eds.), *Developing theories of intention* (pp. 195–225). Mahwah, NJ: Lawrence Erlbaum Associates.

Povinelli, D. J., Bering, J. M., & Giambrone, S. (2003). Chimpanzees' "pointing": Another error of the argument by analogy? In S. Kita (Ed.), *Pointing: Where language, culture, and cognition meet* (pp. 35–68). Mahwah, NJ: Lawrence Erlbaum Associates.

Povinelli, D. J., & Eddy, T. J. (1996). What young chimpanzees know about seeing. *Monographs of the Society for Research in Child Development, 61* (Serial No. 247).

Povinelli, D., & Giambrone, S. (2001). Reasoning about beliefs: A human specialization? *Child Development, 72,* 691–695.

Pratt, C., & Bryant, P. (1990). Young-children understand that looking leads to knowing (so long as they are looking into a single barrel). *Child Development, 61,* 973–982.

Premack, D., & Woodruff, G. (1978). Does the chimpanzee have a theory of mind? *Behavioral and Brain Sciences, 4,* 515–526.

Prinz, W. (2003). Neurons don't represent. *Consciousness and Cognition, 12,* 572–573.

Racine, T. (2004). Wittgenstein's internalistic logic and children's theories of mind. In J. I. M. Carpendale & U. Müller (Eds.), *Social interaction and the development of knowledge* (pp. 275–276). Mahwah, NJ: Lawrence Erlbaum Associates.

Racine, T. P., & Carpendale, J. I. M. (in press). The embodiment of mental states. In W. F. Overton, U. Müller, & J. Newman (Eds.). *Body in mind, mind in body: Developmental perspectives on embodiment and consciousness.* Mahwah, NJ: Lawrence Erlbaum Associates.

Raver, C. C., & Leadbeater, B. J. (1993). The problem of the other in research on theory of mind and social development. *Human Development, 36,* 350–362.

Reddy, V. (1991). Playing with others' expectations: Teasing and mucking about in the first year. In A. Whiten (Ed.), *Natural theories of mind: Evolution, development and simulation of everyday mindreading* (pp. 143–158). Oxford: Basil Blackwell.

Reddy, V. (2001). Mind knowledge in the first year: Understanding attention and intention. In G. Bremner & A. Fogel (Eds.), *Blackwell handbook of infant development* (pp. 241–264). Oxford: Blackwell.

Reddy, V. (2003). On being the object of attention: Implications for self–other consciousness. *Trends in Cognitive Science, 7,* 397–402.

Reddy, V., & Morris, P. (2004). Participants don't need theories: Knowing minds in engagement. *Theory & Psychology, 14,* 647–655.

Repacholi, B. M., & Gopnik, A. (1996–1997). Early reasoning about desires: Evidence from 14- and 18-month-olds. *Developmental Psychology, 33,* 12–21.

Repacholi, B. M., Slaughter, V., Pritchard, M., & Gibbs, V. (2003). Theory of mind, Machiavellianism, and social functioning in childhood. In B. Repocholi & V. Slaughter (Eds.), *Individual differences in theory of mind: Implications for typical and atypical development* (pp. 67–97). New York: Psychology Press.

Richner, E. S., & Nicolopoulou, A. (2001). The narrative construction of differing conceptions of the person in the development of young children's social understanding. *Early Education and Development, 12,* 391–432.

Riggs, K. J., & Peterson, D. M. (2000). Counterfactual thinking in pre-school children: Mental state and causal inferences. In P. Mitchell & K. J. Riggs (Eds.), *Children's reasoning and the mind* (pp. 87–100). Hove: Psychology Press.

Riggs, K. J., Peterson, D. M., Robinson, E. J., & Mitchell, P. (1998). Are errors in false belief tasks symptomatic of a broader difficulty with counterfactuality? *Cognitive Development, 13,* 73–90.

Roberts, R. J., & Pennington, B. F. (1996). An interactive framework for examining prefrontal cognitive processes. *Developmental Neuropsychology, 12,* 105–126.

Robinson, E. J., & Apperly, I. A. (2001). Children's difficulties with partial representations in ambiguous messages and referentially opaque contexts. *Cognitive Development, 16,* 595–615.

Robinson, E. J., & Beck, S. (2000). What is so difficult about counterfactual reasoning? In P. Mitchell & K. J. Riggs (Eds.), *Children's reasoning and the mind* (pp. 101–119). Hove: Psychology Press.

Robinson, E. J., & Robinson, W. P. (1983). Children's uncertainty about the interpretation of ambiguous messages. *Journal of Experimental Child Psychology, 36,* 81–96.

Rochat, P. (2001). Origins of self-concept. In G. Bremner & A. Fogel (Eds.), *Blackwell handbook of infant development* (pp. 191–212). Oxford: Blackwell.

Rochat, P., & Hespos, S. J. (1997). Differential rooting response by neonates: Evidence for an early sense of self. *Early Development and Parenting, 6,* 105–112.

Rochat, P., & Striano, T. (2002). Who's in the mirror? Self–other discrimination in specular images by four- and nine-month-old infants. *Child Development*, 73, 35–46.

Rosnay, M., Pons, F., Harris, P. L., & Morrell, J. M. B. (2004). A lag between understanding false belief and emotion attribution in young children: Relationships with linguistic ability and mothers' mental-state language. *British Journal of Developmental Psychology*, 22, 197–218.

Ross, H. S., Recchia, H. E., & Carpendale, J. I. M. (2005). Making sense of divergent interpretations of conflict and developing an interpretive understanding of mind. *Journal of Cognition and Development*, 6, 571–592.

Ross, L. (1980). The "intuitive scientist" formulation and its developmental implications. In J. R. Flavell & L. Ross (Eds.), *Social cognitive development: Frontiers and possible futures* (pp. 1–42). Cambridge: Cambridge University Press.

Rubin, K. H., Bukowski, W., & Parker, J. G. (1998). Peer interactions, relationships and groups. In W. Damon and N. Eisenberg (Eds.), *Handbook of child psychology* (vol. 3, pp. 619–700). New York: Wiley.

Ruffman, T. (2000). Nonverbal theory of mind: Is it important, is it implicit, is it simulation, is it relevant to autism? In J. W. Astington (Ed.), *Minds in the making: Essays in honor of David R. Olson* (pp. 250–266). Oxford: Blackwell Publishers.

Ruffman, T. (2004). Children's understanding of mind: Constructivist but theory-like. *Behavioral and Brain Sciences*, 27, 129–121.

Ruffman, T., Garnham, W., Import, C., & Connolly, D. (2001). Does eye gaze indicate implicit knowledge of false belief? Charting transitions in knowledge. *Journal of Experimental Child Psychology*, 80, 201–224.

Ruffman, T., & Keenan, T. R. (1996). The belief-based emotion of surprise: The case for a lag in understanding relative to false belief. *Developmental Psychology*, 32, 40–49.

Ruffman, T., Olson, D. R., & Astington, J. W. (1991). Children's understanding of visual ambiguity. *British Journal of Developmental Psychology*, 9, 89–102.

Ruffman, T., Perner, J., Naito, M., Parkin, L., & Clements, W. A. (1998). Older (but not younger) siblings facilitate false belief understanding. *Developmental Psychology*, 34, 161–174.

Ruffman, T., Perner, J., & Parkin, L. (1999). How parenting style affects false belief understanding. *Social Development*, 8, 395–411.

Ruffman, T., Slade, L., & Crowe, E. (2002). The relation between children's and mothers' mental state language and theory-of-mind understanding. *Child Development*, 73, 734–751.

Ruffman, T., Slade, L., Rowlandson, K., Rumsey, C., & Garnham, A. (2003). How language relates to belief, desire, and emotion understanding. *Cognitive Development*, 18, 139–158.

Russell, J. (1987). Rule-following, mental models, and the development view. In M. Chapman & R. A. Dixon (Eds.), *Meaning and the growth of understanding: Wittgenstein's significance for developmental psychology* (pp. 23–48). Berlin: Springer-Verlag.

Russell, J. (1992). The theory theory: So good they named it twice? *Cognitive Development, 7,* 485–519.

Russell, J. (1996). *Agency: Its role in mental development.* Hove, UK: Lawrence Erlbaum Associates, (UK) Taylor & Francis.

Russell, J. (Ed.) (1997). *Autism as an executive disorder.* Oxford: Oxford University Press.

Russell, J., Hala, S., & Hill, E. (2003). The automated windows task: the performance of preschool children, children with autism, and children with moderate learning difficulties. *Cognitive Development, 18,* 111–137.

Russell, J., Jarrold, C., & Potel, D. (1994). What makes strategic deception difficult for children – the deception or the strategy? *British Journal of Developmental Psychology, 12,* 301–314.

Russell, J., Mauthner, N., Sharpe, S., & Tidswell, T. (1991). The windows task as a measure of strategic deception in preschoolers and autistic subjects. *British Journal of Developmental Psychology, 9,* 331–349.

Russell, J., Saltmarsh, R., & Hill, E. J. (1999). What do executive factors contribute to the failure on false belief tasks by children with autism? *Journal of Child Psychology and Psychiatry, 40,* 859–868.

Russell, P. A., Hosie, J. A., Hunter, D. C., Banks, S. J., & Macaulay, M. C. (1997). The development of theory of mind in deaf children. *Journal of Child Psychology and Psychiatry, 38,* 903–910.

Rutter, M. (2000). Genetic studies of autism from the 1970s into the millennium. *Journal of Abnormal Child Psychology, 28,* 3–14.

Sabbagh, M. A., & Callanan, M. A. (1998). Metarepresentation in action: 3-, 4-, and 5-year-olds' developing theories of mind in parent–child conversations. *Developmental Psychology, 34,* 491–502.

Saltmarsh, R., Mitchell, P., & Robinson, E. (1995). Realism and children's early grasp of mental representation – belief-based judgments in the state change task. *Cognition, 57,* 297–325.

Sameroff, A., & Chandler, M. J. (1975). Reproductive risk and the continuum of caretaking casualty. In F. D. Horowitz, M. Hetherington, S. Scarr-Salapatek, & G. Siegel (Eds.), *Review of child development research* (vol. 4). Chicago, IL: The University of Chicago Press.

Samuels, M. C., Brooks, P. J., & Frye, D. (1996). Strategic game playing through the Windows Task. *British Journal of Developmental Psychology, 14,* 159–172.

Savage-Rumbaugh, S. E., Murphy, J., Sevcik, R. A., Brakke, K. E., Williams, S. L., & Rumbaugh, D. M. (1993). Language comprehension in ape and child. *Monographs of the Society for Research in Child Development, 58* (Serial No. 233).

Scaife, M., & Bruner, J. (1975). Capacity for joint visual attention in infant. *Nature, 253,* 256–266.

Scheler, M. (1954). *The nature of sympathy* (trans. by P. Heath). Hamden, CT: Archon Books. (Original work published 1913).

Schneider, W., Schumann-Hengsteler, R., & Sodian, B. (Eds.) (2005). *Young children's cognitive development*. Mahwah, NJ: Lawrence Erlbaum Associates.

Scholl, B. J., & Leslie, A. M. (1999). Modularity, development and "theory of mind". *Mind and Language, 14*, 131–153.

Scholl, B. J., & Leslie, A. M. (2001). Minds, modules, and meta-analysis. *Child Development, 72*, 696–701.

Searle, J. R. (1983). *Intentionality*. Cambridge: Cambridge University Press.

Selman, R. (1980). *The growth of interpersonal understanding*. New York: Academic Press.

Sharrock, W., & Coulter, J. (2004). ToM: A critical commentary. *Theory and Psychology, 14*, 579–600.

Shatz, M. (1975). The development of social cognition. In E. Hetherington (Ed.), *Review of child development research* (vol. 5, pp. 257–323). Chicago: University of Chicago Press.

Shatz, M. (1983). Communication. In J. Flavell & E. Markman (Eds.), *Manual of child psychology: Cognitive development* (4th ed., vol. 3, pp. 495–555). Chichester: Wiley.

Shatz, M. (1994). Theory of mind and the development of social-linguistic intelligence in early childhood. In C. Lewis & P. Mitchell (Eds.), *Children's early understanding of mind: Origins and development* (pp. 311–329). Hove, UK: Lawrence Erlbaum Associates.

Shatz, M., Wellman, H. M., & Silber, S. (1983). The acquisition of mental verbs: A systematic investigation of the first reference to mental state. *Cognition, 14*, 301–321.

Shimmon, K. (2004). Unpublished PhD. Lancaster University, UK.

Shimmon, K., Lewis, C., & Francis, B. (2003). *Unity and diversity in executive skills and false belief: A longitudinal analysis*. Paper presented at the biennial meeting of the Society for Research in Child Development, Tampa, April.

Shinn, M. W. (1900). *The biography of a baby*. Boston and New York: Mifflin Company. (republished 1975).

Shotter, J., & Gregory, S. (1976). On first gaining the idea of oneself as a person. In R. Harré (Ed.), *Life sentences* (pp. 3–9). Chichester: Wiley.

Shultz, T. R. (1974). Development of the appreciation of riddles. *Child Development, 45*, 100–105.

Shultz, T. R., & Pilon, R. (1973). Development of the ability to detect linguistic ambiguity. *Child Development, 44*, 728–733.

Shultz, T. R., Wells, D., & Sarda, M. (1980). The development of the ability to distinguish intended actions from mistakes, reflexes and passive movements. *The British Journal of Social and Clinical Psychology, 19*, 301–310.

Siegal, M. (2004). Social understanding and the cognitive architecture of theory of mind. *Behavioral and Brain Sciences, 27*, 122.

Simpson, A., Riggs, K. J., & Simon, M. (2004). What makes the windows task difficult for young children: Rule inference or rule use? *Journal of Experimental Child Psychology, 87*, 155–170.

Slaughter, V., Dennis, M. J., & Pritchard, M. (2002). Theory of mind and peer acceptance in preschool children. *British Journal of Developmental Psychology, 20*, 545–564.

Slaughter, V., & Gopnik, A. (1996). Conceptual coherence in the child's theory of mind: Training children to understand belief. *Child Development, 34*, 161–174.

Slaughter, V., & McConnell, D. (2003). Emergence of joint attention: Relationships between gaze following, social referencing, imitation, and naming in infancy. *Journal of Genetic Psychology, 164*, 54–71.

Slomkowski, C., & Dunn, J. (1996). Young children's understanding of other people's beliefs and feelings and their connected communication with friends. *Developmental Psychology, 32*, 442–447.

Smith, L. (1996). With knowledge in mind: Novel transformation of the learner or transformation of novel knowledge. *Human Development, 39*, 257–263.

Smith, L. (1999). What Piaget learned from Frege. *Developmental Review, 19*, 133–153.

Smith, P. K. (1986). Exploration, play and social development in boys and girls. In D. J. Hargreaves, & A. M. Colley (Eds.), *The psychology of sex roles*. London: Harper & Row.

Sodian, B. (1990). Understanding verbal communication: Children's ability to deliberately manipulate ambiguity in referential messages. *Cognitive Development, 5*, 209–222.

Sodian, B. (1994). Early deception and the conceptual continuity claim. In C. Lewis & P. Mitchell (Eds.), *Children's early understanding of mind* (pp. 385–402). Hove: Lawrence Erlbaum Associates.

Sodian, B., & Hülsken, C. (2005). The developmental relation of theory of mind and executive functions: A study of advanced theory of mind abilities in children with attention deficit hyperactivity disorder. In W. Schneider, R. Schumann-Hengsteler, & B. Sodian (Eds.), *Young children's cognitive development* (pp. 175–188). Mahwah, NJ: Lawrence Erlbaum Associates.

Sodian, B., Taylor, M., Harris, P. L., & Perner, J. (1991). Early deception and the child's theory of mind – false trails and genuine markers. *Child Development, 62*, 468–483.

Sodian, B., & Wimmer, H. (1987). Children's understanding of inference as a source of knowledge. *Child Development, 58*, 424–433.

Soffer, G. (1999). The other as alter ego: A genetic approach. *Husserl Studies, 15*, 151–166.

Sokol, B., & Lalonde, C. E. (2004). A penny *is* your thoughts? Reflections on a Wittgensteinian proposal. *Behavioral and Brain Sciences, 27*, 123–124.

Sokol, B. W., & Chandler, M. J. (2003). Taking agency seriously in the theories-of-mind enterprise: Exploring children's understanding of interpretation and intention. *British Journal of Educational Psychology Monograph Series II* (Number 2 – Development and Motivation), 125–136.

Sokol, B. W., Chandler, M. J., & Jones, C. (2004). From mechanical to autonomous agency: The relationship between children's moral judgments and their developing theories of mind. In J. A. Baird & B. W. Sokol (Eds.), Connections between theory of mind and sociomoral development. *New Directions for Child and Adolescent Development, 103,* 19–36.

Spelke, E. (1994). Initial knowledge: 6 suggestions. *Cognition, 50,* 431–445.

Steele, H. (2004). The social matrix reloaded: An attachment perspective on Carpendale and Lewis. *Behavioral and Brain Sciences, 27,* 124–125.

Stern, D. (1977). *The first relationship.* Cambridge, MA: Harvard University Press.

Strauss, S., Ziv, M., & Stein, A. (2002). Teaching as a natural cognition and its relations to preschoolers' developing theory of mind. *Cognitive Development, 17,* 1473–1487.

Sullivan, K., & Winner, E. (1993). 3-year-olds understanding of mental states – the influence of trickery. *Journal of Experimental Child Psychology, 56,* 135–148.

Sullivan, K., Zaitchik, D., & Tager-Flusberg, H. (1994). Preschoolers can attribute second-order beliefs. *Developmental Psychology, 30,* 395–402.

Sutton, J., Smith, P. K., & Swettenham, J. (1999a). Bullying and "theory of mind": A critique of the "social skills deficit" view of anti-social behaviour. *Social Development, 8,* 117–127.

Sutton, J., Smith, P. K., & Swettenham, J. (1999b). Social cognition and bullying: Social inadequacy or skilled manipulation? *British Journal of Developmental Psychology, 17,* 435–450.

Sutton, J., Smith, P. K., & Swettenham, J. (2001). "It's easy, it works, and it makes me feel good" – A response to Arsenio and Lemerise. *Social Development, 108,* 74–78.

Symons, D. (2004). Mental state discourse, theory of mind, and the internalization of self–other understanding. *Developmental Review, 24,* 159–188.

Symons, D. K., & Clark, S. E. (2000). A longitudinal study of mother–child relationships and theory of mind during the preschool period. *Social Development, 9,* 3–23.

Tager-Flusberg, H. (2003). Exploring the relationship between theory of mind and social communicative functioning in children with autism. In B. Repacholi & V. Slaughter (Eds.), *Individual differences in theory of mind* (pp. 197–212). Hove: Psychology Press.

Tager-Flusberg, H., Sullivan, K., & Boshart, J. (1997). Executive functions and performance on false belief tasks. *Developmental Neuropsychology, 13,* 487–493.

Talwar, V., & Lee, K. (2002). Emergence of white-lie telling in children between 3 and 7 years of age. *Merrill-Palmer Quarterly, 48,* 160–181.

Tangney, J. P., & Fischer, K. W. (Eds.) (1995). *Self-conscious emotions.* New York: The Guilford Press.

Tardiff, T., & Wellman, H. M. (2000). Acquisition of mental state language in Mandarin- and Cantonese-speaking children. *Developmental Psychology, 36,* 25–43.

Thompson, R. A. (2000). The legacy of early attachments. *Child Development, 71,* 145–152.

Thompson, R. A., & Raikes, H. A. (2004). The mind in the mind of the beholder: Elucidating relational influences on early social understanding. *Behavioral and Brain Sciences, 27*, 126–127.

Tomasello, M. (1995a). Joint attention as social cognition. In C. Moore & P. J. Dunham (Eds.), *Joint attention: Its origins and role in development* (pp. 103–130). Hillsdale, NJ: Lawrence Erlbaum Associates.

Tomasello, M. (1995b). Language is not an instinct. *Cognitive Development, 10*, 131–156.

Tomasello, M. (1998). The return of constructions. *Journal of Child Language, 25*, 431–442.

Tomasello, M. (1999a). *The cultural origins of human cognition.* Cambridge, MA: Harvard University Press.

Tomasello, M. (1999b). Having intentions, understanding intentions, and understanding communicative intentions. In P. D. Zelazo, J. W. Astington, & D. R. Olson (Eds.), *Developing theories of intention* (pp. 63–75). Mahwah, NJ: Lawrence Erlbaum Associates.

Tomasello, M. (1999c). The human adaptation for culture. *Annual Review of Anthropology, 28*, 509–529.

Tomasello, M. (2001). Perceiving intentions and learning words in the second year of life. In M. Tomasello & E. Bates (Eds.), *Language development: The essential readings* (pp. 111–128). Cambridge, MA: Harvard University Press.

Tomasello, M. (2003). *Constructing a language: A usage-based theory of language acquisition.* Cambridge, MA: Harvard University Press.

Tomasello, M., & Call, J. (1997). *Primate cognition.* Oxford: Oxford University Press.

Tomasello, M., Call, J., & Hare, B. (1998). Five primate species follow the visual gaze of conspecifics. *Animal Behavior, 55*, 1063–1069.

Tomasello, M., Call, J., & Hare, B. (2003). Chimpanzees understand psychological states: The question is which ones and to what extent. *Trends in Cognitive Science, 7*, 153–156.

Tomasello, M., & Camaioni, L. (1997). A comparison of the gestural communication of apes and human infants. *Human Development, 40*, 7–24.

Tomasello, M., Carpenter, M., Call, J., Behne, T., & Moll, H. (in press). Understanding and sharing intentions: The origins of cultural cognition. *Behavioral and Brain Sciences.*

Tomasello, M., Kruger, A. C., & Ratner, H. H. (1993). Cultural learning. *Behavioral and Brain Sciences, 16*, 495–552.

Toner, I. J., Moore, L. P., & Emmons, B. A. (1980). Effect of being labelled on subsequent self control in children. *Child Development, 51*, 618–621.

Toner, I. J., & Smith, R. A. (1977). Age and overt verbalisations in delay maintenance behavior in children. *Journal of Experimental Child Psychology, 12*, 334–348.

Tooby, J., & Cosmides, L. (1992). The psychological foundations of culture. In J. H. Barkow, L. Cosmides, & J. Tooby (Eds.), *The adapted mind: Evolutionary psychology and the generation of culture* (pp. 19–136). New York: Oxford University Press.

Tooby, J., & Cosmides, L. (1995). Foreword. In S. Baron-Cohen, *Mindblindness: An essay on autism and theory of mind* (pp. xi–xviii). Cambridge, MA: MIT Press.

Towse, J. N., Redbond, J., Houston-Price, C. M. T., & Cook, S. (2000). Understanding the dimensional change card sort: Perspectives from task success and failure. *Cognitive Development, 15*, 347–365.

Trevarthen, C. (1979). Communication and cooperation in early infancy: A description of primary intersubjectivity. In M. M. Bullowa (Ed.), *Before speech: The beginning of interpersonal communication*. New York: Cambridge University Press.

Trevarthen, C., & Aitken, K. J. (2001). Infant intersubjectivity: Research, theory, and clinical applications. *Journal of Child Psychology and Psychiatry, 42*, 3–48.

Trevarthen, C., & Hubley, P. (1978). Secondary intersubjectivity: Confidence, confiding and acts of meaning in the first year. In A. Lock (Ed.), *Action, gesture and symbol: The emergence of language*. London: Academic Press.

Tronick, E. Z. (2003). Things still to be done on the still-face effect. *Infancy, 4*, 475–482.

Tschudin, A., Call, J., Dunbar, R. I. M., Harris, G., & van der Elst, C. (2001). Comprehension of signs by dolphins (*Tursiops truncatus*). *Journal of Comparative Psychology, 115*, 100–105.

Turnbull, W. (2003). *Language in action: Psychological models of conversation*. Hove, UK: Psychology Press.

Turnbull, W., & Carpendale, J. (1999a). Locating meaning in interaction, not in the brain. *Behavioral and Brain Sciences, 22*, 304–305.

Turnbull, W., & Carpendale, J. I. M. (1999b). A social pragmatic model of talk: Implications for research on the development of children's social understanding. *Human Development, 42*, 328–355.

Turnbull, W., & Carpendale, J. I. M. (2001). Talk and social understanding. *Early Education and Development, 12*, 455–477.

Umiltà, M. A., Kohler, E., Gallese, V., Fogassi, L., Fadiga, L., Keysers, C., & Rizzolatti, G. (2001). "I know what you are doing": A neurophysiological study. *Neuron, 32*, 91–101.

Vaillancourt, T., & Hymel, S. (2004). The social context of children's aggression. In M. M. Moretti, C. L. Odgers, & M. A. Jackson (Eds.), *Girls and aggression: Contributing factors and intervention principles* (pp. 57–73). New York: Kluwer Academic.

Varouxaki, A., Freeman, N. H., Peters, D., & Lewis, C. (1999). Inference neglect and inference denial. *British Journal of Developmental Psychology, 17*, 483–499.

Vasek, M. E. (1986). Lying as a skill: The development of deception in children. In R. W. Mitchell & N. S. Thompson (Eds.), *Deception: Perspectives on human and nonhuman deceit* (pp. 271–292). Albany, NY: State University of New York Press.

Vinden, P. (2004). In defense of enculturation. *Behavior and Brain Sciences, 27,* 127–128.

Vinden, P. G. (1996). Junin Quechua children's understanding of mind. *Child Development, 67,* 1701–1716.

Vinden, P. G. (1999). Children's understanding of mind and emotion: A multicultural study. *Cognition and Emotion, 13,* 19–48.

Vinden, P. G. (2001). Parenting attitudes and children's understanding of mind: A comparison of Korean American and Anglo-American families. *Cognitive Development, 16,* 793–809.

Vygotsky, L. (1986). *Thought and language.* Cambridge: MIT. (Original work published 1934).

Vygotsky, L. S. (1978). *Mind in society: The development of higher psychological processes.* Cambridge, MA: Harvard University Press.

Vygotsky, L. S. (1998). *The collected works of L. S. Vygotsky, Vol. 5, Child psychology.* New York: Plenum Press.

Walden, T., & Ogan, T. (1988). The development of social referencing. *Child Development, 59,* 1230–1240.

Walker-Andrews, A. S., & Hudson, J. A. (2004). Interpretation based on richness of experience: Theory development from a social-constructivist perspective. *Behavior and Brain Sciences, 27,* 128–129.

Walker-Andrews, A. S., & Kahana-Kalman, R. (1999). The understanding of pretence across the second year of life. *British Journal of Developmental Psychology, 17,* 523–536.

Warburton, K. (2004). *Young children's difficulty on the dimensional change card sort: Cognitive vs. social explanations.* Unpublished paper. Department of Psychology, Lancaster University.

Watson, A. C., Nixon, C. L., Wilson, A., & Capagne, L. (1999). Social interaction skills and theory of mind in young children. *Developmental Psychology, 35,* 386–391.

Watson, A. C., Painter, K. M., & Bornstein, M. H. (2001). Longitudinal relations between 2-year-olds' language and 4-year-olds' theory of mind. *Journal of Cognition and Development, 2,* 449–457.

Watson, J. K., Gelman, S. A., & Wellman, H. M. (1998). Young children's understanding of the non-physical nature of thoughts and the physical nature of the brain. *British Journal of Developmental Psychology, 16,* 321–335.

Watson, J. S. (1972). Smiling cooing and "the game". *Merrill Palmer Quarterly, 18,* 323–340.

Wellman, H. M. (1988). First steps in the child's theorizing about the mind. In J. W. Astington, P. L. Harris, & D. R. Olson (Eds.), *Developing theories of mind* (pp. 64–92). New York: Cambridge University Press.

Wellman, H. M. (1990). *The child's theory of mind.* Cambridge, MA: MIT Press.

Wellman, H. M., & Banerjee, M. (1991). Mind and emotions: Children's understanding of the emotional consequences of beliefs and desires. *British Journal of Developmental Psychology*, 9, 191–214.

Wellman, H. M., & Bartsch, K. (1988). Young children's reasoning about beliefs. *Cognition*, 30, 239–277.

Wellman, H. M., & Bartsch, K. (1994). Before belief: Children's early psychological theory. In C. Lewis & P. Mitchell (Eds.), *Children's early understanding of mind: Origins and development* (pp. 331–354). Hove, UK: Lawrence Erlbaum Associates.

Wellman, H. M., & Estes, D. (1986). Early understanding of mental entities: A reexamination of childhood realism. *Child Development*, 57, 910–923.

Wellman, H. M., Cross, D., & Watson, J. (2001). Meta-analysis of theory of mind development: The truth about false belief. *Child Development*, 72, 655–684.

Wellman, H. M., & Liu, D. (2004). Scaling of theory of mind tasks. *Child Development*, 75, 523–541.

Wellman, H. M., & Woolley, J. (1990). From simple desires to ordinary beliefs: The early development of everyday psychology. *Cognition*, 35, 245–275.

Welsh, M. C., Pennington, B. F., & Grossier, D. B. (1991). A normative-developmental study of executive function: A window on prefrontal function in children. *Developmental Neuropsychology*, 7, 131–149.

Werner, H., & Kaplan, B. (1963). *Symbol formation*. New York: Wiley.

Williams, M. (1999). *Wittgenstein, mind and meaning: Toward a social conception of mind*. New York: Routledge.

Wilson-Brune, C., & Woodward, A. L. (2004). What infants know about intentional action and how they might come to know it. *Behavior and Brain Sciences*, 27, 129.

Wimmer, H., & Gschaider, A. (2000). Children's understanding of belief: Why is it important to understand what happened? In P. Mitchell & K. Rigs (Eds.), *Children's reasoning and the mind* (pp. 253–266). Hove, UK: Psychology Press.

Wimmer, H., & Hartl, M. (1991). Against the Cartesian view on mind: Young children's difficulty with own false beliefs. *British Journal of Developmental Psychology*, 9, 125–138.

Wimmer, H., & Perner, J. (1983). Beliefs about beliefs: Representation and constraining function of wrong beliefs in young children's understanding of deception. *Cognition*, 13, 103–128.

Winch, P. (1972). *Ethics and action*. London: Routledge & Kegan Paul.

Wittgenstein, L. (1968). *Philosophical investigations*. Oxford: Blackwell.

Wittgenstein, L. (1981). *Zettel*. Oxford: Basil Blackwell.

Woodfield, A. (1996). Which theoretical concepts do children use? *Philosophical Papers*, 25, 1–20.

Woolfe, T., Want, S. C., & Siegal, M. (2002). Signposts to development: Theory of mind in deaf children. *Child Development*, 73, 768–778.

Wootton, A. J. (1997). *Interaction and the development of mind*. Cambridge, MA: Cambridge University Press.

Wright, D. (1982). Piaget's theory of moral development. In S. Modgil & C. Modgil (Eds.), *Jean Piaget: Consensus and controversy* (pp. 207–217). London: Holt, Rinehart and Winston.

Yasui, M., & Lewis, C. (2005). "*'Oh Great!' can mean nasty*": A message from three-year-olds' understanding of sarcasm. Paper presented at the biennial meeting of the Society for Research in Child Development, Atlanta, March.

Youngblade, L. M., & Dunn, J. (1995). Individual differences in young children's pretend play with mothers and siblings: Links to relationships and understanding other people's feelings and beliefs. *Child Development*, 66, 1472–1492.

Yuill, N. (1997). Children's understanding of traits. In S. Hala (Ed.), *The development of social cognition* (pp. 273–295). Hove, UK: Psychology Press.

Zaitchik, D. (1991). Is only seeing really believing?: Sources of the true belief in the false belief task. *Cognitive Development*, 6, 91–103.

Zelazo, P. D. (2000). Self-reflection and the development of consciously controlled processing. In P. Mitchell & K. Rigs (Eds.), *Children's reasoning and the mind* (pp. 169–189). Hove, UK: Psychology Press.

Zelazo, P. D., & Frye, D. (1998). Cognitive complexity and control: The development of executive function. *Current Directions in Psychological Science*, 7, 121–126.

Zelazo, P. D., & Müller, U. (2002). Executive function in typical and atypical development. In U. Goswami (Ed.), *Handbook of childhood cognitive development* (pp. 445–469). Oxford: Blackwell.

Zelazo, P. D., Frye, D., & Rapus, T. (1996). An age-related dissociation between knowing rules and using them. *Cognitive Development*, 11, 37–63.

Zelazo, P. D., Müller, U., Frye, D., & Marcovitch, S. (2004). The development of executive function in early childhood. *Monographs of the Society for Research in Child Development*, 68 (Serial No. 274).

Zelazo, P. D., Qu, L., & Müller, U. (2005). Hot and cool aspects of executive function: Relations in early development. In: W. Schneider, R. Schumann-Hengsteler, & B. Sodian (Eds.), *Young children's cognitive development: Interrelationships among executive functioning, working memory, verbal ability, and theory of mind* (pp. 71–93). Mahwah, NJ: Lawrence Erlbaum Associates.

Zerwas, S., Balaraman, G., & Brownell, C. (2004). Constructing an understanding of mind with peers. *Behavior and Brain Sciences*, 27, 130.

Ziv, M., & Frye, D. (2004). Children's understanding of teaching: The role of knowledge and belief. *Cognitive Development*, 19, 457–477.

Author Index

Subject Index

* Words marked with an asterisk occur so frequently throughout the book that page references have not always been given.